Kiruna

LAPPLAND

NORR-
BOTTEN

NO
NO

and

$25.00

DATE			

ÅNGERMAN
LAND

·sund

THERN
·RLAND

MEDELPAD   ·Sundsva

HÄLSING-   ·Hudiksval
LAND

GÄSTRIKLAND
·Falun   ·Gävle

UPPLAND

·Upps

MAN-   ·EASTER
ND   Västerås

SÖDER-
MANLAND   ST

·Nyköping

·Linköping
·RGÖTLAND

ERN   Visby
AND   GOT

·almar   ÖLAND   B

GE
·Karlskrona

N GÖTALAND

EYEWITNESS TRAVEL

SWEDEN

EYEWITNESS TRAVEL

SWEDEN

Main Contributors **Ulf Johansson, Mona Neppenstrom, Kaj Sandell**

DK

LONDON, NEW YORK,
MELBOURNE, MUNICH AND DELHI
www.dk.com

Produced for Dorling Kindersley by Streiffert Förlag AB, Stockholm

Senior Editor Bo Streiffert

Project And Picture Editor Guy Engström

Assistant Picture Editor Ebba Mörner

Main Contributors Ulf Johansson, Mona Neppenström, Kaj Sandell

Photographers Peter Hanneberg, Erik Svensson, Jeppe Wikström

Cartographer Stig Söderlind

Illustrators
Stephen Conlin, Gary Cross, Urban Frank, Claire Littlejohn, Jan Rojmar, John Woodcock

English Translation Kate Lambert, Stuart Tudball

Editor of English Edition Jane Hutching

Printed and bound by South China Printing Co Ltd, China

First American edition 1995

14 15 16 17 10 9 8 7 6 5 4 3 2 1

Published in the United States by DK Publishing,
345 Hudson Street, New York, NY 10014

Reprinted with revisions 2008, 2011, 2014

Copyright 2005, 2014 © Dorling Kindersley Limited, London
A Penguin Company

Published in the UK by Dorling Kindersley Limited.

A catalog record for this book is available from
the Library of Congress.
ISSN 1542-1554
ISBN 978-1-4654-0995-9

Floors are referred to throughout in accordance
with European usage; ie the "first floor" is the floor above ground level

MIX
Paper from
responsible sources
FSC™ C018179
www.fsc.org

**The information in this
DK Eyewitness Travel Guide is checked regularly.**
Every effort has been made to ensure that this book is as
up-to-date as possible at the time of going to press. Some details, however, such as
telephone numbers, opening hours, prices, gallery hanging arrangements and
travel information are liable to change. The publishers cannot accept responsibility
for any consequences arising from the use of this book, nor for any material on third
party websites, and cannot guarantee that any website address in this book will be
a suitable source of travel information. We value the views and suggestions of our
readers very highly. Please write to:
Publisher, DK Eyewitness Travel Guides,
Dorling Kindersley, 80 Strand, London WC2R 0RL, UK,
or email: travelguides@dk.com.

Front cover main image: A sailing boat and cottage in the archipelago, Stockholm

◄ Traditional colorful fishing huts and boathouses along the wooden pier at Smögen

Summer-flowering cottongrass in the
mountains of Sylarna

Contents

Introducing
Sweden

Stockholm
Area by Area

Erik XIV's crown in the Treasury at
Stockholm's Royal Palace

Travellers' Needs

Cross-country skiers resting on Åreskutan mountain *(see p263)*

Lingonberries, a much-loved Swedish fruit

Survival Guide

Inner courtyard of Läckö Slott, Västergötland *(see p224)*

Sweden Area by Area

Royal Palace, Stockholm
(see pp58–61)

HOW TO USE THIS GUIDE

This guide helps you to get the most from your visit to Sweden. It provides both expert recommendations and detailed practical information. *Introducing Sweden* maps the country and sets it in its historical and cultural context. The ten regional chapters, including *Stockholm*, describe important sights using maps, photographs and illustrations. Suggestions on restaurants, hotels, shopping and entertainment are in *Travellers' Needs*. The *Survival Guide* has tips on everything from making a local telephone call to using local transportation, as well as information on money, etiquette and safety.

Stockholm

The centre of the capital and its surrounding area has been divided into four sightseeing areas. Each has its own chapter, which opens with a list of the sights to be covered. All sights are numbered and plotted on an area map. The detailed information for each sight follows the map's numerical order, making sights easy to locate within the chapter.

All pages relating to Stockholm have red thumb tabs.

Sights at a Glance lists the chapter's sights by category: Churches, Palaces and Museums, Historic Buildings, Streets and Squares.

A locator map shows where you are in relation to other areas of the city centre.

1 Area Map For easy reference, the sights are numbered and located on a map. Sights in the city centre are also shown on the Stockholm Street Finder on pages 118–23.

A suggested route for a walk is shown in red.

Stars indicate the sights that no visitor should miss.

2 Street-by-Street Map This gives a bird's eye view of the key areas in each chapter.

3 Detailed information The sights in Stockholm are described individually. Addresses, telephone numbers, opening hours and information on admission charges and wheelchair access are also provided for each entry.

Sweden Area by Area

Apart from Stockholm, Sweden has been divided into nine regions, each of which has a separate chapter. The most interesting towns and places to visit have been numbered on a *Regional Map*.

1 Introduction The landscape, history and character of each region is described here, showing how the area has developed over the centuries and what it offers to the visitor today.

Each area of Sweden can be quickly identified by its colour coding, shown on the inside front cover.

2 Regional Map This shows the road network and gives an illustrated overview of the whole region. All interesting places to visit are numbered and there are also useful tips on getting around the region by car and train.

3 Detailed information All the important towns and other places to visit are described individually. They are listed in order, following the numbering on the Regional Map. Within each town or city, there is detailed information on important buildings and other sights.

For all the top sights, a Visitor's Checklist provides the practical information you will need to plan your visit.

Story boxes highlight noteworthy features of the top sights.

4 Sweden's top sights These are given two or more full pages. Historic buildings are dissected to reveal their interiors. The most interesting towns or city centres are shown in a bird's eye view, with sights picked out and described.

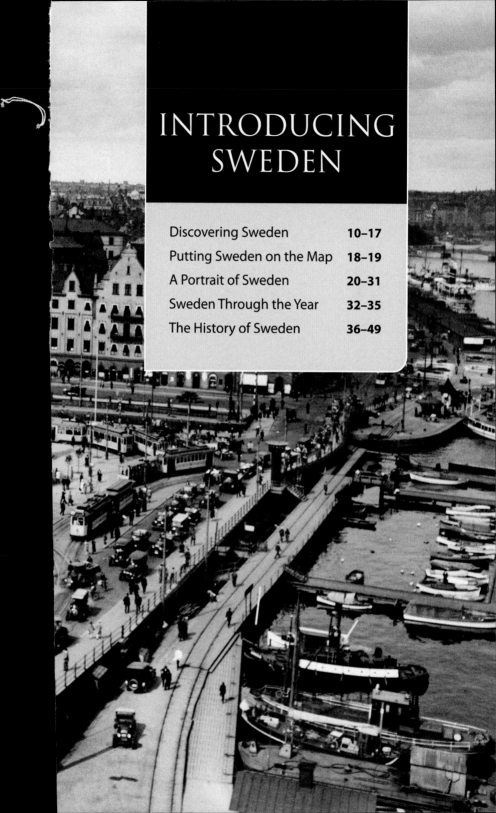

INTRODUCING
SWEDEN

DISCOVERING SWEDEN

The following tours have been created to take in a number of Sweden's highlights. In a country the size of Sweden, some long distance journeys are inevitable in order to reach more far-flung locations such as Lapland; however, the itineraries endeavour to keep travel distances realistic. To begin with, there are three two-day city tours, covering the capital Stockholm, Gothenburg and Malmö. These tours can be done individually or combined to form a seven- or ten-day tour, the latter with added suggestions. The city tours are followed by two seven-day tours taking in some of the most scenic parts of the country: the West Coast and Southern Sweden. Finally, there is a 14-day countrywide tour from south to north. Pick, choose and combine at your leisure.

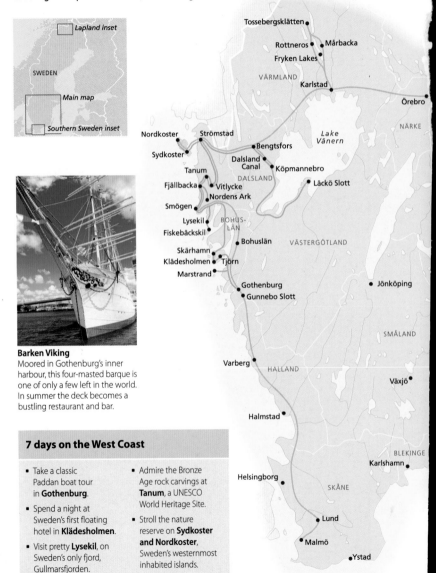

Barken Viking
Moored in Gothenburg's inner harbour, this four-masted barque is one of only a few left in the world. In summer the deck becomes a bustling restaurant and bar.

7 days on the West Coast

- Take a classic Paddan boat tour in **Gothenburg**.

- Spend a night at Sweden's first floating hotel in **Klädesholmen**.

- Visit pretty **Lysekil**, on Sweden's only fjord, Gullmarsfjorden.

- Admire the Bronze Age rock carvings at **Tanum**, a UNESCO World Heritage Site.

- Stroll the nature reserve on **Sydkoster and Nordkoster**, Sweden's westernmost inhabited islands.

14 days in Sweden

- Take a dip at the Moorish-style bath house in **Varberg**, a famous sea-bathing resort.
- Hit the slopes at Midsummer at Europe's northernmost ski resort, **Riksgränsen**.
- See the scenic lakes in rural **Värmland** province.
- Admire the impressive towers of **Örebro Slott**.
- Stroll the narrow cobbled streets of Stockholm's **Gamla Stan**.
- Discover the unique 17th-century warship *Vasa* at **Vasamuseet**.
- Spend a night at **ICEHOTEL** in Lapland (in winter).
- Experience Sami culture and reindeer herding in **Jukkasjärvi**.
- Explore the fishing communities of **Bohuslän**, on the West Coast.

0 kilometres 50
0 miles 50

Jukkasjärvi ↑
See inset map right

Stockholm

Lake Hjälmaren
Gripsholms Slott

SÖDERMANLAND

Björkliden
Riksgränsen
Abisko
Abiskojaure

0 kilometres 50
0 miles 30

LAPPLAND

Kiruna
Jukkasjärvi
Stockholm ↓

Norrköping
Linköping
ÖSTERGÖTLAND

Key
— Sweden tour
— West Coast tour
— Southern Sweden Tour

Västervik

Oskarshamn

Örebro Slott
This castle, on an island in Svartån, is one of Örebro's most popular attractions.

Bjärehalvön

0 kilometres 50
0 miles 30

Sofiero Castle
Söderåsen National Park
SKÅNE

Karlskrona

Helsingborg
Kristianstad

Frostavallen Höör
Åhus
Bosjökloster

DENMARK
Lund
Övedskloster

Malmö
Östarp
Österlen

Skanör
Falsterbo
Marsvinsholms Slott
Ystad
Ale Stenar

7 days in Southern Sweden

- Admire the Turning Torso building in **Malmö**'s Västra Hamnen (Western Harbour).
- Visit the stately home and former Benedictine convent of **Bosjökloster**.
- Enjoy a guided walk through the leafy forests of **Söderåsen National Park**.
- Take a boat tour in **Kristianstad** and explore the wetland centre and eco-museum Vattenriket.
- Marvel at the megalithic monument of **Ale Stenar**.

2 days in Stockholm

Sweden's capital Stockholm, situated on 14 islands, has many must-see sights, including the medieval Old Town (Gamla Stan) and the impressive warship museum Vasamuseet.

- **Arriving** Arlanda, Stockholm's main airport, is located 37 km (23 miles) north of the city. The Arlanda Express train runs non-stop from the main railway station. The city is also served by three smaller airports.

- **Moving on** The journey from Stockholm to Gothenburg takes around 3 hours by express train. Hiring a car or taking a domestic flight are other options.

Day 1

Morning A couple of days in the Swedish capital give you enough time to take in the main sights. Spend a morning in medieval **Gamla Stan** (pp54–67), Stockholm's stroller-friendly Old Town. Don't miss viewing some of the 608 rooms at the **Royal Palace** (pp58–61), and pay a visit to **Livrustkammaren** (p62), Sweden's oldest museum. At noon, be sure to catch the changing of the guard, in the Outer Courtyard. Gamla Stan is replete with cosy eateries, perfect for a lunchtime break.

Afternoon After lunch, amble across **Stortorget** square (p64), past the impressive 700-year-old late-Gothic cathedral **Storkyrkan** (p63), before entering **Riddarholmskyrkan** (p66), site of the royal burial vaults. Next, cross the waters of Riddarfjärden and head to **Stadshuset** (pp106–7), where the Nobel Prize dinners are held. End the day with drinks at the **Grand Hôtel** (p83), where you can enjoy fabulous city views.

Day 2

Morning Take time to discover the treasures of **Vasamuseet** (pp96–7) on the Djurgården

Splendidly frescoed ceiling in Stockholm's Baroque-style Royal Palace

Peninsula. The museum, the city's most popular, displays the *Vasa*, the only preserved 17th-century warship in the world, which capsized in Stockholm's harbour in 1628.

Afternoon Wander around the picturesque open-air museum at **Skansen** (p98), also on Djurgården, exploring historic buildings from across Sweden, as well as local folklore. Get a ferry across to Nybroplan and relax in the bar at **Berns** (p85), a Stockholm drinking and dining institution.

> **To extend your trip…**
> Spend a day trip combining **Drottningholm** palace (pp112–15) and the Viking settlement of **Birka** (pp136–7), and another exploring the **Stockholm Archipelago** (pp116–17) by boat.

2 days in Gothenburg

Gothenburg, Sweden's second city, has an interesting mix of Dutch-style canals, pleasant gardens and excellent shopping facilities.

- **Arriving** Landvetter, Gothenburg's main airport, is located 20 km (13 miles) southeast of the city. There is an airport bus service from the city's main coach and rail terminal. Smaller Gothenburg City airport is used by some low-cost carriers.

- **Moving on** The journey from Gothenburg to Malmö takes just over 3 hours by train. Alternatively, it is possible to hire a car.

Day 1

Morning Start the day at **Trädgårdsföreningen** (p202), a beautiful park where you can admire the flora of five continents, including 1,900 varieties of rose. Next, take a **Paddan Boat Tour** (p209) along the 17th-century canals.

Afternoon After lunch, walk up Kungsportsavenyn, the city's main avenue, viewing Stora Teatern on the way to **Götaplatsen** (pp204–5), Gothenburg's undisputed cultural hub. Admire the collection of Nordic art at **Konstmuseet** (pp204–5) or

Children enjoying the rides at Skansen, the world's first open-air museum

Malmöhus fortress, built in the 1500s and surrounded by a deep moat

catch an exhibition at nearby **Konsthallen** (p205). Continue to **Liseberg** amusement park (p204) for family fun and impressive rides, including the biggest roller coaster in the Nordic countries. The park offers plenty of dining and entertainment options.

Day 2
Morning Spend a morning shopping in **Nordstan** (p303), the largest mall in Scandinavia; those who prefer independent stores can head to the quirky designer boutiques near **Kronhuset** (p201) and the craft shops in **Kronhusbodarna** sheds (p201), Gothenburg's oldest buildings. Make a lunchtime visit to the bustling fish market, **Feskekôrka** (p205), where you can sample delicious West Coast fish and seafood.

Afternoon Venture into peaceful **Slottsskogen** (p208) for an exploratory wander. The park has some interesting old cottages, and the azalea valley is a must in springtime. Stop at **Naturhistoriska Museet** (p208), Gothenburg's oldest museum, inside the park, to see some of the 10 million exhibits.

> **To extend your trip...**
> Take a boat to **Nya Älvsborgs Fästning** (p209), a mid-17th-century fortress at the mouth of the Göta Älv.

2 days in Malmö

Malmö, Sweden's third city and its most ethnically diverse, is located just across the strait from Denmark. It is a vibrant, cosmopolitan centre.

- **Arriving** Malmö is served by Sturup airport, located 28 km (17 miles) to the east; airport buses run from downtown Malmö 30 times a day. Malmö is also easily reached from Copenhagen's airport, Kasturp, which is half an hour away by train.

Day 1
Morning Head for the historic centre, encircled by canals. The main square, **Stortorget** (p182), is surrounded by fine buildings, several of which are open to the public. Take in the impressive façades of **Rådhuset** (p182) and **Jörgen Kocks Hus** (p182), both of which date back to the 16th century, and **Residenset** (p182). Venture into Malmö's 12th-century cathedral **St Petri Kyrka** (p182) to admire the Renaissance altar, before stopping for coffee in **Lilla Torg** (p184), one of the city's most charming squares.

Afternoon Spend the afternoon discovering one of Europe's leading modern art collections at **Moderna Museet** (p182), which is housed inside an old power station.

Day 2
Morning Wander through the pleasant parks of central Malmö, **Slottsparken** (p184) and Kungsparken, strolling along their quaint canals. Make a special stop at **Malmöhus** (p184). An enormous 15th-century structure surrounded by a deep moat, this is the oldest Renaissance castle in Scandinavia and now houses **Malmö Museum** (p184). Don't miss the 18th-century tower with original cannons.

Afternoon A short walk from Malmöhus stands **Kommendantshuset** (p184), a former storage building now used for temporary art shows. Sneak a peek inside for the latest exhibition, then continue to **Västra Hamnen** (Western Harbour) (p185), Malmö's most recent architectural development. This area is located right by the sea, in the city's former shipyard, and it is home to the impressive **Turning Torso** tower (p185), completed in 2005. The building is mainly residential and therefore not open to the public, but it can be admired from the outside. Complete the afternoon with a leisurely stop at one of the seaside promenade bars or restaurants.

> **To extend your trip...**
> Spend a day in quaint **Ystad** (p186), enjoying its medieval architecture.

Malmö's stunning Turning Torso lit up in colour

7 days on the West Coast

- **Airports** Arrive and depart from Gothenburg's Landvetter airport.

- **Transport** The West Coast is best explored by car, although many coastal communities can be reached by train and bus. There are regular ferries from the mainland to many of the islands, including Syd- and Nordkoster. The train journey from Gothenburg to Strömstad takes 3 hours.

- **Booking ahead**
  Day 2: Salt & Sill floating hotel;
  Day 5: Nordens Ark.
  To extend your trip:
  Gunnebo Slott, Dalsland Canal boat trip.

Day 1: Gothenburg
Pick a day from the city itinerary on pages 12–13.

> **To extend your trip...**
> Take a day trip to the Neo-Classical **Gunnebo Slott** (p229), with its beautiful park and garden.

Day 2: Gothenburg to Klädesholmen
Spend the morning exploring Gothenburg further, strolling through the old workers' quarter of **Haga** (p205), now one of the city's trendiest neighbourhoods. Peek into the old wooden houses, home to interesting craft and design shops, then enjoy a coffee in one of the pretty cafés.
     After lunchtime, travel to **Marstrand** (pp220–21), only 45 minutes away by car (1 hour by bus), and pay a visit to Carlstens Fästning, a 17th-century fortress that served as a prison in the 1700s. A guided tour offers a fascinating glimpse into life behind its walls. Spend the night at Salt & Sill, Sweden's first floating hotel; it is located on Klädesholmen, a tiny outcrop on **Tjörn** (p220), one of the West Coast's main islands.

Day 3: Skärhamn to Lysekil
Start the day in **Skärhamn** (p220), the main town on Tjörn. A lively, vibrant community with a scenic location, it is best known for the Nordiska Akvarellmuseet (Nordic Watercolour Museum), housed in an attractive building jutting out into the water. Catch one of the exhibitions before visiting nearby Pilane Gravfält, an Iron Age burial site with impressive stone circles and standing stones on the northwest side of Tjörn. Follow the coastal road north to **Lysekil** (p218). Located in Gullmarsfjorden, Sweden's only real fjord, Lysekil is a charming, long-established seaside resort. Wander through 200-year-old Gammelstan and admire the quaint architecture of the restored 19th-century sea-bathing area.

Day 4: Lysekil to Fjällbacka
Take a short ferry ride across to **Fiskebäckskil** (p219). This seafaring community, dating back to the late 19th century, is home to many picturesque wooden cottages and plenty of local colour. Spend the morning strolling around the village, before returning to Lysekil by ferry. Continue on to **Smögen** (p217), one of Sweden's largest fishing communities, for some delicious seafood, then aim to reach **Fjällbacka** (pp216–17) in the afternoon. Use this village as your base over the next two nights.

Day 5: Fjällbacka and Nordens Ark
A former herring fishing port, Fjällbacka has retained its

Sea-kayaking in the waters of Fjällbacka

seafaring heritage and village atmosphere, despite increasing numbers of visitors. The low-rise wooden houses are painted in bright pastel colours and the harbour area buzzes with restaurants and bars. Try sea-kayaking, or visit some of the outlying islands by ferry. Then take the 3-km (2-mile) trail at nearby nature park **Nordens Ark** (p217), home to several endangered species. During the summer months a guided tour is included.

Day 6: Tanum and Vitlycke
Visit **Tanum** (p216), a UNESCO World Heritage Site renowned for its Bronze Age rock carvings. To view the largest of the rock carvings (200 sq m/2,150 sq ft), visit **Vitlycke Museum** (p216), which also has interesting Bronze Age displays. Further carvings can be viewed at Fossum, Tegneby and Asberget, all in the surrounding area.

Day 7: Koster Islands
Take a morning ferry from **Strömstad** (p215) and explore Sweden's most westerly

Panoramic view of Marstrand, a fashionable seaside resort

For practical information on travelling around Sweden, see pp328–31 inhabited islands, **Sydkoster** and **Nordkoster** *(p215)*, part of a nature reserve and marine national park. Sydkoster is best explored by bike, while its smaller neighbour, Nordkoster, is easy to walk around. Both islands are well known for their varied flora, peaceful atmosphere and quaint fishing huts.

An attractive medieval church in the Swedish coastal town of Åhus

> **To extend your trip…**
> Take a boat trip along the scenic **Dalsland Canal** *(p214)* down to Lake Vänern, or visit the splendid **Läckö Slott** *(p224)* on the lake's southern side.

7 days in Southern Sweden

- **Airports** Arrive and depart from Malmö Sturup airport.
- **Transport** Southern Sweden is best explored by car, although trains and buses connect towns and villages with the main hubs.
- **Booking ahead** Day 3: Höör Stone Age village; Day 4: Söderåsen National Park; Day 5: Vattenriket river tour.

Day 1: Malmö
Pick a day from the city itinerary on page 13.

Day 2: Lund
Explore the historic university town of **Lund** *(p181)*. Start with a visit to Lund Domkyrka, the 12th-century cathedral, home to a 14th-century astronomical clock, then continue on to the university grounds, which feature some of the oldest university buildings in the country. Next, enjoy Kulturen, an open-air museum with many well-preserved cottages and town houses. If there's time, head to Historiska Museet, which has one of Sweden's largest archaeological collections.

Day 3: Bosjökloster, Höör and Frostavallen
Start the morning at **Bosjökloster** *(p180)*, scenically situated on the shore of the Ringsjön lakes. This remarkable set of buildings was originally a Benedictine convent dating back to 1080. Today it's Skåne's most popular stately home, with extensive grounds, a restaurant, café and boat hire. Nearby **Höör** *(p180)* has a Stone Age village where visitors can sample life as it was back then. Continue to the area of **Frostavallen** *(p180)*, one of the most scenic in Skåne, for some late-afternoon canoeing or swimming in Lake Vaxsjön. There are also hiking trails, leisure facilities and plenty of overnight options.

Day 4: Söderåsen National Park and Kristianstad
Take a stroll in **Söderåsen National Park** *(p179)*, which covers a wide variety of landscapes; 1- or 2-hour guided tours give a good overview. Aim to reach the 17th-century town of **Kristianstad** *(p190)* in the afternoon, in time to visit the main attraction there, the Renaissance Heliga Trefaldighetskyrkan church.

A pretty half-timbered house in one of the idyllic alleys in Ystad

Day 5: Kristianstad and Åhus
Kristianstad's wetland centre and eco-museum **Vattenriket** *(p190)* can be explored on a guided river tour. Next, head to **Åhus** *(p190)*, a picturesque coastal community surrounded by sandy beaches. Follow the coastal route south, taking in the rolling, fertile landscape of **Österlen** *(p187)*, in the southeast.

Day 6: Ystad with Ale Stenar and Marsvinsholm Slott
Spend the morning discovering the Hanseatic and Danish influences in **Ystad** *(p186)*. Note the medieval buildings, some dating from the 11th century, and the traditional half-timbered houses found in the old parts of the centre. In the afternoon, visit **Ales Stenar** *(p186)*, a megalithic monument in the shape of a ship, before going on to **Marsvinsholms Slott** *(p186)*, an imposing 14th-century castle with beautiful grounds.

Day 7: Östarp, Övedskloster and Malmö
Pay a visit to **Östarp** *(pp180–81)*, a living open-air museum complete with a charming old-world inn. Next, visit another monastery turned stately home, **Övedskloster** *(pp180–81)*, built in Rococo style and surrounded by an elegant park. In the afternoon, return to Malmö.

> **To extend your trip…**
> Relax in the twin towns of **Skanör** and **Falsterbo** *(p181)*. Visit **Helsingborg** *(p178–9)*, **Sofiero Castle** *(p179)* and **Bjärehalvön** *(p178)*, on Skåne's west coast.

14 days in Sweden

- **Airports** Arrive at Malmö's Sturup airport and return from Kiruna airport via Stockholm.
- **Transport** Due to the size of Sweden, the country is best explored by car, particularly to reach some of the more remote areas. Trains and buses connect smaller towns and villages with the main hubs, while ferries ply the West Coast, Stockholm Archipelago and some of the larger lakes. To reach Lapland, take a domestic flight to Kiruna or the overnight train from Stockholm.
- **Booking ahead** Day 3: Tour of Gunnebo Slott; Day 7: Dalsland Canal Tour; Day 8: Tour of Mårbacka and Rottenros; Day 9: Gripsholms Slott; Days 11–12: Overnight train or domestic flight; Days 12–14: Kungsleden Trail.

Day 1: Malmö
Pick a day from the city itinerary on page 13.

Day 2: Lund
Spend a day exploring medieval **Lund** *(p181)*. This former capital of Denmark is now a thriving university town. Don't miss Kulturen, the open-air museum in the medieval centre, which

Ivy-covered building on the campus of Lund University

The Neo-Classical southern façade of Gunnebo Slott

has well-preserved old town houses and cottages. The university – the second largest in Sweden – boasts some of the oldest university buildings in the country. Make time to visit the cathedral, Lund Domkyrka, where the Gothic altarpiece and astronomical clock are well worth a look.

Day 3: Southern coastal road Lund–Gothenburg
Follow the southern coastal highway north from Lund and make a stop at **Varberg** *(p230)*. A 19th-century spa and sea-bathing resort, Varberg has plenty of seaside charm. Visit the Moorish-style cold bath house and the impressive fortress, Varbergs Fästning. Continue on to **Gunnebo Slott** *(p229)*, a magnificent mansion built in Neo-Classical Swedish style just outside Gothenburg. Tour the mansion, as well as its park and gardens, before ending the day in Gothenburg.

Day 4: Gothenburg
Pick a day from the city itinerary on pages 12–13.

Day 5: Northern coastal road Gothenburg–Strömstad
Continue along the northern coastal route through **Bohuslän** *(pp215–21)*, one of the most picturesque provinces in Sweden, replete with tiny fishing communities and seaside resorts. Pass two of the largest islands along the coast, **Tjörn** *(p220)* and **Orust** *(p220)*, then stretch your legs at **Smögen**

(p217), a lively summer resort. Wander along the wooden quayside and sample the catch of the day – shrimps are truly a delight here. Next, head further north to **Fjällbacka** *(pp216–17)*, another charming seaside village. Admire the quaint wooden houses and amble the narrow streets, soaking up the atmosphere. Take a short drive inland and stop at **Tanum** *(p216)* to view the extraordinary **Vitlycke** Bronze Age rock carvings, a UNESCO World Heritage Site *(p216)*. End the day in **Strömstad** *(p215)*, the northernmost resort on the Swedish West Coast.

Carl Milles's statue of *Poseidon* in Götaplatsen, Gothenburg

Day 6: Koster Islands
Spend a leisurely day on **Sydkoster** and **Nordkoster** *(p215)*. These two islands, easily reached from Strömstad, form a nature reserve that is renowned for its flora, and they're also part of Sweden's first marine

national park, **Kosterhavets** *(p215)*. In the morning, hire a bike to get around Sydkoster, the larger of the two, and take a picnic lunch to enjoy alfresco. Then take the inter-island ferry link to quieter Nordkoster, which is best explored on foot. Return by ferry to Strömstad in the late afternoon.

Day 7: Dalsland Canal
Arrive at Bengtsfors, and start the day with a quick walk around Gammelgården open-air museum before joining the **Dalsland Canal Tour** *(p214)*. The 5½-hour boat trip from Bengtsfors to Köpmannebro, on Lake Vänern, passes some stunning scenery, as well as rock carvings, manor houses and the spectacular Håverud Aqueduct, on its journey through 19 locks. Return to Bengtsfors by bus or train (1 hour), then drive to **Karlstad** *(p238)* or, if using public transport, continue north along Lake Vänern, ending the day in Karlstad.

Day 8: Exploring Värmland
Use Karlstad as a two-night base. Take a day trip around scenic parts of the province of Värmland, home to many artists, writers and poets. Drive north to the **Fryken Lakes** *(p236)*, three striking lakes in the heart of the province. Follow their east side and stop at **Mårbacka** *(p236)*, the family estate of Selma Lagerlöf, the first woman to be awarded the Nobel Prize for Literature. Take a guided tour of the beautiful manor house and gardens. Head north, then cross

Gripsholms Slott, home of the National Portrait Gallery

over to the west side of the lakes at Sunne to reach **Tossebergsklätten** *(p236)*, a hill near the northernmost lake, Övre Fryken, for splendid views of the surrounding landscape. Next, follow the west side of the lakes south to **Rottneros** *(p236)*, another superb manor house with a unique sculpture park and gardens. Return to Karlstad in the evening.

Day 9: Örebro and Gripsholms Slott
Örebro *(pp242–3)*, on Svartån River near Lake Hjälmaren, has a long-standing history and some impressive sights, including the massive 13th-century castle, Örebro Slott, now seat of the county governor. Take a self-guided tour around the Northwest Tower (free admission), then admire the façades of the Neo-Gothic-style town hall and St Nicolai Kyrka.

Spend the afternoon taking in the splendours of **Gripsholms Slott** *(pp138–9)*, one of Sweden's most stunning castles, surrounded by Lake Mälaren. The 16th-century castle has a vast collection of portraits in its National Portrait Gallery and some particularly fine pieces of furniture. End the day in Stockholm.

Days 10–11: Stockholm
Follow the city itineraries on page 12.

Days 12–14: Lapland
Sweden's remote frontier, Lapland offers the visitor the opportunity to get up close and personal with nature and experience the great outdoors.
If visiting in winter, spend a night at ICEHOTEL in **Jukkasjärvi** *(p276)*, sampling Arctic cuisine, experiencing Sami culture and taking in a Northern Lights, snow-mobile or husky-sled tour. Next, move on to one of three ski resorts in the area, **Björkliden**, **Abisko** or **Riksgränsen** *(p279)* for some quality cross-country or downhill skiing.
In summer, spend a couple of days hiking amid the stunning scenery. Take the train (or drive) from **Kiruna** *(p276)*, northern Lapland's main hub, to Abisko, part of the scenic **Kungsleden Trail** *(pp278–9)*, and follow the trail through Abisko National Park to Abiskojaure. Alternatively, continue by train to **Riksgränsen**, where skiing on the high slopes is still possible as late as Midsummer.

Opening one of the 19 locks on the Dalsland Canal

Putting Sweden on the Map

The kingdom of Sweden is one of the largest countries in Europe, covering 449,964 sq km (173,730 sq miles). The most southerly point, Smygehuk, lies at about the same latitude as Edinburgh in Scotland, and the northernmost tip, Treriksröset, is nearly 300 km (186 miles) north of the Arctic Circle. As the crow flies, Sweden is 1,572 km (977 miles) from south to north – the same distance as from Smygehuk to Rome. Sweden shares land borders with Norway to the west and Finland to the east, and water borders with Germany, Poland, Estonia, Latvia, Lithuania, Russia and Denmark, which lies across the Kattegat.

Northern Europe

Key

- ▬ Motorway
- ▬ Major road
- ⋯ Minor road
- — Train line
- – – – Ferry route
- ▬ International border

For additional map symbols *see back flap*

A PORTRAIT OF SWEDEN

Swedes are passionate about nature and the great outdoors, and justly so since their country contains large swathes of Europe's last surviving areas of wilderness. As a nation, Sweden has built its wealth on its natural resources and the ingenuity of its engineers. It has a heritage rich in music, literature and folk traditions, and its people have a deep-rooted sense of peace and democracy.

Few nations in Europe offer such an exceptionally diverse landscape, rich in flora and fauna, as Sweden. From north of the Arctic Circle the country stretches a lengthy 1,572 km (977 miles) south, a distance equal to almost half the length of Europe.

The extreme north is the land of the midnight sun, where daylight lasts for 24 hours in high summer, but is almost non-existent in mid-winter. Moving southwards, the forests and wetlands of Norrland provide habitats for large numbers of elk and a thriving birdlife. In the far south, the rolling plains of Skåne and the area around the great lakes make good arable land.

To the east, the green islands of the Stockholm archipelago contrast with the bare rocky outline of the west coast.

A Country Shaped by Ice

The mountain chain which runs along part of Sweden's border with northern Norway has several peaks more than 2,000 m (6,500 ft) high. It was formed when the ice which covered the country until 10,000 years ago retreated northwards. Several glaciers from this time still linger in the north.

The Climate

Sweden has a relatively mild climate for its northerly location. However, because of the length of the country, the temperature in autumn and spring can vary by more than 20° C (68° F) from one end to the other. Northern Sweden holds the record for the coldest temperature of -53° C (-63° F), while Ultuna, near Uppsala, has recorded the highest temperature of 38° C (100° F).

Start of the annual Vasaloppet race, which attracts some 16,000 skiers

◄ A knight parading during Gotland Medieval Week in Visby

Lars Magnus Ericsson, setting Sweden on the path to industrialization by founding Ericsson in 1876

There are occasional green winters in southern Sweden, but the heaviest snow fell in 1998, with 150 cm (5 ft) accumulating on 4–5 December in Gävle in central Sweden.

Space for All

Sweden covers an area of 449,964 sq km (173,731 sq miles), and with just 9 million inhabitants Swedes have plenty of space. In the forested areas, towns can be few and far between.

Towards the end of the 19th century and thanks largely to the coming of the railways, Sweden began to exploit her rich natural resources. Forestry and copper industries were established and the rivers were harnessed to produce hydro-electricity. Large manufacturing companies began to develop, such as Ericsson, Volvo and Scania, all of which are still in operation today. The needs of industry led to a massive shift in population. Today 85 per cent of the Swedish population lives in the cities and less than 2 per cent is employed in agriculture.

In the post-war period the need for labour led to immigration. Flows of immigrants became even greater at the end of the 20th century with the arrival of refugees from the world's trouble spots.

Government and Politics

Sweden is both a parliamentary democracy and a hereditary monarchy. As the head of state, the king has no political power, but he is considered to be an important representative of Sweden to the rest of the world. Carl XVI Gustaf is the descendant of one of Napoleon's marshals, Jean-Baptiste Bernadotte, who was chosen as the heir to the throne of the last of the Vasa kings, the childless Karl XIII. The Frenchman was crowned in 1818 as Carl XIV Johan, King of Sweden and Norway. Carl XVI Gustaf came to the throne in 1973 and married the German Silvia Sommerlath. Despite doubt over the king's choice of a commoner for his bride, Swedes soon took Queen Silvia to their hearts. The couple's eldest daughter, Crown Princess Victoria, is the heir to the throne.

Sweden's parliament, the Riksdag, has 349 members and is Sweden's legislative assembly. Elections are held every four years.

Since World War II, a balance has prevailed between the socialist and non-socialist parties in parliament. With only a few exceptions, the Social Democrats, as the largest group, have governed, either alone or with smaller supporting parties. Taxation has reached record levels, but the majority of Swedes tend to believe that they get value for money. However, an economic crisis in the 1990s led to cuts in health, education and social care. The environment is a key issue. Swedes have a deep-rooted love of nature, enshrined in the Right of Public Access, which guarantees free access to the forests and countryside and the right to pick berries and mushrooms. There is widespread support for combating pollution.

Emblem of state

Languages and Dialects

While Swedish is the dominant language, Finnish, Tornedalsfinska (the dialect of Finnish spoken in the Torne Valley) and Sami are all official minority languages. The largest of these is Finnish with around 20,000 speakers, while Sami is spoken by about 10,000 people.

Sweden players celebrate after scoring a goal against the United States during the 2011 FIFA Women's World Cup, held in Germany

Despite the general use of standard Swedish, dialects also flourish. The majority is multilingual and Swedes in general are often fluent in English.

Rich Culture

Besides the many specialist museums in the cities, there are more than 1,000 rural museums. Great interest is shown in art and handicrafts which can be seen in the galleries and shops.

Swedes are keen musicians, and many play in local orchestras or sing in choirs. Folk music and dancing enjoy a natural high season from Midsummer to the end of August.

The story of film culture also has a Swedish chapter, thanks to stars such as Greta Garbo, Ingrid Bergman, Max von Sydow and Stellan Skarsgård.

Sheltered archipelagos provide ideal conditions for Sweden's sailing enthusiasts

A Sporting Nation

Sweden's abundance of clean, unpolluted waters makes fishing a popular hobby, and the long coastline, glorious archipelagos and numerous waterways have made it a nation of sailors.

For a small nation Sweden has proud traditions, especially in winter sports. Skiing and ice hockey as well as football, handball, bandy (Russian hockey), tennis and golf, all set Swedish pulses racing, while swimming, athletics, boxing, water sports and motorsports also number several stars at international level.

Sweden on the World Stage

The neutrality which protected Sweden from two world wars has remained a guiding principle. Sweden did not join NATO, choosing instead to focus on its own defence and related industry.

Sweden has been a member of the EU since 1995 and elections to the European Parliament are held every five years. The attitude towards the EU is divided and in 2003, the Swedes voted "no" to adopting the euro by a considerable majority.

Sweden is an enthusiastic advocate for the work of the UN. Its own Dag Hammarskjöld was a celebrated Secretary-General (1953–61), and Swedish troops have been involved in peace initiatives worldwide.

Landscape and Wildlife

Sweden has a remarkably varied landscape. The flat arable land of Skåne in the south gives way to lakes and forests, rugged mountains, fast-flowing rivers and wild open moorland further north, leading to the Arctic tundra. Plant and animal species from both continental Europe and the Arctic thrive. Large areas of wilderness have become enclaves where endangered species such as bears and wolves, snakes and owls have been able to survive the pressure from civilization. The coastline, too, is immensely varied. Marine life is unique, as North Sea fish make their way into the brackish water of the Baltic and mix with species normally only found in fresh water.

Wolves are a threatened species and, despite migration from neighbouring countries, there are only around 300 in Sweden.

Coasts and Islands

Smooth rocks and sandy beaches dominate the west coast, where marine life includes saltwater fish such as cod and haddock. Freshwater pike and whitefish can be found off the northerly stretches of the east coast. On the limestone islands of Öland and Gotland orchid meadows flourish.

The Arable South

The flat lands of Skåne with their fields of crops, willow windbreaks and half-timbered houses topped by storks' nests are a familiar image of Sweden. But just as typical are the stony pastures and juniper slopes of Småland surrounding red cottages, and the meadows and pasture lands of Mälardalen.

Seals declined in number as a result of hunting, pollution and disease. But now populations of grey seals, ringed seals and harbour seals (pictured) are increasing, thanks to their protected status.

Roe deer were almost extinct in the early 19th century. Now they are so common in southern and central Sweden that they are known to raid local gardens in search of food.

Sea eagles, with a wing span of up to 250 cm (8 ft), are Sweden's largest birds of prey. They nest along the east coast and also on lakes in Lappland.

Hedgehogs rely on their 5,000 spines for protection and curl into a ball at the approach of danger. But this is of little effect against cars, and the popular doorstep guest is in decline.

Sweden's Flora

Considering Sweden's unusually rich flora, it is not surprising that the father of botany, Carl von Linné *(see p134)*, was born here. There are more than 2,000 species of flowers alone. After a long cold winter, nature explodes into life with a profusion of blooms, as in the orchid meadows of Öland. Swedes' love of wild flowers is illustrated by the maypoles and garlands used to celebrate Midsummer.

Wood anemones carpeting the forests signal the arrival of spring.

The red water-lily can only be found in some lakes in Tiveden National Park.

King Karl's Spire can grow 1 m (3 ft) tall – an impressive height for an orchid. It is most common in swampy mountain areas.

Forests

More than half of Sweden's land area is covered by forests, with deciduous trees in the south, coniferous forests with pines and spruce further north. Here lingonberries, blueberries and chanterelles grow. This is the home of elk and beaver, and forest birds such as capercaillies and black grouse.

The elk is the big game of the forest. Around 100,000 elk are killed in the annual hunting season and, despite the road warning signs, others die in accidents involving cars.

The brown bear is the largest of Sweden's predators and can weigh up to 300 kg (660 lb). It may look slow, but it moves quickly and is dangerous if disturbed.

The Far North

The mountains and moorlands are characterized by their proximity to the Arctic. With late spring come the migratory birds such as hooper swans and the lesser white-fronted goose, and the mountain flora bursts into flower. Wolves, bears, wolverine and lynx inhabit the national parks.

Reindeer live as domesticated animals in northern Sweden, farmed by Sami in the mountains and forests. In winter the herds move further south to graze.

The ptarmigan lives above the tree line and is often encountered, as it is unafraid of mountain hikers. It follows the changing seasons with up to four changes of plumage.

Sweden's Wooden Houses

The quintessential image of Sweden is the red-and-white painted wooden cottage. Originally, wooden houses were not considered attractive so they were painted red to make them look as though they were built of brick, or yellow to represent stone, and this tradition has continued. Every building from the humblest hut to the most majestic mansion was made of timber from the large tracts of forest. Wood triumphs in the grandiose manor houses of Hälsingland and the decoratively carved merchants' homes of the Stockholm Archipelago. Even today, architects are developing innovative ways of using this classic material.

Bell Tower
Many 18th-century churches had wooden bell towers: Delsbo's, with its elegant onion cupola, dates from 1742.

Hut in Härjedalen
This simple log-built hut in the mountain pasture of Ruändan incorporates the centuries-old tradition of a grass roof.

Interlocking posts bind together the external and interior walls, while the façades are often boarded.

Skogaholm Manor
Built in the 1680s, this Carolean timber house from Närke was originally painted red. In the 1790s, it was given a yellow plaster façade and large windows in line with Gustavian style. It has now been moved to the museum at Skansen.

The façade is clad in pine and painted with a copper-vitriol paint, known as Falun Red, to prevent rotting.

Halsingland's Manor Houses

Reaping the benefits from the lucrative 19th-century timber industry, the forest-owning farmers of Hälsingland built themselves extravagant manor houses. The size of house and magnificence of the painted portico reflected the owner's wealth and status. The interiors were often decorated with wall paintings.

Swedenborg's Pavilion
The miniature manor house of philosopher Emanuel Swedenborg (1688–1772). It is now at Skansen (see p98).

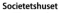

Societetshuset
Decorative wooden buildings, such as this club house for wealthy visitors to the seaside town of Marstrand (see p220), were a feature of the fashionable west coast bathing resorts in the late 19th century.

Modern Wooden Architecture

The Nordic Watercolour Museum *(see p220)* in Skärhamn on the west coast opened in 2000. The Danish architects Bruun/Corfitsen have clad the building's steel and concrete shell with vertical wooden panels in red, using this traditional material in a public setting.

Wooden Lighthouse

Dating from 1840, the wooden lighthouse at Bönan also served as a pilot station. It marked the shipping route into Gävle. The building is now a museum.

Two-storey houses are common in Hälsingland. The finest have an attic floor with half-windows.

Merchant's House in the Archipelago

In the late 19th century Stockholm's upper middle classes spent their summers in the archipelago, where they built magnificent wooden villas with verandas, summer houses, bathing huts and boat houses.

Foundations are a course of cobblestones.

Porticoes and outer doors are particularly richly ornamented and painted. Other details include turned pillars, intricate woodcarving and elegant roofs. The designs vary from parish to parish.

Fishing Cottages at Kungshamn

In fishing villages on the rocky islands of Bohuslän, where space is tight, timber-clad houses in pastel shades crowd in higgledy-piggledy fashion around the harbours.

Decorative Woodwork

More expensive wooden houses dating from around 1900 were often a riot of fretwork and rich ornamentation, known as "carpenter's joy", on verandas, entrances and gables.

Traditions, Customs and Folklore

Since the late 20th century, globalization and the gradual erosion of regional identity have had a major impact on Swedish traditions and lifestyle. Much of the formerly rigid etiquette has been relaxed and today Swedes are more informal when it comes to dress and manners. However, despite this culture shift, Swedes still hold onto their roots, local customs, history and traditions. They are passionate about their little red cottages, the countryside, eating herring at Midsummer and enjoying the first fresh strawberries.

Sami in traditional costume for a celebratory occasion

Feasts and Festivities

Celebrating the high points of the year within the family has again become increasingly important, after a dismissive attitude towards tradition in the 1960s and 70s.

Many traditions have pagan origins, most of them related to the coming and going of seasons, and are an excuse to eat special treats and play games. The most important is Midsummer, the summer solstice feast. Along with dancing and games around the maypole, the light, short night (when all sorts of magic is in the air) can be marked by watching the sun set and rise a few hours apart (or hardly at all in the north). For those who go to bed it is the custom to pick seven different flowers in silence and place them under their pillow; their future partner will appear in their dreams. Walpurgis night, 30 April, is when the last day of winter is chased away with huge bonfires, and songs and speeches welcome spring. Lucia Day, in December, is an intricate mix of pagan and Christian, a festival of light at the onslaught of darkness, which has adopted a Christian martyr as its symbol of hope and bringer of light. Every school, office and church has a Lucia, a girl dressed in white with a red ribbon around her waist symbolizing the martyr's blood, and a crown of candles on her head (see p35).

Easter also has elements of old folk beliefs. Maundy Thursday is the day witches fly to Blåkulla (see p158) to dance with the devil. Today, children dress up, broomsticks and all, and give handmade Easter greetings cards in exchange for sweets. Christmas is preceded by the hectic run-up of Advent, when Swedes go partying and consume vast quantities of glögg (mulled wine usually mixed with cognac or vodka), lussebullar (saffron buns) and pepparkakor (ginger snaps).

Dress and Etiquette

Those who own a folk costume take it out for midsummer, folk dances, weddings and other formal occasions. Each region has its own historic style and there is also a national dress (see p20). The Sami have their own elaborate costumes.

At weddings people are expected to dress up, as specified on the invitation (white tie, black tie or suit). In everyday life, style is more casual, especially in summer.

Although Swedes are more easy-going these days, they are still fond of etiquette. It is important to know how to "skål". Swedes first raise their glass to their female partner at the table, and then to the hostess. People look each other in the eye while raising their glass and saying "skål", looking down as they drink and then re-establishing eye contact before putting down their glass. If the skål is communal, everyone has to look each person around the table in the eye before drinking.

Despite this interest in etiquette, Swedes tend not to observe minor courtesies such as holding open doors or apologizing when they bump into someone. They are very informal when addressing one another; everyone is on first name terms from the start, even when doing business.

Singers and Musicians

More than half a million Swedes sing in a choir, and their passion for song is reflected not just in

Midsummer celebrations with games and dancing round the maypole

singing at parties and the ever-increasing repertoire of drinking songs, but also in the popularity of singing together. There are few 50th birthday parties where each plate doesn't come with a songbook or where friends don't perform songs they have written themselves. Everyone is expected to know works by troubadour Carl Bellman and ballads by Evert Taube *(see p66)*.

Folk music is played at clubs and there are festivals dedicated to folk instruments such as the accordion and hurdy-gurdy. Pageants and history plays have also seen a huge upturn in popularity.

Close to Nature

The Swedes' love of nature is deeply rooted. Many feel, subconsciously, an almost spiritual affinity with the forest, mountains or the sea. Legends and folklore are often linked to nature and many mythical beings are part of country lore. Trolls dwell in the forest, as does the Skogsrå or Huldra (siren), a beautiful young woman who lures men deeper and deeper into the woods and then, once they are lost, she turns around and all there is to be seen is a hollow tree. Women who stroll too far might hear a lovely tune drifting among the trees – that is Näcken, a handsome naked man, playing his fiddle in the middle of gushing streams and, needless to say, it is best to stay away from him. Giants and dwarfs roam the mountains

A tournament during Medieval Week, a popular pageant in Visby

while elves dance in the meadows and marshlands. Some beings have adopted modern guises. The Tomte, who traditionally is a stern, grey little man guarding farmers' barns and livestock, has been transformed into a kindly distributor of Christmas gifts. In the countryside, however, a plate of Christmas porridge is left for him on the doorstep, just to be safe.

There is a strong awareness of the changing seasons, linked to how deeply Swedes long for the bright summer. Spring is a slow affair, building up with the blossoming of one flower at a time, each one eagerly awaited. People know when each bloom is due, hence expressions like "between bird cherry and lilac" (ie "at end of May").

On a more practical note, it is easy to be physically close to nature thanks to the Right of Public Access. This grants everyone access to all land, apart from the immediate surroundings of a house or farm *(see p312)*. Many make the most of this resource, walking, camping, or going mushroom- or berry-picking.

A Country Cottage

The little red cottage is the symbol of paradise. Maybe it is the Swedes' farming roots combined with the brief summer which makes having a holiday house in the countryside or out on an island such a major ambition.

When spring comes, people head out to tend their cottage gardens, and as the autumn nights draw in they are still at their cottages, curled up by the fire. Almost half the population have access to a summer cottage and 20 per cent own one of their own.

Culinary Traditions

People are rediscovering old Swedish dishes and there has been something of a revival in *husmanskost* ("home-cooking"). Few, however, have time to prepare these at home on a daily basis, so childhood favourites such as *kalops* (a slow-cooked meat stew), *köttbullar* (meatballs) and freshly cleaned and fried herring fillets are now often enjoyed in restaurants.

Strawberry cream cake

Swedes drink lots of coffee, and at work the *fika paus* (coffee break) is strictly observed. In fact, *fika* is something everyone does, as proven by the large number of cafés even in small towns. To accompany coffee there is a great variety of *bullar* (buns), cakes, gateaux and biscuits. Home-made sponge cake layered with lots of whipped cream and strawberries is a summer favourite, especially for birthdays.

Painting depicting mythical beings in the forest

Swedish Design

Swedish design first attracted international attention at the 1925 World Exhibition in Paris, when glassware in particular took the world by storm and the concept of "Swedish Grace" was launched. The nation's design tradition is characterized by simplicity and functionality, with a major emphasis on natural materials. Swedish designers and architects are renowned for creating simple, attractive, "human" objects for everyday use. The 20th century marked the beginning of a new golden age, in which Swedish design has won worldwide acclaim.

Stoneware, Hans Hedberg
Swedish ceramics from the 1940s, 50s and 60s, such as this stoneware egg, are popular with collectors around the world.

Armchair (1969), Bruno Mathsson
Bruno Mathsson, one of Sweden's most famous 20th-century furniture designers, is one of the creators of the style that became known as "Swedish Modern". He designed the first version of the Pernilla armchair in 1942.

Pale wood and simplicity is the concept most closely associated with Swedish style.

Rag rugs are an old Swedish weaving tradition adopted by Karin Larsson, whose skill as a textile designer is widely recognized.

Cabinet (1952), Josef Frank
Frank was born in Austria, but worked in Sweden, and was another disciple of the "Swedish Modern" style. He is best known for his printed textiles, but he also designed furniture.

Carpet (1931), Märta Måås-Fjetterström
From 1919, Märta Måås-Fjetterström wove her famous rugs at her studio in Skåne. Her work was inspired by folklore and nature, and she created a design concept that was new but still firmly rooted in tradition.

Silver jug (1953) Sigurd Persson
Persson has an unrivalled ability to handle metal. He made his mark on the history of design with his everyday industrial pieces and exclusive artworks.

Chair (1981), Jonas Bohlin
The *Concrete* chair was the most talked about piece of Swedish furniture in the 1980s. A graduation project, it represented an entirely new approach to furniture design.

Flowers and plants on a windowsill and no curtains typifies the Larssons' ideas on interior decoration.

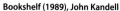

Bookshelf (1989), John Kandell
The *Pilaster* bookshelf stores books horizontally instead of vertically. The lines are simple and typically Scandinavian. The maker, Källemo, is one of Sweden's most unconventional furniture companies.

Gustavian late 18th-century style elements have remained a strong feature in Swedish design through the centuries, but made an international comeback in the 1990s.

Vase, Ann Wåhlström
Wahlström is one of Kosta Boda's new generation of glass designers. Organic, warm and beautiful, *Cyklon* (1998) is an excellent example of contemporary Swedish glass.

Where to See Swedish Design

Asplund
Sibyllegatan 31, Stockholm. **Map** 2 E3.

Nationalmuseum
Södra Blasieholmshamnen, Stockholm. **Map** 4 D2.

Nordiska museet
Djurgårdsvågen 6–16, Stockholm. **Map** 4 F1.

Svenskt Tenn
Strandvägen 5, Stockholm. **Map** 2 E4.

Design Torget
Various major towns and cities, including Vallgatan 14, Gothenburg.

Röhsska Museet
Vasagatan 37–39, Gothenburg.

Malmö Modern
Skeppsbron 3, Malmö.

Glassworks shops
Various, Småland. *(See pp156–7).*

SWEDEN THROUGH THE YEAR

Thanks to Sweden's geographical location, it experiences wide variations in seasons and climate. Winter retains its icy hold on the north until May, when in the south Skåne is often already basking in sunshine. Once spring gets going in the north and the days lengthen, nature soon catches up. Summers can be pleasantly warm throughout Sweden and that is when Swedes head off into the countryside to swim and enjoy the outdoor life, often staying in a summer cottage. The holiday period from late June to August is the height of the tourist season, with the widest range of attractions on offer. In winter, Swedes make for the mountains, which see the first snowfall as early as November. They value festivals, and events such as Christmas, New Year, Easter, Midsummer's Eve and Walpurgis are celebrated with enthusiasm.

An April start for the salmon fly-fishing season in Mörrum

Spring

After the long, dark Swedish winter, spring makes a welcome appearance. In Skåne the migratory birds return and spring flowers bloom in March, while in the north it's mid-May before winter releases its hold. Traditionally eaten before Lent, the *semla* cream bun is a tempting treat. Walpurgis Night, on the last day of April, marks a farewell to winter with folk dancing, torchlight processions, student choirs, bonfires and fireworks.

March
Vasa Ski Race *(early Mar)*. World famous long-distance ski race *(see p249)*.
Stockholm International Boat Show *(early Mar)*. The spring's major boat exhibition at Stockholm International Fairs in Älvsjö.
Åselenappet *(end of Mar)*. Ice-fishing competition, which is the high point of the winter market in Åsele, Lapland.
The "crane dance", Hornborgasjön *(Mar/Apr)*. Several thousand cranes gather on the fields around this lake in Västergötland for their spectacular annual mating dance. Quite a sight to behold.

April
Start of Salmon Fishing Season, Mörrum *(1 Apr)*, Sweden's main salmon river *(see p191)*.
Walpurgis Night *(30 Apr)*. Around the country bonfires welcome in the new season, with students donning their white caps and making merry. In the student town of Uppsala, Walpurgis Night also includes fine student choirs, a fun river-rafting carnival and lots of other events.

May
May Day *(1 May)*. Workers' processions countrywide.
Linné's birthday, Stenbrohult *(23 May)*. The father of botany is commemorated at his childhood home in Småland.
Elite Race *(last weekend in May)*. International trotting competition at Solvalla.
Trollhättan waterfalls *(Sat in May, Jun & Sep; daily Jul & Aug)*. Magnificent falls, usually tamed by the power station, burst into life (3pm).
Stockholm Photography Week *(late May/early Jun)*. An event for professionals, amateurs and lovers of the photographic arts. Held at the Swedish Museum of Photography (Fotografiska), at Stadsgårdshamnen 22.

Summer

The school year finishes in early June and summer comes into its own with Midsummer celebrations and dancing

Walpurgis Night bonfire, at Riddarholmen, Stockholm

Midsummer celebrations at Skansen open-air museum, Stockholm

round the maypole. Evenings are often warm and the nights light, encouraging parties round the clock. In the far north the sun doesn't even set. July is traditionally the main holiday month and favourite spots can become crowded. But Sweden is big and there's room for everyone. The start of the school term at the end of August coincides with two popular culinary festivals celebrating crayfish and fermented Baltic herring.

June

Stockholm Marathon *(early Jun)*. One of the world's ten biggest marathons with up to 21,500 runners.

Archipelago Boat Day, Stockholm *(Jun)*. Classic steamboats assemble at Strömkajen for a round trip to Vaxholm.

National Day *(6 Jun)*. A public holiday since 2005, National Day is celebrated around the country as Swedish Flag Day. The royal family attend the celebrations at Skansen in Stockholm.

Postrodden Mail Boat Race, Grisslehamn *(mid-Jun)*. Rowing race to the Åland islands following the old mail route.

"Vätternrundan" *(mid-Jun)*. Classic cycling race 300 km (190 miles) round Lake Vättern with around 20,000 participants, starting and finishing in Motala.

Midsummer's Eve *(penultimate Sat in Jun)*. A major Swedish festival celebrated by dancing around a flower-bedecked maypole. Midsummer in Dalarna,

Rättvik, Leksand and Mora is especially rich in tradition with folk music and the wearing of colourful national costumes.

Peace and Love Festival *(end of Jun)*. Large music festival, held in Borlänge.

ÅF Offshore Race *(end of Jun/ early Jul)*. Major international sailing race around Gotland, starting in Stockholm and finishing in Sandhamn, in the Stockholm Archipelago.

July

Skule Song Festival *(first weekend in Jul)*. One of Sweden's largest singing festivals, held at the foot of the Skule mountain on the High Coast.

Vansbro Swim *(early Jul)*. Up to 8,700 people take part in the 3-km (2-mile) swim in the Vanån and Västerdal rivers, starting in Vansbro.

Stånga Games, Gotland *(mid-Jul)*. Events featuring Gotland sports such as Square-and-border-ball, The Stone, Gotlandic Pole Throwing and "Hook the Bottom".

Gammelvala Brunskog, Värmland *(end of Jul)*. Week-long festival celebrating the domestic skills of the past. Music, exhibitions, drama and local food.

Storsjöyran Festival *(end of Jul)*. This week-long festival of pop and rock music in "the Republic of Jämtland" also offers drama, exhibitions and street artists.

Music in the Kingdom of Crystal, Småland's Glassworks *(end of Jul)*. Folk music, choral singing, opera, wind bands and jazz in a charming setting.

Kukkolaforsen Whitefish Festival *(last weekend in Jul)*. Celebrations in Sweden and Finland to mark the whitefish reaching the Torneälven river, which forms the border between the two countries. The fish are caught in large nets and eaten grilled or smoked.

August

Skänninge Market, Östergötland *(first Wed & Thu in Aug)*. One of Sweden's most traditional markets, attracting 120,000 visitors to this medieval city.

Gotland Medieval Week *(early Aug)*. Visby is turned into a 14th-century Hanseatic city with tournaments, plays and music and participants in colourful medieval costumes.

Royal Philharmonic Orchestra Outdoor Concert, Stockholm *(mid-Aug)*. This concert on the lawn outside Sjöhistoriska Museet is one of the highlights of the season.

Hjo Accordion Festival *(mid-Aug)*. Accordion players from around the world meet in the small town of Hjo on the shores of Lake Vättern.

Gothenburg Jazz Festival *(end of Aug)*. This three-day festival of swing, jazz, gospel and blues takes place at seven locations around the city.

Crayfish and Fermented Herring *(end of Aug)*. Although there is no longer a statutory start date for eating these delicacies – accompanied by ice-cold schnapps and cheese – this is when Swedes party the most.

Medieval Week tournament in Visby, Gotland

Beech forest in autumn at Söderåsen, Skåne

Autumn

The nights may be drawing in, but the mornings are light and the days often crisp and clear. In late autumn deciduous trees provide a stunning display of colours. It's harvest time in the forests and countryside, and a wide variety of delicious edible mushrooms, as well as blueberries, lingonberries and the red-gold cloudberries of the northern marshes are all ripe for the picking.

September

Oxhälja Market, Filipstad *(early Sep)*. This traditional market takes place in eastern Värmland.

Tjejmilen, Stockholm *(early Sep)*. In a lively atmosphere at Djurgården, Stockholm's royal park, 33,000 women take part in a 10 km run.

Swedish Trotting Derby, Jägersro *(Sep)*. Sweden's top four year-olds compete for

Chanterelles

the derby title on the trotting track in Malmö.

Kivik Apple Market *(end Sep)*. Apples are the focus of this two-day festival, which attracts around 20,000 visitors. Giant art installations created with tons of apples are a particular highlight.

Harvest Festival, Öland *(end Sep/early Oct)*. Sweden's biggest harvest festival takes place over four days around Michaelmas, with around 900 events attracting 200,000 visitors to enjoy local food, concerts and exhibitions.

October

LidingöLoppet *(first weekend in Oct)*. The world's largest cross-country race, with tens of thousands of competitors, including elite runners, senior citizens and children.

Umeå International Jazz Festival *(end Oct)*. This leading jazz festival was first staged in the 1960s.

Climate

Considerable variations in climate from north to south sometimes result in southern Sweden having no snow and temperatures above freezing in winter, while the north is blanketed in thick snow. The differences are less extreme in summer. The effect of the North Atlantic and the Gulf Stream is felt on the west coast in mild damp winds and the highest rainfall.

STOCKHOLM			
°C/°F	22/76		
	13/55	10/50	
9/48		5/41	
1/34			-1/30
			-5/23
6 hrs	8 hrs	3 hrs	1 hrs
30 mm	72 mm	50 mm	39 mm
month **Apr**	**Jul**	**Oct**	**Jan**

GOTHENBURG			
°C/°F	21/70		
	13/55	12/54	
10/50		6/43	
2/36			1/34
			-3/27
6 hrs	8 hrs	3 hrs	1 hrs
41 mm	68 mm	83 mm	61 mm
month **Apr**	**Jul**	**Oct**	**Jan**

Average maximum temperature

Average minimum temperature

Average daily hours of sunshine

Average monthly rainfall

MALMÖ			
°C/°F	21/70		
	13/55	12/54	
10/50		7/45	
2/36			2/36
			-3/27
6 hrs	7 hrs	3 hrs	1 hrs
38 mm	61 mm	57 mm	49 mm
month **Apr**	**Jul**	**Oct**	**Jan**

ÖSTERSUND			
°C/°F	19/66		
		10/50	
5/41		6/43	
-3/27		1/34	-6/21
			-13/9
6 hrs	7 hrs	2 hrs	1 hrs
32 mm	86 mm	45 mm	36 mm
month **Apr**	**Jul**	**Oct**	**Jan**

LULEÅ			
°C/°F	20/68		
		11/52	
4/39		6/43	
-4/25		0/32	-7/19
			-16/3
7 hrs	10 hrs	7 hrs	0.6 hrs
29 mm	50 mm	50 mm	40 mm
month **Apr**	**Jul**	**Oct**	**Jan**

Winter

While Christmas does not always go hand in hand with snow in southern Sweden, there are plenty of opportunities for ice-skating and there's always a chance of a white January. The mountains become a paradise for skiers, while snow cannons help out elsewhere if nature isn't up to the job. From the first day of Advent, the Christmas season is in full swing, culminating in present-giving on Christmas Eve. Restaurants enjoy their busiest time and Lucia processions brighten the winter darkness.

Lucia, the "Queen of Light", with her attendants at Skansen

November

Gustav Adolf Day *(6 Nov)*. Gothenburg celebrates the royal founder of the city on the anniversary of his death *(see p199)*.
St Martin's Day *(10–11 Nov)*. Roast goose and "black soup" containing goose blood are served at parties for St Martin of Tours and Martin Luther.

December

Nobel Day *(10 Dec)*. The year's Nobel Prize laureates are honoured in a ceremony at Konserthuset (Concert Hall) and a banquet in Stadshuset (City Hall) attended by the King and Queen.
Lucia Celebrations *(13 Dec)*. Sweden's chosen Lucia, with her girl attendants and "star boys", serves the Nobel laureates morning coffee with saffron buns and performs traditional songs. In the evening a Lucia procession winds through the capital to celebrations and fireworks at Skansen. Similar Lucia processions take place throughout Sweden and, on a smaller scale, in many homes and schools.
Christmas Markets throughout Sweden *(from early Dec)*. The markets at Skansen and Stortorget in Stockholm are particularly atmospheric.
Christmas *(24–26 Dec)*. Filled with traditions, Christmas is the most important Swedish holiday. The main event is Christmas Eve when an abundant *smörgåsbord* is followed by gifts. Christmas Day often begins with a church service.
New Year *(31 Dec–1 Jan)*. People go out on the town. Celebrations are televised from Skansen, including a traditional midnight reading of Tennyson's *"Ring out wild bells…"* Church bells peal and there are spectacular fireworks displays.

January

Hindersmässan *(end Jan)*. Market in Örebro dating back to medieval times.
Kiruna Snow Festival, *(last week in Jan)*. Renowned festival, especially for its reindeer racing.

February

Jokkmokks Winter Market *(first weekend in Feb)*. Colourful festival with market, reindeer sledding and races.
Gothenburg Boat Show *(early Feb)*. New boats on show at the Swedish Exhibition Centre in Gothenburg.
Vikingarännet *(as soon as the ice holds)*. Long-distance ice-skating race between Stockholm and Uppsala.
Globen Gala *(2nd half of Feb)*. Athletes compete at this top indoor competition.
Spring Salon *(Feb–Mar)*. Annual art exhibition of new talent at Liljevalchs, Stockholm.

Man in traditional outfit at the Jokkmokks Winter Market in Lapland

Public Holidays

New Year's Day (1 Jan)
Epiphany (6 Jan)
Good Friday (Mar/Apr)
Easter Monday (Mar/Apr)
Ascension Day (6th Thu after Easter)
Labour Day (1 May)
National Day (6 Jun)
Midsummer (Jun)
Christmas Day (25 Dec)
Boxing Day (26 Dec)

Frozen Riddarfjärden in Stockholm as a winter park

THE HISTORY OF SWEDEN

Described in the 4th century BC as a land of frozen seas and midnight sun, this northerly nation of reindeer herders also produced the fearsome Viking traders of the 9th century. By the 17th century, Sweden, in its Age of Greatness, ruled supreme over the Baltic region. Vanquished by Russia in 1809, the country adopted a more peaceful role and today is heavily engaged in world affairs.

In the last 100,000 years, Sweden has been covered by thick inland ice on at least three occasions. As the ice retreated northwards for the last time in approximately 12,000 BC, nomadic reindeer hunters moved in to use the newly revealed land, but it was not until 6500 BC that Sweden was entirely free of ice.

Farming was gradually adopted in southern Sweden from 4000 BC, while hunting continued to remain prevalent in the inland areas of Norrland for a long time to come. The first examples of domestic pottery date from this period and burial mounds appeared in the southern provinces.

Finds from the Bronze Age (1800–500 BC) bear witness to increased contact with the outside world. A chieftain society based on power and social alliances began to develop. Magnificent bronze objects, huge burial mounds and cairns with grave goods as well as rock carvings date from this period (see p216).

The transition to the Iron Age in 500 BC saw the first written accounts about Scandinavia. In the 4th century BC the Greek explorer and trader, Phytheas of Massilia, described the journey to "Thule", with its frozen seas and midnight sun. In his *Germania* (AD 98), the Roman Tacitus refers to the *"sviones"* as a powerful people with strong men, weapons and fleets.

With the growth of the Roman Empire, links with the Continent increased and numerous finds show evidence of trade with Rome via the many German tribes in the area north of the Rhine. The fall of Rome and the subsequent period of population migrations saw the rise of small kingdoms across Europe. In Sweden there was a kingdom centred on Uppsala where large *kungshögar* (King's Mounds) can still be seen today (see p135).

From 800 until Christianity reached Sweden in the mid-11th century, the Vikings took the world by storm. As traders, settlers and plunderers, they set sail in search of land, slaves and treasure. They carried out raids throughout Europe, sailed as far as Baghdad and even reached America. Christian monks wrote of attacks on rich monasteries and towns. But the Vikings were more than wild barbarians. They were also hard-working farmers, traders, experienced sailors, craftsmen and shipbuilders.

c. 12,000 BC Thick ice covers the country. As the ice retreats, reindeer herders gradually move into the southernmost coastal area	1500 BC Regional provinces build barrows and cairns to powerful men and women	500 BC Early Iron Age; a worsening climate and a decline in agriculture	Viking ship c. 980	
12000 BC	**4000 BC**	**2000 BC**	**AD**	**500**	**1000**
4000 BC Farming is gradually adopted in the south of the land	3700 BC Burials take place in chambered mounds, creating the first monuments in the Swedish countryside	1800 BC Bronze objects start to be made in Sweden along continental lines	AD 98 Tacitus refers to the *sviones* in his writings	800 The Viking period begins and the trading centre of Birka in Lake Mälaren is founded

◄ Gustav Vasa (1523–60), painting by Cornelius Arendtz

Christianity and the Birth of a Kingdom

During the 11th and 12th centuries several families from different provinces battled for power over the central part of what is known today as Sweden. The country was more like a federation of self-governing provinces, a number of which, for a limited time, had influence over those around them.

Little is known of the kings and chieftains in the early Middle Ages other than brief mentions in sagas. In the 11th century, King Olof Skötkonung (d. 1020) was converted to Christianity and was baptized in 1008, along with his sons Anund Jakob (d. 1050) and Edmund the Old (d. 1060). Thereafter power passed to the Stenkil family, which had strong links with Västergötland where the Christian church had gained the most influence.

The church and the gradual transition to Christianity underway in the 12th century were vital to the growing power of the king. The priests brought with them an administrative tradition, a civil service and a rational system for regulating property. The church also reinforced the strength of the king ideologically through the idea that his power was derived from God.

King Olof Skötkonung's baptism at Husaby well in Västergötland, 1008

Once the Stenkil dynasty came to an end around 1120, the royal houses of Västergötland (Erik) and Östergötland (Sverker) battled for supremacy. Both families died out in the first half of the 13th century at the time when the power of the *riksjarl* (earl) was at its height. The *riksjarl* was the king's most important statesman and the position gained greater influence through Birger Magnusson, known as Birger Jarl, who became *riksjarl* in 1248 under King Erik Eriksson. Until his death in 1266, Birger Jarl was the de facto wielder of power in Sweden, which by then had developed into a medieval kingdom similar to those elsewhere in Europe.

The Hanseatic League and the Bjälbo Dynasty's Power Struggle

The 13th century saw the founding of many of the medieval towns still standing today. Documents show that Stockholm existed as a town in 1252, four years after Birger Jarl became *riksjarl*. In 1289 it was described as the largest town in Sweden, but it was not yet a capital city. Its importance lay in its role as a trading centre, particularly for the German Hanseatic League, during the 14th century. The Hanseatic League had previously established a base in Visby on Gotland, which was one of its most important centres. In some places, the Hansa influence was so great that the king had to prevent Germans from holding more than half of the leading positions in the town.

Through Birger Jarl's son, Valdemar, elected king in 1250, power passed to the Bjälbo dynasty. Valdemar was replaced after a revolt by his brother Magnus Ladulås who was elected king in 1275. During Magnus's reign, Swedish legislation was reformed and the Ordinance of Alsnö of 1280 granted the nobility and church far-reaching privileges and freedom from taxation.

The king's nickname, Ladulås (literally "lock barn"), is said to derive from his ban on nobles from helping themselves to sustenance from peasants' barns when travelling.

On Magnus' death in 1290, his son Birger was still a minor and Sweden was ruled by a regency. Once the king reached his majority in 1303, a power struggle broke out between Birger and his brothers, Dukes Erik and Valdemar. Sweden was divided between the brothers until in 1317 Birger invited Erik and Valdemar to a banquet at Nyköping Castle and had them both imprisoned and left to die. Soon, Birger himself was forced to flee the country after a revolt and Magnus Eriksson, the three year-old son of Duke Erik, was elected king of Sweden in 1319.

Magnus's rule was characterized by severe domestic opposition and financial problems. Sweden also suffered the Black Death in 1350 in which one-third of the population died. The crisis led to the Swedish nobles in 1363 appealing to the Duke of Mecklenburg, whose son Albrecht was hailed king of Sweden the following year.

The Kalmar Union

Albrecht of Mecklenburg came to the throne with the support of the nobility, who reacted with a revolt when he subsequently sought to wield his own power. The nobles were backed by Queen Margareta of

Beheading of 100 members of the Swedish nobility in the Stockholm Bloodbath, 1520

Denmark-Norway and Albrecht was defeated at Fallköping in 1389, after which Denmark, Norway and Sweden came under the rule of Denmark. At a meeting in Kalmar in 1397, Margareta's nephew, Erik of Pomerania, was crowned king of Denmark, Norway and Sweden, thus establishing the Kalmar Union, which lasted until 1523.

The unification period was characterized by conflict in Sweden. Under Erik of Pomerania there was great dissatisfaction with newly-introduced taxes. A peasant revolt, known as the Engelbrekt revolt after its legendary leader, led to Erik being deposed in 1439. The Kalmar Union was unable to control the Council of State or the castles, and Sweden lacked a recognized supreme authority. Subsequent Danish kings were recognized as rulers in Sweden only for a few years and in between the country was controlled by representatives of the nobility.

At the Battle of Brunkeberg in Stockholm in 1471, the Danish King Christian I sought to enforce his power in Sweden, but was defeated by the viceroy, Sten Sture the Elder. A new Danish crusade under Christian II in 1520 culminated in the notorious Stockholm Bloodbath in which 100 Swedish nobles were executed.

1275 Magnus Ladulås elected king of Sweden at Mora Stones

1349–50 Black Death rampages through Sweden

1364 Albrecht of Mecklenburg elected king of Sweden

Queen Margareta

1434 Engelbrekt leads revolt over the taxes and burdens imposed by the Kalmar Union

1520 Swedish nobles executed in the Stockholm Bloodbath

1300 | **1350** | **1400** | **1450**

1280 Ordinance of Alsnö grants freedom from taxation to the nobility

1350 Magnus Eriksson's law applies throughout the land, although cities have their own laws

1397 The Kalmar Union unites the Nordic countries under Queen Margareta

1471 Sten Sture the Elder defeats Danish King Christian I at Brunkeberg

Gustav Vasa making his ceremonial entry into Stockholm, Midsummer Day, 1523

The Vasa Era

Among the nobles fortunate to avoid execution in the Stockholm Bloodbath was the young Gustav Eriksson. At the end of 1520 Gustav organized an army to oust the Danish King Christian from Sweden. Gustav was successful and on 6 June 1523 – later to become Sweden's National Day – he was named king. On Midsummer Day the new monarch, Gustav Vasa, made his ceremonial entry into war-torn Stockholm.

When Gustav Vasa took the throne, he discovered a nation in financial crisis. He called on parliament to pass a controversial law transferring the property of the church to the state, which then became the country's most important source of economic power. Another important result of this policy was the gradual separation from Catholicism and the adoption of the Lutheran State Church, which was to remain tied to the state until 2000.

During his reign, Gustav Vasa implemented tough economic policies in order to

Portrait of Erik XIV (1561)

concentrate central power in Stockholm. This effective dictatorship also resulted in the Swedish parliament's decision in 1544 to make the monarchy hereditary.

Descendants of Gustav Vasa oversaw the rise of Sweden into one of Europe's great powers. During the reign of Gustav's eldest son Erik XIV (r.1561– 69), there were wars against Denmark, Lübeck and Poland. His brothers dethroned him. Erik died in prison, possibly by eating pea soup poisoned by his brother Johan III. During the reign of Karl IX, the third son, Sweden waged war against Denmark and Russia.

Gustav II Adolf and Kristina

When the next king, Gustav II Adolf, came to power in 1611, Sweden was involved in wars against Russia, Poland and Denmark. This reign came to be as remarkable as that of his grandfather and under his rule Sweden steadily increased its influence over the Baltic region. It was also in the 17th century that Stockholm started to develop into the country's political and

1523 Gustav Vasa is chosen as king and marches into Stockholm	**1542** Nils Dacke leads a peasants revolt in Småland	**1560** Gustav Vasa dies		**1568** Erik XIV imprisoned by his brothers at Gripsholms Slott	**1611** Gustav II Adolf becomes king
		Vasa coat of arms		**1577** Erik XIV dies, probably poisoned	

1525	**1550**	**1575**	**1600**

| **1527** Reformation parliament confiscates church property | **1544** Hereditary monarchy established for Gustav Vasa's descendants | **1561** Eric XIV is crowned king and his brothers' powers curbed | **1570** Nordic Seven Years War ends **1569** Johan III crowned in Stockholm | **1587** Johan III's son Sigismund chosen as king of Poland **1612** Axel Oxenstierna made State Chancellor |

administrative centre. In 1630 Gustav II Adolf, with his influential chancellor Axel Oxenstierna, decided to intervene in the Thirty Years War *(see p42)*, first on the side of the Protestants, then in an alliance with France. Sweden had some military successes during the war, but paid a heavy price for winning the bloody battle at Lützen in 1632, as the king was killed in action.

Gustav II Adolf's only child, Kristina, came to the throne at the age of six. During her reign (1633–54), life at court was influenced by the world of science and philosophy. Kristina's reluctance to marry resulted in her cousin, Karl Gustav, becoming Crown Prince. Kristina abdicated and left for Rome, where she converted to Catholicism, a sensation at the time.

The Carolian Era

Karl X Gustav (1654–60) was the first of three Karls to reign. At the height of Sweden's era as a great power, he defeated Denmark by leading his army across the frozen waters of the Great Belt *(see p42)*, thus gaining Sweden's southernmost provinces. Karl XI (1660–97) secured the border and divided

Queen Kristina corresponding with leading scientists and philosophers of the time

Young Karl XII with the widowed queen on his arm leaving the burning Tre Kronor Palace, 1697

the land more evenly between crown, nobility and peasants.

While the body of Karl XI lay in state at Tre Kronor in 1697, a fire broke out which destroyed most of the building. The new monarch was the teenage Karl XII (1697–1718). He faced awesome problems when Denmark, Poland and Russia formed an alliance in 1700 with the aim of crushing the power of Sweden. Karl XII set off to battle.

Denmark and Poland were soon forced to plead for peace, but Russia was a harder nut to crack. A bold push towards Moscow was unsuccessful and the Swedish army suffered a devastating defeat at Poltava in Ukraine in 1709. This marked the beginning of the end of Sweden's Age of Greatness.

Karl XII, possibly the most written about and controversial Swedish monarch, returned to Sweden in 1715 after an absence of 15 years. His plans to regain Sweden's position of dominance never came to fruition and he was killed in Norway in 1718. Sweden was in crisis. Crop failures and epidemics had wiped out one third of the population and the state's finances were drained.

Sweden's Age of Greatness

For more than a century (1611–1721) Sweden was the dominant power in northern Europe, and the Baltic was effectively a Swedish inland sea. The country was at its most powerful after the Peace of Roskilde in 1658, when Sweden acquired seven new provinces. Outside today's frontiers, the Swedish Empire covered Finland, large parts of the Baltic states, and important areas of northern Germany. Over 111 years as a great power Sweden spent 72 of them at war, but the period also marked great cultural development and more efficient state administration. Treasures were brought back as trophies and grand palaces were built.

Swedish Empire

Sweden's empire after the Peace of Roskilde, 1658

The Tre Kronor Castle
Built as a defensive tower in the 1180s, the Tre Kronor castle was the seat of Swedish monarchs from the 1520s and became the administrative centre of the Swedish Empire. Named after the three crowns on the spire, it burned down in 1697.

The columns of troops ride out over the shifting ice towards Danish Lolland.

The Thirty Years War

A major European war raged from 1618–48, largely on German soil. Sweden entered the fray in 1630 and joined forces with France in 1631 against the Austrian Habsburgs. The Swedish army had been reorganized and rearmed by Gustav II Adolf and immediately had successes at the battles of Breitenfeld (1630) and Lützen (1632), where the king was killed in action. Later the Swedes pressed into southern Germany and also captured Prague (1648). Rich cultural treasures were brought home from the war. In 1648 the Peace of Westphalia gave Sweden several important possessions in northern Germany.

The death of Gustav II Adolf at the Battle of Lützen in 1632

Stockholm in 1640
The city's transformation from a small medieval town into a capital city can be seen in the network of straight streets, similar to the present layout.

Karl XI's Triumphs
The ceiling painting in Karl XI's gallery at the Royal Palace *(see p60)* by the French artist Jacques Foucquet (1693) shows in allegoric form the king's victories at Halmstad, Lund and Landskrona.

Karl X Gustav himself leads the Swedish army of 17,000 men.

Field Marshal Count Carl Gustav Wrangel *(see p133)*

The Powerful Nobility
The nobility were very influential in the Empire era and many successful soldiers were ennobled. The Banér family coat of arms from 1651 is adorned by three helmets and barons' crowns.

Karl X Gustav
Portrait of Karl X Gustav (r. 1654–60) as a general. It was in this role that he became known throughout Europe during the final phase of the Thirty Years War.

Crossing the Great Belt
When Denmark declared war on Sweden in autumn 1657, the Swedish army was in Poland. Marching west, it captured the Danish mainland, but without the navy was unable to continue to Copenhagen. However, unusually severe weather froze the sea, making it possible for the soldiers to cross the ice of the Great Belt, and the Danes had to surrender.

Karl XII's Pocket Watch
The warrior king's watch-case dates from 1700. It shows the state coat of arms, as well as those of the 49 provinces that belonged to Sweden at that time.

Karl XII's Last Journey
After he was hit by a fatal bullet at Fredrikshald in Norway (1718), the king's body was taken first to Swedish territory then on to Uddevalla for embalming. Painting by Gustav Cederström (1878).

Gustav III with the white armband he wore when mounting his *coup d'etat* in 1772

The Age of Liberty and the Gustavian Era

A new constitution came into force in 1719 which transferred power from the monarch to parliament. As a result, Sweden developed a system of parliamentary democracy similar to that of Britain at the time.

The "Age of Liberty" coincided with the Enlightenment, with dramatic advances in culture, science and industry. The botanist Carl von Linné became one of the most famous Swedes of his time. Another was the scientist, philosopher and author Emanuel Swedenborg, who is thought to have influenced both Balzac and Baudelaire. The production of textiles expanded in Stockholm, and Sweden's first hospital was constructed on Kungsholmen.

Changes in the balance of power around 1770 gave the new king, Gustav III, an opportunity to strike in an attempt to regain his monarchical powers.

On 19 August 1772 Gustav accompanied the guards' parade to the Royal Palace where, in front of his lifeguards, he declared his intention to mount a *coup d'etat*. The guards and other military units in Stockholm swore allegiance to the king, who tied a white handkerchief round his arm as a badge and rode out into the city to be acclaimed by his people. Absolute power had been restored.

Gustav III was influenced by the Age of Enlightenment and by French culture, which had a great effect on Swedish life (*see pp46–7*). Over the years opposition grew to the king's powers, largely because of his costly war against Russia. In 1792 he was murdered by a nobleman during a masked ball at the Opera House.

Gustav III was succeeded by his son, Gustav IV Adolf. During his reign Sweden was dragged into the Napoleonic wars. After a war against Russia in 1808–9, Sweden lost Finland, which at the time accounted for one-third of Swedish territory. The king was deposed and went into exile.

Napoleon's former marshal, Jean-Baptiste Bernadotte, as King Karl XIV Johan surrounded by his family

---

1719 New constitution transfers power from the king to parliament

1741 Carl von Linné appointed professor at Uppsala

1754 Royal family moves into Royal Palace

1780s Immigrants given religious freedom

1790 Sweden defeats Russia at the Battle of Svenskund

1792 Gustav III is murdered

1809 Sweden loses Finland, Gustav IV Adolf deposed

1720	1740	1760	1780	1800

1738 Parliamentary power is established in the Age of Liberty as the "Hat" party wins elections

Carl von Linné

1772 Gustav III crowned and mounts coup d'etat giving the king absolute power

1778 National costume decreed. Death penalty removed for some crimes

1786 Swedish Academy founded

Newspaper readers outside the *Aftonbladet* office in 1841

The Era of Karl Johan and Bourgeois Liberalism

By the early 19th century the absolute powers of the monarch had been removed for all time, and the privileges of the aristocracy were undermined even more in 1809 with a new constitution that divided power between the king, the government and parliament. With a new class structure and the effect of the French Revolution, a new middle class emerged which also wanted to be more influential. Altercations between middle-class liberals and the conservatives prevailed. One of the best-known newspapers founded at this time was the liberal mouthpiece, *Aftonbladet*.

Difficulties in finding a suitable new monarch led to the choice of one of Napoleon's marshals, Jean-Baptiste Bernadotte, who took on the Swedish name of Karl Johan. Founder of the present royal dynasty, Karl XIV Johan continued to speak French and never fully learned Swedish. His French wife, Desirée, found Stockholm a cultural backwater after Paris. In 1813 a Swedish army, with Karl XIV Johan at its head, became involved in the final battle against

Napoleon. The Battle of Leipzig ended in defeat for France, but more significantly for Sweden, Denmark had to hand over Norway to Sweden. The Norwegians were reluctant to unite with Sweden, but after a display of military power in Norway, a union between the two countries was agreed which lasted from 1814 to 1905.

A long era of peace began, and with it came a dramatic increase in population, which grew by 1 million to 3.5 million by 1850. Many Swedes were driven into poverty because of the shortage of work. Mass emigration followed. From the 1850s to the 1930s about 1.5 million people left Sweden, mostly for North America.

Social Movements and Industrialization

As Sweden was transformed from an agricultural society into an industrialized country, the problems posed by the population surplus were gradually tackled. Its industrial revolution started around 1850, gathering momentum in the late 19th century, and the textile, timber and iron industries provided the main sources of employment. Here the early and fast development of a coherent railway network played an important role.

Swedes heading for a new life in North America

Social movements sprang up in the 19th century which still play an important role in Swedish life. One of the first was the temperance movement, which emerged from a background of alcohol abuse – in the 1820s annual consumption of spirits was 46 litres (80 pints) per person.

810 Parliament chooses ean-Baptiste Bernadotte s Crown Prince

1842 Elementary schools established

1869 Emigration to North America increases due to crop failures

1876 L M Ericsson starts manufacture of telephones

August Strindberg

1905 Parliament dissolves union with Norway

1820	**1840**	**1860**	**1880**	**1900**

1818 Karl XIV Johan is crowned King of Sweden and Norway

1814 Sweden gains Norway in peace treaty with Denmark

1856 Sweden's first railway opens

1850 Sweden has 3.5 million inhabitants; 93,000 live in Stockholm

1879 August Strindberg's novel *The Red Room* is published

1908 Royal Dramatic Theatre opens in Stockholm

The Era of Gustav III

Gustav III (r. 1771–92) is one of the most colourful figures in Swedish history. The king's great interest in art, literature and the theatre made the late 18th century a golden age for Swedish culture, and several academies were founded at this time. After a bloodless revolution in 1772, Gustav III ruled with absolute power and initiated a wide-ranging programme of reform. But his attacks on the privileges of the nobility and his adventurous and costly foreign policy made him powerful enemies. In 1792 he was murdered during a masked ball at Stockholm's Opera House.

The Swedish Academy
The academy was founded by Gustav III in 1786 to preserve the Swedish language. Members received a token depicting the king's head at every meeting.

Gustav III's Coronation 1772
The coronation of the all-powerful monarch in Stockholm's cathedral was a magnificent ceremony, portrayed here by C G Pilo (1782). Every detail was overseen by Gustav himself, who used his flair for the dramatic in politics as well.

A courtier entertains by reading aloud.

Gustav III studies architectural designs.

Court Life at Drottningholm
Hilleström's painting (1779) gives an insight into court life at Drottningholm, where the king resided between June and November. In what is now the Blue Salon, Gustav III and Queen Sofia Magdalena socialized with their inner circle. Behaviour was modelled on the French court and etiquette was even stricter at Drottningholm than at Versailles.

The Battle of Svensksund
Gustav III was not known as a successful warrior king, but in 1790 he led the Swedish fleet to its greatest victory ever, when it defeated Russia in a major maritime battle in the Gulf of Finland.

Life in the Inns
Stockholm abounded with inns, frequently visited by the city's 70,000 inhabitants. J T Sergel's sketch shows a convivial dinner party.

Murder at the Masked Ball

In 1792 Gustav III fell victim to a conspiracy at the Opera House. He was surrounded by masked men and shot by Captain Anckarström on the crowded stage. He died of his wounds 14 days later.

Gustav III's Mask and Cocked Hat

Despite his mask, Gustav III was easy to recognize since he was wearing the badges of two orders of chivalry. The drama intrigued the whole of Europe and inspired Verdi's opera *Un Ballo in Maschera*.

Flogging of the King's Murderer

Among the conspirators, only Anckarström was condemned to death. Before he was taken to his execution in Södermalm, he was flogged on three successive days on the square in front of Riddarhuset.

Queen Sofia Magdalena does her needlework.

Bust of Catherine the Great of Russia, the king's cousin

Gustavian Style

The mid-18th century saw the emergence of Neo-Classicism, with the focus on antiquities and Greek ideals. Gustav III embraced this trend with great enthusiasm and supported the country's talented artists and authors. He established his own Museum of Antiquities *(see p61)* with marble sculptures which he brought home from Italy. In handicrafts, the sweeping lines of Rococo elegance were replaced by the stricter forms of what has become known as Gustavian Style. Rooms at the Royal Palace were renovated with decoration and furnishings adapted to suit this style.

Chair designed in Gustavian style

Swedish Court Costume

In 1778, Gustav III introduced a court costume, based on French lines, for daily wear at court, in order to restrain fashion excesses.

Universal Suffrage

Sweden's population reached 5 million around 1900, despite mass emigration to America. Many people moved to the towns to work in industry, and by the early 20th century Stockholm's population was about 300,000, a fourfold increase since the year 1800.

Increasing social awareness and the rise of the Social Democrat and Liberal parties in the early 20th century gave impetus to the demands for universal suffrage. Authors such as August Strindberg became involved. A political battle ensued which was not resolved until 1921, when universal suffrage was introduced for both sexes.

Branting and Gustav V in conversation, 1909

Another question which was hotly debated in the 19th century was the role of the king and the extent of his powers. In his "courtyard speech" at the Royal Palace in 1914, King Gustav V called for military rearmament. This led to a constitutional crisis and the resignation of the Liberal government. After the 1917 election, the king had to accept a government which contained republican-friendly Social Democrats, including the future prime minister, Hjalmar Branting. By then it was parliament, not the king, that decided what sort of government Sweden should have.

The Growth of the Welfare State

In 1936 the Social Democrats and Farmers' Party formed a coalition which developed what was to become known as the welfare state. The Social Democrat prime minister, Per Albin Hansson (1885–1946), defined the welfare state as a socially conscious society with financial security for all. Reforms introduced under this policy included unemployment benefit, paid holidays and childcare. As a result, poverty in Sweden virtually disappeared during the 1930s and 1940s.

The right of everyone to good housing was also part of welfare state policy. Under the principle of "work-home-centre" a new Stockholm suburb, Vällingby, was built in the early 1950s. The idea was to transform the dormitory suburbs into thriving communities where people would both live and work. The concept was unsuccessful. It soon became apparent that the people who lived there still worked somewhere else, and vice versa. The great shortage of housing in the 1960s led to the "million" programme, which involved the building of a million homes in a very short time.

Calls for democratic reforms in June 1917 led to riots like this one outside the parliament building in Stockholm

1921 Universal suffrage for men and women

1930 Rise of Functionalist style in architecture, stimulated by the Stockholm Exhibition

1940 Swedish-German agreement on transit of German military personnel

1955 Obligatory national health insurance

1958 Women can be ordained as priests

1967 Driving on the right introduced

1920

1940

1960

Selma Lagerlöf, winner of the Nobel Prize for Literature, 1909

1939 Sweden's coalition government declares neutrality in World War II

1952 Stockholm's first underground railway is inaugurated

1950 First public TV broadcast in Sweden

1964 Art exhibition Moderna Museet sh works by Andy Warl Roy Lichtenstein an Claes Oldenburg

The War Years

Sweden declared its neutrality during both World Wars I and II. Its policy of continuing to trade with nations involved in the conflict during World War I provoked a number of countries into imposing a trade blockade on Sweden. The situation became so serious that hunger riots broke out in some towns.

World War II proved an even more difficult balancing exercise for Swedish neutrality, largely because its Nordic neighbours were at war. Through a combination of luck and skill, Sweden remained outside the conflict, but the concessions it had to make were strongly criticized both nationally and internationally.

Neutrality stamp issued in 1942

The policy of non-alignment has not proved an obstacle to Swedish involvement on the international scene, including the United Nations. The country has offered asylum to hundreds of thousands of refugees from wars and political oppression. Prime Minister Olof Palme (1927–86), probably the best-known Swedish politician abroad, was deeply involved in questions of democracy and disarmament, as well as the problems of the Third World. He was renowned for condemning undemocratic acts by right-wing and left-wing dictators. Palme's assassination on the streets of Stockholm in 1986 sent shock waves across the world. The murder has still not been solved.

These areas soon became known as the "new slums" despite high standards of construction.

The Post-War Era

Although the Social Democrats dominated government from the 1930s to the 1970s, the socialist and non-socialist power blocs in Swedish politics have remained fairly evenly matched since World War II.

Important changes took place during the closing decades of the 20th century. These included a new constitution in 1974 which removed the monarch's political powers. In 1995 Sweden joined the European Union after a referendum approved entry by a narrow majority. The start of the new millennium marked a change in the role of the church in Sweden, which severed its connections with the state after more than 400 years.

Today, Sweden, like other developed countries shows signs of economic downturn, even though most people still lead a good, socially secure life. Rapid technical developments and globalization have given Sweden new job opportunities and new inhabitants, as well as a leading international role in technology and innovation.

The centre of Vällingby, which attracted attention among city planners worldwide in the 1950s

1974 The monarch loses all political powers

1980 New constitution gives women the right of succession to the throne

1995 Sweden joins European Union

2000 Öresund Bridge opens between Denmark and Sweden

2003 Sweden rejects the euro

2009 Swedish becomes the official language of Sweden

Crown Princess Victoria

1980	2000	2020

1986 Prime Minister Olof Palme murdered in Stockholm

1973 Gustav VI Adolf dies and is succeeded by his grandson, Carl XVI Gustaf

2003 Foreign Minister Anna Lindh murdered in Stockholm

2000 Swedish church separates from the state

2013 King Carl XVI Gustaf celebrates 40 years as reigning monarch by travelling all over Sweden, visiting all of its 21 counties

2012 Crown Princess Victoria gives birth to Princess Estelle, who becomes second in line to the throne

STOCKHOLM AREA BY AREA

Stockholm at a Glance

Stockholm has around 100 museums covering every conceivable subject, as well as buildings of historic and architectural interest, such as Stadshuset (City Hall). The museum collections range from the treasures and antiquities of Kungliga Slottet (the Royal Palace) to the latest in contemporary art at Moderna museet and the spectacular *Vasa* warship at Vasamuseet. Open spaces abound, and it is even possible to swim in the heart of the city.

Hallwylska Palatset
Thanks to a methodical countess and her impeccable taste, this lavish 1890s' palace has become a magnificent museum with 67,000 exhibits displayed in their original setting.

Vasastaden

City

Stadshuset
This stunning building opened in 1923 is the seat of the capital's government and a symbol of Stockholm. It is also the venue for the annual Nobel Prize festivities.

Kungs-holmen

| 0 metres | 500 |
| 0 yards | 500 |

Gamla

Swimming in the City
In the summer, swimmers bathe in the clean, warm water (about 20 °C/68 °F) in the city centre. Långholmen *(see p108)* has sandy beaches and smooth rocks – an ideal setting for a dip.

Kungliga Slottet
In addition to its own attractions, the Royal Palace has four specialist museums: the Treasury, featuring Erik XIV's orb (1561), the Royal Armoury, Gustav III's Museum of Antiquities, and Tre Kronor Museum.

◄ An aerial view of downtown Stockholm

Nationalmuseum
The Nationalmuseum, Sweden's largest art gallery, has superb collections of 18th- and 19th-century Swedish paintings, as well as applied arts and design, 18th-century French and 17th-century Dutch art. Rubens's *Bacchanal on Andros* dates from the 1630s.

Nordiska Museet
A statue of Karl X Gustav greets visitors arriving at this enormous building. Opened in 1907, it houses many different artifacts illustrating Swedish life and customs.

Skansen
The world's first open-air museum, founded in 1891, shows the Sweden of bygone days with farms and manor houses, urban scenes and craftspeople at work. Nordic fauna and flora are also on display.

Östermalm

Djurgården

Skepps-holmen

öder-malm

Moderna museet
Paradise (1966) by Tinguely/de Saint Phalle marks the way to Moderna museet, which houses remarkable collections of international and Swedish modern art.

Vasamuseet
A fatal capsizal in 1628 and a successful salvage operation 333 years later gave Stockholm its most popular museum. The warship *Vasa* is 95 per cent intact after painstaking renovation.

GAMLA STAN

Relics of Stockholm's early history as a town in the 13th century can still be found on Stadsholmen, the largest island in Gamla Stan (Old Town). The island is a huge area of historical heritage, with the many sights just a few metres apart.

The Royal Palace is the symbol of Sweden's era as a great power in the 17th and early 18th centuries (see pp42–3), and its magnificent state rooms, apartments and artifacts are well matched to the Roman Baroque-style exterior. The historic buildings standing majestically around Slottsbacken underline Stockholm's role as a capital city.

This area has a special atmosphere with much to offer: from the bustling streets of souvenir shops, bookstores and antique shops to elegant palaces, churches and museums. Many medieval cellars are now restaurants and cafés, while the narrow cobbled streets recall a bygone era.

Bridges lead to Riddarholmen, with its 17th-century palaces and royal crypt, and to Helgeandsholmen for the newer splendours of Riksdagshuset (the Parliament building).

Sights at a Glance

Palaces and Museums
1. The Royal Palace (Kungliga Slottet) pp58–61
2. Livrustkammaren
3. Kungliga Myntkabinettet
10. Postmuseum
12. Medeltidsmuseet

Public Buildings
14. Riddarhuset
15. Riksdagshuset

Historic Buildings
4. Tessinska Palatset
12. Wrangelska Palatset

Streets and Squares
6. Stortorget
8. Mårten Trotzigs Gränd
9. Västerlånggatan
13. Evert Taubes Terrass

Churches
5. Storkyrkan
7. Tyska Kyrkan
11. Riddarholms kyrkan

0 metres 250
0 yards 250

See also Street Finder map 3

◄ Bernt Notke's sculpture of St George and the Dragon in Storkyrkan

For keys to symbols see back flap

Street-by-Street: Slottsbacken

Slottsbacken is much more than just a steep hill linking Skeppsbron and the highest part of Gamla Stan (Old Town). It also provides the background for ceremonial processions and the daily changing-of-the-guard, and is the route for visiting heads of state and foreign ambassadors when they have an audience with the king at the Royal Palace. Alongside Slottsbacken the palace displays its most attractive façade, with the entrance to the Treasury (Skattkammaren), State Room (Rikssalen) and Palace Church (Slottskyrkan). Architect Nicodemus Tessin the Younger's ambition to make Stockholm a leading European city in architectural terms was realized in 1799 with the addition of the Obelisk.

The Olaus Petri statue by Storkyrkan stands in front of a tablet telling the cathedral's history since 1264.

Outer Courtyard

Axel Oxenstiernas Palats (1653) is, for Stockholm, an unusual example of the style known as Roman Mannerism. For 30 years, Axel Oxenstierna (1583–1654) himself was a dominant figure in Swedish politics (see p41).

The Obelisk by Louis Jean Desprez was erected in 1799 to thank the citizens for supporting Gustav III's Russian war in 1788–90.

Stock Exchange (see p64)

TRÅNGSUND

STORTORGET

❺ ★ Storkyrkan
An impressive cathedral with a late Gothic interior, it is full of treasures from many different eras.

❻ Stortorget
This square is the heart of the "city between the bridges", with a well dating from 1778. It was the scene of the Stockholm Bloodbath in 1520.

0 metres		100
0 yards		100

2 ★ **Livrustkammaren**
Sweden's oldest museum displays royal weaponry, clothing and carriages from over five centuries. The picture shows Gustav II Adolf's stallion Streiff, from the battle of Lützen in 1632.

Kungsträdgården

Locator Map
See Street Finder map 3

1 ★ **The Royal Palace**
The southern façade has a triumphal central arch with four niches for statues, created by French artists in the 18th century.

Gustav III's statue was sculpted by J T Sergel in 1799 in memory of the "gallant king" who was murdered in 1792.

↓ Slussen

Köpmantorget with statue of St George Slaying the Dragon (1912).

3 **Kungliga Myntkabinettet**
In a 16th-century setting, the Royal Coin Cabinet has the world's largest stamped coin, from 1644.

Key

— Suggested route

Finska Kyrkan, Slottsbacken's oldest building, dates from the 1640s. Originally a royal ball-games court for the palace, since 1725 it has been the religious centre for the Finnish community.

4 **Tessinska Palatset**
Built by and for Nicodemus Tessin the Younger, architect of the Royal Palace, in 1694–7, this palace has been the residence of the Governor of Stockholm County since 1968

❶ The Royal Palace (Kungliga Slottet)

Defensive installations or castles have stood on the island of Stadsholmen ever since the 11th century. The Tre Kronor (Three Crowns) fortress was completed in the mid-13th century, but became a royal residence only during the following century. The Vasa kings turned the fortress into a Renaissance palace which burned to the ground in 1697. In its place the architect Nicodemus Tessin the Younger created a new palace in Baroque style with an Italianate exterior and a French interior toned down to suit Swedish tastes. The palace's 608 rooms were decorated by Europe's foremost artists and craftsmen. Adolf Fredrik was the first king to move into the palace, in 1754. It is no longer the king's private residence, but remains one of the city's leading sights.

★ **Changing the Guard**
Stockholm's most popular tourist event is the daily changing of the guard at midday in the Outer Courtyard.

The Western Staircase
Tessin was especially proud of the two staircases, made from Swedish marble and porphyry. On the western staircase stands a bust of the gifted architect.

Entrance to the Royal Apartments

★ **The Hall of State**
This opulent hall has an atmosphere of ceremonial splendour and forms an ideal setting for Queen Kristina's silver throne, probably the palace's most famous treasure.

Entrance to Treasury and Royal Chapel

KEY

① **The Guest Apartments**

② **The Bernadotte Apartments** are situated on the floor below Karl XI's Gallery.

③ **Tre Kronor Museum** entrance from Lejonbacken (see p61).

④ **Carl Hårleman** played an important role in the design of the palace. His bust adorns this niche.

⑤ **Logården** is the terrace between the palace's east wings.

⑥ **Livrustkammaren** (see p62)

The Royal Chapel
This delightful little church has a rich interior decorated by many different artists. The pulpit is the work of J P Bouchardon.

Official Royal Residence

The king and queen have their offices at the palace, where they hold audiences with visiting dignitaries, and official ceremonies. They travel around the country attending special events, official openings and anniversaries, and they make regular State visits abroad. The king is well known for his interest in the environment while the queen is heavily involved with her work for children, especially the disabled.

King Carl XVI Gustaf and Queen Silvia

Gustav III's State Bedchamber
Sergel's bust of Gustav III (1779) stands in the room where the king died after being shot at the Opera House. The 1770s decor is by J E Rehn.

★ Karl XI's Gallery
One of the most magnificent rooms in the palace, this fine example of Swedish Late Baroque is used for banquets hosted by the king and queen. In the cabinet is this priceless salt-cellar dating from 1627–8.

Gustav III's Museum of Antiquities
The museum's collection includes antique statues brought home by Gustav III from his journey to Rome.

Exploring the Royal Palace

The public areas of the Royal Palace allow visitors to walk through grand rooms of sumptuous furnishings and priceless works of art and craftsmanship. The Hall of State and the Royal Chapel are both characterized by their magnificent lavish decor and Gustav III's Museum of Antiquities contains ancient marble sculptures from the king's journey to Italy. The palace also houses the Treasury with the State regalia; the Tre Kronor Museum, which depicts the palace before the 1697 fire; and the Livrustkammaren *(see p62)*.

The Pillar Hall in the Bernadotte Apartments with original decor

Karl XI's Gallery, the finest example of the Late Baroque period in Sweden

The State Apartments

The Royal Family has lived at Drottningholm Palace (see pp112–15) since 1982, but official functions still take place in the State Apartments, including banquets hosted by the king during visits by foreign heads of state. Other official dinners are held here, as well as the annual festivities in December to honour the Nobel laureates.

The dinners are served in Karl XI's Gallery, the finest example of Swedish Late Baroque, modelled on the Hall of Mirrors at Versailles. Each window is matched with a niche on the inner wall where some of the palace's priceless works of arts and crafts are exhibited. Most remarkable is the salt-cellar made from ivory and gilded silver designed by the Flemish painter Rubens (1577–1640). The room known as "The White Sea"

King Karl XIV Johan's egg cup

serves as a drawing room. Gustav III's State Bedchamber, where the king died after being shot at the Opera House in 1792 *(see pp46–7)*, is the height of Gustavian elegance. Along with Queen Sofia Magdalena's State Bedchamber, it was designed by the architect Jean Eric Rehn. The lintels on the doors to the Don Quixote Room, named after the theme of its tapestries, were made by François Boucher and are among the most treasured pieces.

The Guest Apartments

An imposing part of the palace, these apartments are where visiting heads of state stay. The beautiful rooms include the Meleager Salon, where official gifts and decorations are exchanged, and a large bedroom with a sculpted and gilded bed. Other impressive rooms are the Inner Salon, whose decor was inspired by the excavations in Pompeii, and the Margareta Room, named after the present king's grandmother, which displays some pictures painted by her.

The apartments contain remarkable works of craftsmanship by such 18th-century masters as Georg Haupt, Ephraim Ståhle and Jean-Baptiste Masreliez.

The Bernadotte Apartments

This magnificent suite has earned its name from the gallery displaying portraits of the Bernadotte dynasty. The apartments have some notable ceiling paintings and mid-18th-century chandeliers, and are used for many a ceremonial occasion. The elegant Pillar Hall is the venue for investitures, and the East Octagonal Cabinet with probably the palace's best Rococo decor, is where the king receives foreign ambassadors. Along with the western cabinet, its interior has remained just as it was planned by Carl Hårleman more than 250 years ago.

Oscar II's very masculine Writing Room, dating from the 1870s, also looks much as it did in his day. However, the palace was kept up to date with the latest technical advances: electricity was installed in 1883, and the telephone only one year later.

The Hall of State

Rococo and Classicism were brought together in perfect harmony by the architects Nicodemus Tessin the Younger and Carl Hårleman when they designed the two-storey Hall of State.

The Hall provides a worthy framework for Queen Kristina's silver throne, a gift for the coronation in 1650 and one of the most valuable treasures in the palace. The throne was given to the queen by Magnus Gabriel de la Gardie and was made in Augsburg by the goldsmith Abraham Drentwett.

The canopy was added 100 years later for the coronation of King Adolf Fredrik and was designed by Jean Eric Rehn.

The room is lavishly decorated. The throne is flanked by colossal sculptures of Karl XIV Johan and Gustav II Adolf, while those on the cornice symbolize Peace, Strength, Religion and Justice.

Until 1975 the Hall of State was the scene of the ceremonial opening of the Swedish Parliament (Riksdagen), which included a march past of the royal bodyguard in full regalia. It is now used for official occasions and, like the Royal Chapel, is a venue for summer concerts.

The Hall of State, the most important ceremonial room in the palace

The Royal Chapel

It took 50 years to build the Royal Palace, and a lot of effort went into the interior decoration of the Royal Chapel. The work was carried out largely by Carl Hårleman under the supervision of Tessin. As with the Hall of State, the co-operation between the two produced a magnificent result, enhanced by the contributions of several foreign artists.

A number of remarkable artifacts have been added over the centuries. The most recent was a group of six 17th-century-style bronze crowns, as well as two crystal crowns, given by the Court to King Carl XVI Gustaf and Queen Silvia to mark their marriage in 1976.

It also has some rare relics of the original Tre Kronor fortress: new benches that had been

ordered by Tessin. They had been rescued during the palace fire in 1697 and preserved, but not put in the chapel until the 19th century. The benches were made by Georg Haupt, grandfather of the Georg Haupt who was to create some of the palace's most prized furnishings *(see p86)*.

Gustav III's Museum of Antiquities

Opened in 1794 in memory of the murdered king, the Museum of Antiquities initially housed more than 200 exhibits, mainly acquired during Gustav's Italian journey in 1783–4 and then supplemented with more purchases at a later date.

In 1866 the museum's collection was moved to the city's National Museum *(see pp86–7)*. During the 1950s the main gallery was renovated, followed by the smaller galleries 30 years later, which enabled the collection to be returned to its original setting.

The most prized exhibits are in the main gallery, the best known being the sculpture of Endymion, the eternally sleeping young shepherd and lover of the Moon Goddess Selene. The 18th-century sculptor Johan Tobias Sergel is represented by *The Priestess*, ranked as the collection's second most important piece. She is flanked by two large candelabras.

The Treasury

At the bottom of 56 well-worn steps, below the Hall of State on the south side of the palace, is the entrance to the Treasury (Skattkammaren) where the State regalia, the most potent symbols of the monarchy, are kept. Occasionally, for an important event, King Erik XIV's crown, sceptre, orb and the keys of the kingdom are taken out of their showcase and placed beside the uncrowned King Carl XVI Gustaf. The 1-m (3 ft) high silver baptismal font, which took

Erik XIV's crown, made by Cornelis ver Weiden in Stockholm in 1561

the French silversmith Jean François Cousinet 11 years to make, is over 200 years old and is still used for royal baptisms. Hanging in the Treasury is the only undamaged tapestry among six dating from the 1560s, salvaged from the 1697 fire.

Tre Kronor Museum

A fascinating attraction at the Royal Palace is the Tre Kronor (Three Crowns) Museum, which is housed in the oldest parts of the ruined Tre Kronor fortress, preserved under the north side of the palace. About half of a massive 12th-century defensive wall and brick vaults from the 16th and 17th centuries provide a dramatic setting for the museum which illustrates the palace's history over almost 1,000 years.

Two models of the Tre Kronor fortress show changes made during the second half of the 17th century and how it looked by the time of the fire. Among items rescued from the ashes are a schnapps glass, amber pots and bowls made from mountain crystal.

A glass bowl in the Tre Kronor Museum, saved from the 1697 fire

② Livrust-kammaren

Slottsbacken 3. **Map** 3 C2.
Tel 08-402 30 30. Ⓣ Gamla Stan.
🚌 2, 43, 55, 76. **Open** May: 11am–
5pm daily; Jun: 10am–5pm daily;
Jul–mid-Aug: 10am–6pm daily;
mid-Aug–Apr: 11am–5pm Tue–Sun
(to 8pm Thu). 🅿 🏠 🎥 ♿ ✉
Ⓦ **livrustkammaren.se**

Sweden's oldest museum,
Livrustkammaren (the Royal
Armoury) was founded in 1628
and is full of *objets d'art* and
everyday items used by the
Royal Family over the past five
centuries. The oldest exhibit is
Gustav Vasa's crested helmet
dating from 1542. The museum
also houses a variety of royal
items which illustrate events
in Swedish history. Among
them are Gustav II Adolf's
stuffed stallion, Streiff,
which he rode at the
Battle of Lützen in
1632; Gustav III's
costume from the
notorious masked
ball at which he
was murdered in
1792; and Karl XII's
blue uniform with
the still muddy
boots he was
wearing when he
died at the siege of Fredrikshald
in Norway in 1718.

Coronation ceremonies are
illustrated by costumes such as
those worn by King Gustav III
and Queen Sofia Magdalena
in 1766. The king's attire alone
was adorned with some 2 kg
(4 lb) of silver. The coronation
carriage, originally built in the
17th century, was modernized

for this event. Its renovation
in the 1970s took eight years
and cost 700,000 kronor. The
cellar vault, once used for
firewood, is skilfully lit,
providing an imaginative
setting for the exhibits.

③ Kungliga Myntkabinettet

Slottsbacken 6. **Map** 3 C3.
Tel 08-519 553 00. Ⓣ Gamla Stan.
🚌 2, 43, 55, 76. **Open** 10am–4pm
daily. **Closed** public hols. 🅿 free
Mon. 🎥 by appointment. 🏠 📷 🌐
🎥 ♿ Ⓦ **myntkabinettet.se**

The Royal Coin Cabinet is a
fabulous museum holding a
priceless collection of currency
and highlighting the history of
money from the 10th century
to the present day – from the
little cowrie shell via
the drachma and
denarius to the
current cash card.
The museum also
gives an insight
into the art of
medal design over
the past 600 years
and shows both
traditional portrait
medals and modern
examples such as
those that have been awarded
to Nobel laureates. Visitors can
also see the first Swedish coin,
struck in the late 10th century
by King Olof Skötkonung.
Other rarities include Queen
Kristina's coin from 1644,
weighing 19.7 kg (43 lb) and
reckoned to be the world's
heaviest coin. From the island of
Yap, in Micronesia, the museum
has acquired what
is thought to be
the world's largest
means of payment,
a so-called "rai-
stone" which greets
visitors in the foyer.

The kids'
playroom is great
fun. Among its
highlights are a
pirate ship with a
treasure chest of
gold coins and a
kitsch collection
of piggy banks.

*Sweden's first coin, struck
in about AD 995*

The elegant Baroque garden in Tessinska
Palatset's courtyard

④ Tessinska Palatset

Slottsbacken 4. **Map** 3 C3.
Ⓣ Gamla Stan. 🚌 2, 43, 55, 71, 76.
Closed to the public.

The Tessin Palace at
Slottsbacken is considered to
be the most beautiful private
residence north of Paris. It is
the best-preserved palace
from Sweden's era as a great
power in the 17th century
and was designed by and for
Tessin the Younger (1654–
1728), the nation's most
renowned architect.

Completed in 1697, the
building is located on a narrow
site which widens out towards a
courtyard with a delightful
Baroque garden. The relatively
discreet façade with its beautiful
porch was inspired by the
exterior design of Roman
palaces. The decor and garden
were influenced by Tessin's time
in Paris and Versailles.

Tessin, who became a count
and state councillor, spent large
sums on the building's
ornamentation. Sculptures and
paintings were provided by the
same French masters whose
work had graced the Royal
Palace. Later, however, his son,
Carl Gustaf, had to sell the palace
for financial reasons.

The building was acquired
by the City of Stockholm as a
residence for its governor in
1773. In 1968 it became the
residence of the governor of
the County of Stockholm.

The coronation carriage of King Adolf Fredrik and Queen
Lovisa Ulrika in Livrustkammaren

⑤ Storkyrkan

Trångsund 1. **Map** 3 B3. **Tel** 08-723 30 16. Ⓣ Gamla Stan. 🚌 2, 43, 55, 76. **Open** 10am–4pm daily. ✝ 11am Sun. 🎧 📷 Jul & Aug: daily; Sep–Jun: 10:15am Wed. 📷 ♿ 🌐 **storkyrkan.nu**

Stockholm's 700-year-old cathedral is of great national religious importance. It was from here that the Swedish reformer Olaus Petri (1493–1552) spread his Lutheran message around the kingdom. It is also used for royal ceremonies.

Originally, a small village church was built on this site in the 13th century, probably by the city's founder Birger Jarl. It was replaced in 1306 by a much bigger basilica, St Nicholas, which was altered over the centuries.

The Gothic character of the interior, acquired in the 15th century, was revealed in 1908 when, during restoration work, plaster was removed from the pillars, exposing the characteristic red tiling. The late Baroque period provided the so-called "royal chairs" and the pulpit, while the façade was adapted to bring it into keeping with the rest of the area around the Royal Palace. The 66-m (216-ft) high tower, added in 1743, has four bells, the largest of which weighs about 6 tons.

Storkyrkan's façade in Italian Baroque style, seen from Slottsbacken

The cathedral houses some priceless artistic treasures, including *St George and the Dragon*, regarded as one of the finest late Gothic works of art in Northern Europe. The sculpture, situated to the left of the altar, was carved from oak and moose horn by Lübeck sculptor Bernt Notke. Unveiled in 1489, it commemorates Sten Sture the Elder's victory over the Danes in 1471 *(see p39)*.

The Last Judgment (1696) is a massive Baroque painting by David Klöcker von Ehrenstrahl. The 3.7-m (12-ft) high bronze candelabra before the altar has adorned the cathedral for some 600 years. One of the cathedral's most prized treasures is the silver altar, which was a gift from the diplomat Johan Adler Salvius in the 1650s.

The pews nearest to the chancel, the "royal chairs", were designed by Nicodemus Tessin the Younger in 1684 to be used by royalty on special occasions. In 1705, the pulpit was installed above the grave of Olaus Petri.

On 20 April 1535, a light phenomenon was observed over Stockholm – six rings with sparkling solar halos. *The Parhelion Painting*, recalling the event, hangs in Storkyrkan and is thought to be the oldest portrayal of the capital. It shows the modest skyline dominated by the cathedral, at that time still the basilica of St Nicholas.

In 2010, the cathedral underwent a large-scale renovation ahead of the wedding of Crown

Storkyrkan's silver altar (detail)

The sculpture *St George and the Dragon* by Bernt Notke (1489) in Storkyrkan

Stortorget, the former Stock Exchange, now home of the Nobelmuseet

❻ Stortorget

Map 3 B3. Ⓣ Gamla Stan. 🚌 2, 3, 43, 53, 55, 76. **Nobelmuseet Tel** 08-23 25 06. **Open** Jun–Aug: 10am–6pm daily; Sep–May: 11am–5pm Tue–Sun (to 8pm Tue). **Closed** 21 Jun. 🎨 📷 daily (English). 🏛 ♿ 🎁 ♿
w nobelmuseum.se

It was not until 1778, when the Stock Exchange (Börsen) was completed, that Stortorget ("the big square") in the heart of the Old Town, acquired a more uniform appearance. Its northern side had previously been taken up by several buildings that served as a town hall. Since the early Middle Ages the square had been a natural meeting point with a well and marketplace, lined with wooden stalls on market days.

A pillory belonging to the jail, which was once on nearby Kåkbrinken, used to stand on the square. It is now in the Town Hall on Kungsholmen.

The medieval layout is clear on Stortorget's west side, where the red Schantzska Huset (No. 20) and the narrow Seyfridtska Huset were built around 1650. The Schantzska Huset remains unchanged and has a lovely limestone porch adorned with figures of recumbent Roman warriors. The artist Johan Wendelstam was responsible for most of the notable porches in the Old Town. The 17th-century gable on Grilska Huset (No. 3) is also worth a closer study. Today there are cafés and restaurants in some of the vaulted cellars.

The decision to construct the Stock Exchange was taken in 1667, but the many wars delayed the start of the building by 100 years. The architect was the young and talented Erik Palmstedt (1741–1803), who also created the decorative cover for the old well. Trading on the floor of the Stock Exchange ceased in 1990. In 2001 the **Nobelmuseet** was opened here to mark the centenary of the Prize (see p75). The exhibition explores the work and ideas of more than 700 creative minds by means of short films and original artifacts. On the upper floor, the Swedish Academy holds its ceremonial gatherings, a tradition maintained since Gustav III gave his inauguration speech here in 1786.

❼ Tyska Kyrkan

Svartmangatan 16. **Map** 3 B3. **Tel** 08-411 11 88. Ⓣ Gamla Stan. 🚌 2, 3, 43, 53, 55, 71, 76. **Open** May–Sep: 11am–5pm daily; Oct–Apr: noon–4pm Wed, Fri & Sat. **Closed** during services. 🏛 11am Sun, German. 📷 by arrangement (Swedish & German). ♿

The German Church is an impressive reminder of the almost total influence that Germany had over Stockholm during the 18th century. The Hanseatic League trading organization was in control of the Baltic and its ports, which explains why the basic layout of Gamla Stan resembled that of Lübeck. Germany's political influence was only broken after the Stockholm Bloodbath and Gustav Vasa's accession to the throne in 1523 (see p40), but its cultural and mercantile influence remained strong as German merchants and craftsmen settled in the city.

The church's congregation, which today has some 2,000 members, was founded in 1571. The present twin-aisle church was built in 1638–42, as an extension of a smaller church which the parish had used since 1576.

In German Late Renaissance and Baroque style, the interior

The Stockholm Bloodbath

Stortorget is intimately linked with the Stockholm Bloodbath of November 1520. The Danish king, Christian II, besieged the Swedish Regent, Sten Sture the Younger, until he capitulated and the Swedes chose Christian as their king. The Dane promised an amnesty and ordered a three-day feast at Tre Kronor Fortress. Near the end of the festivities, the revellers were suddenly shut in and arrested for heresy. The next day more than 80 noblemen and Stockholm citizens were beheaded in the square.

Detail of a painting of the Bloodbath (1524)

The royal gallery in the 17th-century Tyska Kyrkan

has a royal gallery, added in 1672 for German members of the royal household. The pulpit (1660) in ebony and alabaster is unique in Sweden and the altar, from the 1640s, is covered with beautiful paintings surrounded by sculptures of the apostles and evangelists.

The sculptures on the south porch by Jobst Hennen date from 1643 and show Jesus, Moses and three figures portraying Faith, Hope and Love.

Mårten Trotzigs Gränd, the narrowest street in the city

❽ Mårten Trotzigs Gränd

Map 3 C4. **T** Gamla Stan. 2, 3, 43, 53, 55, 71, 76.

At only 90 cm (3 ft) wide, Mårten Trotzigs Gränd is the city's narrowest street. Climbing up the 36 steps gives a good impression of how the various parts of the Old Town differ in height and how tightly the houses are packed together.

Mårten Trotzigs Gränd is named after a German merchant called Traubzich who owned two houses here at the end of the 16th century. After being fenced off at both ends for 100 years, the street was reopened in 1945.

❾ Västerlånggatan

Map 3 B3. **T** Gamla Stan. 2, 3, 43, 53, 55, 71, 76.

Once a main road outside the city proper, built along parts of the original town wall, Västerlånggatan now runs through the heart of the Old

Town, and is usually thronging with people – tourists and locals – shopping or strolling. Starting at Mynttorget in the north, by the Chancery Office (Kanslihuset) and Lejonbacken, the lively and atmospheric street finishes at Järntorget in the south, where the export of iron was once controlled. On Järntorget is Bancohuset, which served as the headquarters of the State Bank from 1680 to 1906.

The building at No. 7 has been used by the Swedish Parliament since the mid-1990s. Its late 19th-century façade has a distinctive southern European influence.

No. 27 was built by and for Erik Palmstedt, who also designed the Stock Exchange and the well at Stortorget. No. 29 is a truly venerable building, dating from the early 15th century. The original pointed Gothic arches were revealed during restoration in the 1940s.

No. 33 is a good example of how new materials and techniques in the late 19th century made it possible to fit large shop windows into old houses. The cast-iron columns which can be seen in many other places also date from this period.

No. 68, Von der Lindeska House, has a majestic 17th-century façade and a beautiful porch with sculptures of Neptune and Mercury.

❿ Postmuseum

Lilla Nygatan 6. **Map** 3 B3. **Tel** 010-436 44 39. **T** Gamla Stan. 3, 53. **Open** May–Aug: 11am–4pm Tue–Sun; Sep–Apr: 11am–4pm Tue–Sun (11am–7pm Wed). by arrangement. **postmuseum.posten.se**

An attraction in itself, the Postmuseum building takes up a whole area bought by the Swedish Post Office in 1720.

Västerlånggatan, Gamla Stan's most popular shopping street

About 100 years later the majestic-looking Post Office was built, incorporating parts of the 17th-century buildings. Stockholm's only Post Office until 1869, it was turned into a museum in 1906.

Letters have been sent in Sweden, in an organized way, since 1636, and the museum's permanent exhibits include a portrayal of early "peasant postmen" fighting the Åland Sea in their boat *Simpan*. Also on display is the first post bus which ran in northern Sweden in the early 1920s and a stagecoach used in eastern Sweden.

Mauritian stamp in the Postmuseum

The collection includes Sweden's first stamp-printing press and no less than four million stamps among which are the first Swedish stamps, produced in 1855. Also on show is "Penny Black", the world's first stamp dating from 1840, and some stamps issued by Mauritius in 1847.

There is a philatelic library holding 51,000 volumes and stamp collections, as well as computers and multimedia equipment for research. A special exhibition for children is on display in the basement.

⓫ Riddarholms-kyrkan

Birger Jarls Torg. **Map** 3 A3. **Tel** 08-402 61 30. Ⓣ Gamla Stan. 🚌 1, 3, 14, 53. **Open** mid-May–mid-Sep: 10am–5pm daily. Eng: noon daily. ♿ 🔲

This church on the island of Riddarholmen is best known as a place for royal burials. Its interior is full of ornate sarcophagi and worn gravestones, and in front of the altar are the tombs of the medieval kings Karl Knutsson and Magnus Ladulås.

Built on the site of the late 13th-century Greyfriars abbey, founded by Magnus Ladulås, the majestic brick church was gradually enlarged over the centuries. After a serious fire in 1835, it acquired its present lattice-work cast-iron tower.

Inside, the church is surrounded by splendid burial vaults dating back to the 17th century. The coffins rest on a lower level with space for a memorial above. The most recent was built in 1858–60 for the Bernadotte dynasty.

The vaults contain the remains of all the Swedish sovereigns from Gustav II Adolf in the 17th century to the present day with two exceptions: Queen Kristina was buried at St Peter's in Rome in 1689 and Gustav VI Adolf, who was interred at Haga in 1973 (see p102). The most magnificent sarcophagus is that of the 19th-century king, Karl XIV Johan, which had to be towed here by sledge from his porphyry workshops in northern Sweden. Particularly moving are the

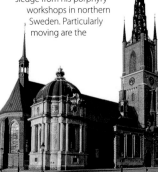

Riddarholmskyrkan and the external burial vault by Tessin and Hårleman

graves of royal children, including the many small tin coffins that surround the last resting place of Gustav II Adolf and his queen, Maria Eleonora.

⓬ Wrangelska Palatset

Birger Jarls Torg 16. **Map** 3 A3. Ⓣ Gamla Stan. 🚌 3, 53. **Closed** to the public.

Only two parts of Gustav Vasa's fortifications from 1530 remain – Birger Jarl's Tower and the southernmost tower of what became the Wrangel Palace. Built as a residence for the nobleman Lars Sparre in 1652–70, it was remodelled a few decades later by Carl Gustaf Wrangel. A field marshal in the Thirty Years War, Wrangel chose Nicodemus Tessin the Elder as his architect. The result was Stockholm's largest privately owned palace.

In 1697 the royal family moved into the palace after the Tre Kronor fortress (see p58) was ravaged by fire. It became known as the King's House, and it was here in the same year that the 15-year-old Karl XII took the oath of office after the death of his father. Gustav III was born here in 1746 and in 1792 his assassin was incarcerated in the dungeons. The Court

of Appeal now uses this building, as well as Rosenhane Palace (Birger Jarls Torg 10) and Hessenstein House (Birger Jarls Torg 2), built in 1630 by Bengt Bengtsson Oxenstierna.

⓭ Evert Taubes Terrass

Norra Riddarholmshamnen. **Map** 3 A3. Ⓣ Gamla Stan. 🚌 3, 53.

A statue of Evert Taube, the much-loved troubadour and ballad writer, stands on the terrace below Wrangelska Palatset looking out over the waters of Riddarfjärden. In an ideal position, given the poet's close links to the sea, the bronze sculpture was created by Willy Gordon in 1990. Close by stands Christer Berg's granite sculpture *Solbåten* (Sun Boat), unveiled in 1966. Inspired by the shape of a shell, from some angles it also resembles a sail.

Evert Taube (1890–1976)

⓮ Riddarhuset

Riddarhustorget 10. **Map** 3 A3. **Tel** 08-723 39 90. Ⓣ Gamla Stan. 🚌 3, 53. **Open** 11:30am–12:30pm Mon–Fri. **Closed** public hols. 📷 📹 by appointment. 🌐 **riddarhuset.se**

Often regarded as one of Stockholm's most beautiful buildings, Riddarhuset (House of Knights) stands on Riddarhustorget, the city's centre until the 19th century.

Wrangelska Palatset, a royal residence after the Tre Kronor fire of 1697

Built in 1641–7 on the initiative of the State Chancellor, Riddarhuset provided the knights with a base for meetings and events. The building is a supreme example of Dutch Baroque design by the architects Simon and Jean de la Vallée, Heinrich Wilhelm and Justus Vingboons.

Over the entrance on the northern façade is the knights' motto *Arte et Marte* (Art and War) with Minerva, Goddess of Art and Science, and Mars, God of War.

The sculptures on the vaulted roof symbolize the knightly virtues. On the south side is *Nobilitas* (Nobility) holding a small Minerva and spear. She is flanked by *Studium* (Diligence) and *Valor* (Bravery). Facing the north is the male equivalent, *Honor*, flanked by *Prudentia* (Prudence) and *Fortitudo* (Strength).

Inside, a magnificent double staircase leads up to the Knights' Room. This has a painted ceiling by David Klöcker Ehrenstrahl (1628– 98) and Riddarhuset's foremost treasure, a sculpted ebony chair, 1623. The walls are covered with coats of arms.

Riddarhuset, built in the 17th century in imposing Dutch Baroque style

⓯ Riksdagshuset

Riksgatan 3 A. **Map** 3 B2. **Tel** 08- 786 40 00. Ⓣ Kungsträdgården. 🚌 3, 43, 53, 62. **Open** tours & meetings in the Chamber. 🎥 daily in summer; weekends in winter; ring for details. 🏛 🚹 🌐 **riksdagen.se**

The Parliament building (Riksdagshuset) and Bank of Sweden (Riksbank) on Helgeandsholmen were inaugurated in 1905 and 1906 respectively. In the 1970s and 1980s the two buildings were combined and restored and a modern extension built to house a new, single debating chamber. The chamber is truly Nordic in its decoration with benches of Swedish birch and wall-panelling in Finnish birch. A large tapestry, *Memory of a Landscape* (1983), by Elisabeth Hasselberg-Olsson, covers 54 sq m (581 sq ft) of wall and took 3,500 hours to make. Parliamentary debates can be watched from the public gallery.

The original two-chamber Parliament is used for meetings of the majority party. The former First Chamber has three paintings by Otte Sköld (1894–1958); the other chamber contains works by Axel Törneman and Georg Pauli. Between the chambers is a 45 m (148 ft) long hall with an elegant display of coats of arms. The Finance Committee meets in the oak-panelled library surrounded by old prints and *Jugendstil* (Art Nouveau-style) lamps. Facing the Norrbro entrance is the original 1905 stairwell with columns, floor, steps and balusters in various marbles. The present entrance was the Bank of Sweden's main hall until 1976.

Medieval stone head of Birger Jarl at Medeltidsmuseet

⓰ Medeltids-museet

Strömparterren, Norrbro. **Map** 3 B2. **Tel** 08-508 317 90. Ⓣ Kungsträd-gården. 🚌 43, 62. **Open** 11am–5pm Tue–Sun (noon–7pm Wed). 🎥 🏛 🏛 🚹 ♿ 🌐 **medeltidsmuseet. stockholm.se**

This fascinating museum of medieval Stockholm is built around some of the capital's archaeological remains, mainly parts of the city wall that date from the 1530s. They were discovered in 1978–80. Completely underground, the dimly-lit, atmospheric museum includes finds evoking Stockholm's early history. Among them is the 22 m (72 ft) long Riddarholm ship, dating from the 1520s, which was found off Riddarholmen in 1930.

The museum provides a good picture of Stockholm's early days. From the entrance, a 350-year-old tunnel leads into a reconstructed medieval world. There is a pillory in the square and gallows with the tools of the executioner's trade. The city has been recreated with a church, harbour and a square. Visitors can also see a 55 m (180 ft) long section of the original city wall, complete with a skeleton which had been concealed there.

The new Parliament building, with the older building behind

CITY

The area known as City today was where, in the mid-18th century, the first stone-built houses and palaces outside Gamla Stan started to appear for the burghers and nobility. After World War II, the run-down buildings around Hötorget were demolished to form what is now Sergels Torg; many homes were replaced by rather dreary office blocks.

In the 21st century, though, the area has livened up and become the true heart and commercial centre of Stockholm.

A hub for public transport and banking, City is the place for the best department stores and shopping malls, exclusive boutiques and nightspots. The centre also has some beautiful parks and pleasant squares which serve as popular meeting places. The unique landscape surrounding Stockholm permeates even City, offering sudden unexpected glimpses of water complete with bustling boat life and a string of anglers along the embankments.

Sights at a Glance

Museums
- ⑤ Dansmuseet
- ⑥ Medelhavsmuseet
- ⑪ Strindbergsmuseet Blå Tornet
- ⑭ Armémuseum
- ⑮ Musikmuseet
- ⑱ Hallwylska Palatset

Churches
- ③ Jacobs Kyrka
- ⑧ Klara Kyrka
- ⑫ Adolf Fredriks Kyrka

Squares
- ② Kungsträdgården

Public Buildings
- ① Nordiska Kompaniet (NK)
- ⑦ Arvfurstens Palats
- ⑬ Kungliga Biblioteket
- ⑯ Hovstallet

Theatres and Concert Halls
- ④ Kungliga Operan
- ⑨ Kulturhuset and Stadsteatern
- ⑩ Konserthuset
- ⑰ Kungliga Dramatiska Teatern

See also Street Finder maps 1, 2 & 3

◀ Statue of Gustav II Adolf in the middle of Gustav Adolfs Torg

For keys to symbols *see back flap*

Street-by-Street: Around Kungsträdgården

With a history going back to the 15th century, the King's Garden (Kungsträdgården) has long been the city's most popular meeting place and recreational centre. Both visitors and Stockholmers gather here for summer concerts and festivals, or just to enjoy a stroll under the lime trees. Around the park is a wealth of shops, including the upmarket department store Nordiska Kompaniet, boutiques, churches, museums and restaurants. A short walk takes you to Gustav Adolfs Torg, flanked by the Royal Opera House and other stately buildings, including the Swedish Foreign Office.

❹ ★ Kungliga Operan
Built in 1898 with a magnificently ornate auditorium, the Royal Opera House replaced an earlier one from the time of Gustav III.

❻ ★ Medelhavsmuseet
This museum near Gustav Adolfs Torg has vast collections from prehistoric cultures around the Mediterranean.

FREDSGATAN

REGERINGSGATAN

Sagerska Palatset

STRÖMGATAN

GUSTAV ADOLFS TORG

STRÖMGATAN

NORRBRO

NORRSTRÖM

Operakällaren
(see p294)

Gustav II Adolf's equestrian statue, designed by L'Archevêques, was unveiled in 1796.

SOPHIA·ALBERTINA
ÆDIFICAVIT·

❼ Arvfurstens Palats
The Swedish Foreign Office is based in this palace, built for Gustav III's sister Sofia Albertina in 1794.

Key

— Suggested route

Queen Kristina's summer house, the cobble-stoned Lantmäteri-backen.

The NK clock, part of the city skyline.

Locator Map
See Street Finder maps 2 & 3

VASASTAN

CITY

Riddarfjärden   GAMLA STAN

Strömmen

Sergels Torg

HAMNGATAN

VÄSTRA TRÄDGÅRDSGATAN

KUNGSTRÄDGÅRDSGATAN

Statue of Karl XIII

Molin's fountain

❶ **Nordiska Kompaniet (NK)**
Designed by Ferdinand Boberg in 1915, the granite palace houses Sweden's most exclusive department store.

❷ **Kungsträdgården**
The king's kitchen garden was sited here in the 15th century. Today it is one of the most popular recreation centres in the city, both in summer and winter.

❸ **Jacobs Kyrka**
Started in 1580, the church was consecrated in 1643. Its stone porches are beautifully crafted.

0 metres   100
0 yards   100

Karl XII's statue by Molin was built in 1868 to mark the 150th anniversary of the king's death.

❶ Nordiska Kompaniet (NK)

Hamngatan 18–20. **Map** 2 D4.
Tel 08-762 80 00. T-centralen.
47, 69, 76. **Open** 10am–8pm Mon–
Fri, 10am–6pm Sat, noon–5pm Sun.

Designed by Ferdinand Boberg,
the granite palace on
Hamngatan houses the
department store Nordiska
Kompaniet (NK). Opened in
1915, NK was – and still is –
aimed at an exclusive clientele.
It made its name as a
showcase for
Swedish arts and
crafts, writing design
history when the
textiles department,
Tetilkammaren, opened
in 1937. The manager
was the textile artist
Astrid Sampe who
commissioned leading

Molin's
fountain

contemporary artists and
designers to supply work. Olle
Baertling, Arne Jacobsen, Alvar
Aalto and Viola Gråsten all
contributed patterns. Sampe
also introduced new fabric
printing techniques.
    Today at NK you can find
almost everything from
perfume, clothing and sporting
equipment to glass, silver and
porcelain, but above all, the
store is, as its founder Josef
Sachs once described it, a
commercial and cultural theatre.

❷ Kungsträdgården

Map 3 B1. Kungsträdgården.
47, 69.

The "King's Garden" is a popular
meeting place for Stockholmers
where there is something for
everyone going on all year
round. This open urban space

is bordered by treelined
promenades, with a modern
fountain in the middle. At the
Strömgatan end there is a
square named after Karl XII with
J P Molin's statue of the warrior
king, unveiled in 1868, at its
centre. In Kungsträdgården
itself there is a statue of Karl XIII
(1809–18) by Erik Göthe. During
the summer, the park is the
venue for food festivals,
concerts, dancing and street
theatre. In winter, the skating
rink attracts children
and grown-ups
alike. Also to be seen
is Molin's fountain, made
from gypsum in 1866
and cast in bronze.
    It is the city's oldest
park, starting as the royal
kitchen garden in the
15th century. During
Erik XIV's reign in the 16th
century, it was transformed into
a formal Renaissance garden.
Queen Kristina built a stone
summer house here in the 17th
century, which stands at
Västra Trädgårdsgatan 2,
by the cobblestoned
Lantmäteribacken.

❸ Jacobs Kyrka

Jakobs Torg 5. **Map** 3 B1. **Tel** 08-723
30 38. Kungsträdgården. 55.
Open noon–4pm Tue, 1–4pm Wed,
11am–6pm Thu, 1–6pm Fri, 2–5pm
Sat. In Eng 6pm Sun.

In medieval times there
was a small chapel where
Kungsträdgården now lies.
Dedicated to St Jacob, the
patron saint of wayfarers, the
chapel and another modest-
sized church were pulled down
by King Gustav Vasa in the 16th
century. His son, Johan III,

wanted to provide two new
churches in Norra Malmen, as
the area was then called, and
work to build the churches of
St Jacob and St Klara *(see p74)*
started in 1580. St Jacob's was
consecrated first, in 1643. It has
been restored several times
since then, in some cases rather
clumsily. However, several
valuable items have been
preserved, including a
baptismal font from 1634 and
some church silver, as well as
porches by the stonemasons
Henrik Blom and Hans Hebel.
    The organ's façade was
created by the architect
Carl Hårleman and the large
painting on the west wall of the
southern nave is by Fredrik
Westin, Sweden's most
distinguished historical painter
of the early 19th century.

Altar in Jacobs Kyrka, dating in part from
the 17th century.

❹ Kungliga Operan

Gustav Adolfs Torg. **Map** 3 B1.
Tel 08-791 44 00. Kungsträdgården. 2, 43, 55, 62, 65. Ticket
Office: **Open** 9am–6pm Mon–Fri,
10am–2pm Sat (open Sun for
performances). In Eng 1pm Sat.
operan.se

Opera has been staged in
Sweden since 18 January
1773, when a performance
took place at Bollhuset at
Slottsbacken. Kungliga Operan
(The Royal Opera House) on
Gustav Adolfs Torg was
inaugurated on 30 September
1782, but by the late 19th
century it had become a fire
hazard. The architect Axel
Anderberg was commissioned
to design a new opera house

View of Kungsträdgården, towards Hamngatan

The splendid golden foyer at Kungliga Operan

which was given to the State in 1898 by a consortium founded by the financier K A Wallenberg.

The colouring of the building in late-Renaissance style is in keeping with the Royal Palace and Parliament building, and some details of the architecture are common to all three. The beautiful staircase with ceiling paintings by Axel Jungstedt was inspired by the Paris Opera. The same artist's portrait of Oscar II hangs in the 28 m (92 ft) long golden foyer, where Carl Larsson was responsible for the decorative paintings. The wings at either side of the stage have been retained, as has the width of the proscenium arch (11.4 m/37 ft). Also saved was J T Sergel's group of angels above the stage. An angel in Vicke Andrén's ceiling painting is holding a sketch of the Opera House.

Gold ceiling in Kungliga Operan

❺ Dansmuseet

Drottninggatan 17. **Map** 3 A1. **Tel** 08-441 76 50. 🚈 Kungsträd-gården. 🚌 52. **Open** 11am–4pm Tue–Fri (Mon–Fri Jun–Aug), noon–4pm Sat & Sun. 🚻 📷 📹 📷 ♿ 🌐 **dansmuseet.se**

Located in the heart of Stockholm, the Dance Museum is housed in a former bank building on Drottninggatan. The museum was originally established in Paris in 1953 by the Swedish aristocrat Rolf de Maré (1888–1964). He was a noted art collector and founder of the renowned avant-garde company Les Ballets Suédois. The collection features all aspects of dance – costumes and masks, scenery sketches, art and posters, books and documents – and includes an archive on popular dance. Apart from the exhibition hall, there is also a data bank – the Rolf de Maré Study Centre – which contains video/DVD facilities, a library and archives. The museum shop stocks Sweden's largest collection of dance DVDs for sale.

❻ Medelhavs-museet

Fredsgatan 2. **Map** 3 B1. **Tel** 08-519 553 80. 🚈 Kungsträdgården. 🚌 3, 43, 52, 62, 65. **Open** noon–8pm Tue–Fri, noon–5pm Sat & Sun. 🚻 📷 📹 📷 ♿ 🌐 **medelhavsmuseet.se**

Gods and people from pre-historic cultures around the Mediterranean rub shoulders in Medelhavsmuseet (the Museum of Mediterranean and Near East Antiquities). Its many treasures include a large group of terracotta figures discovered by archaeologists on Cyprus in the 1930s. There is an extensive display covering ancient Egypt, with bronze weapons, tools and some remarkable mummies. Greek and Islamic culture, Roman and Etruscan art are all represented and complemented by temporary exhibitions.

Medelhavsmuseet is housed in a former bank, built in the 17th century for Gustav Horn, a general in the Thirty Years War. The stairwell, dating from 1905, and the peristyles and colonnade around the upper part of the hall are worth a visit in themselves.

❼ Arvfurstens Palats

Gustav Adolfs Torg 1. **Map** 3 B1. 🚈 Kungsträdgården. 🚌 43, 62. **Closed** to the public.

Opposite the Royal Opera House, on the other side of Gustav Adolfs Torg, stands Arvfurstens Palats (Prince's Palace), built for Gustav III's sister Sofia Albertina and completed in 1794. She commissioned the architect Erik Palmstedt to carry out the work. He was a pupil of Carl Fredrik Adelcrantz, designer of the original opera house.

The palace and its decor are shining examples of the Gustavian style, thanks to the contributions of artists and craftsmen such as Louis Masreliez and Georg Haupt and their pupils Gustaf Adolf Ditzinger, J T Sergel and Gottlieb Iwersson. In 1906 the building was taken over by the Swedish Foreign Office.

Nearby is the elegant Sagerska Palatset (1894) in French Renaissance style, which is used by the prime minister as an official residence.

Arvfurstens Palats (1794), now the Swedish Foreign Office

Edvin Öhrström's obelisk in Sergels Torg, with Kulturhuset to the left

❽ Klara Kyrka

Klara Östra Kyrkogata. **Map** 1 C4.
Tel 08-411 73 24. Ⓣ T-centralen.
🚌 47, 52, 59, 65. **Open** 10am–5pm
Sun–Fri, 5–7:30pm Sat. **Concert** noon
Thu, 6pm Sat. ✝ 5pm Sat, 11am &
2pm Sun (Swahili). 🖼 ♿

The convent of St Klara stood on
the site of the present church
and cemetery until 1527, when it
was pulled down on the orders
of Gustav Vasa. Later, his son
Johan III commissioned a new
church, completed in 1590.
 The church was ravaged by fire
in 1751. Its reconstruction was
planned by two of the period's
most outstanding architects,
Carl Hårleman and Carl Fredrik
Adelcrantz. The pulpit was made
in 1753 to Hårleman's design,
and J T Sergel (*see p87*) created
the angelic figures in the
northern gallery. A pair of
identical angels adorn the
chancel, based on the
gypsum originals.
 In the 1880s, the 116 m
(380 ft) tower was added. The
20th-century church artist,
Olle Hjortzberg, created the
paintings in the vault in 1904.

Interior of Klara Kyrka with decoration by
Olle Hjortzberg

❾ Kulturhuset and Stadsteatern

Sergels Torg 3. **Map** 1 C4. Kulturhuset:
Tel 08-508 315 08. Stadsteatern:
Tel 08-506 202 00. Ⓣ T-centralen.
🚌 52, 59, 69. **Open** 11am–7pm Tue,
Wed & Fri (to 9pm Thu, to 5pm Sat &
Sun). ♿ some areas. 🖥 ✏ 📷 ♿
🌐 **kulturhuset.stockholm.se;**
🌐 **stadsteatern.stockholm.se**

The distinctive glass façade of
Kulturhuset (Cultural Centre)
fronts the southern side of
Sergels Torg. The winning entry
in a Nordic architectural competition, Kulturhuset has become a
symbol of Swedish Modernism.
It was designed by Peter Celsing
and opened in 1974.
 Refurbished to meet the needs
of the new millennium, the
complex contains several
galleries which mount regularly
changing exhibitions. In the
auditorium, a varied programme
of music, dance, drama and
lectures is presented.

In the Children's Room,
youngsters can read books,
draw pictures, listen to stories
or watch films. "Lava" focuses
on youth culture nationwide.
There is a library for fans of
strip cartoons and reading
rooms providing computers,
newspapers and magazines.
 Among the shops here is
Designtorget, selling items
of Swedish design. There are
two cafés: the top-floor Café
Panorama offers diners
fantastic city views, while Café
Ekoteket serves organic and
locally produced food and also
hosts tasting sessions.
 Kulturhuset also houses
Stadsteatern (City Theatre),
whose main auditorium
opened in 1990. This part of
the building was formerly
occupied by Parliament while
its chamber on Helgeands-
holmen was being rebuilt
(*see p67*). The theatre was
designed by architects Lars
Fahlsten and Per Ahrbom and
contains six stages of varying
size and style under one roof.

❿ Konserthuset

Hötorget. **Map** 1 C4. **Tel** 08-786 02 00.
Ⓣ Hötorget. 🚌 1, 56, 59. Ticket
Office: **Open** 11am–6pm Mon–Fri,
11am–3pm Sat, and 2 hours before a
concert. 🖥 🖼 📷 ♿
🌐 **konserthuset.se**

A Nordic version of a Greek
temple, Konserthuset (the
Concert Hall) is a masterpiece
of the architect Ivar Tengbom
(1878–1968) and is an
outstanding example of the

City's Transformation

During the 20th century Stockholm's population grew from 250,000
to more than 1.6 million. By the 1920s it was obvious that the old
heart of the city would not meet
the future needs of business, public
administration and the growth in
traffic. In 1951 a controversial
30-year ongoing programme to
transform the lower Norrmalm city
centre was launched. Slums on
335 of the 600 sites were pulled
down and 78 new buildings were
built. Two-thirds of the area's
buildings were added during
this period.

The first steps towards a new Hötorg
City, 1958

The *Orpheus* sculpture group by Carl Milles at Konserthuset

The Nobel Prizes

Alfred Nobel (1833–96) was an outstanding chemist and inventor. He left his fortune to endow the prestigious Nobel Prizes – consisting of a monetary award and a medal – which have been presented every December since 1901. The ceremony takes place in Konserthuset, where prizes are awarded for physics, chemistry, physiology or medicine, and literature. Since 1969 the Bank of Sweden has given a prize for economic sciences in Nobel's memory. The Nobel Peace Prize is presented in Oslo on the same day. In 1901 each prize was worth 150,000 kr; in 2012 the figure was 8 million kr.

The Nobel Medal, awarded annually

1920s' Neo-Classical style. Tengbom's tradition has been carried on by his son Anders (b. 1911), who was in charge of its renovation in 1970–71, and his grandson Svante (b. 1942), who had a similar task in 1993–6.

Constructed in 1923–6, the main hall has undergone major reconstruction and modernization to overcome acoustical problems. Its interior is very simple in contrast to the Grünewald Hall, by the artist Isaac Grünewald (1889–1946), which is in the more lavish style of an Italian Renaissance palace. The four marble statues in the main foyer are by Carl Milles, creator of the *Orpheus* sculpture group outside.

The Concert Hall is the home of the Swedish Royal Philharmonic Orchestra, which gives some 70 concerts every year, and international star soloists perform regularly. It is also the venue for the Nobel Prize presentations.

⓫ Strindbergs-museet Blå Tornet

Drottninggatan 85. **Map** 1 C3. **Tel** 08-411 53 54. Ⓣ Rådmansgatan. 🚌 52, 65. **Open** Jul–Aug: 10am–4pm Tue–Sun; Sep–Jun: noon–4pm Tue–Sun. 🎧 🎦 1pm Thu–Sun (Swedish only). 🏛 ♿ 🌐 strindbergsmuseet.se

The world-famous dramatist August Strindberg (1849–1912) lived at 24 different addresses in Stockholm over the years. He

moved to the last of these in 1908, and gave it the name Blå Tornet (the Blue Tower). By then he had gained international recognition.

The apartment, now the Strindbergsmuseet, was newly built with central heating, toilet and lift, but lacked a kitchen. Instead he relied on Falkner's Pension, in the same building, for food and other services. On his last few birthdays the great man would stand on his balcony and watch his admirers stage a torchlight procession in his honour.

Opened in 1973, the museum shows the author's home with his bedroom and dining room and his study as it was on his death, as well as 3,000 books, photographic archives, press cuttings and posters. In the adjoining premises, a permanent exhibition portrays Strindberg as author, theatrical director, artist and photographer. Temporary exhibitions and other activities are often held here.

Strindberg's desk and writing materials in his study

⓬ Adolf Fredriks Kyrka

Holländargatan 16. **Map** 1 C3. **Tel** 08-20 70 76. Ⓣ Hötorget. 🚌 52. **Open** 1–7pm Mon, 10am–4pm Tue–Sun. **Concert** 12.15pm Tue. 🎦 7pm Mon, 12.15pm Wed & Thu, 11am Sun. 📷 by appointment. 📱 🏛 ♿

King Adolf Fredrik laid the foundation stone of this church in 1768 on the site of an earlier chapel dedicated to St Olof. Designed by Carl Fredrik Adelcrantz, in Neo-Classical style with traces of Rococo, the church has been built in the shape of a Greek cross and has a central dome.

The interior has undergone a number of changes, but both the altar and pulpit have remained intact. The sculptor Johan Tobias Sergel created the altarpiece and the memorial to the French philosopher

Memorial to Descartes

Descartes who died in Stockholm in 1650. The paintings in the dome were added in 1899–1900 by Julius Kronberg. More recent acquisitions include altar silverware by Sigurd Persson.

The cemetery is the resting place of the assassinated Prime Minister Olof Palme (1927–86). J T Sergel is also buried here.

Armémuseum, with the dome of Hedvig Eleonora Kyrka in the background

⓭ Kungliga Biblioteket

Humlegården. **Map** 2 D3. **Tel** 010-709 30 30. Ⓣ Östermalmstorg. 🚌 1, 2, 55, 56. **Open** 9am–7pm Mon–Thu, 9am–6pm Fri, 11am–5pm Sat; early Jun–mid-Aug: 9am–6pm Mon–Thu, 9am–5pm Fri, 11am–3pm Sat. 📷 by appointment. 🖥 ♿ 🌐 **kb.se**

This is Sweden's national library and an autonomous Government department in its own right. Ever since 1661, when there were only nine printing presses in Sweden, copies of every piece of printed matter have had to be lodged with Kungliga Biblioteket (Royal Library). Since 1993 this requirement has also applied to electronic documents. As there are now some 3,000 printers and publishers in Sweden the volume of material is expanding rapidly. The stock of books is increasing at the rate of 35,000 volumes a year.

The imposing original building, dating from 1865–78, had to be expanded in the 1920s, and again in the 1990s.

The library is in a beautiful setting in Humlegården, created by Gustav II Adolf in 1619 to grow hops for the royal household. Ever since the 18th century, the park has been a favourite recreation area for Stockholmers.

The 13th-century "Devil's Bible" in Kungliga Biblioteket

⓮ Armémuseum

Riddargatan 13. **Map** 2 E4. **Tel** 08-519 563 00. Ⓣ Östermalmstorg. 🚌 62, 69. **Open** 11am–8pm Tue, 11am–5pm Wed–Sun. 📷 🎥 📷 📷 ♿ 🌐 **sfhm.se**

The old armoury on Artillerigården has been the home of the Armémuseum (Royal Army Museum) since 1879. During the 1990s, the 250-year-old building and its displays underwent extensive renovation to create one of the capital's best-planned and most interesting museums.

Exhibits are arranged over three floors. Dramatic life-size settings have been made to portray Sweden's history of war and defence, showing not only what happened in battle but how the lives of the women and children at home were affected. Diaries, intelligence manuals, rifles, flags, banners and even cutlery add a note of reality.

During the summer guardsmen march from here to the Royal Palace at 11:45am daily for the changing of the guard.

⓯ Musikmuseet

Sibyllegatan 2. **Map** 2 E4. **Tel** 08-519 554 90. Ⓣ Östermalmstorg, Kungsträdgården. 🚌 47, 62, 69, 76. **Open** noon–5pm Tue–Sun. 📷 🎥 by appointment only. 📷 📷 ♿ 📷 🌐 **musikmuseet.se**

The Museum of Music opened in the old royal bakery in 1979. Bread was baked here for military personnel in Stockholm from 1640 right up to 1958. It is the capital's oldest preserved industrial building, in the city centre. Today the museum's collection includes about 6,000 instruments, and it also holds Sweden's national musical archive. With 20,000 manuscripts, it is a gold mine for anyone interested in Swedish folk music. The archive is open by appointment only. It hosts a regular programme of temporary exhibitions.

A Swedish cornet, part of the Musikmuseet's collection

⓰ Hovstallet

Väpnargatan 1. **Map** 2 E4. **Tel** 08-402 61 06. Ⓣ Östermalmstorg. 🚌 2, 5, 71, 76. **Open** for guided tours. 📷 2pm Sat & Sun; Jul–Aug: 2pm Mon–Fri. 🌐 **royalcourt.se**

The Royal Mews looks after transport for the Royal Family and Royal Household. It maintains about 40 carriages, a dozen cars, carriage horses, and a few horses used for riding. The royal horses are Swedish half-breeds.

There are many treasures among the carriages, such as the glass-panelled State Coach known as a "Berliner". It was built in Sweden at the Adolf Freyschuss carriage works and made its debut at Oscar II's silver jubilee in 1897. It is still used today on ceremonial occasions.

Incoming foreign ambassadors travel to the Royal Palace for their formal audience with the monarch in Karl XV's coupé. Open horse-drawn carriages from the mid-19th century are normally used for processions.

Ingmar Bergman

The playwright and producer Ingmar Bergman was born at Östermalm in 1918. His long series of masterly films have made him world-famous, but he started his career in the theatre. From 1963–6 he was Director of Kungliga Dramatiska Teatern. His breakthrough as a film producer came with *Smiles of the Summer Night* (1955), and *The Seventh Seal* (1957) was a cinematic milestone. *Fanny and Alexander* (1982) was his last major film, after which he wrote screenplays and published his autobiography, *Magic Lantern*. Ingmar Bergman died in 2007.

Ingmar Bergman at a press conference, 1998

The Hallwylska Palatset courtyard, seen through the gateway arch

⑰ Kungliga Dramatiska Teatern

Nybroplan. **Map** 2 E4. **Tel** 08-667 06 80. Ⓣ Östermalmstorg. 🚌 69, 76. Ticket Office: **Open** noon–7pm Tue–Sat, noon–4pm Sun (except Jun–Aug). 🕐 ♿ ♿ 🖼 ⓦ dramaten.se

When plans were drawn up in the early 20th century to build the present Kungliga Dramatiska Teatern (Royal Dramatic Theatre) at Nybroplan, the State refused to give financial aid, so it was funded by lotteries instead. The results exceeded all expectations, giving the architect Fredrik Lilljekvist generous resources which he used to the full.

The new theatre, known as Dramaten, took six years to build and opened in 1908. The design was lavish, both in the choice of materials and in the contributions by leading Swedish artists.

The Jugendstil façade, inspired by Viennese architecture, is in expensive white marble. Christian Ericsson created the powerful relief frieze, Carl Milles the centre section and John Börjesson the bronze statues *Poetry* and *Drama*. These are complemented in the foyer by *Tragedy* and *Comedy* by Börjesson and Theodor Lundberg respectively.

The ceiling in the foyer is by Carl Larsson, while the upper lobby's back wall was painted by Oscar Björk, and the auditorium's ceiling and stage lintel by Julius Kronberg. Gustav Cederström provided the central painting in the marble foyer.

When Gustav III founded the Royal Dramatic Theatre in 1788 it performed in a building on Slottsbacken. The colour scheme there – blue, white and gold – was chosen for the new venue, but was changed to "theatre red" in the 1930s. The original colours were reinstated in 1988.

⑱ Hallwylska Palatset

Hamngatan 4. **Map** 2 D4. **Tel** 08-519 555 99. Ⓣ Östermalmstorg. 🚌 2, 69, 76. **Open** noon–4pm Tue–Sun (to 7pm Wed); Jul–Aug: 10am–4:30pm Tue–Sun. 🎧 🕐 3pm Sun (in Eng). 🖼 🖼 ⓦ hallwylskamuseet.se

The impressive façade of Hamngatan 4 is nothing in comparison with what is concealed behind the heavy gates. The Hallwyl Palace was built from 1892–7 as a residence for the immensely wealthy Count and Countess Walther and Wilhelmina von Hallwyl. When the Countess died in 1930 the State was left a fantastic gift: an unbelievably ornate palace whose chatelaine had amassed a priceless collection of *objets d'art* over many decades. Eight years later the doors opened on a new museum with 67,000 catalogued items.

Wilhelmina left nothing to chance, often visiting the building site. The architect Isak Gustav Clason (1856–1930) had no worries about cost and nor did the decorative painter and artistic adviser Julius Kronberg. Every detail had to be perfect. A typical example is the billiards room which has gilt-leather wallpaper and walnut panelling, with billiard balls sculpted into the marble fireplace.

The paintings in the gallery, mostly 16th- and 17th-century Flemish, were bought over a period of only two years.

Kungliga Dramatiska Teatern's Jugendstil façade in white marble

BLASIEHOLMEN & SKEPPSHOLMEN

Opposite the Royal Palace on the eastern side of the Norrström channel lies Blasieholmen, a natural springboard to the islands of Skeppsholmen and Kastellholmen.

Several elegant palaces were built at Blasieholmen during Sweden's era as a great power in the 17th and early 18th centuries. But the area's present appearance was acquired in the period between the mid- 19th century, when buildings such as Nationalmuseum were erected, and just before World War I. In the early 1900s, stately residences such as Bååtska Palatset became overshadowed by smart hotels, opulent bank buildings and entertainment venues. Blasieholmen is also the place for auction houses, art galleries, antiques shops and second-hand bookshops. And the quayside is the departure point for sightseeing and archipelago boats.

Skeppsholmen is reached by a wrought-iron bridge with old wooden boats moored next to it. In the middle of the 17th century the island became the base for the Swedish Navy and many of its old buildings were designed as barracks and stores. Today they house some of the city's major museums and cultural institutions, juxtaposed with the avant-garde construction of the Moderna museet.

Sights at a Glance

Museums
1 Östasiatiska museet
2 Moderna museet pp84–5
3 Arkitekturmuseet
7 Nationalmuseum pp86–7

Islands and Squares
6 Kastellholmen
9 Blasieholmstorg
12 Raoul Wallenbergs Torg

Synagogues
10 Synagogan

Hotels and Restaurants
4 af Chapman
8 Grand Hôtel
11 Berns

Concert Halls
13 Musikaliska

Public Buildings
5 Kungliga Konsthögskolan

0 metres 250
0 yards 250

See also Street Finder maps 2, 3 & 4

◀ **af Chapman**, Stockholm's most unusual youth hostel -

For keys to symbols *see back flap*

Street-by-Street: Skeppsholmen

Skeppsholmen has long since lost its importance as a naval base and has been transformed into a centre for culture. Many of the naval buildings have been restored and traditional wooden boats are moored here, but pride of place now goes to the exciting Moderna museet. The island is ideal for a full-day visit, with its location between the waters of Strömmen and Nybroviken acting as a breathing space in the centre of Stockholm. The attractive buildings, the richly wooded English-style park and the view towards Skeppsbron and Strandvägen also make Skeppsholmen a pleasant place for those who would just prefer to have a quiet stroll.

Teater Galeasen is Stockholm's avant-garde theatre for new Swedish and international drama.

Blasieholmen

Skeppsholmsbron (bridge)

❶ ★ Östasiatiska museet
This yellow-enamel dish with a blue dragon is part of a collection of arts and crafts from China, Japan, Korea and India covering the period from the Stone Age to the 1800s.

Skeppsholmen Church (1824–42) in well-preserved Empire style.

Salute battery *(see p82)*

Admiralty House

S V E N S K S U N D V A G E N

V A S T R A B R O B A N K E N

Paradise (1963), a sculpture group by Jean Tinguely and Niki de Saint Phalle for Montreal's World Exposition, has stood outside the site of the Moderna museet since 1972.

Youth Hostel

Swedish Society of Crafts & Design

❹ af Chapman
Built in 1888, the full-rigged former freighter and school ship has served as a popular youth hostel since 1949. Skeppsholmen Church *(left)* and the Admiralty House (1647–50, rebuilt 1844–6) are in the background.

❺ Kungliga Konsthögskolan
The first part of the Royal College of Fine Arts was completed in the 1770s, but it acquired its present appearance in the mid-1990s. This cast-iron boar stands at the entrance.

For hotels and restaurants in this area see pp284–289 and pp294–301

The festival area on the quayside below the Moderna museet is the venue for the popular International Jazz & Blues Festival, which takes place for a week in July each year.

Loading crane built in 1751 – the oldest of its type in Sweden.

Locator Map
See Street Finder map 4

❸ Arkitekturmuseet
The Museum of Architecture highlights thousands of years of building, with a collection of models showing masterpieces worldwide, including this model of the Stockholm City Library by Asplund.

❷ ★ Moderna museet
Designed by Rafael Moneo, the museum was opened in 1998 when Stockholm was Cultural Capital of Europe. It has an exciting collection of modern art, and fine views across the water.

Monument commemorating the battle at Svensksund in 1790 *(see p46)*

Hotel Skeppsholmen is part of a complex of buildings dating back to around 1700. They originally accommodated King Karl XII's bodyguard, but today serve as a hotel and restaurant.

Kastell-holmen

Key

— Suggested route

0 metres   100
0 yards   100

Arkitekturmuseet, housed in the Neo-Classical former naval drill hall

❶ Östasiatiska museet

Tyghusplan. **Map** 4 D2. **Tel** 010-456 12 00. Ⓣ Kungsträdgården. 🚌 65. 🚢 Djurgårdsfärja. **Open** 11am–8pm Tue, 11am–5pm Wed–Sun. 🗝 by appointment only. 📷 ♿
🌐 ostasiatiskamuseet.se

It is not unusual for Western capitals to have a museum devoted to art and archaeology from China, Japan, Korea and India. But it is not every Museum of Far Eastern Antiquities that, like Östasiatiska museet, can claim one of the world's foremost collections of Chinese art outside Asia.

On a visit to the Yellow River valley in China in the early 1920s, the Swedish geologist Johan Gunnar Andersson discovered hitherto unknown dwellings and graves containing objects dating from the New Stone Age.

He was allowed to take a selection of items back to Sweden, and these formed the basis for the museum, founded in 1926. A key figure in its development was the then Crown Prince, later to become

King Gustav VI Adolf, who was both interested in and knowledgeable about archaeology. Later, he bequeathed to the museum his own large collection of ancient Chinese arts and crafts.

The museum has been on Skeppsholmen since 1963, when it was moved into a restored house which had been built in 1699–1700 as a depot for Karl XII's bodyguard.

❷ Moderna museet

See pp84–5.

❸ Arkitekturmuseet

Exercisplan. **Map** 4 E3. **Tel** 08-587 270 00. Ⓣ Kungsträdgården. 🚌 65. 🚢 Djurgårdsfärja. **Open** 10am–8pm Tue, 10am–6pm Wed–Sun. 🎨 (free up to age 19; free for everyone 4–6pm Fri.) 🗝 in English, by appointment only. 📷 💻 🖊 📷 ♿ 🖼
🌐 arkitekturmuseet.se

The Swedish Museum of Architecture shares an entrance hall and restaurant with the Moderna museet. It has also

reclaimed its earlier Neo-Classical home, a one-time naval drill hall.

In the permanent exhibition, more than 100 architectural models guide visitors through the history of Swedish building. They include the oldest and simplest of wooden houses to the highly sophisticated construction techniques and innovative styles of the present day.

It is fascinating to move from an almost 2,000-year-old longhouse to a modern supermarket, interspersed with examples of architecture in Gothenburg from the 17th century to the 1930s.

Models of historic architectural works worldwide, from 2000 BC up to the present day, are also on show.

The museum offers an ambitious programme – albeit only in Swedish – alongside the permanent and temporary exhibitions, including lectures, study days, city walks, guided tours, school visits and family events on Sunday afternoons, which involve model-building.

Chinese Bodhisattva in limestone (c.530), Östasiatiska museet

The Skeppsholmen Cannons

A salute battery of four 57-mm rapid-fire cannons is sited on Skeppsholmen and is still in use. Salutes are fired to mark national and royal special occasions at 12 noon on weekdays and 1pm at weekends: 28 January – the King's name day; 30 April – the King's birthday; 6 June – Sweden's National Day; 14 July – Crown Princess Victoria's birthday; 8 August – the Queen's name day; 23 December – the Queen's birthday.

The salute battery on Skeppsholmen

❹ af Chapman

Västra Brobänken. **Map** 4 D3.
Tel 08-463 22 66. Ⓣ Kunsträd-gården.
🚌 65. ⛴ Djurgårdsfärja. 🅿 ✒ *See Where to Stay p284.*

The sailing ship *af Chapman* is one of Sweden's most attractive and unusual youth hostels. The ship has 125 beds, and there are a further 155 beds in the hostel building facing the gangway.

Visitors staying in more conventional accommodation can still go on board and enjoy *af Chapman*'s special atmosphere. The three-masted ship was built in 1888 at the English port of Whitehaven and used as a freight vessel. She came to Sweden in 1915 and saw service as a sail training ship until 1934. The City of Stockholm bought the vessel after World War II and she has been berthed here since 1949. She is named after Fredrik Henrik af Chapman, a master shipbuilder who was born in

❺ Kungliga Konst-högskolan

Flaggmansvägen 1. **Map** 4 E3.
Tel 08-614 40 00. Ⓣ Kungsträdgården.
🚌 65. ⛴ Djurgårdsfärja. **Open** to the public for special events. 🅿 ♿

A stroll around Skeppsholmen provides an opportunity to have a closer look at the beautifully restored 18th-century naval barracks which now houses Kungliga Konsthögskolan (the Royal Institute of Arts). At the entrance there are two statues depicting a lion and a boar. "In like a lion and out like a pig" is an old saying among the lecturers and the 200 or so students at this college, still rich in tradition.

The college started out in 1735 as an academy for painting and sculpture for the decorators working on Tessin's new Royal Palace. Gustav III granted it a royal charter in 1773. Before it moved here in 1995, the college was located on Fredsgatan as part of Konstakademien, although since 1978 it had

been run independently with departments for painting, sculpture, graphics, computing and video, as well as offering courses for architects.

The college is not normally open to the public, apart from an "open house" once a year. Then visitors can enjoy the beautiful interiors, especially the vaulted 18th-century cellars.

The medieval-style castle on Kastellholmen, built in 1846–8

❻ Kastellholmen

Map 4 F4. Ⓣ Kungsträdgården.
🚌 65. ⛴ Djurgårdsfärja.

Right in the middle of Stockholm, Kastellholmen is a typical archipelago island with granite rocks and steep cliffs. From Skeppsholmen it is reached by a bridge built in 1880. Every morning since 1640 a sailor has hoisted the three-tailed Swedish war flag at the castle. Whenever a visiting naval vessel arrives,

the battery's four cannons fire a welcoming salute from the castle terrace.

The charming brick pavilion by the bridge was built in 1882 for the Royal Skating Club, which used the water between the two islands when it froze.

❼ Nationalmuseum

See pp86–7.

❽ Grand Hôtel

Södra Blasieholmshamnen 8.
Map 3 C1. **Tel** 08-679 35 00. Ⓣ Kungsträdgården. 🚌 55, 62, 65, 76.
🅿 ✒ *See Where to Stay p284 and Where to Eat p294.* 🖥 **grandhotel.se**

Oscar II's head chef, Régis Cadier, founded the Grand Hôtel, Sweden's leading five-star hotel, in 1874. Since 1901, the hotel has accommodated the Nobel Prize winners each year.

Traditional Swedish delicacies are served in an abundant *smörgåsbord* in the elegant Veranda. The hotel also has two, Michelin-starred restaurants and the Cadier Bar, named after its founder.

The hotel has 24 banqueting and conference suites, the best known of which is the lofty *Vinterträdgården* (Winter Garden) which can accommodate 800 people. The *Spegelsalen* (Hall of Mirrors) is a copy of the hall at Versailles and was where the Nobel Prize banquet was held until 1929, when it became too big and was moved to City Hall *(see p106).*

The exclusive Grand Hôtel on Blasieholmen

❷ Moderna museet

The Museum of Modern Art is an airy building, designed by the Catalan architect Rafael Moneo in 1998. The museum has a top-class collection of international and Swedish modern art, as well as photography and film. Built partly underground, the complex includes a cinema and auditorium; the photographic library is the most comprehensive collection of its type in northern Europe and there is also a collection of video art and art documentaries. A wide choice of books on art, photography, film and architecture can be found in the bookshop and the Restaurant MM Mat has attractive views over the water.

Breakfast Outdoors *(1962)*
This sculpture group by Picasso, executed in sandblasted concrete by Carl Nesjar, stands in the museum garden near the entrance.

To Arkitekturmuseet

Bookshop

Restaurant MM Mat

Main entrance to both Moderna museet and Arkitekturmuseet *(see p82).*

Entrance level

Middle level

Pontus Hultén Study Gallery

Cinema

Auditorium

Studio

★ **Marzella** *(1909–10)*
This boldly-coloured portrait by Ernst Ludwig Kirchner (1880–1938) highlights his desire to bring fresh ideas to art by refuting traditional artistic conventions.

Rafael Moneo

Rafael Moneo (b. 1937) is one of the leading contemporary architects. As a young architect, Moneo took part in the project to build the Sydney Opera House. His flair for adapting building design to sensitive surroundings was recognized in 1989 when he was chosen out of 211 entries as the winner of the competition to design the new Moderna museet.

Moderna museet's northern façade

★ **Landscape from Céret** *(1913)*
Inspired by Braque and Picasso, Spanish Cubist artist Juan Gris (1887–1927) developed his own unique take on the discipline, as seen in this vivid, geometric landscape painting.

Gallery Guide

*The large room on the entrance
level is used for temporary
exhibitions. Three rooms on the
same level have an alternating
selection of collections from the
eras 1900–45, 1946–70 and
1971 to the present day. The
middle level has an auditorium,
cinema and study gallery.
Another entrance is at the
lowest level.*

Key

☐ Museum's own collections
☐ Temporary exhibitions
☐ Non-exhibition space

★ **The Child's Brain** *(1914)*
The surrealist Giorgio de Chirico
gave his work the title *The Ghost*,
but in the irrational spirit of the
movement Louis Aragon renamed
it in a pamphlet about the artist's
1927 retrospective.

❾ Blasieholmstorg

Map 3 C1. 🚇 Kungsträdgården.
🚌 2, 55, 62, 65, 71, 76.

Two of the city's oldest palaces
are located in this square,
flanked by two bronze horses.
The palace at No. 8 was built in
the mid-17th century by Field
Marshal Gustaf Horn. It was
rebuilt 100 years later, when it
acquired the character of an
18th-century French palace.
Foreign ambassadors and
ministers lodged here when
they visited the capital, so it
became known as the Ministers'
Palace. Later it became a base
for overseas administration and
soon earned its present name
of Utrikesministerhotellet
(Foreign Ministry Hotel). Parts of
the building
are now used as
offices by the
Musical Academy
and the Swedish
Institute.

Bååtska Palatset
stands nearby at
No. 6. Its exterior
dates from 1669
and was designed
by Tessin the Elder.
In 1876–7 it was partly rebuilt
by F W Scholander for the
Freemasons, who still have
their lodge here.

Another interesting complex
of buildings can be found on
the square at No. 10. The
façade which faces on to
Nybrokajen, along the water's
edge, is an attractive example
of the Neo-Renaissance style
of the 1870s and 1880s.

Bronze horse on
Blasieholmstorg

❿ Synagogan

Wahrendoffsgatan 3B. **Map** 3 C1.
Tel 08-587 858 54. 🚇 Kungsträdgården. 🚌 2, 55, 62, 65, 71, 76.
🕐 all year 9.15am Sat; Jun–Aug:
6.30pm Fri; Hebrew and partly English.
🎫 summer and by appointment. ♿

It took most of the 1860s to
build the Conservative Jewish
community's synagogue on
land reclaimed from the sea.
When it was inaugurated in
1870, the building was
standing on 1,300 piles which
had been driven down to a

Monument to the victims of the Holocaust
during World War II

depth of 15 m (50 ft). It is
built in what the architect,
F W Scholander, called "ancient
Eastern style". The synagogue
can be visited on guided tours
during the summer. Alongside
is the congregation's assembly
room and library. Outside is
a monument erected in 1998
in memory of 8,000 victims
of the Holocaust whose
relations had been
rescued and taken
to Sweden during
World War II.

There is also an
Orthodox synagogue
in the city centre,
reached through
the Jewish Centre
(Judiska Centret) on
Nybrogatan at No. 19.

⓫ Berns

Berzelii Park. **Map** 2 D4. **Tel** 08-566
322 00. 🚇 Kungsträdgården,
Östermalmstorg. 🚌 2, 47, 55, 62, 65,
69, 71, 76. ♿ *Where to Stay p284.*

This has been one of Stockholm's
most legendary restaurants and
entertainment venues since
1863. Both salons, with their
stately galleries, magnificent
crystal chandeliers and elegant
mirrors, were restored to their
original splendour by the British
designer and restaurateur
Terence Conran to mark the
new millennium.

Berns is one of Stockholm's
biggest restaurants with
seating for 400 diners. The
gallery level, with its beautifully
decorated dining rooms, was
made famous by August
Strindberg's novel *The Red
Room* (1879). The building also
has a luxury hotel.

❼ Nationalmuseum

The Nationalmuseum is a landmark on the southern side of Blasieholmen. The location by the Strömmen channel inspired the 19th-century German architect August Stüler to design a building in the Venetian and Florentine Renaissance styles.

Completed in 1866, the museum houses Sweden's largest art collection, with some 16,000 classic paintings and sculptures. Drawings and graphics from the 15th century up to the early 20th century bring the total to 500,000. The applied art and design section has works spanning five centuries, including a 500-year-old tapestry, porcelain and examples of work by master furniture-makers, such as Georg Haupt. Space is devoted to the development of modern Swedish design *(see pp30–31)* from 1900 to today.

The Love Lesson *(1716–17)*
Antoine Watteau's speciality was the so-called *fêtes galantes*, depicting young couples in playful mood.

★ **The Conspiracy of the Batavians under Claudius Civilis** *(1661–2)*
Originally intended for Amsterdam, Rembrandt depicts the Batavians' conspiracy against the Romans, symbolizing the Dutch liberation campaign against Spain.

Level 2

Cupid and Psyche *(1787)*
Johan Tobias Sergel is considered the foremost sculptor of the Gustavian era. This piece is regarded as one of his most triumphant works. The sculpture refers to the victory of love over weakness.

Atrium through levels 1 and 2

Alhambra Vase
Discover the roots of European design development in furniture, embroidery, gold, glass and porcelain, featuring this late-14th Century Alhambra Vase, from Granada in Spain, on show in the permanent Design in Sweden *(1500–1740)* exhibition.

Gravure gallery

Entrance

Entry for wheelchairs

★ The Lady with the Veil
Alexander Roslin's elegant portrait (1769) is often considered to be a glamorized symbol of 18th-century Sweden.

VISITORS' CHECKLIST

Practical Information
Södra Blasieholmshamnen.
Map 4 D2.
Tel 08-519 543 00.
W nationalmuseum.se
Closed for renovations until 2017. Temporarily relocating to Fredsgatan 12; see website for more details. 🅰 🏠 in Eng.
🚻 🎁 ♿ 🛍

Transport
🚌 65; or 2, 55, 62, 76 to Karl XII's Torg. 🚇 Kungsträdgården.

The Upper Staircase
At the back is Carl Larsson's monumental mural *The Entry of King Gustav Vasa of Sweden in Stockholm 1523*. On the opposite wall is his *Midwinter Sacrifice*.

Lamino Armchair *(1955)*
Yngve Ekström's beech and laminated leather armchair, produced by Swedese Möbler, features in the Design in Sweden (1900 to Present) exhibition.

Level 1

Auditorium

Entrance level

Key
- ▢ Painting and sculpture
- ▢ Applied art and design
- ▢ Temporary exhibitions
- ▢ Non-exhibition space
- ▢ No admission

Gallery Guide
The Nationalmuseum is undergoing extensive renovations aimed at creating larger public spaces, and will be closed until 2017. During this time, a number of artworks from the Nationalmuseum's collections will be on display in rotating temporary exhibitions at the Royal Academy of Fine Arts (Konstakademien) at Fredsgatan 12. In addition, some other works from the collection will appear at other museums in the city. Check the website for more details.

⑫ Raoul Wallenbergs Torg

Map 2 E4. 🚇 Östermalmstorg. 🚌 2, 47, 55, 62, 69, 71, 76.

This square is dedicated to Raoul Wallenberg (1912–unknown), who during World War II worked as a diplomat at the Swedish Embassy in Budapest. By using Swedish "protective passports" and safe houses throughout the city he helped a large number of Hungarian Jews to escape deportation to the Nazi concentration camps.

In 1945, when Budapest was liberated, Wallenberg was imprisoned by the Soviet Union and according to Russian sources he died in Moscow's Lubianka prison in 1947. His fate has never been satisfactorily explained despite strenuous efforts by the Swedes to seek the truth.

The small square adjoins Berzelii Park and Nybroplan and faces the Nybrokajen waterfront. The definitive design of the square has been hotly debated because it is set in an architecturally sensitive area, but great efforts have been made to ensure that it remains a worthy memorial to Raoul Wallenberg.

⑬ Musikaliska

Nybrokajen 11. **Map** 3 C1. **Tel** 08-407 16 00. 🚇 Kungsträdgården, Östermalmstorg. 🚌 47, 62, 69, 76. 🚢 Djurgårdsfärja. **Open** for concerts (phone for details). ♿
W rikskonserter.se

Constructed in the 1870s, this building facing the waters of Nybroviken once housed the Musical Academy. Its concert hall, opened in 1878, was the first in the country, and was used to present the inaugural Nobel Prize in 1901. Designed in Neo-Renaissance style with cast-iron pillars, the hall has a royal box and galleries, and can seat up to 600 people.

It is run by the state musical organization, Rikskonserter, and is a popular venue for chamber and choral concerts, jazz and folk music.

MALMARNA & FURTHER AFIELD

As Stockholm grew, the heart of the city, Gamla Stan, became cramped and building spread out to the surrounding areas, known as "Malmarna" (the "ore hills"). Parts of these now make up present-day Stockholm.

Södermalm came into the ownership of the city in 1436. Much of Stockholm's old charm can still be found in the areas around Fjällgatan, Mosebacke and Mariaberget. To the north, the Norrmalm area expanded rapidly and became known as Stockholm's northern suburb in the 17th century. The once-rural Östermalm was transformed

in the late 19th century into an affluent residential area with grand, wide boulevards, contrasting with the 1930s Functionalist style of the adjoining Gärdet district.

To the west is Kungsholmen, the centre for local government, with distinguished buildings such as Stadshuset (the City Hall) and Rådhuset (the Law Court). National-stadsparken (the National City Park), a green area of ecological and cultural interest surrounding the city and reaching into its central districts, offers lovely walking routes and many of the city's foremost museums.

Sights at a Glance

1. *Historiska museet (pp90–91)*
2. Strandvägen
3. Junibacken
4. *Nordiska museet (pp94–5)*
5. Biologiska museet
6. *Vasamuseet (pp96–7)*
7. Spritmuseum
8. ABBA Museum
9. Gröna Lund
10. Skansen
11. Waldemarsudde
12. Thielska Galleriet
13. Etnografiska museet
14. Tekniska museet
15. Sjöhistoriska museet
16. Kaknästornet
17. Tessinparken & Nedre Gärdet
18. Millesgården
19. Stadion
20. Naturhistoriska Riksmuseet
21. Hagaparken
22. Ulriksdal
23. Bellevueparken
24. Karlbergs Slott
25. Judiska museet
26. Observatoriemuseet
27. Stadsbiblioteket
28. *Stadshuset (pp106–107)*
29. Västerbron
30. Långholmen
31. Stockholms Stadsmuseum
32. Katarinahissen
33. Katarina Kyrka
34. *Fjällgatan (p110)*
35. Vita Bergen
36. Ericsson Globen
37. Skogskyrkogården
38. *Drottningholm (pp112–15)*
39. *Stockholm Archipelago (pp116–17)*

Key

- ▢ Stockholm City Centre
- ═ Motorway
- ═ Major road
- ═ Minor road

◀ An old-fashioned ride at Gröna Lund, Sweden's oldest amusement park

For keys to symbols *see back flap*

❶ Historiska museet

The Swedish History Museum, Historiska museet, was opened in 1943. It was designed by Bengt Romare and Georg Sherman. Bror Marklund (1907–77) was responsible for the decoration around the entrance and the richly detailed bronze gateways depicting events in early Swedish history. The museum originally made its name with its exhibits from the Viking era, as well as its outstanding collections from the early Middle Ages. Contemporary church textiles are also on show. Many of Historiska museet's gold treasures have been gathered together to form one of Stockholm's most remarkable sights, Guldrummet (the Gold Room).

Exhibitions documenting the history of Sweden through the ages.

Upper floor

Courtyard

Ground floor

Rosen-gården

Bronze Age Find
This Bronze Age artifact, thought to be a percussion instrument, was discovered in a bog in southern Sweden in 1847.

The Bäckaskog Woman
The 155 cm (5 ft) tall Bäckaskog woman lived around 5000 BC. She died at the age of 40–50 and was buried sitting in a cramped pit.

★ The Alunda Elk
This 21 cm (8 inch) stone axe, discovered in 1920 at Alunda in central Sweden, resembles an elk's head. It is a ceremonial axe, probably made in Finland or Karelia in around 2000 BC.

The Viking Era
This is the world's largest Viking exhibition, with more than 4,000 artifacts. The Vikings were most famous as warriors, but they were also keen traders.

For hotels and restaurants in this area see pp284–289 and pp294–301

The Skog Tapestry
This once hung in the wooden church at Skog in northern Sweden. It is one of the museum's oldest textile treasures.

Baroque Hall

★ **Maria from Viklau**
This gilded wooden Madonna figure is the best-preserved example from Sweden's early medieval period. It is found in the medieval exhibition on the upper floor.

Stairs descending to the Gold Room

Main entrance

Gallery Guide

The exhibitions are divided chronologically on two floors with the prehistoric section on the ground floor and the Middle Ages on the upper floor, where there is also a Baroque Hall. In the basement, reached by a staircase from the entrance hall, is the Gold Room with stunning gold and silver objects.

Key

- Prehistoric Era
- Middle Ages and Baroque
- Temporary exhibitions
- Non-exhibition space

★ **The Gold Room**
Since the early 1990s the museum's many priceless gold artifacts have been on show in Guldrummet (the Gold Room), a 700 sq m (7,500 sq ft) underground vault built with 250 tons of reinforced concrete to ensure security. The room is in two circular sections. The inner section houses the main collection, with 50 kg (110 lb) of gold treasures and 250 kg (550 lb) of silver from the Bronze Age to the Middle Ages.

The Elisabeth Reliquary was originally a drinking goblet which was mounted with gold and precious stones in the 11th century. In about 1230 a silver cover was added to enclose the skull of St Elisabeth. Sweden seized it in Wurzburg in 1631, as a trophy in the Thirty Years War.

The Gold Collars were found between 1827 and 1864; the three-ringed collar in a stone quarry in eastern Sweden, the five-ringed in a ditch on the island of Öland, and the seven-ringed hanging on a spike in a barn.

The underground Gold Room in Historiska Museet

Strandvägen with its stately houses and boats along the quayside

❷ Strandvägen

Map 4 E1. 🚌 69, 76. Ⓣ
Östermalmstorg, Karlaplan. 🚋 7.

In the early 1900s Stockholm's
10 richest citizens – seven of
whom were wholesale
merchants – lived in palatial
new houses along Strandvägen.
Before 1897, when a major
exhibition was held just across
the water on Djurgården, this
muddy, hilly stretch known as
Ladugårdslands Strandgata
aspired to becoming "a street,
the like of which will not be
found anywhere else in Europe".
It was a long process. Even after
all the grand buildings had
been completed, the wooden
quay erected in the 1860s was
something of an eyesore. It
was still used up to the 1940s
by boats bringing firewood
from the archipelago islands.

Nevertheless, the renamed
Strandvägen, with its three rows
of lime trees, soon became the
elegant boulevard envisaged
and, then as now, it was a
popular place for a stroll, to
admire the elegant façades,
watch the boats and to see
and be seen.

The financiers behind this
and other housing projects in
the early 1900s were wealthy
and could call on the best
architects, including I G Clason
(1856–1930). Clason was
influenced by Italian and French
Renaissance styles for his work on
No. 19–21 (Thaveniuska Huset)
and No. 29–35 (Bünszowska
Huset), where he designed
gateways made of ships'
timbers. No. 55 (Von Rosenska
Palatset) is also by Clason.

❸ Junibacken

Galärvarvsvägen. **Map** 4 F1. **Tel** 08-587
230 00. 🚌 44, 69. 🚋 7. 🚢
Djurgårdsfärja. **Open** Sep–May:
10am–5pm Tue–Sun; Jun & Aug:
10am–5pm daily; Jul: 9am–6pm daily.
🏷️ 🏪 ♿ 👶 ♿ 🅦 junibacken.se

They are all here – Pippi
Longstocking, Mardie, Karlsson
on the Roof, Emil, Nils Karlsson
Pyssling, Ronja the robber's
daughter, the Lionheart
Brothers and many more
favourite characters from Astrid
Lindgren's children's books. In
accordance with the popular
novelist's wishes, visitors can
also meet the creations of other
Swedish children's authors.
When she heard about Staffan
Götesam's project for a
children's cultural centre she
was adamant it should not be
just an Astrid Lindgren museum.

Nevertheless Junibacken is
still something of a tribute to
the much-loved author. It was
officially opened by the Royal
Family in the summer of 1996

and has become one of the city's
most popular tourist attractions.
A mini-train takes visitors from a
mock-up of the station at
Vimmerby (the author's home
town) to meet some of her
characters, finishing with a visit
to Pippi's home in Villekulla
Cottage, where children can
play in the different rooms.

There is also a well-stocked
children's bookshop and
a restaurant.

❹ Nordiska museet

See pp94–5.

❺ Biologiska museet

Lejonslätten. **Tel** 08-442 82 15. 🚌 44.
🚋 7. **Open** Apr–Sep: 11am–4pm
daily; Oct–Mar: noon–3pm Tue–Fri,
10am–3pm Sat–Sun. 🏷️ 🏪 by appt.
🏪 🅦 skansen.se

The National Romantic
influences of the late 19th
century inspired the architect

Wooden Boats Along Strandvagen

Until the 1940s sailing vessels used to carry firewood from Roslagen on
the Baltic coast to the quayside at Strandvägen. This trade had lost its
importance by the 1950s, and boating enthusiasts started buying up
these old vessels. Some were
renovated and sailed to the
Caribbean, others became illegal
drinking or gambling clubs on
Strandvägen. New harbour
regulations led to the formation
of two associations to administer
the boats. The wooden boats
moored along Strandvägen
today are owned by people
who want to preserve a piece
of the area's cultural heritage.

Old wooden boats along the Strandvägen quay

Astrid Lindgren and Pippi Longstocking

Astrid Lindgren wrote around 100 children's books which have been translated into 74 languages, making her one of the world's most-read children's authors. Publishers turned down her first book about Pippi Longstocking, but she went on to win a children's book competition two years later, in 1945. Her headstrong and tough character Pippi soon won the hearts of children worldwide.

Astrid Lindgren (1907–2002)

Born on 14 November 1907 in Vimmerby in southern Sweden, Astrid stopped writing books at 85, but her characters live on at Junibacken.

Agi Lindegren when he was commissioned to design Biologiska museet (Museum of Biology) in the 1890s. He based his plans on the simple lines of the medieval Norwegian stave churches.

The man behind the museum was the zoologist, hunter and conservationist Gustaf Kolthoff (1845–1913). In 1892, he persuaded the industrialist C F Liljevalch – who later financed the nearby art gallery – to form a company with the aim "to develop and maintain a biological museum to include all the Scandinavian mammals and birds as stuffed specimens in natural surroundings". Within a few months of opening in autumn 1893, Gustaf Kolthoff had delivered a couple of thousand stuffed animals, as well as birds' nests, young and eggs, to the museum. Many of the creatures are shown against a diorama background, with about 250 species of Scandinavian birds and land mammals in their respective biotypes. Kolthoff's friend, the artist Bruno Liljefors, was responsible for the paintings.

Since 1970 the Museum of Biology has belonged to the Skansen Foundation. During the 1990s it underwent extensive renovation and was reopened on 13 November 1993 – exactly 100 years after its original inauguration.

❻ Vasamuseet

See pp96–7.

❼ Spritmuseum

Djurgårdsvägen 38. **Tel** 08-121 313 00. 🚇 Karlaplan. 🚌 44, 69, 76. 🚋 7. 🚢 Djurgårdsfärja. **Open** 10am–4pm daily (Jun–Aug: to 6pm). 🅿 📷 ♿ ⓦ **spritmuseum.se**

Schnapps label, Spritmuseum

The Spritmuseum (Spirits Museum) is located in Stockholm's two remaining 18th-century naval buildings on the island of Djurgården, close to the Vasamuseet. The exhibits explore the Swedish people's relationship with alcohol. Visitors follow a through-the-year itinerary, discovering the pleasure that can be derived from sipping a chilled beer on a park bench on a summer's evening, as well as the warming effects of a glass of red wine during the winter months. The visit also illustrates the processes linked to alcohol production, attitudes towards drinking and the art of the traditional Swedish drinking song.

The museum hosts temporary exhibitions, too. Past successes include the Absolut Art Collection, a compilation of the images used in Absolut Vodka's advertising campaigns. Such artworks were commissioned from the likes of Andy Warhol, Keith Haring, Ralph Steadman and Pierre et Gilles.

Another highlight of the Spritmuseum is the elegant restaurant, with its enviable location right on the water.

❽ ABBA Museum

Djurgårdsvägen 68. 🚌 44. 🚋 7. 🚢 Djurgårdsfärja. **Open** noon–8pm daily (May–Aug: from 10am). 🅿 📷 🎒 ♿ ⓦ **abbathemuseum.com**

This museum is dedicated to ABBA, Sweden's best-known and loved pop band, which enjoyed enormous success all over the world during the 1970s.

In addition to stage costumes, gold records, an audio guide with fascinating insights into life as a band and original press cuttings (many sourced from the private scrapbook of band member Björn Ulvaeus's father), the ABBA Museum delivers a delightfully interactive experience. Visitors can sit at a piano that is connected to Benny Andersson's own piano in his music studio; when the composer tinkles the ivories, the museum piano also starts playing. Other fun experiences include auditioning to be ABBA's fifth member at a perfect replica of the band's Polar Studio and recording a music video.

Biologiska museet's wooden façade, inspired by Nordic medieval design

❹ Nordiska museet

Resembling an extravagant Renaissance castle, Nordiska museet portrays everyday life in Sweden from the 1520s to the present day. It was created by Artur Hazelius (1833–1901), who was also the founder of Skansen *(see p98)*. In 1872, he started to collect objects which would remind future generations of the old Nordic farming culture.

The present museum, designed by Isak Gustav Clason, was opened in 1907. Today it has more than 1.5 million exhibits, with everything from luxury clothing and priceless jewellery to everyday items, furniture and children's toys, and replicas of period homes.

Doll's Houses
The doll's houses show typical homes from the 17th century to modern times. This example illustrates one from 1860.

State Bedchamber from Ulvsunda Castle
At the end of the 17th century, the lord of the manor at Ulvsunda would accommodate prominent guests in this prestigious bedchamber.

Level 3

Corridor to staircase

Level 2 (Main Hall)

Ground floor

Obelisk with the inscription: "The day may dawn when not even all our gold is enough to form a picture of a bygone era."

Equestrian statue of Karl X Gustav

Main entrance

Gallery Guide

The museum is arranged over four floors. From the entrance, stairs lead up to the temporary exhibitions in the Main Hall on Level 2. Floor 3 houses the Strindberg Collection, Doll's Houses, Table Settings, Traditions and the Fashion and Textile Galleries. On the fourth floor are sections dealing with Folk Art, Interiors, Swedish Homes, Small Objects and a section covering the Sami People and Culture.

★ Table Settings
In the mid-17th century, table settings were a feast for the eyes. A swan is the centrepiece at this meal.

The Proposal
This painting, in the Interiors section, is by Knut Ekwall (1843–1912) and depicts a town flat in the 1880s. The room is heavily decorated with *objets d'art*, ornaments and textiles.

VISITORS' CHECKLIST

Practical Information
Djurgårdsvägen 6–16.
Map 4 F2.
Tel 08-519 546 00.
Open 10am–5pm daily.
Closed some holidays. 🅿 🅰
🅰 Eng. 🔲 🔲 🔲 🔲 🔲
🆆 nordiskamuseet.se

Transport
🚌 44, 69, 76. 🚋 7.
🚢 Djurgårdsfärja.

Bridal Crown
It used to be a tradition of the church to lend a crown like this to brides as a symbol of innocence.

Level 4

Children's
Playworld

★ Strindberg Collection
This picture, *Snowstorm at Sea* (1894), by the writer August Strindberg *(see p75)*, is among the museum's collection of 16 of his paintings.

Key

☐	Folk art
☐	Small Objects 1700–1900
☐	Swedish Homes, Interiors
☐	Table Settings, Traditions
☐	Strindberg Collection
☐	Fashion Gallery
☐	Doll's Houses
☐	Textile Gallery
☐	The Sami People
☐	Temporary exhibitions
☐	Library and Reference room
☐	Non-exhibition space

★ Main Hall
As visitors enter this huge hall, they are greeted by a monumental statue of King Gustav Vasa. It was made in painted and gilded oak by Carl Milles in 1924.

Entrance with access for
pushchairs, prams and wheelchairs

❻ Vasamuseet

After a maiden voyage of just 1,300 m (1,422 yd) in calm weather, the warship *Vasa* capsized in Stockholm's harbour on 10 August 1628. About 30 people went down with what was supposed to be the pride of the navy, only 100 m (109 yd) off the southern tip of Djurgården. Almost all the guns were salvaged from the vessel in the 17th century and it was not until 1956 that a private researcher's persistent search led to the rediscovery of *Vasa*. A complex operation began to salvage the wreck, followed by a 17-year conservation programme. The city's most popular museum opened in 1990, less than a nautical mile from the scene of the disaster. The museum has undergone reconstruction, and its plan may differ from the illustration shown.

Gun-port Lion
More than 200 carved ornaments and 500 sculpted figures decorate *Vasa*.

★ Lion Figurehead
King Gustav II Adolf, who commissioned *Vasa*, was known as the Lion of the North. So a springing lion was the obvious choice for the figurehead. It is 4 m (13 ft) long and weighs 450 kg (990 lb).

Emperor Titus
Carvings of 20 Roman emperors stand on parade on *Vasa*.

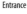
Entrance

KEY

① **Information desk**

② **To the restaurant**

③ **The main mast** was originally 52 m (170 ft) high.

④ **Exit to Museifartygen**

⑤ **Reconstruction of the upper gun deck**

⑥ **Main film auditorium**

Bronze Cannon
More than 50 of *Vasa's* 64 original cannons were salvaged in the 17th century. Three bronze cannons are on display in the museum.

★ **Stern**
Vasa's stern was badly damaged, but has been painstakingly restored to reveal the ship's magnificent ornamentation.

VISITORS' CHECKLIST

Practical Information
Galärvarvsvägen 14.
Map 4 F2.
Tel 08-519 548 00. **Open**
10am–5pm daily (Wed until 8pm); 1 Jun–31 Aug: 8:30am–6pm daily. **Closed** 1 Jan, 23–25 Dec. English. **Films** with English subtitles every hour.
vasamuseet.se

Transport
44, 69. Djurgårdsfärja. 7.

Gun Ports
Vasa carried more heavy cannons on its two gun-decks than earlier ships of the same size. This contributed to its capsizing.

The Salvage Operation

The marine archaeologist Anders Franzén had been looking for *Vasa* for many years. On 25 August 1956 his patience was rewarded when he brought up a piece of blackened oak on his plumb line. From the autumn of 1957, it took divers two years to clear space beneath the hull for the lifting cables. The first lift using six cables was a success, after which *Vasa* was raised in 16 stages into shallow water. Plugs were inserted into holes left by rusted iron bolts, then the final lift began and on 4 May 1961 *Vasa* was towed into dry dock.

Vasa in dry dock after being salvaged in 1961

Gun Deck
Although visitors cannot board the ship, there is a full-size replica of a part of the upper gun deck, which gives a good idea of what conditions on board were like.

Hornborgastugan, a 19th-century timber cottage at Skansen

❾ Gröna Lund

Lilla Allmänna Gränd 9. **Tel** 010-708 91 00. 🚌 44. 🚊 7. 🚢 Djurgårdsfärja. **Open** late Apr–mid-Sep: opening hours vary. 🅿️🍽️♿ **w** gronalund.com

A tavern called Gröna Lund (Green Grove) existed on this site in the 18th century, and it was one of the haunts of the renowned troubadour Carl Michael Bellman *(see p99)*.

Jakob Schultheis used the tavern's name for the modest-sized funfair which he opened here in 1883 with a two-level horse-drawn roundabout as the main attraction. Today Gröna Lund is Sweden's oldest amusement park.

The 130-day season, starting around the end of April, is short but hectic. Gröna Lund draws up to 18,000 visitors a day to its attractions, which include a thrilling roller- coaster and haunted house. Popular attraction "Insane", is a vertical roller-coaster that can reach speeds of 60 km per hour (47 miles per hour), and it is

Gröna Lund funfair seen from Kastellholmen

considered to be one of the highest and longest of its kind in the world.

The park also has restaurants and cafés, two stages, a cabaret restaurant, a theatre and beautiful gardens.

Nearby is Liljevalchs Konsthall, a gallery featuring collections of Swedish, Nordic and international art. It also holds temporary exhibitions, including the annual Spring Salon.

❿ Skansen

Djurgårdsslätten 49. **Tel** 08-442 80 00. 🚌 44. 🚊 7. 🚢 Djurgårdsfärja. **Open** daily. Mar–Apr & Oct: 10am–4pm; May–Jun & Sep: 10am–8pm; Jul–Aug: 10am–10pm; Nov–Dec: 10am–3pm. **Closed** 24 Dec. 🅿️🍽️ Jun–Aug. 🍽️♿ Seglora Kyrka 📞 call for details. **w** skansen.se

The world's first open-air museum, Skansen was established in 1891 to show an increasingly industrialized society how people once lived. It comprises around 150 houses and farm buildings from all over Sweden. But it is not just a museum, Skansen also plays an important role in nurturing the country's folklore and traditions. Sweden's National Day, Walpurgis Night, Midsummer, Christmas and New Year's Eve celebrations take place here *(see pp32–5)*.

In the Town Quarter, complete with 19th-century wooden town houses, glass-blowers, bookbinders and other craftspeople demonstrate their skills. The 300-year-old Älvros farmhouse, from the Härjedalen region, represents rural life with

an intriguing collection of everyday tools. At the other end of the scale, Skogaholms Herrgård *(see p26)*, a Carolean manor from 1680, shows how the wealthy lived. The shingle-roofed Seglora Church (1729) is popular for weddings.

Nordic animals such as elk and wolves can be seen in the zoo, and exotic snakes in the aquarium.

⓫ Waldemarsudde

Prins Eugens Väg 6. **Tel** 08-545 837 00. 🚊 7. **Open** 11am–5pm Tue–Sun. 🅿️🍽️♿ **w** waldemarsudde.com

Prince Eugen's Waldemarsudde, which passed into State ownership after his death in 1947, is one of Sweden's most visited art galleries. The prince was trained as a military officer, but became a successful artist and was one of the leading landscape painters of his generation. He produced monumental paintings for several of the city's important buildings, including Kungliga Operan and Stadshuset. Among his own works hanging in Waldemarsudde, his former palace, are three of his most prized paintings: *Spring* (1891), *The Old Castle* (1893) and *The Cloud* (1896).

Together with works by his contemporaries, the gallery holds an impressive collection of early 20th-century Swedish art. Oscar Björck, Carl Fredrik Hill, Richard Bergh, Nils Kreuger, Eugène Jansson, Bruno Liljefors and Anders Zorn are all featured.

Prince Eugen was a generous patron to the next generation – the group known as "The Young Ones" – so works by younger artists, including Isaac Grünewald, Einar Jolin, Sigrid Hjertén and Leander Engström are also in the collection. Sculptors of the same era are well represented, particularly Per Hasselberg, whose works can be seen in both the gallery and the park.

Prince Eugen and his architect, Ferdinand Boberg, drew up the sketches for the palace, completed in 1905.

Hornsgatan (1902) by Eugène Jansson, in Thielska Galleriet

The same architect was called in later to design the gallery, which was finished in 1913. This now includes parts of the collection of some 2,000 works, as well as the Prince's own paintings.

The guest apartments remain largely unchanged, and the two upper floors with the Prince's studio at the top are used for temporary exhibitions. The buildings are surrounded by beautiful gardens.

⑫ Thielska Galleriet

Sjötullsbacken 6–8. **Tel** 08-662 58 84. 🚌 69. **Open** noon–5pm Tue–Fri (to 7pm Wed & Thu), 11am–5pm Sat & Sun. 🅿️ 🎫 by appointment. 🖥️ 🌐 thielska-galleriet.se

When the magnificent apartments of the banker Ernest Thiel (1860–1947) on Strand-vägen started to overflow with his comprehensive collection of Nordic art from the late 19th and early 20th centuries, he commissioned the architect Ferdinand Boberg to design a dignified villa on Djurgården.

However, during World War I Thiel lost most of his fortune. His collection was bought by the State, which opened Thielska Galleriet in his villa in 1926.

Thiel was regarded as something of a rebel in the banking world. He was parti-cularly fond of works by painters belonging to the Artists' Union, which had been formed in 1886 to counter the influence of the traditionalist Konstakademien (Royal Academy of the Arts).

There are paintings by all the major Swedish artists who formed an artists' colony at Grèz-sur-Loing, south of Paris, including Carl Larsson, Bruno Liljefors, Karl Nordström and August Strindberg.

In additon, the gallery features works by Eugène Jansson, Anders Zorn and Prince Eugen, as well as wooden figures by Axel Petersson and sculptures by Christian Eriksson. Thiel also acquired pieces by foreign artists, not least his good friend Edvard Munch.

⑬ Etnografiska museet

Djurgårdsbrunnsvägen 34. **Tel** 010-456 12 00. 🚌 69. **Open** 11am–5pm Tue–Sun (to 8pm Wed). 🎫 🖥️ 🌀 📷 🅿️ 🌐 etnografiska.se

The National Museum of Ethnography is a showcase for the collections brought home to Sweden by enterprising travellers and scientists from the 18th century to the present day. All are arranged in imaginative displays designed to provide a better understanding of the unknown or unfamiliar from around the world.

Another aspect of the museum's work is to reflect the multicultural influences on Sweden brought about by the large-scale immigration into the country during the late 20th century.

The explorer Sven Hedin (1865–1952), who was the last Swede to be ennobled (in 1902), contributed many exhibits to the museum, including Buddha figures and Chinese costumes, as well as Mongolian temple tents donated by leaders of the Kalmuck people in western China to King Gustav V. Another section of interest shows masks and totem poles from western Canada.

A Japanese tea house was opened in 1990, which is a work of art in itself. Here, visitors to the museum can take part in traditional tea ceremonies during the summer.

The museum runs an exten-sive educational programme with lectures, courses and workshops. In addition to the permanent exhibitions, the museum also displays themed temporary exhibits.

The MatMekka restaurant, located in the museum, offers a menu of Swedish and international dishes made with organic and locally produced ingredients.

An Immortal Troubadour

Carl Michael Bellman (1740–95) was a much-loved troubadour. Gustav III gave him a job as secretary of a lottery, but he was best known around Stockholm's many taverns – particularly on Djurgården. His works about the drunken watchmaker Jean Fredman and his contemporaries (*Fredman's Epistles* and *Fredman's Songs*) have never lost their popularity and form part of Sweden's musical heritage. A bust of Bellman was unveiled on Djurgården in 1829 in the presence of Queen Desideria.

Bust of Bellman by J N Byström (1829)

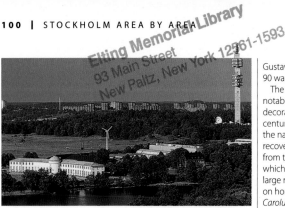

Kaknästornet with the buildings of Sjöhistoriska museet, Tekniska museet and Folkens museum Etnografiska in the foreground

⓮ Tekniska museet

Museivägen 7. **Tel** 08-450 56 00. 🚌 69. **Open** 10am–5pm Mon–Tue, Thu–Fri, 10am–8pm Wed, 11am–5pm Sat & Sun. **Closed** 1 Jan, Midsummer, 24, 25 & 31 Dec. 🅿️ 🎫 by appointment. 🖥️ 📷 ♿ 🌐 tekniskamuseet.se

The Museum of Science and Technology contains a wealth of exhibits connected with Sweden's technical and industrial history. It also houses the science centre, Teknorama, with hands-on experiments designed for children and young people.

The machinery hall features the country's oldest preserved steam engine. Built in 1832, it was used in a coal mine in southern Sweden. The classic model T-Ford and early Swedish cars from Volvo, Scania and Saab are also on display. Swinging from above is Sweden's first commercial aircraft, built in 1924. There is another rarity – the scientist Emanuel Swedenborg's model of a "flying machine" (1716).

The museum also has sections on electric power, computing, technology in the home, and the Swedish forestry, mining, iron and steel industries.

Tekniska museet's machinery hall with historic aircraft

⓯ Sjöhistoriska museet

Djurgårdsbrunnsvägen 24. **Tel** 08-519 549 00. 🚌 69. **Open** 10am–5pm daily. 🅿️ 📷 🛍️ 📷 ♿ 🌐 sjohistoriska.se

The National Maritime Museum focuses on shipping, shipbuilding and naval defence. It is housed in an attractive building, designed by the architect Ragnar Östberg in 1938, in a beautiful location by the calm waters of Djurgårdsbrunnsviken.

There are some 100,000 exhibits, including more than 1,500 model ships. The oldest Swedish model is a reproduction of the "Cathedral ship" from the early 1600s. The model collection comprises every conceivable type of ship from small coasters to oil tankers, coal vessels, dinghies, full-riggers and submarines. A series of models on a scale of 1:200 shows the development of ships in Scandinavia since the Iron Age.

Life-size settings provide a good idea of life on board the various ships. Among them are the exquisite original cabin and elegant stern from the royal schooner *Amphion*. Designed by the leading shipbuilder F H af Chapman and built at the Djurgården shipyard, *Amphion* was

Figurehead, about 1850

Gustav III's flagship in the 1788–90 war with Russia.

The museum has some notable examples of ship decoration from the late 17th century. They include part of the national coat of arms recovered by divers in the 1920s from the stern of the *Riksäpplet*, which sank at Dalarö in 1676. A large relief portrayal of Karl XI on horseback from the stern of *Carolus XI* – an 82-cannon ship launched from the shipyard in 1678 – is also on show. It is thought that the relief was removed some years later when the ship was renamed *Sverige*. There are many fine figureheads in the collection, including one depicting Amphion, the son of Zeus, playing his lyre, which adorned the schooner of the same name.

The museum often hosts temporary exhibitions focusing on themes such as piracy, shipping and treasure recovered from shipwrecks.

Linked to the museum is the Swedish Marine Archaeology Archive, containing an extensive collection of maritime documents and photographs. There is a special children's section with a workshop which is open on Saturdays and in school holidays. On the gable facing Djurgårdsbrunnsviken is *The Sailor*, a monument to the victims of naval warfare by Nils Sjögren.

⓰ Kaknästornet

Ladugårdsgärdet. **Tel** 08-667 21 80. 🚌 69, 69K. **Open** 10am–9pm Mon–Sat; 10am–6pm Sun. 🅿️ 🎫 by appointment. 🖥️ 📷 📷 ♿ 🌐 kaknastornet.se

Anchored by 72 steel poles, driven 8 m (26 ft) into the rock, the 34-storey Kaknästornet soars to a height of 155 m (508 ft). The tower, designed by the architects Bengt Lindroos and Hans Borgström, was opened in

1967. It was erected as a centre for the country's television and radio broadcasting and also contains technical equipment to conduct conferences by satellite between European cities. Five dishes to the left of the tower – the largest of which has a diameter of 13 m (43 ft) – relay signals to and from satellites. The main hall containing the transmitters and receivers has been blasted out of the rock below the dishes.

The observation points on levels 30 and 31 provide a spectacular view of the city, and the restaurant on the 28th floor has panoramic windows. It is reached by two lifts, travelling at 18 km/h (11 mph). There is a tourist information office at the entrance, selling souvenirs, maps and the Stockholm Card (see p319). Decorative features include a wall relief by Walter Bengtsson, which was inspired by the tower's daunting technology.

⑰ Tessinparken & Nedre Gärdet

Map 2 F2. Ⓣ Karlaplan, Gärdet.
🚌 1, 4, 62, 72.

Three generations of the Tessin family of architects have given their name to this park which opened at Lower Gärdet in 1931. Tessinparken runs from north to south and is attractively designed with lawns, play areas, paths and ponds. The adjoining houses, built between 1932 and

1937, have their own gardens and blend in such a way that they give the impression of being part of the park itself.

The earliest houses, nearest to Valhallavägen, still show signs of 1920s Classicism, although Gärdet's real hallmark is Functionalism. The lower white houses along Askrikegatan, marking the northern boundary of the park, are Functionalist in style and noticeably different from other buildings in Gärdet. Some 60 different architects were involved in designing the Gärdet development, including Sture Frölén.

A granite statue of a woman with a suitcase, *Housewife's Holiday*, stands in the part of Tessin Park adjoining Valhallavägen. It was made by Olof Thorwald Ohlsson in the 1970s. At the other end of the park is a colourful concrete statue, *The Egg*, by Egon Möller-Nielsen.

Millesgården, home of the sculptor Carl Milles in the early 20th century

⑱ Millesgården

Herserudsvägen 32, Lidingö.
Ⓣ Ropsten, then bus 201, 202, 204, 206, 208, 212, or train to Torsvik. **Tel** 08-446 75 90. **Open** May–Sep: 11am–5pm daily; Oct–Apr: noon–5pm Tue–Sun. 🎫 🅿 by appointment. 🅿 ♿ ♿
Ⓦ **millesgarden.se**

Carl Milles (1875–1955) was one of the 20th century's greatest Swedish sculptors and the best known internationally. From 1931 he lived for 20 years in the USA, where he became a prolific monumental sculptor with works such as the *Meeting of the Waters* fountain in St Louis and the *Resurrection* fountain in the National Memorial Park outside Washington DC. In Stockholm visitors can see 15 of his public works, including the *Orpheus* fountain in front of Konserthuset (see p75).

In 1906 Milles purchased land on the island of Lidingö on which he built a house, completed in 1908. He lived here with his wife until 1931, and also after his return from the USA. In 1936 he and his wife donated the property to the people of Sweden. Millesgården extends over a series of terraces filled with sculptures and includes Milles' studios with originals and replicas of his work. There is a magnificent garden – a work of art in itself – and a fine view over the water.

Tessinparken, surrounded by Functionalist-style housing dating from the late 1930s

Running track at Stadion, built in 1912

⑲ Stadion

Lidingövägen 1–3. **Map** 2 E2.
Tel 08- 508 283 51. Ⓣ Stadion.
🚌 4, 55, 72, 73. **Open** 8am–4pm daily.
🚶 during events. ♿

A new main arena was built for the 1912 Olympic Games in Stockholm, the towers of which have become a familiar landmark on the capital's skyline. The architect of Stadion, Torben Grut (1871–1945), followed the National Romantic influences of the day. The complex is richly decorated. The clock tower has two figures by Carl Fagerberg, *Ask and Embla,* the counterparts of Adam and Eve in Nordic mythology. There are also busts of Victor Balck, the man behind the 1912 Olympics, and P H Ling, the father of Swedish gymnastics.

Four notable sculptures were added in the 1930s. The painter and gymnast Bruno Liljefors created *Play* at the main entrance, Carl Eldh made *The Runners*, and Carl Fagerberg provided *Relay Runners* and *The Shot-Putter*.

Stadion has continued to be an important venue for athletics events and can hold up to 35,000 spectators. The European Athletics Championships were held here in 1958, and an international athletics gala is staged every summer. In 1990 it hosted the World Equestrian Championships.

The arena is also used as a venue for concerts by internationally renowned bands.

⑳ Naturhistoriska Riksmuseet

5 km (3 miles) N of city centre along road 264. **Tel** 08-519 540 00. Ⓣ Universitetet. 🚌 40, 540. **Open** 10am–8pm Tue, 10am–7pm Wed–Fri, 11am–7pm Sat & Sun. 🎦 🅿 by appointment. 🖥 📷 🎨 🛍 ♿
🅦 **nrm.se**

Completed in 1916, the vast Naturhistoriska Riksmuseet (Swedish Museum of Natural History) was designed by Axel Anderberg and decorated by Carl Fagerberg. The museum is a venerable institution, founded in 1739 by Carl von Linné *(see p134)* as part of Vetenskapsakademien (the Academy of Science). It is one of the 10 largest museums of its kind in the world. Over the centuries, the number of exhibits has risen to 17 million.

During the 1990s it was modernized and there are both permanent and temporary exhibitions on a wide range of themes from dinosaurs and sea creatures to the "Marvels of the Human Body". The hugely popular Cosmonova opened at the

Polar bear, Naturhistoriska Riksmuseet

same time. Both a planetarium and an IMAX cinema, its screen is 25 times the size of a conventional one. The *Vega Monument* was erected in front of the museum in 1930 to mark the 50th anniversary of explorer Adolf Erik Nordenskiöld's return from the first voyage through the Northeast Passage in his ship *Vega.* Designed by Ivar Johnsson, it is an obelisk in granite topped with a copper ship.

㉑ Hagaparken

4 km (2.5 miles) N of city centre, along E4. 🚌 515. Haga Parkmuseum: **Tel** 08-27 42 52. **Open** Oct–May: 10am– 3pm daily. Gustav III's Paviljong: **Tel** 08-402 61 30. 📷 every hour Jun–Sep: noon–3pm Tue–Sun. Fjärils- & Fågelhuset: **Tel** 08-730 39 81. **Open** Apr–Sep: 10am–4pm Tue–Fri, 11am– 5:30pm Sat & Sun; Oct–Mar: 10am– 3pm Tue–Fri, 11am–4pm Sat & Sun. **Closed** Midsummer's Eve. 🖥 🍴 in Koppartälten and Fjärils- & Fågelhuset and Café Vasaslätten.

King Gustav Vasa decided to create a royal park in the popular Haga area in the mid-18th century. The king's vision was realized by the architect of the moment, Fredrik Magnus Piper. The result was an English-style park with some very unusual buildings, including the Chinese Pagoda and the Roman battle tent, Koppartälten. A royal palace inspired by Versailles in France was also planned, but construction came to a halt after the king's death and it remained unfinished.

Gustav III's Pavilion, a Gustavian masterpiece designed by Olof Tempelman, with an interior by Louis Masreliéz, is the park's greatest architectural attraction, while Fjärils- & Fågelhuset has colourful, exotic butterflies and

Hagaparken's Roman battle tent, designed by Louis Jean Desprez (1790)

birds flying freely around a tropical greenhouse.

Haga Slott, built in 1802–04 for Gustav IV Adolf, was the childhood home of the present monarch, Carl XVI Gustaf, and his sisters. Now it is used for government receptions and to accommodate visiting heads of state.

Hagaparken is very popular with Stockholmers. The park is part of the Royal National City Park (Ekoparken), an oasis of nature and culture close to the city centre (see box).

Exotic butterflies in the greenhouses at Hagaparken

㉒ Ulriksdal

7 km (4 miles) N of Stockholm. **Tel** 08-402 61 30. 🚌 503. Palace: **Open** Jun–mid-Sep: Tue–Sun for guided tours only. 🕐 noon, 1pm, 2pm & 3pm. Orangery: **Open** Jun–Aug: noon–4pm Tue–Sun. 🎨📷📹 📅♿️📧 🌐 kungahuset.se/royalpalaces

Situated on a headland in the bay of Edsviken, Ulriksdal's attractive buildings and leafy surroundings are well worth a visit. At the entrance to the grounds is one of Stockholm's best-known restaurants, Ulriksdals Wärdshus (see p300).

The original palace was built in the 1640s and designed by Hans Jakob Kristler in German/Dutch Renaissance style. The owner, Marshal of the Realm Jakob de la Gardie, named the palace Jakobsdal. It was bought in 1669 by the Dowager Queen Hedvig Eleonora. Fifteen years later, she donated the palace to her grandson Ulrik as a christening gift, and it was renamed Ulriksdal.

Around this time the architect Tessin the Elder suggested some rebuilding work, but only a few of his proposals saw

Ulriksdal with its magnificent 18th-century Baroque exterior

the light of day. In the 18th century the palace acquired its Baroque exterior.

After being a popular place for festivities in the time of Gustav III (1746–92), it began to lose its glamour. Interest was revived under Karl XV (1826–72), and furnishings and handicrafts many hundreds of years old are on shown his rooms.

The park was laid out in the mid-17th century. It has 300-year-old lime trees, as well as one of Europe's most northerly beechwoods. Carl Milles's two sculptures of wild boars stand by the pool in front of the palace. A stream is

crossed by a footbridge, which is supported by Per Lundgren's Moors Dragging the Nets.

More art can be seen in the Orangery, designed by Tessin the Elder in the 1660s for Queen Hedvig Eleonora. It now houses a sculpture museum.

The palace chapel, a popular place for weddings, was designed by F W Scholander and built in 1865 in Dutch Neo-Renaissance style. The riding school, built in 1671, was converted into a theatre by Carl Hårleman and C F Adelcrantz in the 1750s, and performances continue to be staged in the theatre every summer.

The Royal National City Park (Ekoparken)

Ekoparken – the world's first National City Park – was established by the Swedish Parliament in 1995. Its creation has enabled the capital to safeguard the ecology of its "green lung", a 27 sq km (10.5 sq miles) area for recreation and outdoor activities.

The park threads through Stockholm's central districts, including Skeppsholmen and the southern part of Djurgården, and continues northwest to northern Djurgården, Hagaparken, Brunnsviken and Ulriksdal. It also encompasses the tiny islands of Fjäderholmarna (see p116). Much of the park was a royal hunting ground as early as the 16th century, scattered with beautiful palaces and other sights.

Haga Forum, at the southern entrance to Hagaparken, provides plenty of information about the park.

There are also boat tours on Brunnsviken, with stops at some of the sights. For further details, telephone 08-587 140 40 or visit www.nationalstadsparken.se.

Breeding herons at Isbladskärret, part of Ekoparken's rich bird-life

Karlbergs Slott, a palace dating from the 1630s – now one of Sweden's military academies

㉓ Bellevueparken

South of Brunnsviken Lake, Ekoparken.
🚌 2, 40, 53. Carl Eldhs Ateljémuseum:
Lögbodavägen 10, Bellevueparken.
Tel 08-612 65 60. **Open** May–Aug:
11am–4pm Tue–Sun; Sep & Oct:
11am–4pm Sat & Sun. 🎨 📷 1:30pm
in English. 🔲 📷 ♿ ✉

This park is part of Ekoparken
(see p103), Stockholm's Royal
National City Park. Built by
architect Fredrik Magnus Piper,
Bellevue offers winding paths,
groves, tree-lined avenues and
open green areas. It also boasts
200-year-old lime trees and rare
medicinal plants. The name
(French for "beautiful view") came
from Baron Carl Sparre who
purchased a villa on Bellevue
Hill in 1782. Today the villa is
used as a conference centre.
  On Bellevue Hill is the
Lögbodavägen viewpoint,
which looks out over the
Brunnsviken inlet and is close
to the monument *The Young
Strindberg in the Archipelago*
by Carl Eldh (1873–1954). This
sculptor's studio, in an unusual
wooden building dating from
1919, is now preserved as the
Carl Eldhs Ateljémuseum and
is located nearby. Eldh was
one of Sweden's most prolific
sculptors, and his works can
be seen at 30 public sites
around Stockholm. The plaster
casts of these sculptures are
on show in his studio and
include the *Branting Monument*
at Norra Bantorget, the statue

of Strindberg in Tegnérparken
and *The Runners* at Stadion *(see
p102)*. Also here are drawings,
tools and other personal
belongings of the artist.

㉔ Karlbergs Slott

Karlsbergs Slottsväg. 🚇 St Eriksplan.
🚌 42, 72 to Karlberg station, then
15-min walk. Park **Open** 6am–10pm
daily.

Admiral Karl Karlsson
Gyllenhielm started to build
Karlbergs Slott in the 1630s,
during the Thirty Years War. From
1670 the palace was extended
and rebuilt by Magnus Gabriel
de la Gardie, an important
political and military figure at
the time, with Jean de la Vallée
as his architect. When Karlberg
became royal property in 1688,
it was one of Sweden's most
majestic palaces. It was where
the "hero King" Karl XII (1682–
1718) grew up, and it was here
that he lay in state after his death
at the Battle of Fredrikshald *(see
p41)*. In 1792 the architect
C C Gjörwell converted
the property into the Royal
War Academy, which later
became the Karlberg Military
School, and since 1999 it has
been the site for one of the
country's military academies.
  The interior decorations
include Carl Carove's
magnificent stucco-work
which can be seen in the
grand hall. The palace

church has been renovated
several times, but the
17th-century lanterns are
original. De la Gardie's wood-
panelled "rarities room" is now
the sacristy, but once it housed
his collection of valuables.

㉕ Judiska museet

Hälsingegatan 2. **Map** 1 A2.
Tel 08-557 735 60. 🚇 Odenplan.
🚌 2, 4, 47, 72. **Open** noon–4pm
Mon–Fri & Sun. 🎨 📷 in English by
appointment. 🔲 📷 ♿
🌐 **judiska-museet.se**

In 1774 Aaron Isaac became the
first Jewish immigrant to settle
in Stockholm and practise his
religion. Today, half of Sweden's
Jewish population of around
18,000 live in the Stockholm
area. Judiska museet depicts
the history of the Swedish
Jews from Isaac's time to the
present. It focuses on Judaism
as a religion, its integration
into Swedish society and the
Holocaust. A comprehensive
collection of pictures and

An eight-stemmed *chanuki* (candlestick) at
Judiska museet

other items provide an insight into Jewish life in Sweden with its traditions and customs. The beautiful *Torah* (the five books of Moses), the bridal canopy, and the collection of eight-stemmed *chanukis* (candlesticks) are just some of the museum's treasured spiritual artifacts.

The old observatory (1748–53) at the top of the Observatory hill

㉖ Observatorie-museet

Drottninggatan 120. **Map** 1 B2. **Tel** 08-545 483 90. Ⓣ Odenplan. ▦ 40, 42, 65, 72. **Open** Oct–Mar: 6–9pm Tue & Thu, noon–3pm Sun. **Closed** Jul. ▨ 6pm Tue includes telescope observation if sky is clear; in Eng by appointment. ▣ ▨ ▨
Ⓦ observatoriet.kva.se

A number of institutions connected with science and education can be found on and around the hill of Brunkeberg. The oldest is the former observatory designed by Carl Hårleman for the Royal Swedish Academy of Sciences and opened in 1753. In 1931, astronomical research was moved to Saltsjöbaden in the Stockholm archipelago and replaced by Observatoriemuseet (the Observatory Museum). Here visitors can see the observation room with its instruments, the two median rooms and the weather room. From October to March, visitors can admire the stars using the telescope (Tue & Thu only).

The grove which surrounds the old observatory began to take shape in the 18th century. It is an idyllic enclosed area, first opened to the public in the 20th century. On top of

Gunnar Asplund

Gunnar Asplund (1885–1940) was a dominant figure among Swedish and internationally renowned architects in the 1930s. His first major commission was the chapel at the Skogskyrkogården Cemetery, designed in National Romantic style. His last work was Heliga Korsets Kapell, the cemetery's crematorium (1935–40). Regarded as a masterpiece in the Functionalist style, it has earned a place on the UNESCO World Heritage list *(see p111)*. Asplund designed Stads-biblioteket (City Library, 1920–28). He pioneered the Functionalist style as chief architect for the Stockholm Exhibition in 1930.

Stockholm Exhibition, by Gunnar Asplund, 1930

Brunkeberg is Sigrid Fridman's statue *The Centaur*.

A park stretches down to Sveavägen, where a pond is fed by a hillside stream. The statue *Dancing Youth* is by Ivar Johnsson. At the southern entrance of the park is Nils Möllerberg's sculpture *Youth*.

㉗ Stadsbiblioteket

Sveavägen 73. **Map** 1 B2. **Tel** 08-508 310 60. Ⓣ Odenplan, Rådmansgatan. ▦ 4, 42, 52, 53, 59, 72. **Open** 9am–9pm Mon–Thu, 9am–7pm Fri, noon–4pm Sat & Sun (mid-Jun–mid-Aug: 9am–7pm Mon–Fri, noon–4pm Sat). ▨ Ⓦ biblioteket.stockholm.se

Gunnar Asplund's masterpiece, Stadsbiblioteket (City Library), is one of the capital's most architecturally important buildings. Asplund, the champion of the Functionalist

style prevalent in the 1930s, designed a public library which was dominated by Classical ideals. It was opened in 1928.

Internally, the furnishings and many of the light fittings were designed by Asplund himself. The work of Swedish artists is well represented: in the entrance hall are Ivar Johnsson's stucco reliefs with themes from Homer's *Iliad*; the sparkling mural in the children's section, *John Blund*, is by Nils Dardel; and the depiction of the stars in the heavens by Ulf Munthe. The door lintels, door handles and drinking fountains are by Nils Sjögren. Hilding Linnquist was responsible for the giant-sized tapestry, and also for four mural paintings using ancient fresco techniques.

The library lends more than a million books every year and also organizes author sessions and other events.

Stadsbiblioteket, in Neo-Classical style, designed by Gunnar Asplund

⊗ Stadshuset

Probably Sweden's biggest architectural project of the 20th century, the City Hall was completed in 1923 and has become a symbol of Stockholm. It was designed by Ragnar Östberg (1866–1945), the leading architect of the Swedish National Romantic style, and displays influences of both the Nordic Gothic and Northern Italian schools. Several leading Swedish artists contributed to the rich interior design. The building contains the Council Chamber and 250 offices for city admin-istrative staff. The annual Nobel Prize festivities take place in the Blue Hall.

★ The Golden Hall
The Byzantine-inspired wall mosaics by Einar Forseth (1892–1988) are made up of 18.6 million pieces of glass and gold. The northern wall's theme is *Queen of Lake Mälaren*.

KEY

① **Stairway to the gallery**

② **Norra Trapptornet**, crowned by a sun.

③ **Courtyard**

④ **Marriage room**

⑤ **Engelbrekt the Freedom Fighter** by Christian Eriksson (1858–1935).

★ The Blue Hall
The banqueting room is made from handmade bricks. The name is from the initial plan to paint the bricks blue, but the architect changed his mind.

Three Crowns
Sweden's heraldic symbol, Tre Kronor, dating from the 14th century, tops the 106 m (348 ft) tower.

The Council Chamber
Stockholm's 101 councillors meet in this magnificent chamber, which contains furnishings designed by Carl Malmsten.

The Dance
The steps leading to Riddarfjärden are flanked by two statues by Carl Eldh. *Dansen* is the figure of a woman, *Sången* (The Song) of a man.

★ The Prince's Gallery
A fresco, *The City on the Water*, in the Prince's Gallery, was painted by Prince Eugen (*see p98*), who donated it to the City Hall.

Västerbron bridge, opened in 1935, linking Kungsholmen with Södermalm across Lake Mälaren

㉙ Västerbron

🚌 4, 40, 77.

As Stockholm expanded and car-use increased in the 1920s, it became necessary to build an additional bridge between the northern and southern shores of Lake Mälaren. German experts dominated the architectural competition launched in 1930, but their plans were implemented by Swedish architects and engineers and Västerbron bridge was completed in 1935. Twenty years later it was broadened to increase its capacity.

The attractive design blends well with the landscape. The bridge is built in two spans of 168 m (551 ft) and 204 m (669 ft) with a vertical clearance of 26 m (85 ft). There are footpaths and cycle lanes on each side and a walk to the centre of Västerbron is rewarded with a magnificent view of central Stockholm.

Exercise yard in the former royal prison on Långholmen

㉚ Långholmen

🚇 Hornstull, then 10 min walk.
🚌 4, 40, 66. 📷 🚲

Below the majestic Västerbron bridge is the island of Långholmen, which is linked to Södermalm by two bridges. Långholmen is best known for the various prisons which have been located here since 1724. During the 20th century it was the site of the largest prison in Sweden, housing 620 inmates. The prison closed in 1975, since when the island has become a popular recreational area.

The prison buildings have been demolished, but the former royal jail dating from 1835 remains. The one-time cells now form both a hotel and a prison museum. There is also a youth hostel and an excellent restaurant, as well as a museum to the poet C M Bellman (see p99) with a café in the gardens which run down towards Riddarfjärden.

Långholmen's park has an open-air theatre, and offers excellent swimming both from the beaches and the rocks.

㉛ Stockholms Stadsmuseum

Ryssgården. **Map** 3 B5. **Tel** 08-508 316 00. 🚇 Slussen. 🚌 2, 3, 43, 53, 55, 76. **Open** 11am–5pm Tue–Sun (to 8pm Thu). 📷 🏛 🖼 🎁 👶 ♿ 🚻
🌐 stadsmuseum.stockholm.se

Hemmed in between the traffic roundabouts of Slussen and the steep hill up to Mosebacke Torg is Stockholms Stadsmuseum (City Museum). It is housed in a late-17th-century building originally designed by Tessin the Elder as Södra Stadshuset (Southern City Hall). After a fire, it was completed by Tessin the Younger in 1685. It has been used for various purposes over the centuries, including law courts and dungeons, schools and city-hall cellars, theatres and churches, until in the 1930s it became the city museum.

The museum documents the history of Stockholm. The city's main stages of development are described in a slideshow and a series of four permanent exhibitions. The first starts with the Stockholm Bloodbath of 1520 (see p64) and continues through the 17th century. The eventful 18th century is illustrated with exhibits that include the Lohe Treasure – 20 kg (44 lb) of silver discovered in Gamla Stan in 1937. The other sections depict industrialization in the 19th century and the tremendous growth in the 20th century with the emergence of a new city centre and new suburbs. The museum also organizes tours that take in the locations mentioned in writer Stieg Larsson's popular *Millennium* trilogy.

The 18th-century Lohe Treasure at Stockholms Stadsmuseum

The library has a large picture archive and a Stockholm reference room. There are children's activities, concerts and lectures.

⁂ Katarinahissen

Stadsgården. **Map** 3 C5. **Tel** 08-642 47 85. 🅣 Slussen. 🚌 2, 3, 43, 53, 55, 59. **Closed** to the public. 🚫 〰

Katarinahissen is the oldest of Stockholm's "high-rise" attractions. The 38 m (125 ft) high lift was opened to the public in March 1883 and is still a prominent silhouette on the Söder skyline. The first Swedish neon sign was erected here in 1909 – a legendary advertisement for Stomatol toothpaste. Since the 1930s, the sign has been placed on a nearby rooftop.

The original lift was driven by steam, but it switched to electricity in 1915. In the 1930s it was replaced by a new lift. In its first year of operation, the lift was used by more than a million passengers, but its record year was 1945, when it carried a total of 1.8 million people between Slussen and Mosebacke Torg.

Although the original lift is no longer in use, there is another less iconic lift that takes diners up to a gourmet restaurant, Gondolen *(see p295)*. The views from here are spectacular.

Katarina Kyrka (1695) after its extensive restoration due to a devastating fire in 1990

㉝ Katarina Kyrka

Högbergsgatan 13. **Tel** 08-743 68 00. 🅣 Slussen, Medborgarplatsen. 🚌 2, 3, 53, 71, 76. **Open** 11am–5pm Mon– Sat, 10am–5pm Sun. 📷 by appointment. 🎵 12.15pm Tue & Thu (organ music), 11am Wed & Sun. 🖥 📷 ♿ 🌐 **svenskakyrkan.se**

The buildings surrounding the hilltop on Katarinaberget date partly from the 18th century, although there have been churches on the site since the late 14th century. The most impressive of all the buildings is the 17th-century Katarina Kyrka, designed by one of the era's greatest architects, Jean de la Vallée (1620–96). King Karl X Gustaf was also deeply involved in the project, and specified that the church should have a central nave with the altar and pulpit positioned right in the middle. Construction began in 1656 and the church was finally completed in 1695. In 1723 it was badly damaged by fire, along with large parts of the surrounding area, but it was restored over the next couple of decades. The architect Göran Josua Adelcranz designed a larger, octagonal tower.

Major restoration was carried out in the 20th century, and a new copper roof was added in 1988. Then two years later, on the night of 16 May 1990, there was another fire and the interior and virtually all its fittings were destroyed. Only the outer walls survived.

The architectural practice of Ove Hidemark was commissioned to design a new church which, as far as possible, was to be a faithful reconstruction of the original.

In order to carry out such a detailed reconstruction, the architects resorted to the use of 17th-century building techniques. Experts and craftsmen skilfully joined heavy timbering on to the central dome in the traditional way, and the church's central arch was rebuilt with bricks specially made in 17th-century style.

In 1995, Katarina Kyrka was reconsecrated and, in the eyes of many people, looked more beautiful than ever. The altar was sited exactly where it was originally planned.

The reconstruction cost 270 million kronor, of which 145 million kronor was covered by insurance. The remainder was raised through public donations.

Katarinahissen with Stockholms Stadsmuseum in the background

㉞ Fjällgatan

Per Anders Fogelström (1917–98), pro bably Söder's best-known author, wrote: "Fjällgatan must be the city's most beautiful street. It's an old-fashioned narrow street which runs along the hilltop with well-maintained cobblestones … and with street lights jutting out from the houses. Then the street opens up and gives a fantastic view of the city and the water…" This area offers an experience of the authentic Söder and its unique atmosphere.

The Heights of Söder
With its 300-year-old houses and terraced gardens, the Söder hilltop stands like a giant stage-set behind Stadsgården harbour.

0 meters		100
0 yards		100

Fjällgatan
Most of the houses were built along this picturesque street after a devastating fire in 1723. No. 34 is said to be the area's oldest.

Viewpoint with magnificent vista across the city.

Café

Katarina Vägen

FJÄLLGATAN

STIGBERGSGATAN

Stigberget

Norwegian Church

Mamsell Josabeth's Steps were named after Josabeth Sjöbert (1812–82), a local painter.

Tjärhovsplan

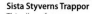

Sista Styverns Trappor
This alley of steps was once known as Mikaelsgränd after a 17th-century executioner. Later it was named after the inn on the harbour, Sista Styvern ("The Last Penny").

Söder Cottages
Typical well-preserved cottages can be found along Stigbergsgatan. One of them is No. 17, the house of the blockmaker Olof Krok during the 1730s.

Key
— Suggested route

⑤ Vita Bergen

Södermalm. 🚌 2, 3, 55, 66, 76.

Today famous for its popular open-air theatre performances, this park is also an opportunity to see houses originally built for workers at Söder's harbours and factories. They were simple homes, often with a small garden and surrounded by a fence. In 1736 the building of new wooden houses was forbidden because of the fire risk, but slum districts, as this was then, were exempted.

Around 1900, when Sofia Kyrka was built, the area was turned into a leafy hillside park with allotment-garden cottages to the east. The park has a bronze statue, *Elsa Borg*, by Astri Bergman Taube (1972), wife of the great troubadour Evert Taube (*see p66*).

㊱ Ericsson Globen

3 km (2 miles) S of Stockholm.
🚇 Globen. 🚌 4, 164, 150, 807.
Tel 08-508 353 00. **Open** during events. 🚡 gondola ride. 📷 by appt.
📱 ♿ 🏠 ♿ 🌐 **globen.se**

In 1989 Stockholm acquired a new symbol in the shape of the indoor arena Ericsson Globen, which has a circumference of 690 m (2,260 ft) and a height of 85 m (279 ft). The arena offers a wide programme of events, from international sports to performances by musicians and bands from around the world.

The spectacular Skyview ride enables visitors to travel up the outside wall of the arena in glass gondolas.

Skyview's glass gondolas taking visitors to the top of the Ericsson Globen

Chapel of the Holy Cross by Gunnar Asplund at Skogskyrkogården

㊲ Skogskyrko-gården

6 km (3.5 miles) S of Stockholm. **Tel** 08-508 317 30. 🚇 Skogskyrko-gården. 🕐 Jun–Aug by appt (call 08-508 316 59). 📱 ♿ 🌐 **skogskyrkogarden.se**

Nature and architecture have combined to give the Skogskyrkogården Cemetery a place on the UNESCO World Heritage list. The cemetery is the creation of architects Gunnar Asplund (*see p105*) and Sigurd Lewerentz, winners of a design competition for the site in 1915. It is set amid pinewoods which provide a sombre framework for the various chapels and crematorium, all of which are important examples of Sweden's National Romantic and Functionalist styles.

Epitaph to Gunnar Asplund

Asplund's first work, Skogskapellet (Woodland Chapel), featuring a steep shingled roof, was opened at the same time as the cemetery in 1920, and was decorated by Carl Milles. This was followed five years later by Uppståndelse-kapellet (the Resurrection Chapel), designed by Lewerentz.

In 1940 Asplund's last masterpiece, Skogskrematoriet (Woodland Crematorium), was completed, along with its three chapels representing Faith, Hope and the Holy Cross. John Lundqvist's *The Resurrection* stands in the pillared hall of Heliga Korsets Kapell, the largest of the chapels, where there is also a mural painted by Sven Erixson. Adjoining the chapel is Asplund's black granite cross. The Hill of Meditation lies to the west. Skogskyrkogården is the final resting place of Greta Garbo.

Greta Garbo

The legendary Greta Garbo, one of the 20th century's outstanding film stars, was born in 1905 in a humble part of Södermalm. At the age of 17 she joined the theatre academy of Dramaten and made her film debut in *Peter the Tramp*. Her breakthrough came in 1924 in Mauritz Stiller's film of Selma Lagerlöf's book *The Atonement of Gösta Berling*. The following year she moved to Hollywood, where she soon became the reigning star. Garbo appeared in 24 films, including *Anna Karenina* (1935) and *Camille* (1936). She never married and lived a solitary life until her death in 1990. Her ashes were interred at the Skogskyrkogården Cemetery in 1999.

Garbo in *As You Desire Me* (1932)

㉚ Drottningholm

The unique Baroque and Rococo environment of
Drottningholm – its palace, theatre, park and Chinese
Pavilion – have been perfectly preserved. This royal palace
emerged in its present form towards the end of the 17th
century, and was one of the most lavish buildings of its era.
Contemporary Italian and French architecture inspired
Tessin the Elder (1615–81) in his design, which was also
intended to glorify royal power. The project was completed
by Tessin the Younger, while architects such as Carl
Hårleman and Jean Eric Rehn finished the interiors.
The Royal Family uses parts of the palace as their private
residence. Drottningholm was designated a UNESCO
World Heritage Site in 1991.

Baroque Garden
The bronze statue of *Hercules* (1680s)
by the Dutch Renaissance sculptor
Adrian de Vries adorns the parterre
in the palace's Baroque Gardens.

**Upper South
Bodyguard Room**
This ante-room to the State
Room, used for ceremonial
occasions, was decorated
with stucco works by
Giovanni and Carlo Carove,
and ceiling paintings by
Johan Sylvius.

Writing Table by Georg Haupt
Standing in the Queen's Room is this masterpiece
(1770) commissioned by King Adolf Fredrik as a gift
to Queen Lovisa Ulrika. Textiles for the walls and
furnishings date from the 1970s.

KEY

① **Apartments of the Royal Family**

② **The Palace Church** in the
northern cupola was completed by
Hårleman in the 1720s.

★ **Queen Lovisa Ulrika's Library**
The Queen commissioned Jean Eric Rehn (1717–93) to decorate this splendid library, which illustrates her influence on art and science in Sweden in the 18th century.

Entrance

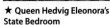

★ **Queen Hedvig Eleonora's State Bedroom**
Morning receptions (*"levées"*) were held in this lavish Baroque room designed by Tessin the Elder. It took about 15 years for Sweden's foremost artists and craftsmen to decorate the room, which was completed in 1683.

★ **Staircase**
Trompe-l'oeil paintings by Johan Sylvius adorn the walls, giving the impression that the already spacious interior stretches further into the palace.

Exploring Drottningholm

The Palace of Drottningholm, a UNESCO World Heritage Site, is complemented by the Court Theatre (Slottsteatern), the world's oldest theatre still in active use, the Theatre Museum (Teatermuseum) and the elegant Chinese Pavilion (Kina Slott). The complex is situated on the shores of Lake Mälaren, surrounded by Baroque and Rococo gardens, and lush English-style parkland. In summer there are jousting tournaments, and the theatre stages opera and ballet.

Drottningholm Palace Area

Stockholm

0 metres 250
0 yards 250

Sights

① Palace
② Chinese Pavilion
③ Palace Park
④ Court Theatre and Theatre Museum

Karl XI's gallery at Drottningholm, featuring the victory at Lund, 1667

The Palace Apartments

The first thing that meets the eye on entering the apartments is a Baroque corridor with a view that frames part of the gardens in all their splendour. The central part of the palace is dominated by the staircase, crowned by a lantern with ceiling paintings by Ehrenstrahl. There are examples of Baroque stucco work by Giovanni and Carlo Carove. Marble statues of the nine muses and their protector, Apollo, are placed at the corners of the balustrades.

Medallion symbolizing life and death

The Green Salon is reached from the lower vestibule via the Lower Northern Bodyguard Room. This is the beginning of the main ceremonial suite, which continues with Karl X's Gallery where paintings illustrate his major military exploit, the crossing of the iced-over Store Bælt (Great Belt) by the Swedish army in 1658. Queen Hedvig Eleonora (1636–1715) held audiences in the Ehrenstrahl Salon, named after the artist whose paintings dominate the walls. More prominent guests were received in the State Bedroom which later in Queen Lovisa Ulrika's time was in fact used for sleeping. Her Meissen porcelain can be seen in the Blue Cabinet; the Library has her collection of more than 2,000 books. Behind the Upper Northern Bodyguard Room, with a ceiling by Johan Sylvius, is a Gustavian drawing room with a bureau by Johan Niklas Eckstein. In 1777, following Gustav III's assumption of power, the Blue Salon was decorated in the Neo-Classical style.

The Chinese Salon was used as a private bedroom by King Adolf Fredrik. It is directly above the Queen's State Bedroom and there is a hidden staircase linking the two floors. The "bureau" opposite the tiled stove is also a sofa bed. The Oscar Room was refurbished by Oscar I (1799–1859) and is adorned by a tapestry dating from the 1630s. After the General's Room, Karl XI's Gallery commemorating the victory at Lund (1667), and the Golden Salon, comes the Queen's Salon. Just as the adjoining State Room has portraits of all the European monarchs, the portraits in the Queen's Salon are of European queens. This floor finishes with the Upper South Bodyguard Room, an ante-room to the State Room and lavishly decorated by the Carove stucco artists and the ceiling painter Johan Sylvius.

The Chinese Pavilion

On her 33rd birthday in 1753 Queen Lovisa Ulrika was given a Chinese pavilion by her husband, King Adolf Fredrik. It had been manufactured in Stockholm and the previous night it was shipped to Drottningholm and assembled a short distance from the palace. It had to be taken down after 10 years because rot had set in, and was replaced by the

The Chinese Pavilion, an extravaganza in blue and gold

For hotels and restaurants in this area see pp284–289 and pp294–301

Chinese Pavilion (Kina Slott) which is still one of the major attractions at Drottningholm. The polished-tile building was designed by D F Adelcrantz (1716–96).

At this time there was great European interest in all things Chinese. In 1733 the newly formed East India Company made its first journey to China. After Lovisa Ulrika's death in 1782 this interest waned, but it was rekindled in the 1840s. The Chinese Pavilion is a mixture of what was considered 250 years ago to be typical Chinese style along with artifacts from China and Japan. Efforts have been made to restore the interior to its original state with the help of a 1777 inventory.

Four smaller pavilions belong to the building. In the northeastern pavilion the king had his lathe and a carpenter's bench. Alongside is the

Tiled stove in a cabinet in the Chinese Pavilion

Confidencen pavilion, where meals were taken if he wished to be left undisturbed. The food was prepared in the basement, the floor opened and the dining table hauled up. The adjoining Turkish-style "watch tent" was built as a barracks for Gustav III's dragoons. It now houses a museum about the estate.

The Palace Park

The palace's three gardens are each of a completely different character but still combine to provide a unified whole. The symmetrical formal garden started to take shape in 1640. The garden was designed to stimulate all senses with sights, sounds and smells. It starts by the palace terrace with its "embroidery" parterre and continues as far as the Hercules statue. The water parterre is situated on slightly higher ground and is broken up with waterfalls and topiaries. The sculptures, mainly carved by the

Flemish sculptor Adrian de Vries (1560–1626) were war trophies from Prague in 1648 and from Fredriksborg Castle in Denmark in 1659.

The avenues of chestnut trees were laid out when the Chinese Pavilion was completed, as well as the Rococo-inspired garden area – a cross between the formal main garden and the freer composition of the English park. The English park has natural paths and a stream with small islands, along with trees and bushes at "natural" irregular intervals. Gustav III is reputed to have been responsible for its design and also planned several buildings. Not all his plans were realized, but he added four statues which he had bought during his travels in Italy.

The first 300 of a total of 846 lime trees were planted in the avenues flanking the Baroque garden as early as 1684.

The Court Theatre and Theatre Museum

The designer of the Chinese Pavilion, Carl Fredrik Adelcrantz, was also responsible for the Drottningholm Court Theatre (Slottsteatern), which dates from 1766. The theatre was commissioned by Queen Lovisa

The magnificent 18th-century stage in the Drottningholm Court Theatre

Ulrika, but Adelcrantz did not have the same resources as the architects of the palace itself. This simple wooden building with a plaster façade is now the world's oldest theatre still preserved in its original condition. The interior and fittings are masterpieces of simple functionality. The pilasters, for example, are made from gypsum and the supports from papier mâché. The scenery, with its wooden hand-driven machinery, is still in working order.

After Gustav III's death in 1792 the theatre fell into disuse until the 1920s, when the machinery ropes were replaced, electric lighting was installed, and the original wings were refurbished.

The scenery is adapted to 18th-century plays. It can be changed in just a few seconds with the help of up to 30 scene-shifters. The sound effects are simple but authentic: a wooden box filled with stones creates realistic thunder, a wooden cylinder covered in tent cloth produces a howling wind. Every summer there are about 30 performances, mainly opera and ballet from the 18th century. The theatre is open daily for visitors to the palace.

A Theatre Museum and shop are housed in Duke Carl's pavilion, built in the 1780s. The museum focuses on 18th-century theatre, with decoration sketches, paintings, scenery models and costumes. A *Commedia dell'arte* room contains paintings by Pehr Hilleström and sketches for Gustav III's dramatic productions by Louis Jean Desprez.

Court Theatre stage machinery dating from 1766

㊴ The Stockholm Archipelago

Extending 80 km (50 miles) east from the sheltered waters of Stockholm to the open sea, the archipelago encompasses tens of thousands of islands of all shapes and sizes, some inhabited, others not. Many of the inner archipelago's larger islands, such as Värmdö, Ingarö and Ljusterö, are linked to the mainland by bridges and car ferries, making them in parts little more than city suburbs. But the majority of the archipelago islands, with their traditional wooden houses, cosy hotels and youth hostels, and summer sailing regattas, can be reached by an extensive network of scheduled ferries departing from Stockholm, Vaxholm, Stavsnäs and Dalarö.

Passengers boarding steamships on a Stockholm wharf on Archipelago Boat Day

Archipelago Highlights

① Fjäderholmarna
② Vaxholm
③ Grinda
④ Finnhamn
⑤ Möja
⑥ Sandhamn
⑦ Utö

🦞 Fjäderholmarna

6 km (4 miles) E of Stockholm. **Tel** 08-718 01 00. 🚢 May–Sep from Nybrokajen and Slussen.

With the inclusion of the Fjäderholmarna islands in the Royal National City Park (see p103), the city's "green lung" has acquired a small part of the archipelago. The main island, Stora Fjäderholmen, is only 25 minutes by boat from Nybrokajen or Slussen.

There was an inn here as long ago as the 1600s, conveniently sited for islanders on their way to the city to sell their wares. Today there is an attractive harbour, restaurants, an art gallery and museums devoted to boating and angling as well as the Baltic Sea Museum, home to virtually every type of aquatic creature from Stockholm to Landsort. Local handicrafts include metalwork, weaving, wood-carving and glassmaking. The other three islands have a rich birdlife and one, Libertas, has Sweden's last remaining gas-powered lighthouse.

🏛 Vaxholm

25 km (16 miles) NE of Stockholm. **Tel** 08-541 314 80. 🚌 670. 🚢 from Strömkajen and Nybrokajen. Vaxholm Fortress and Vaxholm Fortress Museum: **Tel** 08-541 718 90. **Open** mid-Jun–Sep: 11:30am–5:30pm daily.

The archipelago's main community, Vaxholm, is easily reached by boat from Stockholm on a delightful one-hour journey through the archipelago. Vaxholm Fortress, on the nearby island of Vaxholmen, guards this busy port. First fortified in 1548 by Gustav Vasa, the more recent 19th-century citadel houses a military museum.

Two of Stockholm's best-known architects have left their mark on Vaxholm. The law courts were given their present appearance in 1925

The Fjäderholmarna islands, a popular summer excursion just 25 minutes by boat from the city

Vaxholm Fortress, strategically sited on the approach to Vaxholm

by Cyrillus Johansson, and the hotel on the headland, by Erik Lallerstedt (1899), has Jugendstil ornamentation.

The wooden buildings and shops around the square and along Hamngatan provide a pleasant stroll.

⛵ Grinda

30 km (19 miles) E of Stockholm. **Tel** 08-542 490 72. 🚌 670 from Östra station to Vaxholm, then boat. 🚢 from Strömkajen and Nybrokajen. 🛏 🚻 (summer only).

Grinda is a leafy island, typical of the inner archipelago, about one and a half hours by boat from the city. It has some excellent beaches and rocks for swimming, as well as good fishing. The architect Ernst Stenhammar, who designed the Grand Hôtel in Stockholm (see p83), built a large Jugendstil

Sandhamn, the yachting centre in Stockholm's outer archipelago

villa here, which is now a pub and restaurant with guest rooms. There are chalets to rent, a campsite and a youth hostel in a former barracks. Boats can be hired.

🏝 Finnhamn

40 km (25 miles) NE of Stockholm.
Tel 08-542 462 12. 🚢 from Strömka-jen and Nybrokajen. 📱 ✂ 📷

Finnish ships used to moor at Finnhamn on their way to and from Stockholm. This attractive group of islands lies two and a half hours by boat from Stockholm at the point where the softer scenery of the inner archipelago gives way to the harsher landscape of the outer islands. As on Grinda, the main island has a wooden villa designed by Ernst Stenhammar (1912). Today it is the largest youth hostel in the archipelago. There is a restaurant, chalets to rent and a campsite. Smaller islands nearby are accessible by rowing boat.

🏝 Möja

50 km (31 miles) E of Stockholm.
Tel 08-571 640 53. 🚌 670 to Vaxholm, then boat. 🚢 from Strömkajen and Nybrokajen. 📱 ✂ 📷

Fishing and strawberry-growing were the mainstays of this idyllic corner of the archipelago. Now there are few Möja strawberry growers and only one professional fisherman among the island's 300 inhabitants. Instead, picturesque harbours attract the sailing fraternity in particular. Nature reserves on and around Möja shelter a rich abundance of wildlife. Services on the island are good in the summer, with cottages, boats and kayaks for hire, and guest houses.

🏝 Sandhamn

50 km (31 miles) E of Stockholm.
Tel 08-571 530 00. 🚌 433, 434 from Slussen to Stavsnäs, then boat. 🚢 from Nybrokajen. 📱 ✂ 📷
🌐 destinationsandhamn.se

Over the past 200 years the village of Sandhamn has been a favourite meeting point for sailors. The Royal Swedish Yacht Club is based in Seglarrestaurangen (Sailors' Restaurant), and every summer the world's yachting elite arrive to take part in the Round Gotland Race.

A pretty village with narrow alleys and houses adorned with decorative carvings, Sandhamn has shops, crafts centres and a swimming pool. About 100 people live here permanently. The Customs House, built in 1752, is a listed heritage building and the former home of poet and artist Elias Sehlstedt (1808–74).

Although camping is not permitted, there is no shortage of hotel, bed-and-breakfast and chalet accommodation. There are also great sandy beaches.

VISITORS' CHECKLIST

Practical Information
🏛 Vaxholm: Archipelago fair (mid-Aug). 🎫 Sandhamn: Round Gotland Yacht Race (late Jun/early Jul), Sandhamn Regatta (3rd week in July), Vaxholm: Archipelago Boat Day (1st Wed in Jun).
🌐 stockholmtown.com

Transport
🚇 SL traffic information in Eng, 08-600 10 00. 🚢 Strömma Kanalbolaget, 08-587 140 00; Vaxholmsbolaget, 08-679 58 30.

🏝 Utö

50 km (31 miles) SE of Stockholm.
Tel 08-501 574 10. 🚢 in summer, from Strömkajen. ✂ 📷
🌐 utoturistbyra.se

No other island in the archipelago has as rich a history as Utö, which was inhabited before the Viking era. In the 12th century the islanders started to mine iron ore; this activity continued until 1879. Their story is told in the Mining Museum adjoining the hotel. Today's holiday homes along Lurgatan were built as miners' cottages in the 18th century. A windmill, built in 1791, provides an unrivalled view of the island.

Utö is one of the best seaside resorts in the Stockholm area, and is ideal for a weekend or full-day excursion.

A range of accommodation options is available. Bicycles, rowing boats and canoes can be hired. The bakery is renowned for its delicious "Utölimpa" bread.

Excursions by Steamboat

Traditional steamboats are a familiar feature on the waters around Stockholm. Both in the archipelago and on Lake Mälaren visitors can still enjoy the tranquil atmosphere of a steamboat voyage. One of the veterans, *SS Blidösund*, built in 1911, is operated by voluntary organizations and serves mostly the northern archipelago. Some routes, for example Stockholm–Mariefred, are operated partly or completely by steamers. Most of the other passenger boats from the early 20th century have been fitted with oil-fired engines, but still provide a nostalgic journey back in time.

SS Blidösund, one of the oldest in Stockholm's fleet of steamboats

STOCKHOLM STREET FINDER

Key to Street Finder

- Major sight
- Place of interest
- Other building
- 🚊 Train station
- Ⓣ Tunnelbana station
- Ferry boarding point
- Tram stop
- Bus station

- ℹ️ Tourist information office
- ➕ Hospital
- Police station
- ✝️ Church
- Synagogue
- ✵ Viewpoint
- Railway line
- Pedestrian street

Scale of Map Pages 1–2

0 metres 200
0 yards 200

Scale of Map Pages 3–4

0 metres 200
0 yards 200

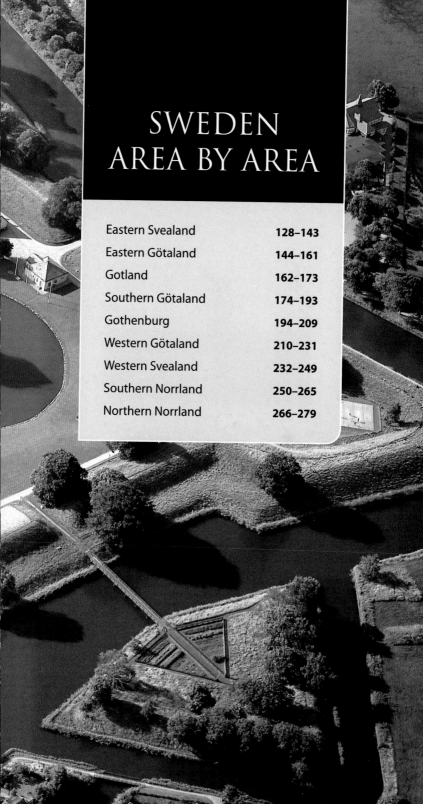

SWEDEN
AREA BY AREA

Sweden at a Glance

Sweden is a long country, traditionally divided into Norrland, Svealand and Götaland. In Norrland the landscape is characterized by its proximity to the Arctic, with mountains in the west, rivers running east towards the coast, and an interior of forest or marshland. With the exception of the larger towns along the coast, the area is sparsely populated. In Svealand the countryside is hilly, with lakes and rivers interspersed with farmland. Island archipelagos lie offshore. The population is concentrated in Mälardalen, centring on Stockholm. Götaland, comprising the southern part of the country, offers the most variation with differing landscapes and a high urban and rural population.

The Mountains of Härjedalen are a haven for outdoor activities in both summer and winter *(see pp264–5)*.

The Fryken Lakes in Värmland are edged by superb manor houses such as Rottneros, whose park overlooking Mellanfryken contains an outstanding collection of statues, including works by Carl Milles *(see p236)*.

Götaplatsen, Gothenburg's finest square, features Carl Milles' statue *Poseidon* with Konstmuseet in the background *(see p204)*.

Fiskebäckskil, with its red fishermen's huts and white wooden houses, is typical of the coastal villages of Bohuslän *(see p219)*.

Österlen, on the southeastern coast of Skåne, is characterized by rolling agricultural land and the half-timbered farmhouses typical of the area *(see p187)*.

Gä

Öste

Ste
Sjö

Sve

Mo
Sil

Karlstad

Vänern

Vättern

Jönköping

Skagerrak

Gothenburg   Borås

Varberg

Va

Kattegat

Halmstad

Karlsh

Helsingborg

Malmö

◄ Aerial view of the fortified citadel in Landskrona

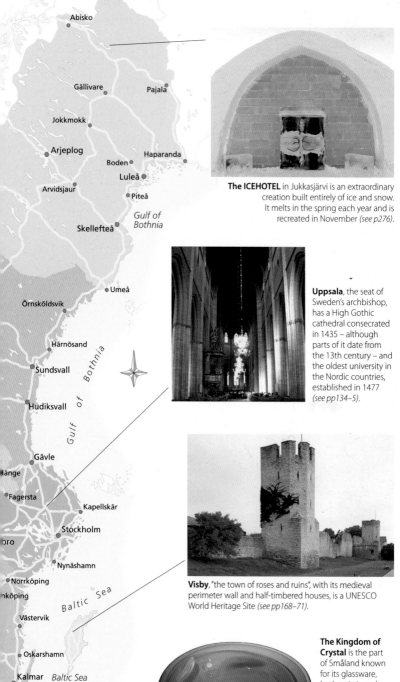

The ICEHOTEL in Jukkasjärvi is an extraordinary creation built entirely of ice and snow. It melts in the spring each year and is recreated in November *(see p276)*.

Uppsala, the seat of Sweden's archbishop, has a High Gothic cathedral consecrated in 1435 – although parts of it date from the 13th century – and the oldest university in the Nordic countries, established in 1477 *(see pp134–5)*.

Visby, "the town of roses and ruins", with its medieval perimeter wall and half-timbered houses, is a UNESCO World Heritage Site *(see pp168–71)*.

The Kingdom of Crystal is the part of Småland known for its glassware, both artistic and practical. The plate, *Amber*, was designed by Göran Wärff at Kosta Glasbruk in 2003 *(see pp156–7)*.

EASTERN SVEALAND

The waterways of Lake Mälaren and the vast archipelago extending to the Baltic both divide and unite the provinces of Uppland, Södermanland and Västmanland. This is a land of verdant islands and glittering bays, splendid castles and little wooden towns, and a cultural heritage that predates the Vikings. With Stockholm at the centre, the region is home to one-third of Sweden's population.

This area was the cradle of ancient Svea, as can be seen in the rock carvings, burial mounds and standing stones in the shapes of ships that dot the landscape. It was from the town of Birka on Lake Mälaren and from Roslagen in Uppland that the Vikings headed east on plundering raids and trading missions around Europe and beyond *(see p37)*. The centre of the ancient pagan Æsir cult in Uppsala held out against Christianity until the 12th century. Many beautiful, small medieval churches testify to the fact that Christianity finally dominated. They are richly decorated with paintings depicting biblical scenes for the benefit of the local congregations. Uppsala itself became a cathedral city and the seat of the archbishop in 1273.

The many castles and fortresses which guard the waterways are an eye-catching sight. Several of these date back to the Middle Ages, but the most important, such as Skokloster, are the result of the great wealth which flooded into the country after Sweden's victories in the various European wars of the 17th century *(see pp41–3)*. Shipping brought further prosperity to the region, with centres such as Arboga lying on the iron route between Bergslagen, Stockholm and the Uppland harbours. There are well-preserved ironworks in all three provinces, including Engelsbergs Bruk, a UNESCO World Heritage Site.

The extensive archipelago straddles the coasts of Uppland and Södermanland, and Lake Mälaren itself is so full of islands that the archipelago appears to continue uninterrupted.

All the architectural sights and natural attractions of Eastern Svealand are best enjoyed at a slow pace by bicycle or boat, or on foot.

The flat skerries of the outer archipelago

◄ Traditional houses and church in Mariefred, on Lake Malaren

Exploring Eastern Svealand

This, the heartland of Sweden, offers as many tempting treats as the most well-stocked Swedish *smörgåsbord*. Whether travelling by car, bus, train, bicycle or on foot, visitors will enjoy frequent glimpses of lakes and bays, as water is a constant presence. This makes travelling by boat an unbeatable way of discovering Eastern Svealand's history and culture and enjoying the area's natural beauty. There are hundreds of canoe trails, and canoes and boats can be hired all over the region. For walkers, Sörmlandsleden, Upplandsleden and Bruksleden in Västmanland offer more than 1,500 km (940 miles) of stunning trails.

Botanist Carl von Linné's Hammarby, outside Uppsala *(see p135)*

Julita Gård, a Södermanland estate and open-air museum

Sights at a Glance

Key
- Motorway
- Major road
- Minor road
- Main railway
- Minor railway

One of the traditional steamers of the
archipelago and Lake Mälaren

Ceiling fresco by Albertus Pictor, Härkeberga
Church (see p136)

Getting Around

Destinations on both sides of Lake Mälaren can
be reached quickly via the major motorways.
Travelling north–south, the E4 is a good road,
although Stockholm can be a bottleneck at times.
The minor roads tend to offer motorists a more
pleasurable experience. The railway network serves
many locations, but in Roslagen in Uppland and
the more remote areas the main option is the bus.
Summer offers the opportunity to take to the water,
with good connections to the archipelago on high-
speed ferries or traditional steamers.

Österbybruk's English gardens with estate offices and clock tower

❶ Österbybruk

Uppland. 🗺 2,200. 🚹 1 Jun–31 Aug: Ånghammaren 0295-214 92. 🚌 817, 823 from Uppsala. 🚗 💻 🚲
Vallonsmedjan: **Open** Jun–Aug: daily. 📷 by appointment, 0295-200 72. Liljeforsateljén: **Open** May–mid-Jun, mid-Aug–Sep: noon–4pm Sat & Sun; mid-Jun–mid-Aug: noon–5pm daily. 🎪 Hurdy-Gurdy Festival (weekend before Midsummer), Fire Festival (2nd weekend Aug).

Iron played a key role in the region and nowhere is this more apparent than at Österbybruk. It is the area's oldest ironworks, dating back to the 15th century, but things only really took off when Dutchman Louis de Geer bought the foundry in 1643. With the help of migrant Walloon blacksmiths, he developed the iron industry so crucial to Sweden's position as a great power.

As the world's only fully preserved Walloon forge, the 15th-century **Vallonsmedjan** uses puppets, sound and light to recreate life in the hammer mills. Around it are charming 18th- and 19th-century streets.

The 18th-century manor house was home to wildlife painter Bruno Liljefors in the early 20th century. In summer, his popular animal paintings are exhibited in **Liljeforsateljén** in the gardens.

Dannemora Gruva was the mine on which local ironworking was built. Gaping opencast pits such as Storrymningen are relics of an industry that has gone on here since the Middle Ages. Above the mine is the building

in which Mårten Triewald built Sweden's first steam engine in 1726.

🏛 **Dannemora Gruva**
2 km (1 mile) west of Österbybruk.
Tel 0295-214 92. **Open** Jun–Sep: daily.
🚗 💻

❷ Forsmarks Bruk

Uppland. 🚌 826, 832, 851 from Uppsala. 🚹 next to Brukscaféet, Jun–Aug: 0173-500 15. **Open** 10am–4.30pm Mon–Fri, 10am–3pm Sat & Sun. 📷 mid-Jun–mid-Aug: 10am (call to book). 🚗 💻 🚲 🐾 ♿

The historic ironworks of Forsmarks Bruk retains its well-preserved streets with their beautiful, whitewashed rows of houses and a manor house built in 1767–74. The manor is set in English-style gardens.

The nuclear power station of **Forsmarks Kärnkraftverk** lies on the coast, 3 km (2 miles) from the ironworks. It provides one-seventh of Sweden's electricity. Guided tours include such features as the vast biotest lake where the environmental impact of the cooling water is studied.

Louis de Geer's Walloon ironworks empire also included the impressively preserved **Lövstabruk**.

🏭 **Forsmarks Kärnkraftverk**
3 km (2 miles) north of Forsmark. 🚹 0173-812 68. **Open** Mon–Fri. 📷 mid-May–mid-Aug: tours from Forsmarks Bruk; other times by appointment. ♿

🏛 **Lövstabruk**
16 km (10 miles) north from Forsmark. 🚹 summer: 0173-500 15. **Open** summer: daily (manor). 🚗 💻 🚲 ♿

❸ Öregrund

Uppland. 🗺 1,600. 🚌 639 from Stockholm. 🚹 Jun–Aug: Harbour Office 0173–305 55; all year round: Östhammar Tourist Office, Rådhusgatan 6, Östhammar, 0173–178 50. ♿
🎪 Östhammar Music Festival (early Jul), Roslagsloppet speedboat race (late Jul/early Aug). 🌐 **roslagen.se**

The twin towns of Öregrund and Östhammar are closely linked geographically and historically. At the end of the 15th century, the citizens of Östhammar founded Öregrund in order to obtain a better harbour. Seafaring and iron-exporting became vital to the town. In 1719, Öregrund was burned by the Russians, but the wooden buildings were rebuilt according to a town plan from 1744. The Town Hall is from 1829. At the end of the 19th century, the sleepy area became a seaside resort and continues to attract visitors to this day.

The Öregrund and Östhammar region is home to many well-preserved old ironworking communities, including **Harg** and **Gimo**. Built in 1763–70, Gimo Manor was the first in Sweden to be designed in Gustavian style by Jean Eric Rehn.

Outside Gimo lies **Skäfthammars Kyrka**, a medieval church particularly renowned for its lectern, which was built for the Gimo smiths.

🏛 **Skäfthammars Kyrka**
Gimo, 16 km (10 miles) southeast of Östhammar. **Tel** 0173-404 27.
Open call for info.

Öregrund Church's shingle-clad, free-standing bell tower (1719)

Albert Engström's studio on the granite cliffs outside Grisslehamn

❹ Grisslehamn

Uppland. 🚹 4,700. 🚌 637 from Norrtälje. 🛈 Engströmsgården 0175-331 02. 🚣 🎣 Postrodden boat race to Åland (Jun).

The choppy Åland Sea constantly batters the red granite cliffs of northern Väddö at Grisslehamn. This is the closest point in Sweden to Finland and the reason for the town's existence. Today's ferry crossing to Eckerö takes only two hours, but things were much tougher in the 17th and 18th centuries when this was the main link with the eastern outposts of the Swedish empire. Until 1876, the post was rowed across the water by local fishermen in open boats. To commemorate the "post rowers", a race is held across the Åland Sea every year in similar boats.

Today, apart from those making the ferry crossing, the sleepy fishing port of Grisslehamn attracts Väddö's many holidaymakers. Delicious fresh fish can be bought from the red sheds on the harbourside.

In 1902, painter and writer Albert Engström (d. 1940) moved to Grisslehamn. He became much loved for his priceless characters such as the tramp, Kolingen, and the Roslagen figure, Österman. The **Albert Engströmsmuseet**, a reconstruction of his home containing Engström's art and memorabilia, was moved to Augustberg in 2006.

🏛 Albert Engströmsmuseet
Augustberg. **Tel** 0175-331 02. **Open** late Jun–Aug; rest of year by appointment only. 🚗 🎣 🖥

❺ Norrtälje

Uppland. 🚹 17,000. 🚌 676 from Stockholm. 🛈 Danskes Gränd 4, 0176-719 90. 🎷 Norrtälje Jazz Festival (late Jun/early Jul).
W norrtalje.se

An idyllic town, built of wood, Norrtälje is the natural hub of Roslagen, the area which covers large parts of the Uppland coast. Norrtälje received its town charter from Gustav II Adolf in 1622, when an important armaments factory was established here. In the second half of the 19th century, the town became a seaside resort, not least due to the health-giving properties of the mud found in Norrtälje Bay.

Thousands of summer residents from Stockholm still head for Norrtälje. The town centre and the buildings along the Norrtäljeån river retain their 18th-century features. The church was built in 1726 and the Town Hall dates from 1792. Attractions include **Roslagsmuseet** in the old armaments factory, focusing on seafaring and coastal life. **Pythagoras** is an unusual museum in a former diesel engine factory and one of Sweden's best preserved industrial relics.

Viking ship in Norrtälje

🏛 Roslagsmuseet
Hantverkargatan 23. **Tel** 0176-576 30. **Closed** for renovations until 2014. ♿

🏛 Pythagoras
Verkstadsgatan 6. **Tel** 0176-100 50. **Open** mid-Jun–mid-Aug: daily. 🚗 🎣 🖥

❻ Skokloster

Uppland. **Tel** 08-402 30 60. 🚆 SL train from Stockholm to Bålsta, then bus 894. 🚌 from Sigtuna. **Open** May: 11am–4pm Sat & Sun; Jun–Aug: 11am–5pm daily. 🚗 🎣 🍴 🖥

One of the best preserved Baroque castles in Europe, Skokloster, on Lake Mälaren, contains a unique collection of furniture, art, weapons, textiles and books. Construction was started in 1654 for army commander Carl Gustav Wrangel, who accumulated incredible treasures during the Thirty Years War (1618–48). This magnificent building was a way for Wrangel to show off his success, but he only ever lived here for a few weeks. Time seems to have stood still at the castle: the Banquet Hall, for example, remains incomplete, with all the tools lying where the craftsmen left them. The most sumptuous rooms are the armoury and library.

Next to the castle is Sweden's second oldest brick church. Built in the 13th century for nuns of the Cistercian order, it still contains a 13th-century triumphal cross. In the 17th century, it became the Wrangel family church. The churchyard contains several runestones, some of which are signed by the Viking runemaster, Fot, who was active in the mid-11th century.

The Baroque Skokloster Castle, beautifully situated on Lake Mälaren

❼ Uppsala

The city of learning on the idyllic Fyrisån river long remained a small town despite becoming the seat of the archbishop in 1273, having the first university in Scandinavia in 1477 and being the venue for parliaments and coronations. Scientists such as Carl von Linné and Anders Celsius gained the university worldwide glory, but as late as 1800 the town had only 4,000 inhabitants. It wasn't until 20th-century industrialization and the expansion in education that Uppsala grew into Sweden's fourth largest city. The Gothic cathedral, castle, historic university buildings, botanical gardens and ancient Gamla (Old) Uppsala make this one of Sweden's foremost sights.

The cathedral's twin spires, restored in the 19th century

🏛 Domkyrkan

Domkyrkoplan 2. **Tel** 018-430 36 30. **Open** daily. 🎧 🔊 💻 📷 daily. ♿ 🔊 Skattkammaren: **Open** daily. 📷

The first sight on approaching Uppsala is the 119 m (390 ft) high twin spires of the largest cathedral in the Nordic region. The building, with its impressive, colonnaded Gothic nave, was consecrated in 1435. Many monarchs have been crowned here and kings Gustav Vasa and Johan III, as well as botanist Carl von Linné and theosophist Emanuel Swedenborg (1688–1772), are buried here. The chapel contains the remains of St Erik, patron saint of Sweden, in a golden shrine.

The cathedral treasury, Skattkammaren, in the north tower has a superb collection of textiles and silver.

🏛 Gustavianum

Akademigatan 3. **Tel** 018-471 75 71. **Open** Tue–Sun. **Closed** public holidays. 📷 📷 Sat & Sun (also Eng). 🏛 ♿ 📷

Named after King Gustav II Adolf, who donated both funds and land, this is the oldest preserved building of Uppsala University. The unusual dome was built in 1662 for Olof Rudbeck's Theatrum Anatomicum. This is an amphitheatre with standing room for 200 spectators – students and paying members of the public – who would gather here to watch dissections of executed criminals. The room which visitors see today is largely a faithful reconstruction.

The Gustavianum mounts exhibitions connected with the work of the university since its foundation in 1477. One of the gems on show is the Augsburg Art Cabinet from the early 17th century. It is a kind of universal museum showing the world view of the time in miniature. Various archaeological collections from Egypt and the Classical world are also on display.

🏛 Universitetshuset

St Olofsgatan/Övre Slottsgatan. **Tel** 018-471 17 15. **Open** Mon–Fri and for events. ♿

The university's imposing main building was constructed in 1887 in Neo-Renaissance style. It contains an attractive auditorium.

🏛 Carolina Rediviva

Dag Hammarskjölds Väg 1. **Tel** 018-471 39 18. **Open** Mon–Sat (mid-May–mid-Sep also Sun). **Closed** public holidays. 📷 mid-May–mid-Sep. ♿

In 1841, the 200-year-old university library moved into this specially designed building which houses 5 million printed books and 4 km (2 miles) of shelving holding manuscripts. Rarities include the Silver Bible from the 6th century and Olaus Magnus's *Carta Marina* (1539).

🏛 Uppsala Slott

Slottsbacken. **Tel** 018-727 24 85. 📷 phone for info. Konstmuseet: **Open** Tue–Sun. House of Peace (museum): **Tel** 018-50 00 08. 📷 💻 📷 📷

Standing on a glacial ridge, this Vasa castle competes with the cathedral for domination of the city. Established as a fortress in 1549, it was added to several times, but never finished. A disastrous city fire in 1702 destroyed much of the castle and restoration work was started by Carl Hårleman. The castle now houses Uppsala's art museum, the governor's

Carl Von Linné

Bust of Carl von Linné, 1707–78

"God created, Linné organized," goes the saying about the Swedish king of plants. It is thanks to Linné's ground-breaking *Systema Naturae*, first published in 1735, that the world has the familiar system of binomial nomenclature, giving all plants and animals two Latin names. In 1741, Linné, also known as Linnaeus, became professor of medicine at Uppsala and his spirit has suffused the city ever since. At his country house in Hammarby, Linné tutored students. It was not unknown for him to greet them dressed only in his nightshirt, for the morning's nature walk. According to Linné "nature does not wait for powder and wigs".

Burial mounds next to Gamla Uppsala church

residence and the House of Peace, a museum that explores world conflicts and Sweden's long history of neutrality.

Botaniska Trädgården

Villavägen 8. **Tel** 018-471 28 38. **Open** daily. **Closed** public holidays. greenhouse.

The botanical gardens have had an educational function since the end of the 18th century. They hold more than 130,000 plants, many exotic, in a beautiful setting that includes several greenhouses, one of which is tropical. The first garden was established on the banks of the Fyrisån river by Olof Rudbeck in 1655. In 1741, Carl von Linné took it over and made it one of the leading gardens of its time. Lovingly restored, it is now known as the Linné garden. After a donation from Gustav III in the late 18th century, teaching was switched to the castle garden, where the Linneanum, housing the orangery, opened in 1807.

Gamla Uppsala

Route 290 or E4, 5 km north of the centre. Disagården: **Tel** 018-16 91 30. Gamla Uppsala Museum: **Tel** 018-23 93 00. **Open** mid-May–Aug: daily. Sun.

Gamla Uppsala and its museum are like a time capsule. Royal burial mounds rise up from the plain as they have done for 1,500 years. This was a centre for worshipping the Norse gods long into the 11th century, with a temple which, according to Adam of Bremen's description from 1070, was clad entirely in gold and contained images of Odin, Thor and Frey. Every nine years, a bloody festival was celebrated with men, stallions and dogs sacrificed around the temple. In the early 12th century, the heathen temple gave way to a Christian church, then a cathedral. But in 1273, the seat of the diocese moved to Uppsala and the cathedral became a parish church of which only small parts remain. Nearby is Disagården, an open-air museum focusing on the life of local farmers in the 19th century.

Linné's Hammarby

13 km (8 miles) southeast of Uppsala. **Tel** 018-471 28 38. **Open** May–Sep: Gardens: daily. Museum: Tue–Sun. **Closed** Whitsun, Midsummer's Eve.

Linné bought Hammarby farm in 1758, because he thought the air in Uppsala was bad for his health. The estate was his rural retreat, where he was able to cultivate plants that could not tolerate the moist soil in the botanical gardens. The farm is now owned by the state and run by Uppsala University.

VISITORS' CHECKLIST

Practical Information
Uppsala. 200,000.
Kungsgatan 59, 018-727 48 00.
Vaksala market (Sat).
Walpurgis Night celebrations (30 Apr), Culture Night (2nd Sat in Sep). **destinationuppsala.se**

Transport
25 km (16 miles) south of the centre. Kungsgatan.

Uppsala City Centre

① Domkyrkan
② Gustavianum
③ Universitetshuset
④ Carolina Rediviva
⑤ Uppsala Slott/Konstmuseet
⑥ Botaniska Trädgården

For keys to symbols see back flap

Steninge Slott near Sigtuna, one of the best examples of a 17th-century Carolian country house

❽ Sigtuna

Uppland. 🏛 42,000. ✈ 🚉 to Märsta C, then bus. 🚌 🛈 🚢 Stora Gatan 33, 08-594 806 50. 🛷 Sigtuna Meeting (last Sat & Sun in Aug).
🌐 sigtuna.se

Sweden's second oldest town after Birka was founded in 980 and soon became a centre of Christianity. Ruins of three of the original seven churches in medieval Sigtuna, St Per, St Lars and St Olof, still remain. The attractive main street, Stora Gatan, is lined with colourful wooden buildings and follows the original route. Still in use today is the 13th-century church of St Maria, with its medieval paintings. It is the oldest brick-built church in Mälardalen.

Sigtuna has Sweden's smallest town hall, built in 1744, and Lundströmska Gården, an early 20th-century home furnished in the style of the period. There are around 150 11th-century rune stones in the surrounding region.

The area is also well-endowed with stately homes. These include Skokloster (see p133) and the royal palace of **Rosersberg**, with some of Europe's best-kept interiors from the period 1795–1825.

East of Sigtuna is **Steninge Slott**, architect Tessin the Younger's Italianate Baroque masterpiece built in the 1690s. The attractive gardens contain a monument to Count Axel von Fersen, renowned not least for his romance with the French queen Marie Antoinette, and a cultural centre and art gallery.

🏠 **Rosersbergs Slott**
15 km (9 miles) from Sigtuna.
Tel 08-590 350 39. **Open** Jun–Aug: 11am–4pm daily. 🎨 🚻 11am & 1pm in Eng. 🚻 🎨

🏠 **Steninge Slott**
7 km (4 miles) east of Sigtuna.
Tel 08-592 595 00. Palace:
Open Jun–Aug daily. 🎨 🚻 🎨 🚻

❾ Enköping

Uppland. 🏛 39,000. ✈ 🚉 🚌
🛈 Gustav Adolfs Plan, 0171-625 040.
🌐 enkoping.se

This centrally located town on Lake Mälaren calls itself Sweden's "nearest town". Another name is "Horseradish Town" from the vegetable production which made the town known in the 19th century. And Enköping remains a city of greenery with its inviting parks.

Enköping was granted a town charter in 1300. It was a spiritual centre with three churches and a monastery. Of these, only the largely remodelled Vårfrukyrkan remains.

Northeast of the town, the medieval church of **Härkeberga** is a real gem. At the end of the 15th century, its star chamber was decorated by the master painter Albertus Pictor with colourful representations of biblical stories (see p131).

🏠 **Härkeberga Kyrka**
10 km (6 miles) northeast of Enköping. **Open** Mar–Oct: daily.

Triumphal cross, Härkeberga Kyrka

❿ Birka

Uppland. 🚢 from Stockholm during summer season only. Birkamuseet:
Tel 08-560 514 45. **Open** May–Sep: 11am–3pm Mon–Fri, 10:30am–4pm Sat & Sun (Jul–mid-Aug: 10:30am–6:30pm daily). 🎨 🚻 🚻 🎨 🚻 🎨

The trading post of Birka on the island of Björkö in Lake Mälaren was established in the 8th century and is thought to be the oldest town in Scandinavia. The founder was the Svea king, who had his royal residence on nearby Adelsö. About 100 years later, Birka is described by a writer as having "many rich merchants and an abundance of all types of goods and a great deal of money and valuables". It was thought to have had 1,000 inhabitants, including craftsmen of every kind, whose products attracted merchants from distant countries.

The town was planned on uncomplicated lines. People lived in modest houses which stood in rows overlooking the long jetties. At these lay the ships which took the Vikings out on trading missions and war expeditions. In 830 the arrival of a monk named Ansgar marked the start of Sweden's conversion to Christianity. But Birka's moment of greatness soon passed. In the

Iron Age burial ground at Birka on the island of Björkö in Lake Mälaren

10th century, the town was abandoned in favour of Sigtuna, on the nearby mainland.

Today, Björkö is a green island with meadows and juniper-covered slopes. It has a fascinating museum and ongoing archaeological digs. The museum shows how Birka would have looked in its heyday, along with some of the finds. Visitors can also share in the day's discoveries when digs are in progress.

In summer, services are held in the Ansgar Chapel. There is a harbour, restaurant, and good places to swim.

Testing the laws of nature at Tom Tits Experiment, Södertälje

⑪ Södertälje

Stockholms län. 🗺 89,000. ✈ 🚌 🚆
🛈 Saltsjögatan 1, 08-523 060 30.
🌐 **sodertalje.nu**

Good communications are the key to the economic success of Södertälje, one of Sweden's oldest cities. In the 9th century, a rise in land levels rendered the sound between the Baltic Sea and Lake Mälaren unnavigable and so Tälje became a reloading point. The small town flourished in the Middle Ages but fires, war and plague almost eradicated it in the 17th and 18th centuries. Fortunes improved with the construction of the canal pin 1819, and with the arrival of the railway in 1860 industrialization took off. The town grew quickly. Today, major companies such as vehicle-maker Scania and pharmaceuticals giant Astra Zeneca form the basis of a booming commercial life.

Södertälje's history is the focus of **Torekällbergets museet**, an open-air museum with animals, historic buildings and a craft quarter. **Marcus Wallenberg-hallen** contains a large collection of veteran vehicles from Scania's 100-year production history.

Tom Tits Experiment is a science centre with many fun activities, both indoors and outdoors, for kids of all ages.

🏛 **Torekällbergets museet**
Tel 08-523 021 18. **Open** daily. 🖥 🅿

🏛 **Marcus Wallenberg-hallen**
Tel 08-553 825 00. **Open** 8am–4:45pm Mon–Fri. **Closed** public holidays.

🏛 **Tom Tits Experiment**
Storgatan 33. **Tel** 08-550 225 00. **Open** 10am–5pm daily (7pm Thu, 6pm Sat & Sun). **Closed** 1 Jan, 23–26 Dec & 31 Dec. 🅿 🖥 🅿 🎏 🚻 🌐 **tomtit.se**

⑫ Ytterjärna

Stockholms län. 🚌 to Järna, then bus.
🛈 Kulturhuset, 08-554 302 00.
Open 10am–5pm daily. **Closed** public holidays. 🎏 🖥 🅿 🚻

Since the 1960s, Ytterjärna has become the centre for Swedish anthroposophists, followers of the teachings of Austrian philosopher Rudolf Steiner (1861–1925). Anthroposophists focus on the development of the whole human being, particularly in the fields of art, music, farming and medicine. There are a number of Steiner organizations here, including schools, the Vidarkliniken hospital, biodynamic farms and market gardens. Kulturhuset is renowned as a centre for art, music and theatre, and for the building's audacious design by architect Erik Asmussen, with its intertwined dialogue of colour and shape inside and out.

Neat wooden houses lining the harbour canal in Trosa

⑬ Trosa

Södermanland. 🗺 5,500. 🚌 to Vagnhärad or Södertälje, then bus.
🛈 Rådstugan Torget, 0156-522 22.
🎪 🛍 Trosa Market (2nd Sat in Jun).
🎭 Dance at the harbour (Wed in Jul–1st week in Aug). 🌐 **trosa.com**

Known as the end of the World, idyllic Trosa is something of a geographical dead end if you are not venturing into the wonderful Trosa archipelago beyond. Like so many coastal towns, it was burned to the ground by the Russians in 1719, although the church dating from 1711 was spared. Pretty groups of red wooden buildings can be found mainly in Kåkstan, where Garvaregården is an arts and crafts museum. The main square, with its miniature town hall and market, is a focal point for the town.

Nearby, **Tullgarns Slott** was the favourite summer residence of Gustav V (1858–1950). The beautiful 18th-century palace has magnificent interiors and English-style gardens.

🏰 **Tullgarns Slott**
On E4, 10 km (6 miles) north of Trosa.
Tel 08-551 720 11. **Open** May & Sep: Sat & Sun, Jun–Aug: Tue–Sun. 🅿 🎏

Kulturhuset by Erik Asmussen, in the anthroposophists' Ytterjärna

Nyköpingshus, site of the fatal Nyköping Banquet in 1317

⑭ Nyköping

Södermanland. 🚇 33,000. ✈ 🚗 🚌
ℹ Rådhuset, Stora Torget, 0155-24 80
00. 🎭 🎨 Nyköping Banquet (Jul).
🌐 nykoping.se

Södermanland's county town is probably best known for the notorious Nyköping Banquet in 1317. King Birger invited the Dukes Erik and Valdemar to a banquet at which the disputes between the brothers were to be resolved. Instead, Birger had the dukes thrown into Nyköpinghus's dungeon, where they were left to die. The story is retold in summer in a colourful pageant at the castle. A fire in 1665 destroyed the original castle and only the tower remains. In the adjoining county governor's residence, the **Sörmlands Museum** contains a lively mix of historical exhibitions.

A pleasant way to see the sights in the summer is to take the Tuffis tourist train which departs from Stora Torget. On the coast north of the town, Nynäs Slott nature reserve is also worth a visit.

🏛 Sörmlands Museum
Nyköpingshus. **Tel** 0155-24 57 00.
Open Jun–Aug: daily (call ahead for opening hours). 🎨 📷

⑮ Flen

Södermanland. 🚇 6,200. 🚗 🚌
ℹ Sveavägen 1, 0157-190 15;
Malmköping (summer) 0157-202 04.
🎪 Malma Market (last Sat & Sun in Jul).
🎨 Flen Festival (2nd weekend in Jun).

One of the youngest towns in Sweden, Flen only gained its town charter in 1949. Although the town itself has little to offer,

it is a good starting point for the attractions in the area.

Environs
On Lake Valdemaren, just east of the town, lies Stenhammar's beautiful castle, renowned as the residence of Prince Vilhelm in the early 1900s. The castle is now used by Carl XVI Gustav and is not open to the public. Northeast of Flen is the prime minister's summer residence, **Harpsund**, where the gardens are open to visitors. The old regimental town of Malmköping has **Malmahed**, a former military site, now a museum and nature centre. There are several military museums, as well as **Museispårvägen**, displaying veteran trams and other public transport vehicles. Visitors can enjoy a short tram ride through the countryside.

🚋 Museispårvägen
Malmköping, 17 km (11 miles) north of Flen, road 55. **Tel** 0157-204 30.
Open late May–end Jun: weekends only; end Jun–mid-Aug: daily (call for opening hours). 🎨

⑯ Mariefred

Södermanland. 🚇 4,700. 🚗 🚌
ℹ Rådhuset, 0159-297 90. 🎭
🚂 Steam Day (1st Sat in Jun),
Medieval Festival (3rd Sat & Sun in Jul).
🌐 mariefred.se

This town should ideally be approached from the water to get the best view of the splendid **Gripsholms Slott**. The first fortress on this site was built in the 1380s by the Lord High Chancellor, Bo Jonsson Grip, who gave the castle its name. Work on the present building, initiated by Gustav Vasa, started in 1537, but extensive alterations were made by Gustav III in the late 18th century. It was during this period that the National Portrait Gallery was set up. It now contains 4,000 portraits, representing the celebrities of the past 500 years.

Gripsholms Slott has a number of well-preserved interiors from various periods, with highlights including Gustav III's theatre and the White Salon. The town of Mariefred, which grew up in the shadow of the castle, derives its name from a medieval Carthusian monastery.

Volvo taxi (1950),
Museispårvägen

An inn has stood on the site of the monastery since the early 17th century.

The peaceful old streets of Mariefred with their delightful wooden buildings are a pleasure to stroll around. Art enthusiasts should head for Grafikens Hus on a hill leading up to the former royal farm, where stables and haylofts have been converted into attractive galleries.

Mariefred Town Hall (1784), site of the town's tourist office

One of the best ways to visit Mariefred is by boat. The 1903 steamer *S/S Mariefred* plies the three-and-a-half-hour voyage from Stockholm. There is a Railway Museum in the town and **ÖSLJ** (Östra Södermanlands Järnväg museum society) operates narrow-gauge steam trains from the harbour on a 20-minute trip to Läggesta and, on certain days, on to Taxinge.

🏠 Gripsholms Slott
500 m (546 yd) southwest of the centre. **Tel** 0159-101 94. **Open** early May–Sep: daily; other times: by appointment only. 🎨 🏠
🏠 **W** gripsholmsslott.se

🚂 ÖSLJ
500 m (546 yd) west of the centre. **Tel** 0159-210 00. **Open** 1 May–Sep: varies so call ahead for days and times. 🎨 🏠 **W** oslj.nu

Bedchamber of Duke Karl (Karl IX, 1550–1611), Gripsholms Slott

⑰ Strängnäs

Södermanland. 🚂 15,000. 🚌 🚃
🛈 Eskilstunavägen 2, 0152-296 94. **Open** Jun–Aug. 🎨 Strängnäs market (2nd Sat in Oct). **W** strangnas.se

As keeper of the keys of the Kingdom, Strängnäs was an important centre in the Middle Ages. It was mentioned as an episcopal see as early as 1120 and is dominated by the imposing tower of its Gothic cathedral, **Domkyrkan**, completed in 1280. It was here that Gustav Vasa was chosen as king on 6 June 1523, the date which was to become Sweden's National Day. Quaint wooden buildings surround the cathedral. To its east is Roggeborgen, the bishop's palace from the 1480s.

Gyllenhjelmsgatan, the street that runs from the city centre to the mighty gates of the cathedral, was described by

Red-painted, 18th-century wooden buildings in central Strängnäs

the poet Bo Setterlind as the most beautiful in Sweden.

Strängnäs Municipality includes the largest island in Lake Mälaren, **Selaön**. There are more rune stones here than in any other part of Södermanland, indicating that this was a major cultural centre in ancient times. Nowadays the island has no connections to the mainland.

The renovated Mälsåkers Palace dating from the 17th century is another of Selaön's attractions.

🏠 Domkyrkan
Biskopsgränd 2. **Tel** 0152-245 00. **Open** daily. 🎨 by appointment. 🏠 Wed & Sun.

⑱ Mälardalen's Castles

See pp140–41.

⑲ Eskilstuna

Södermanland. 🚂 95,000. 🚌 🚃
🛈 Tullgatan 4, 016-710 1000. **W** eskilstuna.se

The town is named after St Eskil, the Englishman who became Svealand's first Christian bishop and built his church on the riverbank along Eskilstunaån at

A Sumatran tiger, one of many exotic animals at Eskilstuna's Parken Zoo

the end of the 10th century. During Sweden's Age of Greatness in the 17th century, Eskilstuna flourished after Karl X Gustav gave master smith Reinhold Rademacher a 20-year monopoly on the manufacture of items such as cannons, knives and scissors. Rademachergatan still has a few forges kept as they were in the 1650s, where visitors can try their hand at being a blacksmith.

Today's modern industrial town and centre of learning features more than 200 items of public art, including Carl Milles's *Hand of God (see p101)* in Stadsparken.

Parken Zoo is one of Sweden's leading zoos, as well as a popular amusement park with a heated outdoor pool. The entrance is guarded by the Phantom, whose Skull Cave is a magnet for youngsters and comic fans alike.

Environs
North of Eskilstuna is **Torshälla**, a small town of cobbled streets and well-kept wooden houses. The magnificent 12th-century church dominates the old quarter. Northeast of Torshälla is **Sunbyholms Slott** *(see p140)* from where a 10-minute walk leads to **Sigurdsristningen**, Sweden's finest rock carving, which is thought to date back to 1040.

🦅 Parken Zoo

1 km (half a mile) west of the centre. **Tel** 016-100 100. Zoo: **Open** early May–mid-Sep: 10am–5pm daily (Jun–mid-Aug: to 6pm). Amusement Park: **Open** May: Sat & Sun; Jun–mid-Aug: daily; mid-Aug–mid-Sep: Fri–Sun. 🎨 🏠 🏠 🎨 🏠 🏠

⑱ A Tour of Mälardalen's Castles

There are more than 100 sturdy castles, opulent palaces and ravishing country houses around Lake Mälaren. Often strategically located near Iron Age and Viking settlements, they highlight the significance of this extensive waterway. Wik's 15th-century castle and the Vasa kings' solid, 16th-century fortress of Gripsholm show how long the need for defences lasted. From the mid-17th century, the grand palaces of Sweden's Age of Greatness, such as Skokloster, predominated, as manifestations of their owners' wealth and power. Many have excellent museums.

⑤ Engsö
The medieval castle was reworked in French Rococo style in the 1740s. It has many beautiful interiors from various periods and a major art collection. The castle grounds are a nature reserve full of wildlife.

⑥ Tidö
Lord Chancellor Axel Oxenstierna's country house, built in 1642, is a fine example of a Baroque manor. It is noted for its handsome state apartment and 43 inlaid wooden doors. A museum displays 30,000 antique toys.

④ Grönsöö
The grand manor from the early 17th century stands guard high above Lake Mälaren. It is still occupied by the von Ehrenheim family, and its grounds represent 400 years of garden history.

⑦ Strömsholm
Equestrianism dates from the 16th century at Strömsholm, with its beautiful pastureland and bridle paths. The palace was built in the 1670s in Carolian Baroque style.

Key

▬ Suggested route

═ Other roads

🏠 Other castles open to the public

Tips for Drivers

This tour, taking in the ten suggested palaces, involves a trip of more than 500 km (300 miles), lasting three days, despite the generally good roads. An option is to select a group of palaces close to each other. For more information, see www.malarslott.nu
Tel Mälarslott, 016-48 06 80.

⑧ Gripsholm
Gustav Vasa's brick Renaissance castle (*see p138*), started in 1540, is a symbol of Swedish independence. Visitors have access to 60 rooms from various periods, the highlight of which is Gustav III's theatre, and the National Portrait Gallery.

0 kilometres 15

0 miles 10

For hotels and restaurants in this area see pp284–289 and pp294–301

③ Wik

This 15th-century castle is Svealand's best-preserved late-medieval fortress. With its solid walls and moat, Wik was considered impregnable. It was remodelled in 1656–60. Today, Wik is a hotel and conference centre.

② Skokloster

Field Marshal Carl Gustaf Wrangel's 17th-century showpiece contains treasures from his campaigns, as well as exceptional collections of art, furniture, textiles, weapons and books *(see p133)*.

① Steninge

Built in the 1690s, the palace was designed by Nicodemus Tessin the Younger in the style of an Italian villa *(see p136)*.

⑩ Drottningholm

This royal palace, built in the 17th century, was one of the most lavish undertakings in Sweden. With its theatre, gardens and Chinese Pavilion, Drottningholm is a UNESCO World Heritage Site *(see pp112–15)*.

⑨ Sturehof

This stylish 18th-century country house in Botkyrka was designed by C F Adelcrantz for Gustav III's finance minister, Johan Liljekrantz, who owned the renowned Marieberg porcelain factory. The building houses a collection of the factory's famously stunning tiled stoves.

⑳ Julita Gård

Södermanland. **Tel** 0150-48 75 00.
🚉 🚌 Mälarbanan to Eskilstuna, then bus 404, 405. **Open** May–Sep daily.

This extensive Södermanland estate on Lake Öljaren is said to be the world's largest open-air museum. It was created in the first half of the 20th century by the romantic Lieutenant Arthur Bäckström and in 1941 was donated to Stockholm's Nordiska Museet. Julita is a working estate farm with parks and gardens, and an 18th-century manor house built on the site of a medieval Cistercian monastery.

The estate has a collection of buildings reflecting rural life in Södermanland. Threatened national species of cow, pig, sheep, hen and duck are cared for at the Swedish agricultural museum. There is also a dairy museum. Children are welcome to pop into the house of the much-loved children's literary character, Pettson, and his cat Findus.

Julita Gård's buildings representing rural life in Södermanland

㉑ Arboga

Västmanland. 🏘 11,000. 🚆 🚉 🚌 🚍 ℹ 🏛 Medieval Festival (Aug).

Red-painted iron warehouses, Ladbron quay and the railway line recall Arboga's great age as the chief shipping port for iron from Bergslagen. Fahlströmska Gården is a typical 16th-century warehouse with a huge loft.

Arboga was an important town in medieval times and the site of Sweden's first parliament in 1435. Churches from the period include the hospital chapel on Stortorget, which has been preserved as a town hall. The 14th-century **Heliga Trefaldighets Kyrka** on Järntorget has a splendid Baroque pulpit by Burchardt Precht.

Anundshögen, the 7th-century burial mound of King Bröt-Anund, with a stone ship in the foreground

⓴ Köping

Västmanland. 🖼 18,000. 🚉 🚌
i Barnhemsgatan 2, 0221-256 55.
🎭 Köpingsfesten Festival (28–30 May).

The port of Köping on Lake
Mälaren has been a vital link for
transporting products to and
from the mines and forests of
Bergslagen since medieval
times. The city burned down in
1889, but buildings to the west
of the river were saved, including
the 17th-century **Nyströmska
Gården**, a joiner's yard where
visitors can see how the town's
special tilt-top table was made.
Other attractions include the
motor museum, **Bil och
Teknikhistoriska Samlingarna**.
East of Köping is the 11th-
century church of Munktorp.

🏛 **Bil och Teknikhistoriska
Samlingarna**
Glasgatan 19. **Tel** 0221-206 00.
Open May–Sep: 10am–6pm Tue–Sun.
Pre-booked groups all year round.
Closed Midsummer. 🖼 🖵 📷

㉓ Västerås

Västmanland. 🖼 140,000. 🚉 🚌 ✈
i Kopporbergvägen 1, 021-39 01 00.
🎭 City Festival (1st week Jul), Power
meet (Jul).

Strategically situated at the
point where the Svartån river
runs into Lake Mälaren, the
county town of Västerås has
been an important trading
centre since Viking times.
Construction of the castle
and cathedral began in the
13th century and in 1527
Parliament was convened here.
The cathedral, **Domkyrkan**,
contains the sarcophagus of
Erik XIV (r.1561–69), the
unfortunate king who was
allegedly poisoned by his

brother Johan III, by pea soup
laced with arsenic.
Around the cathedral lies the
town's old centre of learning,
where Johannes Rudbeckius
opened Sweden's first upper
secondary school in 1623.
In the 17th and 18th centuries
Västerås became a major port
for the Bergslagen region. Today
it is an industrial centre and
headquarters of the engineering
giant Asea-Brown-Boveri (ABB).
To the east of the town lies
the 7th-century Anundshögen
mound where Bröt-Anund, the
king who settled Bergslagen,
is said to be buried. Standing
stones in the shapes of ships
50 m (164 ft) long can be seen
around the mound. The area was
a major Viking meeting place.
Northwest of the town is
Skultuna Messingsbruk,
Europe's oldest active
brassworks, founded in 1607
and renowned for its cannons
and stylish candlesticks.

🏛 **Domkyrkan**
Västra Kyrkogatan 6. **Tel** 021-81 46 11.
Open daily. 🖵

🏛 **Skultuna Messingsbruk**
16 km (10 miles) NW of Västerås.
Tel 021-783 01. **Open** Tue–Sun.
🖵 tel for info. 🖵 📷

㉔ Sala

Västmanland. 🖼 12,000. 🚉 🚌
i Stora Torget, 0224-74 78 02.
🎭 Autumn market (last Fri & Sat in
Sep). 🌐 sala.se/turism

During the 16th century, the
silver mine in Sala was one of the
richest in the world; 200,000 kg
(440,000 lb) were mined up to
1570, providing valuable funds
for the state coffers. The
Silvergruvan mine is open to
the public down to levels of 60 m

(200 ft) and 155 m (508 ft). There
are beautiful walks around the
old pits and canals, and silver
treasure hunts are organized
in the mine for children.
Aguélimuseet showcases
the work of Sala's own artist,
Orientalist Ivan Aguéli (1869–
1917), and other Modernists.

🏛 **Silvergruvan**
Drottning Christinas Väg. **Tel** 0224-677
250. **Open** 1–4pm Tue–Fri, 11am–4pm
Sat & Sun (May–Sep: 10am–5pm
daily). **Closed** Midsummer Eve.
🖼 🗓 🖵 🗓 📷

🏛 **Aguélimuseet**
Vasagatan 17. **Tel** 0224-138 20. **Open**
11am–4pm Wed–Sat. 🖼 🗓 🖵 📷

Hauling plant at the Sala silver mine, in use
until 1908

㉕ Fagersta

Västmanland. 🖼 12,500. 🚉
i Norbergsvägen 19, 0223-131 00.

Iron-working has shaped
Fagersta since the outset. In
Dunshammar, just south of the
town, Iron Age blast furnaces
show how iron used to be
extracted from bog ore. Today
Fagersta is home to metal-
manufacturing and stainless-
steel industries.
At the UNESCO World
Heritage Site of **Engelsbergs
Bruk**, the historic blast furnace
and ironworks have been
preserved in full working order
and give a remarkable
impression of how the site,
which consists of about

50 buildings, operated between the 17th and 19th centuries.

Oljeön, the world's oldest preserved oil refinery (1875–1902), lies 1.5 km (1 mile) from the ironworks.

Running through Fagersta is the 200-year-old Strömsholm canal from Lake Mälaren to Smedjebacken in Dalarna. Completed in 1795, it was a vital transport link for the Bergslagen foundries. Twenty-six locks, six of them in Fagersta, raise boats a total of 100 m (330 ft). Passenger ferries operate on the canal.

Engelsbergs Bruk
15 km (10 miles) E of Fagersta. **Tel** 0223-131 00. **Open** early May–mid-Jun: Sat & Sun; mid-Jun–Aug: daily; Sep: Sat & Sun.

The Engelsberg Bruk ironworks, founded in 1681 and now a UNESCO World Heritage Site

㉖ Kopparberg

Västmanland. 3,300. Gruvstugutorget, 0580-805 55. Gold panning competitions (end Jun). **ljusnarsberg.se**

The discovery of copper in the early 17th century attracted miners from Falun, who brought with them the name of their old mine and called the place Nya Kopparberget (New Copper Hill). The 2.5 km (2 mile) Kopparstigen (Copper Trail) takes in 28 places of interest, and provides a good view of the many mine buildings. Along the way is **Kopparbergs Miljömuseer**, a complex including a goldsmiths' museum, postal museum and 1880s photography studio. The 17th-century courthouse and unusually large and impressive wooden church from 1635 are also worth looking at.

Kopparbergs Miljömuseer
Gruvstugutorget. **Tel** 0580-805 55. **Open** Jun–Aug: daily.

㉗ Grythyttan

Västmanland. 1,700. **Tel** 0591-340 60. to Örebro, then bus.

A local vein of silver brought prosperity and town status to Grythyttan in 1649, but when the silver ran out 33 years later, the town charter was withdrawn. Today, Grythyttan has awakened from its long slumber and is now a gastronomic centre.

It all started when the inn, built in 1640, was given a new lease of life in the 1970s, thanks to inspired innkeeper Carl Jan Granqvist. Now, in addition to Grythyttan's wooden houses and red-painted church, there is a catering college centred on **Måltidens Hus i Norden**. It occupies Sweden's spectacular pavilion built for EXPO 1992 in Seville. A varied range of activities offers something for everyone interested in food and cooking, alongside exhibitions and a cookery book museum.

South of Grythyttan lies **Loka Brunn**, a classic Swedish

Grythyttan's inn with its beautifully renovated 17th-century interior

spa founded in the 1720s. The site has state-of-the-art facilities, but the old spa, with its gardens and spring, has been preserved in the Swedish spa museum. You can sample the spring water and view the restored bathhouse, pharmacy, clinic and royal kitchen built in 1761.

Måltidens Hus i Norden
Sörälgsvägen 4. **Tel** 0591-340 60. **Open** end of Jun–mid-Aug: daily; other times: Mon–Fri. exhibition.

Loka Brunn
15 km (9 miles) S of Grythyttan. **Tel** 0591-631 00. Pool: **Open** daily. Museum: **Open** summer only. museum.

㉘ Nora

Västmanland. 6,500. to Örebro, then bus. Station House on Norasjön side, 0587-811 20. Nora Festival (1st week in Jul), Noramarken fair (4th weekend in Aug). **nora.se**

This idyllic wooden town is an ideal place to stroll around, with its cobbled streets and charming shops, many in 18th-century buildings. **Göthlinska Gården** (1793) is an interesting museum furnished in the style of a middle-class family home from around 1900.

The highlight of the Nora mining area's monuments is **Pershyttan**, 3 km (2 miles) west of the centre, where the charcoal blast furnace dates from 1856. In summer, a steam train operates from Nora on the Nora Bergslags Veteranjärnväg, Sweden's first normal-gauge railway. Nora's train sheds house historic steam trains, diesel engines and carriages.

Kopparberg's old mining community, now an idyllic wooden village

EASTERN GÖTALAND

The three provinces of Östergötland, Småland and Öland, which make up Eastern Götaland, each retain their own distinctive character. Östergötland is the agricultural heart of Sweden, Småland is the centre of glassmaking and Öland attracts sun-seekers and nature lovers. They are all popular tourist areas typified by their little red cottages and historical sights, quiet lakes and great coastlines.

In north Östergötland, the major towns of Norrköping and Linköping are almost part of Greater Stockholm. Once beyond the steep hills of Kolmården, which form the northern border, flat agricultural land extends as far as the eye can see. Besides being the granary of Sweden, this is historical soil – it was here that the royal Folkung dynasty had its roots and it was here that Birgitta Gudmarsson (St Bridget) advised the political and religious leaders of the 14th century.

The hills north of Gränna and the ruins of Brahehus castle mark the beginning of Småland. For a long time Småland formed the border with Denmark and it was from this region that Nils Dacke led a peasants' revolt in the 16th century. The land is poorer and stonier than Östergötland with small farms and crofters. Mass emigration drained the area of thousands of people during the famine of the 19th century. However, Småland has had its success stories: it is the ideal location for one of its major industries, glassworking, which relies on timber and water. The landscape has also been immortalized in the books of Astrid Lindgren, who was born in the province and turned the place where she grew up into a playground for her popular children's characters, Emil and Pippi Longstocking.

The region's archipelago is a favourite with boat-lovers, stretching south from the Sankta Annas islands in Östergötland through the Kalmarsund between Småland and Öland. Thanks to Ölandsbron bridge, the long narrow island of Öland is easily accessible. Holiday-makers are drawn to its sandy beaches, while botanists head for the Alvar plain and ornithologists for Ottenby bird station.

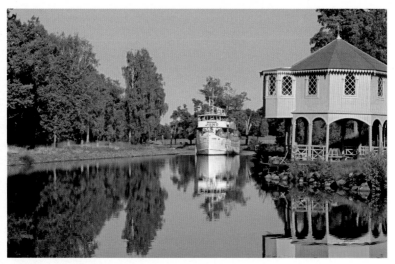

The peaceful Göta Canal at Borensberg

◀ Sailing boats in Västervik harbour, Småland

Exploring Eastern Götaland

This is too big an area to explore in just a few days, but by leaving the major roads and heading cross-country it is possible to have a taste of the different provinces. The Royal Route, or Eriksgatan, created in 2005, has a historical theme and is marked on maps of the region available in any service station or tourist office. Cycling is also an excellent way to see the region, and cruising in comfort on the Göta Canal *(see pp150–51)* offers an unforgettable experience. For a tour of the Kingdom of Crystal *(see p156)* a car is almost essential, but otherwise Småland has countless canoeing routes, lakes for swimming and sights along small forested roads ideally explored by bike.

The mythical Omberg on Lake Vättern seen from Brahehus castle *(see p154)*

Key

═══ Motorway
─── Major road
∷∷∷ Minor road
╍╍╍ Main railway
─── Minor railway
△ Summit

Getting Around

The main artery for traffic in this part of the country is the E4 which passes west of Växjö, via the cities of Norrköping, Linköping and Jönköping, on its way south towards Helsingborg. The E22 runs along the coast, leaving the E4 at Norrköping and continuing via Västervik and Kalmar to Malmö. The larger towns, both on the coast and inland, can be reached by train, but local buses or a car will be needed to visit places in the countryside. There are domestic flights to all major cities.

For additional map symbols *see back flap*

Örebro
MEDEVI BRUNN ⑤
Övralid
Motala
VADSTENA ⑥
Mjölby
OMBERG ⑦
Vättern
Ödeshög
Boxholm
Tranås
Visingsö
⑧ GRÄNNA
Somn
Gothenburg
Bankeryd
Aneby
JÖNKÖPING ⑨
Huskvarna
Forserum
Taberg 343m
EKSJÖ ⑩
Nässjö
Stensjön
Vaggeryd
Vetlanda
Skillingaryd
Gnosjö
Sävsjö
Gislaved
Anderstorp
Vrigstad
Smålandsstenar
Värnamo
SMÅLAND
Vidöstern
Bor
Lammhult
Nissan
Helgasjön
Rydaholm
Lagan
Alvesta
KIN
Bölmen
VÄXJÖ
Ljungby
Hovmantor
Vislanda
Rott
Halmstad
Åsnen
Traryd
Tingsr
Strömsnäsbruk
Älmhult
120
Mien
Helsingborg
Karlshamn

0 kilometres   50
0 miles   30

Katrineholm

Rejmyre

55

Stockholm

nspang Åby E4

1 KOLMÅRDENS
DJURPARK

Skärblacka *Glan* **2** NORRKÖPING

Roxen **4** 209

oro GÖTA CANAL Söderköping Arkösund

3 LINKÖPING
E22

TERGÖTLAND

Valdemarsvik

34 Åtvidaberg

forsa

sa *Asunden* Edsbruk

Överum Loftahammar

Horn Gamleby

34

Södra Vi 40 **14** VÄSTERVIK
Ankarsrum

MERBY **13**

Mariannelund E22

Hultsfred

Målilla Kristdala Fårtö

Mörlunda OSKARSHAMN **20** BYXELKROK
34 37 **15**

Fågelfors **16** BLÅ
JUNGFRUN

hult Högsby Påskallavik Löttorp
37 34 136

Mönsterås

Målerås 125 ÖLAND

31 Pataholm *Kalmarsund* **19** BORGHOLM

RYSTAL Nybro Soliden
25 25 136

21 ÖLANDS
MUSEUM

Emmaboda KALMAR **17** **18** FÄRJESTADEN

Mörbylånga

Vissefjärda **22** STORA
ALVARET
28

Torsås Kastlösa
E22 136

Karlskrona Grönhögen **23** EKETORPS BORG

24 ÖLAND'S SOUTHERN
CAPE

Alvastra Monastery, founded by French
Cistercians in 1143

Grazing land on Öland with some of the island's 400 preserved
windmills in the background

Sights at a Glance

1 Kolmårdens Djurpark
2 Norrköping
3 Linköping
4 *Göta Canal pp150–51*
5 Medevi Brunn
6 Vadstena
7 Omberg
8 Gränna
9 Jönköping
10 Eksjö
11 Växjö
13 Vimmerby
14 Västervik
15 Oskarshamn
16 Blå Jungfrun
17 Kalmar
18 Färjestaden
19 Borgholm
20 Byxelkrok
21 Ölands Museum
22 Stora Alvaret
23 Eketorps Borg
24 Öland's Southern Cape

Tour
12 Kingdom of Crystal

Lion on the prowl in the Safari Park at Kolmårdens Djurpark

❶ Kolmårdens Djurpark

Östergötland. Junction from E4, 12 km (7 miles) N of Norrköping. 🚌 🚈
ℹ️ 010-708 70 00. **Open** May: 10am–5pm daily; Jun–Aug: 10am–6pm daily; Sep: 10am–5pm Sat–Sun. 🎫 🚻 ♿ ☕ 🅿️ W **kolmarden.com**

Kolmårdens Djurpark is no ordinary zoo, even the animal enclosures are large and attractively landscaped.

There is a drive-through Safari Park which brings visitors close to the creatures of the savannah who live here alongside Nordic species such as brown bears and wolves.

A Dolphinarium offers spectacular shows with trained dolphins. Snakes and crocodiles inhabit the outdoor Tropicarium, while the Aparium is designed so that the apes can be viewed indoors and out. Tiger World, offers a unique walk-through experience in close proximity to the big cats. A cable-car ride provides a bird's-eye view of the grounds.

There are a variety of accomodation options available for visitors including African tents on the savannah.

❷ Norrköping

Östergötland. E4. 🚏 128,000. 🚌 🚈
ℹ️ Dalsgatan 9, 011-15 50 00.
🎭 Norrköping International Horse Show (4th week in May), National Day Festival (first week in Jun).
W **destination.norrkoping.se**

In the 17th century the skills of entrepreneur Louis de Geer, combined with water power from the Motala Ström river system, transformed Norrköping into Sweden's first industrial town. Norrköping and neighbouring Linköping make up Sweden's fourth largest urban region.

Although Norrköping is an industrial town, the mix of old and new buildings, parks and trams make it an attractive place to visit. On a small island in Motala Ström sits **Arbetets museet** (Museum of Labour), in an old spinning mill known as Strykjärnet (the Iron).

Environs

The area has a long history of habitation - around 1,650 carvings, some dating back to 1000 BC, can be seen at **Himmelstalund** on the edge of town. About 10 km (6 miles) south of Norrköping on the E4 is the 17th-century **Löfstad Slott** with its beautiful English-style park. The castle remains as it was in 1926 on the death of the owner, Emelie Piper.

🏛️ **Arbetets museet**
Laxholmen. **Tel** 011-18 98 00.
Open daily. **Closed** public hols.
🚻 ☕ ♿ 🅿️

🏠 **Löfstad Slott**
10 km (6 miles) S of Norrköping.
Tel 011-33 50 67. **Open** Jun–Aug: daily; May: Sat, Sun, public holidays; Apr, Sep, Oct: Sun; Nov–Mar: phone for info. 🎫 🚻 ♿ 🅿️

Strykjärnet (the Iron) in Norrköping, housing Arbetets museet

❸ Linköping

Östergötland. E4. 🚏 150,000. 🚌 🚈
🚏 ℹ️ Storgatan 15, 013-190 00 70.
🎭 Ekenäs Castle Tournament (Whitsun), Folk Music Festival (Oct).
W **visitlinkoping.se**

The county capital and cathedral city of Linköping lies in the middle of the Östgöta plain. First populated 3,000 years ago, it is now Sweden's fifth largest city, and is known for its university and high-tech industry.

Construction of the **Domkyrkan** (Cathedral) started in the mid-13th century. The interior contains superb medieval stone carvings. The Renaissance altarpiece is by the Dutch painter M J Van Heemskerck (1498–1574).

The old town open-air museum, **Gamla Linköping**, is a collection of 80 buildings from the city and surrounding area. This charming setting, complete with picturesque wooden buildings, cobbled streets and gardens, is a window on a past way of life.

Malmen, site of Sweden's first military flying school (1911), is now home to the **Flygvapenmuseum** (Swedish Air Force Museum). Exhibits include examples of Swedish military aircraft.

Environs

Kaga Kyrka, one of the region's best-preserved medieval churches, is located on the Svartån river south of Linköping. Dating from the 12th century, its walls are decorated with frescoes.

On Erlången lake, 10 km (6 miles) southeast of the centre, lies the castle of **Sturefors**, which is renowned for its 18th-century interiors and beautiful grounds. The castle is a private residence, but parts of the grounds are open to the public.

🏠 **Domkyrkan**
St Persgatan. **Tel** 013-20 50 50.
Open daily. 📷 phone for info. ♿ 🏠

🏠 **Gamla Linköping**
2 km (3 miles) west of the centre.
Tel 013-12 11 10. **Open** daily. 🅿️
🚻 ☕

Flygvapenmuseum
4 km (3 miles) west of the centre.
Tel 013-28 35 67. **Open** Sep–May:
Tue–Sun; Jun–Aug: daily.
phone for details.

❹ Göta Canal
See pp150–51.

❺ Medevi Brunn
Östergötland. Road 50.
0141-911 00. Grötlunken marching
band processions (Jun/Jul).

In the 17th-century the scientist
and doctor Urban Hjärne
analyzed water from the Medevi
spring and declared it to be
"superior to other medication".
Thus began the transformation
of Medevi Brunn into a health
spa. Today, the season at Medevi
starts at Midsummer and lasts
for seven weeks, during which
time the traditional brass
sextet Brunnsorkester
performs daily concerts.
    South of Medevi, on the edge
of Lake Vättern, lies **Övralid**, the
former home of poet and Nobel
laureate Verner von Heidenstam
(1859–1940). Designed by Heidenstam himself, the house has
stunning views across the lake.

Övralid
10 km (6 miles) N of Motala, Road 50.
Tel 0141-22 05 56, 22 00 36. **Open** 15
May–31 Aug: daily. 10am–5pm
on the hour.

Medevi Brunn, the first health spa in the
Nordic countries

Vadstena Slott, built in 1545 for protection against the Danes

❻ Vadstena
Östergötland. Road 50. 5,500.
Castle, 0143-31571.
St Bridget Festival (3rd week in
May), Vadstena Academy Opera
performances (Jul). **vadstena.com**

Situated on Lake Vättern,
Vadstena is dominated by the
abbey, which dates back to the
14th century and St Bridget,
and the mid-16th-century
castle of the Vasa kings.
Cobbled streets, wooden
buildings and glorious gardens
add to the town's character.
    The stately **Vadstena Slott**
was built in 1545 as a fortress
against the Danes and is
surrounded by a moat. As well
as being a museum, the castle
also hosts opera, theatre
performances and concerts.
    The abbey area encompasses
the original abbey, Vadstena
Kloster, established in 1384 and
dissolved after the Reformation
in 1595, and **Vadstena
Klosterkyrka** (1430). This abbey
church houses the relics of
St Bridget and a life-like wooden
sculpture of the saint. It is also
the site of the Pax Mariae
convent, which was founded
in the 1980s and is home to
around ten nuns.

Environs
Less than 20 km (12 miles)
south of Vadstena towards
Skänninge is **Bjälbo Kyrka**,
a late-12th-century church.
Bjälbo is said to be the birth-
place of the founder of
Stockholm, Birger Jarl.

Vadstena Slott
100 m (110 yd) SW of the centre.
Tel 0143-62 16 00. **Open** Sep–May:
Mon–Fri; Jun–Aug: daily.
Jun–Aug.

Vadstena Klosterkyrka
Open daily. **Tel** 0143-31570, 0143-
298 50. Sun. Jun–Aug.

St Bridget, Sweden's Patron Saint
At the age of only 13, Bridget (c.1303–73) was married to local
dignitary Ulf Gudmarsson. She became lady of the manor of Ulvåsa in
Östergötland and the mother of eight children. Even as a child, she
had religious visions and as an adult
made pilgrimages to Santiago de
Compostela in Spain in 1341–2, Rome
in 1349 and Jerusalem in 1372–3.
Some of her visions also had political
themes and Bridget became
influential in the political arena.
In 1370 she gained the Pope's
permission to found a monastic order,
the Brigittine Order. The first nuns
were ordained in 1384. Bridget died
on returning to Rome following her
pilgrimage to Jerusalem in 1374.
Her remains
were taken to Vadstena in 1374.
Canonized in 1391, Bridget is the
patron saint of Sweden, and in 1999
became the patron saint of Europe.

Sculpture of St Bridget in Vadstena
Klosterkyrka

❹ Göta Canal

Opened in 1832, the Göta Canal provided a vital link for transporting timber and iron between Stockholm and Gothenburg. But it was another 100 years before leisure traffic took off on the waterway. Today in summer, the canal bustles with small craft and passenger boats and it is possible to cruise the entire length on the classic *M/S Diana* (1931), *Wilhelm Tham* (1912) and *Juno* (1874). Other boats take passengers along shorter stretches and there are numerous special packages available, such as combining cycling holidays with canal trips. There are guest marinas offering services along the entire length of the canal. Motala is regarded as the "capital" of the canal, and the man behind its construction, Baltzar von Platen (1766–1829), is buried here.

Building the Canal
Karl XIV Johan inspects construction near Berg in Östergötland with Crown Prince Oscar. Baltzar von Platen is standing bare-headed to the left of the king.

Lock-keeper
Several of the lock gates along the stretch of canal which lies in Västergötland are still worked by hand by friendly and patient lock-keepers.

Key

≡ Motorway

▬ Other road

xxx Canal

KEY

① **Karlsborgs Fästning** (see p225), towers above the canal.

② **Sjötorp** on Lake Vänern marks the end point of the canal in Västergötland.

③ **The lake of Roxen** is home to some 260 species of birds, including wetland species, as well as some rarer varieties.

④ **Mem** is the first lock in the canal system on the journey west.

Borensberg
The long-established Göta Hotell is an idyllic summer spot on the canal. Built in 1894, it offers food and accommodation to passers-by.

Bergs Slussar
The staircase of seven locks at Berg raises boats a total of 18 m (59 ft). The spectacle of opening the lock gates always attracts an audience.

Canal Boats
From May to August traditional white boats such as *M/S Juno* ply the canal. Built in 1874, *Juno* is one of the oldest boats afloat with sleeping accommodation still in use.

Climbing from the Baltic to Lake Vanern

"The Blue Band of Sweden" as the Göta Canal is known, is the high point of Swedish engineering history. It took 58,000 men, mainly soldiers, and 22 years to build a waterway across Sweden from the Baltic Sea to join the already completed Trollhättan Canal *(see p221)*, and provide a route through to the Kattegatt. The problem was not simply digging the canal, but coping with a difference in height of around 92 m (301 ft). Completing this mammoth project took more than just spades and advantage was taken of the latest technological innovations – dredgers, hoists, cranes, pile drivers, mortar mills and optical instruments. Most of the machinery was imported from England, but as the project grew, and with it the need for mechanical equipment, Baltzar von Platen eventually took the initiative to set up a factory in Motala where the mechanical equipment could be made or modified. The canal has 58 locks between Mem on the Baltic and Sjötorp on Lake Vänern.

From Mem the canal begins its climb to reach the highest point between Lakes Vättern and Vänern

View over Lake Vättern from Hjässan, the highest point of Omberg

➐ Omberg

Östergötland. 20 km (12 miles) S of Vadstena. 🚌 ⓘ Naturum, Stocklycke, 0144-332 45. **Open** call to check opening times. 🅿 🅱
w visitostergotland.info

Rising mountain-like from the wide Östgöta plains is Omberg. Its highest point is 175 m (574 ft) above Lake Vättern. It is the legendary home of Queen Omma, whose name means "steam" and indeed the fog that often surrounds the hill gives it a mythical quality. Orchid marshes, beech woodlands and ancient forest flourish on the limestone-rich rock. Walking trails cross the area. To the south lies author Ellen Key's home, **Strand**, and the nature reserves of Bokskogen and Stora Lund. On the plains southeast of Omberg is the ruin of **Alvastra Kloster** where St Bridget (see p149) once stayed.

To the east, Omberg slopes down to Lake **Tåkern**, barely 1 m (3 ft) deep and favoured by flocks of geese and cranes in spring and autumn. The **Rökstenen** at Röks Kyrka is a large 9th-century runestone.

🏠 Strand
10 km (6 miles) N of Ödeshög. **Tel** 0144-330 30. **Open** 15 Apr–Midsummer, mid-Aug–mid-Sep: Tue–Sun. 🅿

➑ Gränna

Småland. E4. 🚶 2,600. 🚌 ⓘ Brahegatan 38, 0390-410 10. 🎭 Andrée Festival (2nd week in Jul), County Festival (3rd week in Jul). **w** grm.se

Gränna was at its height in the 17th century in the days of Count Per Brahe, who founded the town and whose plan is still evident today. On the square in the centre of town, **Grenna Museum** has fascinating tales to tell of the tragic expedition to the North Pole headed by the town's famous son Salomon August Andrée in the hot-air balloon *Örnen*. Inspired by Andrée, Gränna has become a centre for balloon flights. The town is also known for its *polkagris* (peppermint rock), an ideal souvenir. The red and white sweet originated in 1859 when widow Amalia Eriksson started a rock factory in the town.

Along the beautiful stretch of the E4 beside Lake Vättern, just north of Gränna, lies the ruined **Brahehus** castle, built for Count Per Brahe in the 1640s. On a clear day Brahehus offers magnificent views over Vättern towards Västergötland on the other side of the lake and **Visingsö**. This flat island can be reached by boat from Gränna. It is the largest island in Lake Vättern, 14 km (9 miles) long and 3 km (2 miles) wide with a

Polkagris

population of 800. In the 12th and 13th centuries the island was the seat of Sweden's first kings, including Magnus Ladulås. Per Brahe built the castle, Visingsborgs Slott, now a ruin and a church on the island in the 17th century. The boat trip from Gränna takes about 25 minutes and the service is frequent in the summer months.

🏛 Grenna Museum
Brahegatan 38–40. **Tel** 0390-410 15. **Open** daily. **Closed** 1 Jan, 24, 25, 31 Dec. 🎭 🅱 🅿 🅱

➒ Jönköping

Småland. E4. 🚶 130,000. 🚊 🚌 ✈ ⓘ Railway station, 036-10 50 50. 🎭 Jönköping Market (dates vary, but usually between May and Jul). **w** jonkoping.se

King Magnus Ladulås granted Jönköping its charter in 1284, by which time the town was already an important trading centre. For a long time Småland formed Sweden's southern border with Denmark, but when the Danes invaded in 1612 the people set fire to their town and fled to Visingsö.

In the 19th century Jönköping became synonymous with matchstick production; the Lundström brothers opened their first factory here in the 1840s. In the old part of town, **Tändsticksmuseet** (the Match Museum) is set in a former match factory (1848). The historic Västra Storgatan 37 houses **Viktor Rydbergs**

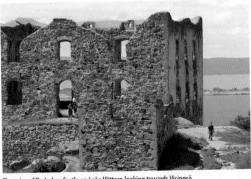
The ruins of Brahehus Castle on Lake Vättern looking towards Visingsö

◀ Passenger boat on the Göta Canal at Borensberg

Museum. Local history comes under the spotlight at **Jönköpings Läns Museum**. The museum also has a display of work by the local artist John Bauer, as well as contemporary art.

Environs

Just outside Jönköping, **Hakarps Kyrka** is famous for its paintings by Edvard Orm. **Taberg**, south of Jönköping, is known as "the Alps of Småland" and is 343 m (1,125 ft) above sea level. The countryside is stunning, with extensive views over Lake Vättern. Sights include a mine and an industrial museum and there are hiking trails and overnight accommodation.

🏛 **Tändsticksmuseet**
Tändsticksgränd 27. **Tel** 036-10 55 43.
Open daily (Sep–May: Tue–Sat).
Closed public hols & eves of public hols. 🐾 📷 📍

🏛 **Jönköpings Läns Museum**
Dag Hammarskjölds Plats 2. **Tel** 036-30 18 00. **Open** Tue–Sun. 🐾 📷 🖥 📍

⑩ Eksjö

Småland. Road 32/40. 🚗 16,000.
🚉 🚌 ℹ Norra Storgatan 29b, 0381-361 70. 🎖 Guard-mounting Parade (summer), Ränneslättsloppet Motocross Race (end Sep), Christmas Market (Dec). 🌐 **visiteksjo.se**

The small town of Eksjö, in the highlands of southern Sweden, is the country's most genuine wooden town. This was border country until the 17th century and Eksjö was burned down by its own people in conjunction with a Danish retreat. In the 1560s Erik XIV drew up a new town plan for Eksjö, which largely remains today. Gamla Stan (the Old Town) escaped the fire and its buildings remain intact and have been sympathetically renovated.

Environs

About 13 km (8 miles) east of Eksjö, the **Skurugata** nature reserve encompasses an impressive canyon in porphyritic rock, 800 m (2,625 ft) long and 35 m (115 ft) deep. From Eksjö to the neighbouring town of

Nässjö is just over 20 km (12 miles). Nässjö owes its existence to the coming of the railway in the 1860s. At that time the village had 57 inhabitants; today it has nearly 30,000 and the railway companies Statens Järnvägar and Banverket are still the main employers. Sights in Nässjö include **Järnvägs-museum** (the Railway Museum) and Hembygdsparken with its woodlands and collection of 18th- and 19th-century buildings.

🏛 **Järnvägsmuseum**
Brogatan 10, Nässjö. **Tel** 0380-722 07.
Open Jun–Aug: 11am–3pm Tue–Sun. 📍

⑪ Växjö

Småland. Road 23/25/27/30.
🚗 62,000. 🚉 🚌 ✈ ℹ Residenset, Stortorget, 0470-73 32 80. 🌐 **vaxjo.se**

A bishopric as early as the 12th century, Växjö was granted its town charter by King Magnus Erikson in 1342. For some time the town lay on the border with Denmark and it was from here that Nils Dacke led his peasant revolt against the King of Sweden in the 16th century. Devastating fires, the most recent in 1843, destroyed the town, which has since been rebuilt. The cathedral dates originally from the end of the

The twin steeples of Växjö's 12th-century cathedral

12th century, but has been remodelled over the centuries. It contains an altar-piece in glass and wood made in 2002 by the glass artist Bertil Vallien.
Smålands Museum, with Sveriges Glasmuseum (Glass Museum), depicts the history of the county of Kronoberg and the development of the glassworks. Next to it is **Utvandrarnas Hus**, which focuses on the mass emigration in the 19th century.

🏛 **Smålands Museum**
Södra Järnvägsgatan 2. **Tel** 0470-70 42 00. **Open** Jun–Aug: daily; Sep–May: Tue–Sun. **Closed** public holidays. 🐾 📷 📍 🖥 ♿

🏛 **Utvandrarnas Hus**
Vilhelm Mobergs Gata 4. **Tel** 0470-201 20. **Open** Sep–Apr: Tue–Sat; May–Aug: daily. 🐾 📷 🖥 📍 ♿

Emigration to America

Disillusioned by poverty, religious intolerance and political discontent, many Swedes in the late 1860s dreamed of a better life in North America. Famine in Sweden, combined with the end of the Civil War in the fast expanding USA, prompted around 100,000 Swedes to emigrate in 1868–71, the majority from southern Sweden, particularly the barren lands of Småland. Another major wave followed in the 1880s when 350,000 people left Sweden.
    Nobel Prize-winner Vilhelm Moberg's epic trilogy The Emigrants describes the tough life Swedish emigrants faced in their new land.
    Emigration to the USA tailed off with the Depression of the 1930s, but by then 1.2 million Swedes had already left their homeland.

Emigrants on the Way to Gothenburg, Geskel Saloman (1821–1902)

⑫ A Tour through the Kingdom of Crystal

Växjö, home to the Swedish Glass Museum, is an ideal starting point for a tour of at least nine of the famous glassworks set in the beautiful countryside between Växjö and Nybro. Access to timber and water accounts for the concentration of glassworks in this area of Småland, where forest, lakes and waterways dominate the landscape. The glassworks are mostly only 20–30 km (12–20 miles) apart, and many have shops offering discounted items and displays of the designers' latest creations.

① Bergdala
Bergdala's signature is blue-edged glass, but designers are pushing the boundaries when it comes to colour and shape. The temperature of the smelting oven is a constant 1,150° C (2,102° F).

③ Kosta
The oldest glassworks, Kosta (1742), like Boda and Åfors, has attracted some of Sweden's foremost contemporary designers. Shown here is the entrance to the original office.

② Strömbergshyttan
Studioglas was established in 1987 by three master glassblowers, who work with young designers to create ground-breaking works of art.

Key

▬ Suggested route

═ Other roads

④ Åfors
Bertil Vallien, Ulrica Hydman-Vallien and upcoming artist Ludvig Löfgren work for the glassworks in Fina Stugan, one of the area's most exciting galleries. Glass eggs are by Ulrica Hydman-Vallien.

Tips for Drivers
Tour length: Växjö–Nybro, road 25, approx. 85 km (53 miles). Well signposted.
Places to eat: Many glassworks have a café/restaurant and some of the larger ones hold herring evenings. Check opening times.

0 kilometres   10
0 miles   5

For hotels and restaurants in this area see pp284–289 and pp294–301

⑧ Orrefors

The glassworks was founded in 1898 and has become the flagship of Swedish glassmaking, producing functional, decorative items and *objets d'art*. The work of Orrefors over the years is on show in its museum.

Crystal bowl by Simon Gate (1883–1945)

⑨ Målerås

The employees bought this glassworks from Kosta in 1981. It is famous for its crystal animal reliefs by glass artist and master etcher Mats Jonasson.

⑦ Pukeberg

The glassworks was founded in 1871. Extensive production in this beautiful old setting has mainly been focused on lighting and domestic glassware using traditional methods.

⑤ Johansfors

This glassworks is known as the Eden of the Kingdom of Crystal, symbolized by Christopher Ramsey's *Astrakhan Apple*. Glassblowing is demonstrated daily and there is a museum.

⑥ Boda

The traditional Boda glassworks has been converted into a Kosta Boda factory shop, museum and exhibition area with a special focus on local artist Erik Höglund.

⑬ Vimmerby

Småland. Road 33/34. 🚇 9,000.
🚉 🚌 🄸 Rådhuset 1, 0492-310 10.
🎪 Holiday Race (2nd week in Jul).

The small town of Vimmerby began as a marketplace on the "King's Road" between Stockholm and Kalmar. It was strategically important and constantly fought over by the Danes, who burned it to the ground on many occasions. Few old buildings remain, but along Storgatan there is the austere Neo-Classical-style Rådhuset (Town Hall) from the 1820s. Like the houses of Tenngjutar-gården and Grankvistgården, it is one of Vimmerby's historical monuments.

For many years Vimmerby has been associated with Astrid Lindgren *(see p93)*, who was born in Näs and set many of her popular children's books in this area. All her beloved characters can be encountered in **Astrid Lindgrens Värld** (Astrid Lindgren's World). The park also includes the Astrid Lindgren Centre with an exhibition about the author's life and work.

Environs

Norra Kvill National Park, 20 km (12 miles) northwest of Vimmerby, is an area of virgin forest in the highlands of Småland containing pine trees over 350 years old. The park slopes down to a small lake, Stora Idegölen, with waterlilies and bogbean.

🏠 **Astrid Lindgrens Värld**
Fabriksgatan. **Tel** 0492-798 00.
Open 15 May–end of Aug: daily.
🈺 🅿 📷 ♻ 🏠 ♿ 🅆 alv.se

Miniature house in Astrid Lindgrens Värld, Vimmerby

Picturesque red cottages on Båtsmansgränd in Västervik

⑭ Västervik

Småland. E22. 🔺 21,000. 🚆 🚌 🚢
ℹ️ Rådhuset, Stora Torget, 0490-254
040. 🎵 Song Festival (Jul).
🌐 **vastervik.com**

Strategically sited at the mouth
of Gamlebyviken Bay, Västervik
was the subject of frequent
Danish attacks, despite
protection from the once
mighty fortress of Stegeholm.
The last attack in 1677 destroyed
the town. Rebuilt, it became a
major seafaring centre. The area
known as Gamla Norr contains
the oldest preserved houses in
Västervik, including Aspagården
and the former poor-house,
Cederflychtska Huset.
Västerviks Museum outlines
the history of the town. Part of
the museum is in the open air
with a nature exhibition and
traditional buildings. The railway
line was closed in 1984, but
train enthusiasts have reopened
the 70-km (43-mile) stretch
from Västervik to Hultfred, to
preserve it as part of Sweden's
industrial heritage.

The annual Folk Festival first
took place in 1966 and has
since grown to become a
major event. It is held in the
ruins of Stegeholm fortress.

Lunds By, just outside
Västervik, is the region's oldest
and best preserved village,
comprising eight small red
cottages around a square.
It was chosen as a location
to film Astrid Lindgren's book
The Bullerby Children.

🏛 Västerviks Museum
Kulbacken. **Tel** 0490-211 77. **Open**
Jun–Aug: daily; Sep–May: Mon–Fri,
Sun. 🅿️ 🚻 📷

⑮ Oskarshamn

Småland. E22. 🔺 18,000. 🚆 🚌
ℹ️ Hantverksgatan 3, 0491-770 72.
🎵 Oskarshamn Harbour Festival
(end Jul). 🌐 **oskarshamn.com**

King Oskar I gave his name
to this town, previously known
as Döderhultsvik, which gained
its charter in 1856. Oskarshamn
grew up around the harbour
and today is still an important
place with a lively seafaring
industry. The old areas of
Besväret and Fnyket have
wooden 19th-century houses
and are ideal for a leisurely
exploration on foot. There
are great views over the water
and the island Blå Jungfrun
from Långa Soffan, an extra-
ordinarily long 72-m (79-yd)
bench built close to the
harbour in 1867.

Oskarshamn has several
museums. On display at
Döderhultarmuseet are the
original wooden figures by
sculptor Axel Petersson, also
known as "Döderhultarn",
together with a description of
his life in late-19th-century
Småland. **Oskarshamns
Sjöfartsmuseum** (Maritime

Museum) has a superb
collection of local maritime
history. **Biologiska museet** has a
botanical collection that focuses
mainly on Swedish plants.

Environs
Stensjö By is a cultural museum
showing how a village looked in
the 18th century. Just under
40 km (25 miles) west of
Oskarshamn at Högsby there is
the **Bråbygden** nature reserve
and a permanent exhibition
about film star Greta Garbo,
whose mother came from here.

🏛 Döderhultarmuseet
Hantverksgatan 18. **Tel** 0491-880 40.
Open Jun–Aug: daily; Sep–May: Tue–
Sat. 🅿️ 🚻 📷 📷 ♿

🏛 Oskarshamns Sjöfartsmuseum
Hantverksgatan 18. **Tel** 0491-880 40.
Open Tue–Sat (Jun–Aug: daily).
🅿️ 🚻 📷 📷 ♿

🏛 Biologiska museet
Åsaområdet, Hus B (Hantverksgatan
64), plan 3. **Tel** 0491-771 61.
Open Tue–Fri. 🌐 **bimon.se**

⑯ Blå Jungfrun

Småland. 20 km (12 miles) E of
Oskarshamn. 🚢 from Oskarshamn &
Byxelkrok. ℹ️ Oskarshamn Tourist
Office, 0491-770 72.

In the northern part of
Kalmarsund, the sound
separating the mainland from
the island of Öland, the national
park Blå Jungfrun (the Blue
Maiden) encompasses an island
about 800 m (875 yd) in
diameter and the waters
surrounding it. Blå Jungfrun's
highest point is 86 m (282 ft)
above sea level, making it easily
visible from the mainland and
from Öland.

According to legend, the
island is the site of Blåkulla,
home of the witches, and is the
subject of many a dark tale.
Carl von Linné (*see p134*)
described it as "horrible".
Others have found it
romantic, including the poet
Verner von Heidenstam, who
was married here in
1896. The island is
mainly bare pink
granite, polished
smooth by ice and

An expressive carved wooden figure by "Döderhultarn"
Axel Petersson (1865–1925)

Medieval Kalmar Slott, a beautifully preserved castle rebuilt in Renaissance style in the 16th century

water, with deciduous forest in the south and a population of black guillemots. It is unlikely that it was inhabited, although a stone labyrinth was built here and there are caves. Boats run from Oskarshamn or Byxelkrok (*see p160*) to Blå Jungfrun, once a day, weather permitting. The journey takes 90 minutes from Oskarshamn with a three-and-a-half-hour stay on the island.

⑰ Kalmar

Småland. E22. 🚏 35,000. 🚉 🚌 ✈
ℹ Ölandskajen 9, 0480-41 77 00.
🎭 Kalmar Market (1st week in Jul), Kalmar City Festival (2nd weekend in Aug). 🌐 **kalmar.com**

Founded in the 12th century, Kalmar's key position on Kalmarsund made it a flourishing trading post as well as a target for Danish attack. To prevent the latter, **Kalmar Slott** was built in 1200 and it was here in the castle that the Kalmar Union was formed in 1397, binding the Scandinavian kingdoms for 130 years (*see p39*). In 1523 Gustav Vasa gained control of Kalmar and fortified the town.

Today, the magnificent Renaissance castle has been restored and contains furnished apartments and exhibitions. With its twisting streets and 17th and 18th-century buildings, the area around the castle, Gamla Stan (Old Town), is made for walking. Next to the castle is **Kalmar Konstmuseum** (Art Museum) showing Swedish art.

The Italian Baroque **Domkyrkan** (cathedral) on the island of Kvarnholmen dates from the second half of the 17th century and was designed by Tessin the Elder. In front of

it is the square Stortorget, restored to its original austere appearance. Kvarnholmen is also home to **Kalmar Läns Museum** with the man-of-war *Kronan* and out on "Kattrumpan" **Kalmar Sjöfartsmuseum**, featuring 5,000 maritime exhibits.

Environs
Ölandsbron, the bridge across Kalmarsund, opened in 1972 and provided a major boost for tourism to Öland. The bridge is 6,072 m (19,921 ft) long, 13 m (43 ft) wide and a sight in its own right. Nearly 35 km (22 miles) north of Kalmar on the coast is the idyllic village of **Pataholm**, a shipbuilding and seafaring community dating from the Middle Ages, with well-preserved historic buildings and cobbled streets.

🏰 **Kalmar Slott**
Kungsgatan 1. **Tel** 0480-45 14 90
Open May–Sep: daily; other times: weekends. 🔲 🔲 🔲 🔲

🏛 **Kalmar Konstmuseum**
Slottsvägen 1D. **Tel** 0480-42 62 82.
Open Tue–Sun. **Closed** some public hols. 🔲 🔲 pre-book.

🏛 **Kalmar Läns Museum**
Skeppsbrogatan 51. **Tel** 0480-45 13 00.
Open daily. **Closed** some public hols. 🔲 🔲 pre-book. 🔲 🔲

⑱ Färjestaden

Öland. Road 136. 🚏 4,500. 🚌
ℹ Turistvägen, 0485-56 06 00.
🎭 Victoria Day (14 Jul).

The Ölandsbron Bridge connects Färjestaden on Öland with the mainland. Since the bridge's arrival in the 1970s, Färjestaden has more or less become a suburb of Kalmar. The first turning to the north

in Färjestaden leads to **Ölands Djurpark**, a popular destination for families. The zoo has 200 species of animals, a water world and amusement park, circus and theatre performances.

Beijershamn, south of Färjestaden, is an interesting reed-covered birdwatching area with wetland and archipelago species. Not far from here is **Karlevistenen**, a remarkable 11th-century runestone dedicated to a hero named Sibbe the Wise.

Vickleby village street, on road 136 to the south, is the epitome of idyllic Öland. Next to the church is Capellagården School of Craft and Design, founded by furniture designer Carl Malmsten in the 1950s and currently a centre for various design-related courses. The school exhibits and sells students' work.

East of Färjestaden, in the forest, is the Iron Age fort of **Gråborg** with the medieval ruins of St Knut's chapel just outside it.

🦓 **Ölands Djurpark**
3 km (2 miles) N of Färjestaden.
Tel 0485-392 22, info 0485-308 73.
Open early May–Sep: 10am–4pm daily. 🔲 🔲 🔲 🔲 🔲

A gigantic clown at the entrance to Ölands Djurpark

Solliden, the king's summer residence, whose park is open to the public

⑲ Borgholm

Öland. Road 136. ⛰ 3,200. 🚌
ℹ Sandgatan 25, 0485-890 00.
🎪 Victoria Day 14 Jul.

In summer Borgholm town centre bustles with shoppers and boats fill the guest harbour. Borgholm became a seaside resort at the end of the 19th century and some of the older buildings still have their ornamented wooden verandas where gentlemen enjoyed their coffee and punsch at the beginning of the last century.

Dominating the town is **Borgholms Slottsruin**, a vast ruined medieval castle with an eventful historical past. There is a museum inside. Guides recount the history of the ruins and offer special tours for children in summer. Also in summer, the castle stage is a popular venue for concerts.

Environs
Just south of the centre lies **Sollidens Slott**, the summer residence of the Swedish royal family, completed in 1906. On 14 July each year, the birthday of Crown Princess Victoria is celebrated here with various events. Exhibitions are held in the pavilion and there is a palace gift shop.

Störlinge Kvarnrad, a row of seven windmills on the eastern coast road, is just a sample of the 400 windmills still standing on the island. There is around 150 km (93 miles) of beaches around Borgholm, two of the best being Köpingsvik and Böda.

🏛 Borgholms Slottsruin
1 km (half a mile) S of Borgholm.
Tel 0485-123 33. **Open** Apr–Sep: daily;
Oct–Mar: by appointment. 🚫 📷 🏠
🚫 📷 ♿

🏛 Solliden
1.5 km (1 mile) S of Borgholm.
Tel 0485-153 56. **Open** mid-May–
mid-Sep: daily. 🚫 📷 ▢ 🏠 ♿

⑳ Byxelkrok

Öland. Road 136. ⛰ 200. 🚌
ℹ Öland Tourist Information,
0485-560 600.

Almost at the northernmost end of Öland's west coast on Kalmarsund is the popular old fishing village of Byxelkrok. Boats to Blå Jungfrun (see p158) depart from here.

About 5 km (3 miles) to the north is **Neptuni Åkrar**, an area of ridged stones resemb-ling ploughed fields with several ancient monuments, including the Iron Age stone ship Forgalla-skeppet.

Löttorp, the largest town in northern Öland, is home to a paradise for car-mad children – **Lådbilslandet** (Boxcar Country),

The island Blå Jungfrun (see p158) seen from Byxelkrok harbour

Glabo Gocart. Here youngsters can race round the 6-km (4-mile) course in motorized vehicles, attend driving school or enjoy the playground.

Böda, 10 km (6 miles) north of Löttorp, has wonderful sandy beaches. It is also the site of **Skäftekärr Järnåldersby**, a reconstructed Iron Age village. Complete with goods, animals, houses and people, it provides a fascinating insight into Iron Age life.

The village also has an arboretum featuring a collection of Thuja occidentalis planted in the late 19th century.

🏛 Lådbilslandet
40 km (25 miles) N of Borgholm.
Tel 0485-203 35. **Open** mid-Jun–mid-
Aug: daily. 🚫 📷 ▢ 🏠

🏛 Skäftekärr Järnåldersby
50 km (31 miles) N of Borgholm.
Tel 0485-221 11. **Open** end Jun–Aug:
daily; other times: call to check.
🚫 📷 ▢ 🏠

㉑ Ölands Museum

Öland. 20 km (12 miles) NE of
Färjestaden. 🚌 ℹ 0485-56 10 22.
Open May–Aug: 11am–5.30pm daily;
Sep: 11am–5pm weekends. 🚫 📷
▢ 🏠

Himmelsberga, in the centre of the island, is home to Ölands Museum, an open-air museum of art and cultural history. It centres around a well-preserved linear village with 18th- and 19th-century farms. The interiors of the houses show how life was once lived, and pigs, chickens and sheep are kept in the grounds. A shop sells crafts and books about Öland. Next to the museum is a gallery showing work by local artists. North of Himmelsberga, **Gärdslösa Kyrka** is one of the most interesting churches on Öland. It dates from the mid-13th century and has excellent limestone murals, a beautiful votive ship and a 17th-century pulpit.

The fort of **Ismantorps Borg** in Långlöt has been

dated to the 5th century. Archaeological finds show that it was probably an important marketplace and cult site. It is encircled by a wall up to 6 m (19 ft) thick and 3 m (10 ft) high with nine gates.

Öland's best preserved row of windmills can be seen in Lerkaka, just to the south of Himmelsberga. The interesting **Lerkaka Linmuseum** shows how linen is made.

🏛 **Lerkaka Linmuseum**
25 km (16 miles) NE of Färjestaden. **Tel** 0485-56 20 90. **Open** Midsummer–Aug: daily.

㉒ Stora Alvaret

Öland. 🚌 *i* Ölands Turist, 0485-56 06 00.

The extraordinary limestone plain of Stora Alvaret dominates southern Öland. Here, the bedrock is around 400 million years old and is covered in a thin layer of soil that was used from prehistoric times as grazing land. In the year 2000 the area was declared a UNESCO World Heritage Site.

In spring the ground is covered in pasque flowers (*Pulsatilla pratensis*). The dominant species include meadow oat-grass (*Helictotrichon pratense*), sheep's fescue (*Festuca ovina*) and a moss species, *kalkbackmossa* (*Homalothecium lutescens*). Juniper bushes are common and lichen inches over bare rock.

The extreme climate has created almost desert-like conditions to which the flora and fauna have had to adapt.

Mountain and Mediterranean plants grow here as well as a unique species of rock-rose (*Helianthemum oelandicum*). The island is a resting place for cranes, but conditions on the plain are so harsh that only a few birds, such as the skylark and wheatear, have succeeded in adapting to the environment.

㉓ Eketorps Borg

Öland. 🚌 *i* 0485-66 20 00. **Open** May–Aug; see website for hours. **Closed** Midsummer's Eve. 🅿 🚾 **eketorp.se**

The only one of Öland's ancient forts to have been completely excavated, Eketorps Borg was built in three stages. It originated in the 4th century to protect the population and was later converted into a fortified farming village with military functions, but was abandoned in the 7th century. It was thrust into use again at the end of the 12th century in the war between the royal houses of Erik and Sverker.

The fort has been partly reconstructed to show how people lived and worked in the Iron Age. In the museum the numerous artifacts uncovered on the site are on display, including jewellery and weapons.

Around 10 km (6 miles) north of Eketorp lies **Seby Gravfält** with no fewer than 285 visible ancient monuments in the form of different kinds of burial sites, mainly dating from the Iron Age.

Långe Jan at Öland's Southern Cape, Sweden's tallest lighthouse

㉔ Öland's Southern Cape

Öland. 🚌 *i* Ottenby Naturum, 0485-66 12 00 (Jun–Aug: daily). 🅿

In the mid-16th century the area around Öland's southern cape became a royal hunting ground and even today descendants of the fallow deer introduced by Johan III in 1569 can be spotted. The northern boundary of his land is marked by Karl X's wall, built in the 1650s to prevent local people and their animals from entering the grounds. To the south, Sweden's oldest and tallest lighthouse, **Långe Jan**, stands to attention, 41.6 m (136 ft) high, and offers amazing views.

At the southernmost tip of the island is a nature reserve, Ottenby Naturum, and **Ottenby Fågelstation** (the bird station). Ornithologists come here to study migratory birds close up and conduct research. The station has several bird-related exhibitions and offers guided tours around the nature reserve.

🐦 **Ottenby Fågelstation**
Öland's Southern Cape. **Tel** 0485-66 10 93. **Open** Mar–Oct: daily. 🅿 🚻 Set guided bird tours mid-Mar–mid-Nov. 🖥

Look out for hedgehogs, a threatened species

The mighty walls of Eketorps Borg, a partly reconstructed Iron Age fort

GOTLAND

Sweden's largest island, Gotland is a popular holiday destination, favoured for its mild climate, sandy beaches, distinctive landscape and beautiful walled town of Visby. It is known as the "Pearl of the Baltic". The island's strategic position made it an important trading centre especially in the Middle Ages. Gotland celebrates its heritage with enthusiasm in the annual Visby Medieval Week.

In geological terms, Gotland is fairly old. It consists of layers of rocks which were deposited in a tropical sea during the Silurian period around 400 million years ago. Fossils can still be found washed up along the shore. At the northern and southernmost tips of the island, the limestone comes to the surface and plant life is sparse. In the centre of the island forest dominates. The high limestone cliffs with their large bird population are broken by sandy beaches beloved by sun-worshippers, and standing offshore are numerous extraordinary sea stacks, known as *raukar*.

The long, warm autumns and mild winters allow trees such as walnut and apricot to survive in sheltered spots. No less than 35 different orchids can be found on the island and the flower meadows which blossom at Midsummer are typical of Gotland. The island's fauna lacks the large mammals of the mainland. The odd fallow deer is probably an escapee from an enclosure, but there is a herd of *russ,* Gotland's little wild ponies, as well as foxes and wild rabbits.

A wealth of archaeological finds have been uncovered on the island, from the ship burials of the Bronze Age to the silver treasure of the Viking period. More than 90 medieval churches dot the landscape and the museums have numerous artifacts from the Hanseatic period and the Danish King Valdemar Atterdag's capture of Visby in 1361. Visby itself is a UNESCO World Heritage Site.

Gotlanders have their own dialect, *Gutamål*, and their own traditions. These are especially reflected in the games of the annual Gotland Olympics and in the Medieval Week in Visby *(see p33)*, a 21st-century recreation of the Middle Ages with tournaments, jesters and fair maidens.

Hoburgen in southern Gotland, a 35-m (115-ft) high limestone cliff containing red "Hoburg" marble

◀ Almedalen Park and the spires of Domkyrkan Sta Maria, Visby

Exploring Gotland

A visit to Gotland naturally begins in Visby, where the ferry terminal and airport are located. To experience this unusual part of Sweden it is best to strike out into the countryside and discover the exceptional landscape with its distinctive flora, long sandy beaches, curious limestone sea stacks and multitude of medieval churches. Hiring a bike and cycling round Gotland is a popular way of seeing the island. There are almost no hills and car-free country lanes constantly lead to new hideaways. There is plenty of bed-and-breakfast accommodation and the island has many good campsites for those with tents or caravans. Bookings should be made well in advance for the month of July.

A ruined medieval church towering above the Visby rooftops

Sights at a Glance

1 Fårö
2 Bunge
3 Slite
4 Tingstäde
5 Lummelundagrottan
6 Bro Kyrka
7 *Visby pp168–71*
8 Roma
9 Ljugarn
10 Lojsta
11 Fröjel Kyrka
12 Karlsöarna
13 Petes
14 Hoburgen
15 Gotska Sandön

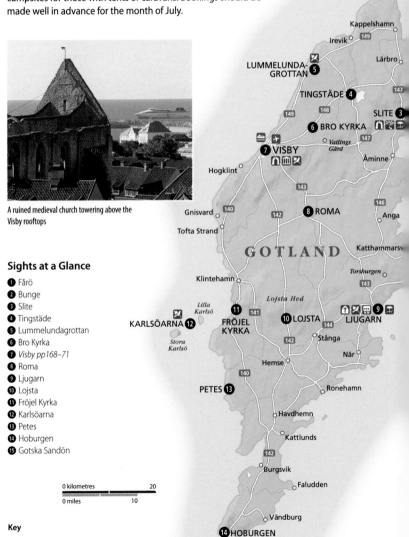

Kappelshamn
Irevik
Kappelshamn 149
Lärbro
LUMMELUNDA-GROTTAN 5
TINGSTÄDE 4
147
148
SLITE 3
149
6 BRO KYRKA
147
7 VISBY
Vatlings Gård
Hogklint
Åminne
143
Gnisvard 140
142
8 ROMA
146
Anga
Tofta Strand

G O T L A N D
Katthammars

Torsburgen
Klintehamn
Lojsta Hed
143

Lilla Karlsö
141
11 FRÖJEL KYRKA
10 LOJSTA
9 LJUGARN
KARLSÖARNA 12
144
Stora Karlsö
142
Stånga
När
Hemse
140
Ronehamn
PETES 13

Havdhemn

Kattlunds
142

Burgsvik
Faludden

0 kilometres   20
0 miles   10

Vändburg
14 HOBURGEN

Key

━━━ Motorway

━━━ Major road

═══ Minor road

For additional map symbols *see back flap*

Sheep in front of a typical Gotland farmhouse, today a tempting renovation project for incomers from the mainland

Getting Around

The most common way to get to Gotland is by ferry or fast catamaran, either from Nynäshamn or Oskarshamn. In summer there are several crossings a day to Visby. Another option is to arrive by air on one of the daily flights from Stockholm, Norrköping or Nyköping. On Gotland, the only means of public transport is the bus. Services outside Visby are infrequent with perhaps just one morning and one afternoon bus, making a car or a bike a necessity for getting around. Bicycles can be hired at the ferry terminal and elsewhere around the island.

One of Gotland's many long sandy beaches attracting hundreds of thousands of visitors to the island every summer

❶ Fårö

Gotland. 🚶 600. 🚢 ℹ️ Mar–Sep: at Fårö church 0498-22 40 22; Oct–Feb: Visby Tourist Office, 0498-20 17 00.
Ⓦ **gotland.info**

A summer paradise for visitors from the mainland and further afield, Fårö appears exotic even to a Gotlander from the main island. Lying at the northern tip of Gotland, the little island of Fårö has a language and traditions all of its own. During the summer car ferries shuttle back and forth on the 15-minute trip from Fårösund to Broa. At other times of year the service is more limited.

Sparse, low pine forest and moorland with swamp and marshland cover the island. There are sheep everywhere. Off the main road between Broa and Fårö lighthouse there are plenty of cattle grids, which prevent the sheep from straying.

Off the northwest coast are the spectacular limestone stacks, known as *raukar*, of Langhammars and Digerhuvud. The sand dune of Ullahau is at the northern end of the island, and Sudersand's long sandy beach is popular with holiday-makers. The easternmost cape of Holmudden is topped by the 30-m (98-ft) high lighthouse, Fårö Fyr. Roughly in the centre of the island, **Fårö Kyrka** offers stunning views over the inlet of Kyrkviken. The church contains votive paintings dating from 1618 and 1767, depicting seal hunters miraculously being rescued from the sea.

🏛 **Fårö Kyrka**
5 km (3 miles) N of Broa. **Tel** 0498-22 10 74. **Open** Jun–Aug: daily; Sep–May: Sat & Sun. 🏛 📷 by appointment.

"The coffee pot", an eroded limestone stack on Fårö's coast

❷ Bunge

Gotland. Road 148. 🚌 900. 🚐
ℹ️ Fårösund, 0498-22 11 12.
🎪 Tournament (2nd week in Jul).

The village of Bunge is renowned for its 14th-century church **Bunge Kyrka**, built in Gothic style. Its tower was constructed in the 13th century to defend an earlier church – holes from pikes and arrows in the north wall bear witness to past battles.

Inside are beautiful limestone paintings dating from around 1400, which are thought to depict the Teutonic Knights fighting the Vitalien brothers, pirates of Mecklenburg who occupied Gotland in the 1390s. In the chancel is a poor box in limestone signed by stonemason Lafrans Botvidarson. Like the font, it dates from the 13th century.

Next to the church is **Bungemuseet**, one of Sweden's largest rural museums. It was created in 1917 by Bunge schoolteacher Theodor Erlandsson, who wanted to show how the people of Gotland used to live. In the fields next to the school he gathered together cottages, buildings and cultural objects from different parts of Gotland covering the 17th, 18th and 19th centuries as well as four carved stones from the 8th century. The museum hosts many events in the summer,

8th-century picture stone, Bungemuseet

including medieval tournaments, markets and handicraft festivals. In Snäckersstugan cottage, with the date 1700 carved into the gable, visitors can enjoy a cup of coffee and attempt to make out the Gotland proverbs painted on the ceiling.

Just north of Bunge is the busy **Fårösund**, one of the larger towns in northern Gotland with around 1,000 inhabitants. For many years the area was dominated by the military and countless young men were drilled here in defence of the island. Since the coastal artillery unit was disbanded in 2000 with the loss of many jobs, the area risks going into decline.

🏛 Bunge Kyrka
60 km (37 miles) N of Visby.
Tel 0498-22 10 74 (Tue & Fri). **Open** mid-Jun–Aug: daily. 🏛 every other Sun.

🏛 Bungemuseet
2 km (1 mile) E of Bunge. **Tel** 0498-22 10 18. **Open** Jun–Sep: daily. 📷 ring for appointment. 📷 🖥 📷

❸ Slite

Gotland. Road 147. 🚗 1,500. 🚌 ⛴
ℹ️ Gotlands Tourist Information Centre, 0498-20 17 00. 🏌 Golf round Gotland (2nd week in May).

Occupying a stunning setting in a bay facing its own archipelago is the town of Slite. It is the second largest community in Gotland. Slite had a long and troubled history from the Viking

Majestic limestone stack at Kyllaj, Slite Bay

period onwards, and development only really took off in the late 19th century with an upturn in seafaring. Today the town is dominated by a cement factory.

In summer, the fine sandy beaches, harbour, tennis courts, stunning stone stacks and lime kiln attract holiday-makers. The islands offshore are perfect for short trips, including Enholmen with Karlsvärd fortress, which dates from 1853–6.

Environs
On the opposite side of the bay is Hellvi, with the delightful old harbour of **Kyllaj**. The quiet beach is in a beautiful setting overlooking weathered sea stacks. Strandridaregården, the 18th-century coastguard's house, now belongs to Bungemuseet.

Northwest of Slite is **Lärbro Kyrka**, a mid-13th century church with an 11th-century watch tower next to it. In the churchyard are buried 44 of the former prisoners of war who came from the German concentration camps to the hospital at Lärbro in 1945.

St Olofsholm, nearby, is dedicated to Olav the Holy who visited Gotland in 1029 to convert the island to Christianity. In medieval times it was a place of pilgrimage. This is also the site of Ytterholmen's large group of limestone stacks and a glorious pebble beach.

🏛 Lärbro Kyrka
10 km (6 miles) N of Slite. **Tel** 0498-22 51 25. **Open** 15 May–30 Sep: daily.
🏛 every other Sun. 📷 🖥 📷 ♿

Buildings at Bungemuseet with thatched roofs of Gotland sedge

For hotels and restaurants in this area see pp284–289 and pp294–301

❹ Tingstäde

23 km (14 miles) N of Visby. 🚌 280.
🚌 ℹ️ Gotland Tourist Information
Centre, 0498-20 17 00. 📷 Nature trail
with lady's slipper in flower (early Jun).

Halfway between Visby and
Fårösund on road 148 lies
Tingstäde, a community
best-known for its sea rescue
radio station and its marsh.
The church dating from the
13th and 14th centuries has
one of the highest towers
on the island.

Tingstäde marsh is, in fact,
a shallow lake and popular,
child-friendly bathing spot.
Submerged in the centre of the
lake is Bulverket, a 10th–11th-
century fortress surrounded
by a palisade of 1,500 stakes.

❺ Lummelunda-grottan

Road 149, 13 km (8 miles) N of Visby.
🚌 ℹ️ 1 May–Sep: 0498-27 30 50,
other times ring to book. 🎫
obligatory. Cave adventure must be
pre-booked. 🚌 📷 🎫 ♿

In 1948 two local school boys
discovered an opening in the
ground in Martebo marsh and
crawled in. They had chanced
upon the entrance to a giant
network of caves and
passageways, now Gotland's
main tourist attraction. Today
the entrance is at Lummelundas
Bruk. Exploration of the caves
continues, but the part which
is open for viewing provides
a fantastic show of stalactites
and stalagmites, magic mirrors
of water and spine-tinglingly
tight openings. The geological
museum, Silurum, is located
at the entrance.

A painting on wood in Bro Kyrka showing Adam and Eve in paradise

Immediately to the
south of the caves is
Krusmyntagården, a
herb garden designed
in traditional monastic
style with wonderful
views over the sea.

🗺️ Krusmyntagården
Road 149, 10 km (6 miles)
N of Visby. **Tel** 0498-29 69 00.
Open Jun–Aug: daily.
🚌 📷 🎫 📷

❻ Bro Kyrka

Road 148, 11 km (7 miles) NE of Visby.
🚌 **Tel** 0498-27 05 60. **Open** mid-
May–mid-Sep: 10am–5pm daily. 🎫
every other Sun.

Tradition has it that Bro Kyrka
is built over a votive well and
in medieval times it was a
famous votive church,
particularly among sailors.
The building dates from the
13th and 14th centuries. Inside,
the prayer chamber contains
5th-century picture stones.

About 1 km (half a mile)
north of Bro Kyrka, on road
148, are two picture stones
known as "Bro Stajnkällingar".
According to legend, two
elderly women were turned
to stone for arguing on the
way to the Christmas Mass.

From Bro, a turning leads
to Fole church on road 147,
and a short detour takes
you to **Vatlings Gård**. The
estate has Gotland's best-
preserved medieval stone
house outside Visby and
is well worth a visit.

🚌 Vatlings Gård
Road 147, 18 km 18 km (11 miles) E of
Visby. **Open** daily. **Tel** 0498-29 27 00.

Roma Kungsgård, built in 1733 using materials
from Roma Kloster

❼ Visby

See pp168–71.

❽ Roma

18 km (11 miles) SE of Visby. 🚌
ℹ️ Roma Kungsgård: 070-543 33 34.
Open 10am–4pm daily.

Cistercian monks from Nydala
monastery in Småland founded
Roma Kloster in 1164. The
monastery was built on the
pattern of the French mother
monastery and became a
religious centre for the entire
Baltic region. The three-aisle
church in the Fontenay style
was completed in the 13th
century. The monastery was
abandoned during the
Reformation in 1530 and
ended up in the ownership of
the Danish crown as a royal
manor under Visborg Castle.

When Gotland came under
Swedish rule in 1645, the
monastery was practically in
ruins. The county governor
used materials from the site
to build his residence, **Roma
Kungsgård**, in 1733. Only the
church remained intact, and
that was used as a stable. In
1822, Roma Kungsgård was
rented to the crown and
served as an army store.

The ruins of Roma monastery
are a popular tourist attraction.
Even today they bear witness
to the monks' skill in
construction techniques.
The beautiful vaulted
ceilings are reminiscent
of Roman aqueducts.

In the summer, Romateatern
performs Shakespearian
plays on an open-air stage
set among the ruins.

❼ Street-by-Street: Visby

A town of roses and ruins, the walled city of Visby is a UNESCO World Heritage Site as well as a popular party town in summer, when it fills up with holiday-makers from the mainland. Its cobbled streets are lined with picturesque cottages, haunting medieval ruins and a multitude of cafés and bars. Away from the busy, more touristy parts of Strandgatan, Stora Torget and around the pleasure boat harbour, the evocative ambience recalls the town's medieval history *(see p171)*. This is also evident from the imposing town wall and its many towers, including Kruttornet (the Gunpowder Tower).

Konstmuseet
Visby Town Wall by Hanna Pauli (1864–1940) is on display in the Museum of Art.

★ Gotlands Museum
The Historical Museum is devoted to Gotland's past from ancient times to modern day. The Science Centre and Natural History Museum are in the same building.

Burmeisterska Huset
Hans Burmeister, a wealthy merchant from Lübeck, built this house in the 17th century. It is one of the best-preserved examples of its kind in Visby.

Visby town wall has 19 towers and gates, including Kruttornet (Gunpowder Tower).

Key

— Suggested route

| 0 metres | | 100 |
| 0 yards | | 100 |

For hotels and restaurants in this area see pp284–289 and pp294–301

Kapitelhusgården
In this leafy medieval courtyard setting, the public can try their hand at medieval crafts. During the summer, it can become busy, especially during Medieval Week.

VISITORS' CHECKLIST

Practical Information
Gotland. 22,000. Gotlands Tourist Information Centre, Skeppsbron 4–6, 0498-20 17 00. Midsummer Week (Jun), Medieval Week (early Aug), Gotland Chamber Music Festival (Jul), Visby Day (first Sat in Oct), Gotland Grand National (first weekend in Nov).
W gotland.info

Transport

St Drotten, the sister church to St Lars.

otaniska ädgården

STORA TORGET

★ Domkyrkan Sta Maria
Completed in 1225, the cathedral was the church of the German merchants. It is the only one of Visby's 17 medieval churches which is not in ruins.

St Lars, also known as the church of Sta Anna after the mother of the Virgin Mary.

Söderport

Around Stora Torget
Entertainment focuses on the main square, Stora Torget. Munkkällaren, with a terrace on the square, is one of the many restaurants and bars here.

Ruins of Sta Karin (St Catherine's) Church
Franciscan monks built the church and monastery of Sta Karin in 1233. Dominicans rebuilt it in the 14th century. But in 1525 was destroyed by an army from Lübeck.

Exploring Visby

Within the walls, Visby is relatively small and all the sights are within easy walking distance. The main streets run north to south: Strandgatan with historic sights and nightlife spots, St Hansgatan with its many churches, and Adelsgatan, the shopping street leading from Söderport (South Gate) to Stora Torget, the main square. North of here are quieter residential streets and alleyways, making for a lovely stroll. Near Norderport (North Gate) it is possible to climb up on the ramparts and admire the magnificent wall.

Visby Town Centre

◻ Street-by-Street: Visby, see pp168–9

Medieval vaulted street in Visby, a UNESCO World Heritage Site

The Heart of the Town

The medieval inner town of Visby is shaped by its mighty town wall, almost 3.5 km (2 miles) in length. Construction of the wall began at the end of the 13th century. It was originally 5.5 m (18 ft) high and designed to protect against attack from the sea. On the inland side, the wall was surrounded by a deep moat. Within the ramparts, narrow cobbled streets are lined with tightly-packed houses, wealthy merchants' homes and the ruins of historic churches. UNESCO described the town as the "best fortified commercial city in northern Europe" and declared it a World Heritage Site in 1995.

Just outside the wall is Almedalen, the former site of the Hanseatic harbour. Today the area is a park. South of Almedalen is Visby marina, which throngs with boats, especially during Medieval Week in August.

⬚ Around Stora Torget

At the heart of Visby lies Stora Torget (Big Square) from which the roads to the town gates radiate. This is still a focal point for visitors to Visby, despite the development of a modern town centre outside Österport, and there is a lively market here in summer. Several medieval houses surround the square, including the restaurants of Gutekällaren, with its characteristic stepped gable, and Munkkällaren, with its deep vaulted cellars and inner courtyard.

The ruins of the church of Sta Karin (St Catherine), dating from the 1230s, form a dramatic backdrop on the southern side of Stora Torget. In the shadow of the ruins is Rosengård, a café where generations have ordered coffee and delicious pastries.

⬚ Gotlands Museum

Strandgatan 14. **Tel** 0498-29 27 00. **Open** 15 May–14 Sep: daily; 15 Sep–14 May: Tue–Sun. ⬚⬚⬚⬚⬚⬚⬚ **w** gotlandsmuseum.se

Gotland's long history going back to prehistoric times has made this collection one of Sweden's richest regional museums. It is housed in a former royal distillery, built in the 1770s.

The Hall of Picture Stones contains an impressive array of carved stones from the 5th–11th centuries, some of which feature runic inscriptions. Next door, the Gravkammaren (Grave Room) shows burial customs from ancient times to the Vikings. Several skeletons are on display, including the 8,000-years-old Stenkyrkamannen (Stenkyrka Man). One of the most remarkable sights is the collection of Viking silver treasure – no fewer than 700 items have been recovered from sites around the island.

Church art is well represented. The museum holds the original, Gothic Öja Madonna (Öja church in southern Gotland has to make do with a copy). A large gallery displays medieval furniture, as well as collections from later periods.

The museum also houses Fenomenalen, a hands-on science centre.

Picture stones from the 5th–11th centuries in Gotlands Museum

Visby's medieval town wall, approximately 3.5 km (2 miles) long and up to 5.5 m (18 ft) high

Ruins of St Nicolai

St Nicolaigatan. **Tel** Visby Tourist Office, 0498-20 17 00.

The ruins of St Nicolai are all that remains of a Dominican monastery founded in Visby in 1228. The Black Friars expanded it and built a Gothic cathedral which they dedicated to the patron saint of sailors and merchants, St Nicholas. When the people of Lübeck stormed Visby in 1525 much of the cathedral was destroyed.

Between 1929 and 1990 a pageant, *Petrus de Dacia*, was performed here every summer. This Gotlander was a famous mystic and author, and prior of the Dominican monastery at the end of the 13th century. Today, musical and theatrical events are staged in the ruins and the Gotland Chamber Music Festival is usually held here each summer. The audience sit protected from wind and weather by the remaining part of the roof.

Ruins of Helge And

Helge Ands Plan. Gotlands Länsmuseum, 0498-29 27 00.

Helgeandstiftelserna was a religious order founded during the early 13th century to take care of the poor and the sick. The ruin of Helge And (Church of the Holy Spirit) is one of Visby's most remarkable church ruins and dates from this period. The octagonal building has two floors opening onto a choir. Two large staircases lead up to the first floor. It was designed in this way to allow patients from the hospital to reach the church via a passage from the upper floor. Today the ruins are used for cultural events and are open to visitors during the summer.

Botaniska Trädgården

Visby. **Tel** 0498-26 94 77.
Open 24 hrs daily. **Closed** Nights in Medieval Week.

Gotland's Botanical Garden was founded in 1856 by the Badande Wännerna (Society of the Bathing Friends), a gentlemen's club formed in 1814 to work for the benefit of the public. The society also established Gotland's first school and set up its first bank.

To reach the garden, follow the promenade along the shore from the harbour and go through Kärleksporten (Gate of Love) in the northwest corner of the town wall.

Inside the gate, the lush park offers a spice-scented herb garden and a pretty rose garden (at its peak Jul–Aug). There are over 16,000 species including many plants and trees that are exotic to the Nordic countries, such as walnut, mulberry and ginkgo. In its midst stand the ivy-clad ruins of St Olof's church and there is a water-lily pond and a small pavilion making an ideal resting place.

Visby's Early History

Archaeological finds, including Roman, Arabic and Russian coins, show that Gotland had a lively foreign trade already in Viking times. At the end of the 12th century, trade with Germany took off and the Hanseatic League was formed – a mercantile and political association between German merchants and towns around the North Sea and the Baltic. The League was centred on Visby and the town enjoyed a boom in the 13th century with people coming from all around to settle here. Towards the end of the century a trading-political power struggle on Gotland led to internal strife and the gradual decline of Visby. Poor harvests and the Black Death contributed to the decline, as did the introduction of large ships capable of travelling longer distances. In 1361 Visby was captured by Valdemar Atterdag and Gotland succumbed to Danish rule. Then in 1525 Visby was plundered by its rival Hanseatic town, Lübeck, and buildings were destroyed or abandoned.

Valdemar Atterdag pillaging Visby in 1361

The small community of Ljugarn with typical Gotland limestone houses close to the sea

flourishing port and limeworks. In the early 1800s lime baron Axel Hägg bought Katthamra manor, which he had rebuilt and decorated in Empire style. Today there is a hotel and youth hostel here, but the manor house itself is a private home.

9 Ljugarn

40 km (25 miles) SW of Visby.
300. Visby Tourist Office, 0498-20 17 00.

This cheerful resort was Gotland's first and makes a good centre for touring the southeast of the island. There was a harbour here long before Russian forces raided Ljugarn on their way to laying waste to the east coast of Sweden in 1714–18. By 1900, the small community, with its long sandy beach, limestone sea stacks and guesthouse, had become a popular bathing spot.

South of Ljugarn is the 13th–14th century **Lau Kyrka**. One of Gotland's largest churches, it has a triumphal crucifix from the 13th century and excellent acoustics for the concerts held there.

Northwest of Ljugarn, **Torsburgen** fortress was built in the 3rd or 4th century and is one of the largest of its kind in Scandinavia. It is protected by naturally steep slopes and a wall 7 m (23 ft) high and up to 24 m (79 ft) wide. To reach it, take the forest road from the 146 towards Östergarn, 2 km (1 mile) east of Kräklingbo church.

About 6 km (4 miles) south of Ljugarn, at **Guffride**, are seven Bronze Age stone-settings, in the form of ships, and are the largest on Gotland. Open to tourists is the 11th Century Church of Garde, southwest of Ljugarn. The Church features paintings in the Byzantine style.

The idyllic **Katthammarsvik**, north of Ljugarn, was once a

10 Lojsta

15 km (9 miles) S of Visby. 120.
Visby Tourist Office, 0498-20 17 00.
Gotland pony judging (4th week in Jul).

Like so many of Gotland's churches, **Lojsta Kyrka** dates from the mid-13th century. The choir and the nave have ornamental paintings and the figures above the triumphal arch are by the master known as "Egypticus" in the mid-14th century.

On **Lojsta Hed**, an area of forest and heath north of the church, lives a herd of semi-wild Gotland ponies (russ), the stubborn little horse native to the island. The animals are owned by local farmers and by Gotlands Läns Hushållningssällskap. Several annual events are organized, such as the release of the stallion in early June, and the high point of the year, the Gotland pony judging at the end of July.

About 2.5 km (2 miles) from Lojsta towards Etelhem is a large building with a sedge roof, **Lojstahallen**. This is an excellent reconstruction of a late-Iron Age hall building. Next to it is a medieval fortress, Lojsta Slott.

11 Fröjel Kyrka

40 km (25 miles) S of Visby.
Tel 0498-24 00 05. **Open** daily.
every 3rd Sun.

In a stunning location, high up overlooking the sea, is the saddle-roof church of Fröjel Kyrka, built in the 12th and 13th centuries. Inside is an impressive triumphal crucifix by the craftsman who created the rood screen of Öja church. The churchyard has an ancient maze which shows that the site was used long before the arrival of Christianity.

North of the church lies the magnificent **Gannarve Skeppssättning** (Gannarve Ship Barrow), which is considered to be one of the best in Gotland. This has been dated to the late Bronze Age (1000–300 BC) and is 30 m (98 ft) long and 5 m (16 ft) wide.

The splendid Gannarve Bronze Age stone ship barrow

12 Karlsöarna

Gotland. Stora Karlsö from Klintehamn. Visby Tourist Office, 0498-20 17 00. Lilla Karlsö from Klintehamn. 0498-48 52 48, summer: 0498-24 11 39.

Many myths have been spun around Stora and Lilla Karlsö, the rocky islands 6.5 km (4 miles) off the west coast of Gotland.

Stora Karlsö covers 2.5 sq km (1 sq mile) and is a nature

Thin-billed (or common) murres at Stora Karlso, Gotland

reserve with steep cliffs, caves such as "Stora Förvar", moorland, leafy groves, and rare flowers and birds. Here, between the bare rocks in May and June, the orchids *Adam och Eva (Dactylorhiza sambucina)* and *Sankt Pers nycklar (Orchis mascula)* form carpets of blooms. Sea birds such as auks, gulls and eider duck can be seen. Razorbills lay their eggs among the stones on the beach, while guillemots prefer the shelves of the steep cliffs.

A guided tour takes a couple of hours and is included in the price of the boat crossing. There is also a museum in Norderhamn.

Like Stora Karlsö, **Lilla Karlsö** is also a nature reserve. The island has been grazed by sheep since the Bronze Age. It is home to guillemots, razorbills, cormorants and gulls. Eider duck, little terns, Sandwich terns and velvet scoters nest on the flat land. The Swedish Society for Nature Conservation organizes guided tours. There is a youth hostel on the island – book in advance.

Petes Museigård, typical 18th- and 19th-century Gotland houses

⑬ Petes

Gotland. 🚌 🛈 Länsmuseet på Gotland, 0498-29 27 00. **Open** mid-Jun–mid-Aug: 11:30am–2:30pm daily.

To the southwest of Gotland, just before Hablingbo church on coastal road 140, there is a turning to the seaside community of Petes. Here, the well-preserved houses show Gotland's architecture from the 18th and 19th centuries.

For younger visitors, **Barnens Petes** displays classic toys such as stilts, hobby horses, hoops, wooden rifles and wooden dolls.

The unbroken sandy beaches of Gotska Sandön

⑭ Hoburgen

80 km (50 miles) S of Visby. 🚌

Far to the south lies Hoburgen, a 35-m (115-ft) high steep cliff of fossil-rich limestone with seams of the local red Hoburgen marble. On the clifftop is a lighthouse built in 1846. From here it is 176 km (97 miles) to the northernmost lighthouse on the island of Fårö.

Below the lighthouse is Sweden's most famous sea stack, Hoburgsgubben (the Old Man of Hoburg), guarding the caves of Skattkammaren (the Treasure Chamber) and Sängkammaren (the Bed Chamber).

Hoburgen is a favourite spot for ornithologists who come to study the multitude of birds which swoop over Gotland's southernmost outpost all year round. In summer there is a restaurant nearby.

Profile of Hoburgsgubben, the "Old Man of Hoburg"

⑮ Gotska Sandön

🛈 Visby Tourist Office, 0498-20 17 00; booking: 0498-24 04 50. 🚌 from Nynäshamn and Fårösund.

Just 40 km (25 miles) north of Fårö lies the most isolated island in the Baltic, Gotska Sandön. It is one of Sweden's national parks and features a unique landscape of deserted, constantly changing sandy beaches and dunes, pine forests and a rich flora. There are migratory birds, unusual beetles, but only one mammal, the hare. The island became a national park in 1909.

Gotska Sandön has been inhabited since the dawn of civilization, although the population has never been large. Colonies of grey seals led seal hunters to settle on the island and the dangerous waters offshore attracted wreck plunderers. In the 17th and 18th centuries sheep were grazed here and later crops were grown. As recently as the 1950s a few lighthouse keepers and their families (and one female teacher) lived here, but now the lighthouse is automated and the only permanent resident is a caretaker.

There is no harbour and boat traffic from Fårösund or Nynäshamn is infrequent and dependent on the weather. It is possible to camp or stay in a shared sleeping hut or cottage. Accommodation must be booked before arrival.

SOUTHERN GÖTALAND

Sweden's two southernmost provinces, Skåne and Blekinge, together form Southern Götaland, with the country's third largest city, Malmö, as the region's main town and gateway to Europe. The gentle, undulating landscape retains its Danish atmosphere from times past. Castles and medieval and Viking sites abound, and the historic naval port of Karlskrona is a UNESCO World Heritage Site.

The province of Skåne has an undeserved reputation for being completely flat, but apart from the plain of Söderslätt the countryside is surprisingly hilly with the rocky ridges of Söderåsen, Linderödsåsen and Romeleåsen dividing the region. To the northwest, the area is bounded by the imposing Hallandsåsen ridge.

The province of Blekinge, criss-crossed by rivers and lakes, is known as the Garden of Sweden. It has its own island archipelago with sheltered harbours beloved by sailors. North, towards the border with Småland, the slightly wild forest landscape predominates.

Throughout Southern Götaland the Danish influence prior to 1645 *(see p41)* is still evident, not least in the architecture, which differs greatly from elsewhere in Sweden. A common sight in rural Skåne is the traditional, often half-timbered farmhouse with a thatched roof, built around a cobbled courtyard. Castles and manor houses, in many cases built by the Danish nobility, are a feature of the countryside. In the coastal communities, former fishing huts are today cherished by their summer residents.

Southern Götaland differs from the rest of Sweden in atmosphere, too. The people of Skåne are known for being relaxed and for loving good food – and in large quantities – something which has lent this part of the country its inn culture, which has its equivalent in the Danish *kroen* just across Öresund.

Having been sparring partners in the long-distant past, Sweden and Denmark are now linked by the Öresund Bridge from Malmö to Copenhagen. Both sides of the sound are now collaborating over the creation of a visionary new Swedish-Danish region, Örestad.

Ales Stenar, a stone ship on Skåne's south coast, thought to be a late Viking grave or cult site

◀ Malmö at dusk, with the spectacular Turning Torso skyscraper in the background

Exploring Southern Götaland

As well as arable fields and willow windbreaks, this southernmost part of Sweden has its share of gently rolling hills, forests and lakes. The region is ideal for cycling through the country from village to village, discovering manor houses and castles along the way, walking through nature reserves or along the Skåneleden trail, canoeing, fishing, swimming in the many small lakes and rivers, driving, or sailing along the coast and putting into shore at fishing harbours on tiny islands. Towns such as Lund and Malmö offer a wealth of history, best discovered on foot, Karlskrona is renowned for its naval port and maritime past, and Trelleborg has a reconstructed Viking fortress.

Spiral beech trees in Trollskogen forest, Torna Hällestad

Sights at a Glance

Statue of the founder of Karlskrona, Karl XI, in front of Trefaldighetskyrkan

The 8-km (5-mile) long Öresund Bridge, completed in 2000, linking Sweden with Denmark and Continental Europe

Key

- Motorway
- Major road
- Minor road
- Main railway
- Minor railway

0 kilometres   30

0 miles   20

Getting Around

The E20 motorway across the Öresund Bridge from Continental Europe joins the E6, E22 and E65 south of Malmö and continues north to Helsingborg where it meets the E4 to Stockholm. The region has several airports and there are train connections to the large towns. Local commuter trains serve districts around the major cities. Ferries from Germany operate to Trelleborg and Ystad and there are frequent ferries from Denmark to Helsingborg.

Hovs Hallar, a nature reserve on the bay of Laholmsbukten

❶ Bjärehalvön

Skåne. Road 105. �m 🚗 🚲
ℹ Båstad Tourist Office 0431-750 45,
Torekov Tourist Office 0431-36 31 80.
🎭 Båstad Chamber Music Festival
(4th week in Jun), Swedish Open
Tennis Tournament (Jul).
W bastad.com

There are several popular resorts surrounding the peninsula of Bjärehalvön, between the bays of Skälderviken and Laholmsbukten. The medieval town of **Båstad** is now best known for hosting the annual Swedish Open tennis tournament, but it also has beautiful old houses and glorious beaches. Just over 10 km (6 miles) to the west is the old fishing village of **Torekov**. Boat trips run from Torekov to the nature reserve **Hallands Väderö**, a remnant of the Hallandsåsen ridge now left 3 km (2 miles) out to sea. Of special note is the alder marsh.

On the northern cape of the peninsula is **Hovs Hallar**, a geologically interesting area with dramatic rocks and caves. The area is a nature reserve popular with birdwatchers and walkers. Hovs Hallar is the westernmost end of the Hallandsåsen ridge, which forms the border between the Bjärehalvön peninsula and Halland *(see p211)*. With its meadows and varied flora, the ridge is ideal for walking.

West of Båstad along the coast is **Norrvikens Trädgårdar**, a paradise for garden lovers

Fruit trees in blossom at Norrvikens Trädgårdar gardens

created by architect Rudolf Abelin in the early 20th century. There are several different gardens, including a Baroque garden and a Japanese garden.

The town of **Ängelholm**, nestling between the Bjärehalvön and Kullahalvön peninsulas at the end of the bay of Skälderviken, has a sandy beach 6 km (4 miles) long. Historically, Ängelholm was known for its pottery industry and today clay cuckoos, the town's symbol, are made here.

🌳 Norrvikens Trädgårdar
5 km (3 miles) W of Båstad.
Open Jun–Aug: daily. 🍴 🛍 🎦

❷ Kullabygden

Skåne. Road 111/112. 🚗 🚌
ℹ Centralgatan 20, Höganäs,
042-33 77 74. 🎭 Music in
Kullabygden (2nd week in Jul), Kulla
Market in Jonstorp (first week in Jul).

The beautiful Kullen Peninsula has been inhabited since the Iron and Bronze Ages. Today, the pretty medieval fishing villages of Arild, Mölle, Höganäs and Viken have become popular seaside resorts. Höganäs is best known for its ceramics.

Just outside Arild lies **Brunnby Kyrka**, parts of which are 12th-century. The church contains impressive ceiling paintings. **Krapperups Slott**, north of Höganäs, dates from the mid-16th century; the castle houses an art gallery and museum.

🏰 Krapperups Slott
7 km (4 miles) N of Höganäs. **Tel** 042-
34 41 90. Castle: **Open** by appointment.
Gallery & museum: **Open** Apr–May:
Sat & Sun, Jun–mid-Aug: daily. 🎦 🛍
🎦 **W** krapperup.se

❸ Helsingborg

Skåne. E4. 🚆 130,000. 🚢 🚗 🚌 🛥
ℹ Kungsgatan 11, 042-10 43 50.
🎭 Helsingborg Festival (late Jul), Horse
Festival (last weekend in Jul); Antiques
Fair (end of Jul). **W** helsingborgs
turistbyra.skane.org

Known as the "Pearl of the Sound", Helsingborg is a lively town, spectacularly located on

Tycho Brahe

Astronomer Tycho Brahe was born in Skåne in 1546 into a Danish noble family. At the age of 13 he was sent to university in Copenhagen to study philosophy and went on to study at several German universities. Inspired by an eclipse of the sun in 1560, he took up astronomy. He believed that the old methods of measurement to determine the position of the planets were not sufficiently exact and designed a new system. In 1572 he observed a new bright star in the constellation Cassiopeia. His discoveries in astronomy paved the way for a new view of the universe. In recognition, the Danish king granted Brahe the island of Ven, where he had an observatory built *(see p179)* which became the finest in Europe. Following a difference of opinion with the Danish court, Brahe went into exile and settled in Prague, where he died in Prague in 1601.

Statue of Tycho Brahe in St Ibbs Kyrka on Ven island

Tycho Brahe's underground observatory on the island of Ven

the shores of the Öresund within sight of the Danish coast. The town's strategic position at the narrowest point of the sound led to a stormy history, and the 34-m (111-ft) tower **Kärnan** is all that remains of its 12th-century fortress. The brick tower of the town hall (1897) also features on the skyline. It was designed by architect Alfred Hellerström and contains glass paintings by Gustav Cederström.

Jacob Hansen's half-timbered house, built in 1641, is the oldest house in Helsingborg. The **Dunkers Kulturhus**, by Danish architect Kim Utzon, encompasses a museum, art gallery and theatre under one roof.

The open-air **Fredriksdal Friluftsmuseum** displays historical buildings from the region and has a botanical garden containing the wild plants of Skåne.

Environs
Ramlösa Brunn, 5 km (3 miles) southeast of Helsingborg, is known for its spring water, discovered in the late 19th century and now on offer in the Water Pavilion.

The castle of **Sofiero** was bequeathed to Helsingborg municipality by Gustav VI Adolf. The park is particularly famous for its Royal Gardens containing more than 300 varieties of rhododendron.

🏰 **Kärnan**
Slottshagen. **Tel** 042-10 59 91.
Open Jun–Aug: daily. 🎫

Helsingborg's renovated tower, Kärnan, dating from the 12th century

🏛 **Dunkers Kulturhus**
Kungsgatan 11. **Tel** 042-10 74 00.
Open Tue–Sun. 🎫 🛒 💻

🏛 **Fredriksdals Friluftsmuseum**
Gisela Trapps Vag. **Tel** 042-10 45 00.
Open daily. 🛒 💻 ♿

🏰 **Sofiero**
Sofierovägen, 5 km (3 miles) N of the centre. **Tel** 042-10 25 00.
Parken: **Open** Apr– Sep: daily. 🎫 🚫
Slottet: **Open** Jun–Aug: guided tours only. 🎫 📷

❹ Klippan

Skåne. Road 21. 🏘 8,000. 🚉 🚌
ℹ Storgatan 46, 0435-282 00.
🎪 Åby Market (3rd Tue–Wed in Jun), Ljungbyhed old-time market (3rd Fri–Sat in Aug).

Located on the Söderåsen ridge, 30 km (19 miles) east of Helsingborg, Klippan is known for having Sweden's oldest operating paper mill, built in the 16th century.

Söderåsen National Park offers leafy forests, dramatic screes, babbling brooks and breathtaking views from Kopparhatten and Hjortsprånget. The Skåneleden trail runs through the park.

The 17th-century mansion **Vrams Gunnarstorp**, 10 km (6 miles) west of Klippan, is built in the Dutch Renaissance style. The stunning park with its acclaimed hornbeam avenue is open to the public.

❺ Landskrona

Skåne. 🏘 27,000. 🚉 🚌
ℹ Skeppsbron 2, 0418-47 30 00.
🎪 Vallå-kraträffen Customized Car Festival (mid-Aug), Gardening Festival (Aug).

The shipbuilding town of Landskrona was granted its charter in the 15th century.

In 1549, the Danish king Christian III built the **Landskrona Slott Citadellet** (Citadel) as protection against the Swedes. This substantial fortress surrounded by a moat dominates the town. Most of the sights can be found in the area around it, including **Landskrona Museum**, with its local history collection, and Konsthallen (Art Gallery) surrounded by a sculpture park.

Environs
In the sound between Sweden and Denmark lies the island of **Ven**, where Tycho Brahe set up his underground observatory, Stjärneborg, in the 1580s. The Tycho Brahe Museum features multimedia shows about the observatory.

There is a ruined castle on Ven, Uraniborg, and at the highest point of the island stands the medieval church of St Ibb. Steep Backafallen is the place for the most spectacular views.

The island can be reached by regular ferries from Landskrona all year round and by fishing boat from Råå during the summer.

🏰 **Landskrona Slott Citadellet**
Slottsgatan. **Tel** 0418-44 82 50.
Open courtyard and exhibition: daily. 📷 daily in summer.
🌐 citadellet.com

🏛 **Landskrona Museum**
Slottsgatan. **Tel** 0418-47 31 20.
Open Tue–Sun. **Closed** Easter Saturday, Saturday before Whitsun, Midsummer Eve, 24, 25 & 31 Dec.

🌊 **Ven**
In Öresund 7 km (4 miles) W of Landskrona. ⛴ from Landskrona.
Tel 0418-47 30 00, 0418-724 20.
Tycho Brahe Museum: **Tel** 0418-725 30. **Open** May–Sep: daily. 🎫
📷 pre-book. 💻 📷 ♿

Bosjökloster, originally an 11th-century Benedictine convent

❻ Frostavallen

Skåne. 3 km (2 miles) N of Höör on road 21. 🚉 to Höör. 🚌 ℹ️ Höör Tourist Office, 0413-275 75.
🌐 turisthoor.se

The beautiful countryside around Höör in central Skåne offers something for everyone, from hiking, canoeing and swimming to fishing from the shore or by boat on Vaxsjön lake. With its many restaurants, cafés, hotels and campsites, Frostavallen is ideal for a day trip or a longer stay. There are playgrounds and all kinds of leisure equipment are available for hire.

Nearby is **Skånes Djurpark**, a zoo specializing in Nordic animals. Popular with children, it has more than 1,000 wild and domesticated Nordic animals. Watch lynx being fed or enjoy a pony ride.

A different kind of experience is offered at **Höörs Stenåldersby**, where visitors can see for themselves what life was like in a Stone Age village. Flint-knapping and bow-making can be tried.

🎫 Skånes Djurpark
Frostavallen. **Tel** 0413-55 30 60. **Open** daily. 🎨 📷 📠 summertime. 🏠 ♿

🏛 Höörs Stenåldersby
Next to Skånes Djurpark. **Tel** 0413-55 32 70. **Open** Jul by appointment.

❼ Bosjökloster

Skåne. Road 23. **Tel** 0413-250 48. 🚌
Open daily. May, Jun & Sep: 11am–5pm; Jul & Aug: 10:30am–5:30pm.
🎨 📷 📠 Park: **Open** daily.
May–Sep: 8am–7pm; Oct–Apr: 10am–5pm. 🎯 Game Fair (last weekend in Aug). 🌐 bosjokloster.se

On a peninsula between the lakes of Östra and Västra Ringsjön lies one of Sweden's most remarkable houses. Bosjökloster was built around 1080 as a convent and soon became one of the wealthiest in Skåne. Rich families paid a great deal to secure a place for their daughters, often donating goods and land. This all came to an end with the Danish Reformation in 1536 and its possessions were transferred into private ownership.

In 1875–9 Bosjökloster was reconstructed to a design by architect Helgo Zettervall and became the prime example of his skill for renovating Swedish manors and palaces.

In the early 20th century the property was bought by Count Philip Bonde and today it is owned by his grandson.

The family opened the house to the public in 1962 and is now it is one of the most popular stately homes in Skåne with parks and gardens, a restaurant, café, mini-zoo, boats for hire and fishing, too. The park features a 1,000-year-old oak tree. The oldest room in the house, Stensalen, is devoted to exhibitions of arts and crafts.

❽ Östarp

Skåne. Near road 11. 🚌 Kulturens Östarp **Tel** 046-350 400. **Open** 1 May–16 Jun: 11am–5pm Sat, Sun & public hols; 18 Jun–18 Aug: 11am–5pm Tue–Sun; 24 Aug–1 Sep: 11am–5pm Sat & Sun. 🌐 kulturen.com/ovriga-besoksmal/kulturens-ostarp

In the Middle Ages the town of Östarp was owned by a monastery, but it fell to the crown during the Reformation in the 16th century and was later destroyed. All that remained of the town was Östarps Gamlegård, built in 1812. Bought by Kulturen in Lund in 1923, today this former farmhouse forms the centre-piece of the open-air Kulturens Östarp. It is a living museum using horses rather than machinery to farm the land.

The countryside around Östarp is dotted with castles and stately homes, and Lake Vombsjön is a paradise for birdwatchers and fishermen alike. On the eastern shore of the lake is **Övedskloster**, a beautiful 18th-century manor house set in an elegant park. The main house, "Stora huset", is one of the most stunning Rococo-style houses in Sweden. It was designed by Carl Hårleman and completed in 1776. The park, modelled on Versailles, is open to the public in the summer. Surrounding the estate are woods and meadows, as well as a village of half-timbered houses.

🏛 Övedskloster
Road 11 from Lund towards Sjöbo. **Tel** 046-630 63. **Open** daily (park only). 🏇 Horse trials (early Sep).

The 18th-century windmill at Kulturens Östarp museum

Old buildings of Lund preserved by the open-air museum of Kulturen

⑨ Lund

Skåne. E 22. 🏔 85,000. ✈ SturUp. 🚉 🚌 ℹ️ Botulfsgatan 1a, 046-35 50 40. 🎭 Walpurgis Night (30 Apr & 1 May), Cultural Evening (3rd Sat in Sep). 🌐 visitlund.se

Founded by King Sven Tveskägg more than 1,000 years ago, the university town of Lund was once Denmark's capital. In the Middle Ages it was a religious, political and cultural centre and site of a cathedral, **Lund Domkyrka**, which was consecrated in 1145. Over the centuries it has been rebuilt, most recently by Helgo Zettervall, 1860–80. Look out for the 14th-century astronomical clock and a sculpture in the crypt of the giant Finn supporting the cathedral's vaulting.

Lund University was established in 1666, in the grounds of the bishop's palace, Lundagård. Now the university is the second largest seat of learning in Sweden with around 47,000 students.

In the heart of the partly medieval city centre lies **Kulturen**, an open-air museum with perfectly preserved streets, cottages and town houses. Kulturen also has extensive historical collections. The 14th-century chapel of Laurentii-kapellet, in central Lund, is thought to have been the library of the monastery of St Laurence.

Historiska Museet, containing Domkyrkomuseet, is one of Sweden's largest museums of archaeology, and includes an exhibition devoted to the history of the cathedral.

Lunds Konsthall, designed by Klas Anshelm, displays contemporary art, while the **Museum of Sketches** shows the development of the creative process through a series of original sketches and models.

Environs

The spring flowers are magnificent at **Dalby Söderskog**, a national park 10 km (6 miles) southeast of Lund, where there is a forest of elm, ash and oak trees.

Established as a royal stud in 1661 by King Carl X Gustaf, **Flyinge Kungsgård**, 16 km (10 miles) northeast of Lund, combines historic buildings with cutting-edge architecture.

🏛 **Lunds Domkyrka**
Kyrkogatan. **Tel** 046-35 87 00.
Open daily. 📷 🚻 ♿

🏛 **Kulturen**
Tegnerplatsen. **Tel** 046-35 04 00. **Open** May–Aug: daily; Sep–Apr: Tue–Sun. 🅿️ 🍴 🛒 ✏️ 📷 ♿ 🌐 kulturen.com

🏛 **Historiska Museet**
Krafts Torg 1. **Tel** 046-222 79 44. **Open** Sun–Tue. 🅿️ 📷 🌐 luhm.lu.se

🏛 **Lunds Konsthall**
Mårtenstorget 3. **Tel** 046-35 52 95.
Open Tue–Sun. 📷 Thu & Sun.
🅿️ 🍴 ♿ 🌐 lundskonsthall.se

🏛 **Museum of Sketches**
Finngatan 2. **Tel** 046-222 72 83.
Open Tue–Sun. 📷 🌐 adk.lu.se

🏛 **Flyinge Kungsgård**
Kungsgård, Flyinge. **Tel** 046-64900.
Open daily. 🐎 🌐 flyinge.se

⑩ Skanör/Falsterbo

Skåne. Road 100. 🏔 7,000. ✈ Sturup. 🚌 ℹ️ Videholms allé 1a, Höllviken, 040-42 54 54. 🎭 Foteviken Viking Week (last week in Jun), Falsterbo Horse Show (Jul), Sandcastle Competition (last Sun in Jul), Falsterbo Bird Show (late summer). 🌐 vellinge.se/turism

Today the twin towns at the far end of Skåne's southwestern cape are idyllic seaside resorts, but they owe their development to the lucrative herring industry in the Middle Ages.

Sights include the ruins of the 14th-century fort of **Falsterbohus**, **Falsterbo Museum** with its local history collection, and **Falsterbo Konsthall**, an art gallery in the old railway station. On the headland is **Falsterbo Lighthouse**, built in 1793 and still in working order. It is now a historical monument. Skanör Town Hall dates from 1777 and the church is 13th-century.

Bärnstensmuseet, the Amber Museum in Höllviken, near the Viking earthworks of Kämpinge Vall, is well worth a visit.

Giant Finn in the cathedral

🏛 **Bärnstensmuseet**
Kämpinge, 10 km (6 miles) E of Falsterbo. 🚌 **Tel** 040-45 45 04.
Open Mon–Sat. 🅿️ 📷 🌐 brost.se

The low, single-storey houses in the small town of Skanör

⑪ Malmö

Sweden's gateway to Europe, Malmö is the country's third largest city. It was founded in the mid-13th century. Under Danish rule from 1397 to 1658, Malmö was an important town, but once it was returned to Sweden its position waned until an upturn in its fortunes at the end of the 18th century. Today, thanks largely to the Öresund Bridge and associated development, Malmö is once more in the spotlight. The city has a lively, distinctly European atmosphere and has become a centre for contemporary art and design. The old town is centred on Stortorget with its historic Town Hall and governor's residence.

Stortorget with Residenset (left) and Rådhuset (right)

🏛 Rådhuset

Stortorget. **Closed** to the public.
The centre of Malmö is the square Stortorget, laid out in the 1530s by the town's mayor Jörgen Kock. Stortorget is dominated by Rådhuset, the town hall, originally built in Renaissance Dutch style in 1546. The cellar remains of the medieval building, which served both as a prison and an inn. In 1860 architect Helgo Zettervall renovated the town hall, giving it a completely new look. A number of changes were made in the cellars, (including the removal of the prisoners). The inn is still standing today and is one of the most popular bars in Malmö.

🏛 Jörgen Kocks Hus

Stortorget. **Closed** to the public.
Stortorget also contains Jörgen Kocks Hus, a large six-storey building with a stepped gable roof, constructed in 1525. Jörgen Kock, appointed mint-master for Denmark in 1518. Four years later he was elected mayor of the city becoming one of the most powerful men in Malmö. He was involved in the rebellion over the Danish

succession and was captured and sentenced to death, but escaped and was reinstated as mayor of Malmö in 1540.

🏛 Residenset

Stortorget. **Closed** to the public.
In the mid-18th century two buildings Kungshuset and Gyllenpalmska Huset were combined to form the new governor's residence. Around 100 years later the building was given a new façade by architect F W Scholander, to which Helgo Zettervall adapted his extensive redesign of the town hall. Today the building is the home of the county governor.

🏛 St Petri Kyrka

Göran Olsgatan 4. **Tel** 040-27 90 56.
Open daily. 🔲 🏛 ⓦ svenska kyrkan.se/malmo/stpetri
In a street behind Stortorget is Malmö's cathedral, St Petri Kyrka. Built in the 12th century, the church, modelled on St Mary's in Lübeck, is made from red brick. The high tower, constructed in the late 19th century, after two 15th-century towers collapsed, is prominent in Malmö's skyline. The church used to contain limestone

paintings, removed during renovation in the mid-19th century. Only the paintings in Krämarkapellet (the Tradesman's Chapel) are preserved.
The cathedral has treasures from the 16th and 17th centuries when Malmö's prosperity was high. The magnificent 15-m (49-ft) high altar in Renaissance style is beautifully ornamented, painted and gilded. The pulpit dating from 1599 is in sandstone and black limestone. Later additions include the organ front, a masterpiece created to a design approved by Gustav III in 1785. The original medieval organ is said to be the oldest working organ in the world and is now in Malmö Museum.

🏛 Moderna Museet Malmö

Gasverksgatan 22. **Tel** 040-685 79 37.
Open 11am–6pm Tue–Sun. **Closed** some public holidays. 🔲 🔲 🔲
ⓦ **modernamuseet.se/sv/malmo**

The Moderna museet in Stockholm is one of Europe's leading museums of modern and contemporary art, and the only one north of Amsterdam with an international collection that covers the entire 20th century.
In autumn 2009, the Moderna museet opened a second branch in Malmö, housed in an old power station that was built in 1900. Architecturally striking in its combination of past and present design styles, this gallery hosts rotating exhibitions that range from the Russian avant-garde to contemporary Swedish art.

Moderna Museet Malmö, occupying an old power station

City library Stadsbiblioteket

🏛 **Malmö Konsthall**

St Johannesgatan 7. **Tel** 040-34 60 00.
Open daily. **Closed** Midsummer Eve,
Midsummer, 24, 25 & 31 Dec.
📷 daily. 🛈 ✏ 📷 ♿
🌐 konsthall.malmo.se

Malmö Konsthall (Art Hall) is
one of Europe's largest spaces
for contemporary art. It arranges
and hosts exhibitions with an
international focus that range
from modern classics to current
artistic experiments.

Past exhibitions have featured
the work of such artists as
Edvard Munch, Paul Klee, Joan
Miró, Alberto Giacometti, Keith
Haring, Andres Serrano, Louise
Bourgeois, Peter Greenaway and
Tony Cragg. Associated special
events organized by the gallery
include theatre performances,
films, poetry readings, lectures
and debates, as well as
extensive educational activities
for both children and adults.

The Konsthall opened in 1975
and was designed by architect
Klas Anshelm with a keen eye for
three main elements: flexibility,
spaciousness and light.

🏛 **Stadsbiblioteket**

Kung Oscars Väg. **Tel** 040-660 85 00.
Open daily. **Closed** public holidays.
📷 📖 ♿

The City Library moved into the
"castle" on Kung Oscars Väg in
1946, but by the 1960s there was
talk of expansion. Finally, in 1999,
the new state-of-the-art library
opened. The famous Danish

architect Henning Larsen
renovated and extended the
old edifice, adding the cylindrical
entrance building and the airy
Calendar of Light hall.

The library offers free access
to computer terminals, Wi-Fi
and a media collection. Tools
for digital needs such as
editing, scanning and printing
are available in the Learning
Centre. The library puts on
events for people of all ages
and draws almost one million
visitors a year.

VISITORS' CHECKLIST

Practical Information
Skåne. E6/E22. 🚗 305,000.
🛈 opposite Central Station,
Skeppsbron 2, 040-34 12 00.
🎭 Malmö Festival (Aug), Malmö
City Horse Show (mid-Aug).
🌐 **malmotown.com**

Transport
✈ 30 km (19 miles) E of centre.
🚉 Skeppsbron. 🚌 Skeppsbron 10.

Central Malmö

① Rådhuset
② Jörgen Kocks Hus
③ Residenset
④ St Petri Kyrka
⑤ Humanitetens Hus
⑥ Moderna Museet
   Malmö
⑦ Malmö Konsthall
⑧ Stadsbiblioteket
⑨ Malmöhus/Malmö
   Museum
⑩ Kommendanthuset
⑪ Teknikens och
   Sjöfartens Hus

0 metres 500
0 yards 500

For keys to symbols *see back flap*

Exploring Malmö

The centre of Malmö, where most of the sights are located, is compact and easy to explore on foot. Start at Västra Hamnen, near the fortress of Malmöhus, and walk towards the centre, in the direction of the tower of St Petri Kyrka on Stortorget. Lilla Torg and Möllevångstorget are lively squares, and the beautiful parks, such as Slottsparken or Pildammsparken, are a delight to wander through. While the centre retains its old-town atmosphere, futuristic projects are taking shape on the outskirts as part of the visionary new Öresund region.

Malmöhus fortress, built in 1537 and now the home of Malmö Museum

🏛 Malmöhus/Malmö Museum

Malmöhusvägen. **Tel** 040-34 44 00. **Open** daily. **Closed** 1 Jan, 1 May, Midsummer Eve, Midsummer, 24, 25 & 31 Dec. 🅿 📷 by appointment. 📷 🚻 👤 partly. Ebbas Hus: Snapperupsgatan 10. **Open** Wed & Sat.

Originally built by Erik of Pomerania in 1434, the fortress of Malmöhus was largely destroyed as a result of the war. It was rebuilt by Christian III in 1537. Today it is the oldest preserved Scandinavian Renaissance castle in the Nordic region. Originally, it was a fortified royal manor and mint. After the 17th century the fortress was reinforced with bastions, but it fell into disrepair and through most of the 18th and 19th centuries served as a

Calendar of Light hall in Malmö's award-winning library

prison. The solid brick fort is surrounded by a deep moat. Extensive restoration work was carried out in 1932, after which Malmö Museum moved into the building. The museum's collections cover archaeology, ethnography, the history of art and handicrafts, and zoology.

Stadsmuseet (the City Museum) illustrates the history of Malmö and surrounding Skåne with tools, weapons and domestic objects. It contains models, a large textiles collection and an ethnographical collection.

The aquarium housed in the Malmö Museum is a popular destination for families and school groups. They come to observe typical marine life from the waters of southern Sweden, as well as tropical fish such as piranhas and the unusual lungfish, which can live without water and hybernate for several years. There are also a jellyfish aquarium, terrariums with snakes and creepy-crawlies and a Nocturnal Hall filled with bats.

Some of the rooms in the fortress can also be seen. Another popular attraction is the 18th-century tower with its 7.5-m (25-ft) thick walls and original cannons.

Malmö's smallest museum, Ebbas Hus, was donated to the city by its owner Ebba Olsson, and now belongs to Malmö Museum. The museum is a tiny terraced house that has been preserved just as it was in the early 20th century.

Malmö Museer also runs Teknikens och Sjöfartens Hus, Kommendanthuset and Malmö Konstmuseum, which can all be visited on a single ticket.

🏛 Kommendanthuset

Malmöhusvägen. **Tel** 040-34 44 00. **Open** daily. **Closed** 1 Jan, 1 May, Midsummer Eve, Midsummer, 24, 25 & 31 Dec. 🅿 📷 🚻 👤

In the latter part of the 18th century the storage buildings in the Malmöhus courtyard had fallen into disrepair and Gustav III ordered the construction of a new armoury. It was built outside the fortress in the Banér bastion and was completed in 1794. By 1814 the fortress's military days were over and it had become a prison. Kommendanthuset (the Governor's House) became the quarters first for the prison's doctor and priest and later the prison governor.

In the 20th century the city of Malmö took over the building and restored it to its original appearance, incorporating it into Malmö Museer. It now houses Fotografins rum, an exhibition hall for photography. It also organizes a number of events and activities aimed at children and young people.

🏛 Teknikens och Sjöfartens Hus

Malmöhusvägen. **Tel** 040-34 44 00. **Open** daily. **Closed** 1 Jan, 1 May, Midsummer Eve, Midsummer, 24, 25 & 31 Dec. 🅿 📷 🚻 👤

The Museum of Technology and Seafaring is also part of Malmö Museer. Its exhibits cover virtually everything to do with technological development and seafaring, as well as the history of roadbuilding and aviation, engines, and steam engines in particular, just to name a few

The 8-km (5-mile) long Öresund Bridge between Sweden and Denmark, carrying a motorway and railway line

examples on display. Among the exhibits is the delta-winged fighter plane J35 Draken from the 1960s. The technically curious can satisfy their urge to experiment in the *kunskapstivoli* interactive test lab.

The museum also covers the industrial and seafaring history of Skåne. Here, the star exhibits include experiencing the *U3* submarine and the steam launch *Schebo*. For those who have never been in a submarine, it is an opportunity not to be missed. This exhibit is very popular with children.

The shipbuilding and shipping industry and the development of the ports from the 17th century onwards are highlighted, as is ferry traffic, so vital to Skåne. There is also an interactive knowledge park, where you can do your own science experiments.

🏛 Limhamn

5 km (3 miles) SW of the centre.
ℹ️ Malmö Tourist Office,
040-34 12 00. 🅿️

On the southern edge of Malmö lies Limhamn, a shipping port for lime since the 16th century. Nowadays Limhamn is home to one of southern Sweden's largest marinas, with spectacular views over the Öresund Bridge.

One of Limhamn's sights is the early-19th century small, blue Soldat-torpet (soldier's house), which shows how soldiers used to live. The cottage was inhabited until

1956. The Limhamn Museum Society runs various events at Midsummer and Christmas. Another fascinating sight is the disused limestone quarry, a huge gaping hole that is now a nature reserve.

⚓ The Öresund Bridge

E20. 6 km (3 miles) SW of the centre.
The idea of a bridge between Sweden and Denmark had been discussed for more than 100 years, but it was only in 1991 that both countries agreed on how and where this dream could be realized.

Opened in July 2000, the Öresund Bridge is 8-km (5-mile) long linking Lernacken in Sweden, southwest of Malmö, and the 4-km (2.5-mile) long Danish artificial island of Peberholm, south of Saltholm. The highest part rests on four pylons, 204 m (670 ft) tall and the roadway is around 30 m (100 ft) wide. The E20 runs along the upper level with a railway along the lower level. It is the longest cable-stayed bridge to carry both a railway and motorway.

On the west side of Peberholm the link plunges into a 4-km (2.5-mile) long tunnel leading to Copenhagen's international airport. The journey by train from Malmö to Copenhagen takes 35 minutes.

The Öresund Region

As part of the EU's vision for a Europe without borders, the Öresund Region project aims to integrate southern Skåne in Sweden with the area around Copenhagen in Denmark, allowing people to cross from one country to another without restrictions. The construction of the Öresund Bridge and tunnel has brought with it enormous benefits for Malmö. It has made the region considerably more attractive to business, cultural exchanges between the two countries are easier and the improved communications have brought more visitors.

Architect Santiago Calatrava's stunning Turning Torso tower, in the Western Harbour, is an expression of the region's faith in the future. Completed in 2005, the 190 m (623 ft) sculptural high rise consists of nine cubes twisting skyward. The Western Harbour waterfront, which has developed into a residential area with offices and services, is internationally recognized as a model for sustainable urban regeneration.

The Turning Torso building soaring 190 m (623 ft) high

Trelleborgen, a reconstructed Viking fortress

⑫ Trelleborg

Skåne. E22. 🏛 43,000. 🚌 🚆 ⛴
🛈 Kontinentgatan 2, 0410-733 320.
🎭 Viking Battle (1st weekend in Jul),
Smygehuk Jazz Festival (mid-Jul),
Palm Festival (last weekend in Aug),
Michaelmas Market.
W soderslatt.com

The town of Trelleborg was at its
most prosperous in the Middle
Ages, when German merchants
came to trade salt for herring.
Some of the old Skåne houses
can be seen in the quarter
around Gamla Torg (Old Square)
and in Klostergränden, where
the ruins of a 13th-century
Franciscan monastery still stand.
Stadsparken, the town park,
boasts a gorgeous rose garden
and is worth a visit.
 Trelleborgen is a reconstruction of a Viking fortress. It is
situated exactly where a fortress
thought to have been built by
King Harald Blue Tooth in the
10th century, and excavated
1,000 years later, once stood.
There is also a Viking museum.
 Other sights of interest
include **Trelleborgs Museum**,
focusing on local history,
Trelleborgs Sjöfartsmuseum
(Seafaring Museum) and **Axel
Ebbes Konsthall** (art gallery),
with its collection of sculptures
by Skåne artist Axel Ebbe.

Environs
A short distance west of
Trelleborg lies the village of
Skegrie and beside the E6 is
Skegriedösen, a Stone Age
burial mound. The rectangular
grave chamber is formed from
four stone blocks with a giant
pointed block as a roof,
surrounded by 17 foot-stones.
This type of Stone Age burial

site is only found in southern
and western Sweden.

🏛 **Trelleborgen**
Västra Vallgatan 6. **Tel** 0410-73 30 21.
Open daily. 🔲 🔲 🔲

🏛 **Trelleborgs Museum**
Stortorget 1. **Tel** 0410-733 045.
Open Tue–Sun. 🔲 🔲 🔲 🔲

🏛 **Trelleborgs Sjöfartsmuseum**
Gråbrödersgatan 12. **Tel** 0410-195 45.
Open Apr–Nov: Sat & Sun.

🏛 **Axel Ebbes Konsthall**
Hesekillegatan 1. **Tel** 0410-733 056.
Open Jun–Aug: Tue–Sun. 🔲 🔲 🔲

⑬ Ystad

Skåne. E65. 🏛 29,000. 🚌 🚆 ⛴
🛈 St Knuts Torg, 0411-57 76 81.
W visitystadosterlen.se

In Ystad the impact of Danish
rule and contact with the
German Hanseatic League is
apparent and the medieval
church and monastery
communities have also left their
mark on the town. Among the
many old buildings is the

Apoteksgården, one of Ystad's many fine
half-timbered houses

13th-century **Sta Mariakyrkan**,
where every night the watch-
man in the tower declares that
all is well by blowing his horn.
In **Karl XII's Hus** on Stora
Västergatan the warrior king is
said to have spent the night in
1715 following his return from
Turkey *(see p41)*.
 Ystad has a number of
museums, including **Ystads
Konstmuseum** (Art Museum),
Charlotta Berlins Museum (an
intact home of a 17th-century
nobleman) and a military
museum. A fine theatre on the
harbourside offers a varied
repertoire ranging from opera
to stand-up comedy.

Environs
High above the fishing
community of Kåseberga lies the
stone ship **Ales Stenar**. The 67-m
(220-ft) monument comprises
59 stones. This mystical place is
well worth a visit.
 Bollerups Borg, 20 km
(12 miles) east of Ystad, is a
13th-century fortress which has
been rebuilt several times. The
fort is owned by an agricultural
college, but is open to the public.
 Sandhammaren is best known
for its sandy beaches, but in the
past was feared by sailors as
new reefs were constantly
forming around the cape. The
lighthouse dates from 1862.
 Marsvinsholms Slott is an
estate dating back to the 14th
century. The castle is not open
to the public, but during the
summer visitors can enjoy the
sculpture park within the castle's
grounds or see a play (in
Swedish) at the open-air theatre.
 Valleberga Kyrka, 17 km
(11 miles) east of Ystad, is the
only round church in Skåne.
It has a 12th-century font
by Majestatis.

🏛 **Ystads Konstmuseum**
St Knuts Torg. **Tel** 0411-577 285. **Open**
Tue–Sun. **Closed** public holidays. 🔲
🔲 🔲 **W konstmuseet.ystad.se**

🏛 **Ales Stenar**
Kåseberga. Road 9, 20 km (12 miles) E
of Ystad. **Tel** 0411-57 76 81. **Open** daily.

🏛 **Marsvinsholms Slott**
On E65, 12 km (8 miles) NW of Ystad.
Tel 0411-577 681. House: **Closed** to the
public. Park: **Open** daily. 🔲 in summer.

⑭ A Tour of Österlen

The name Österlen means "the land to the east" and refers to the southeast corner of Skåne from Ravlunda south to Ystad and west to the Linderödsåsen ridge. The land is the most fertile in Sweden and across the rolling plains are many of the country's most treasured ancient monuments, grandest castles and forts and oldest churches. Along the coast, idyllic fishing villages are dotted like pearls on a string and the entire region has become a haven for painters and writers.

Apple orchard in spring, Kivik

① Brösarps Backar
This nature reserve is awash with rare flowers. The sight of anemones and cowslips blooming in spring is particularly spectacular. The area has lots of walking trails.

② Kivik
Kivik is best known for its annual market and apple orchards, but it is also a charming fishing village with winding streets and half-timbered houses.

⑤ Tomelilla
Tomelilla is an ideal starting point for a tour of Skåne's rolling countryside. The town is also famous for its art museum, located in an idyllic rural setting.

③ Simrishamn
Old low-rise houses give the town its character. Craftsmen lived around the square, Lilla Torg, and fishermen made their home by the harbour.

Key

▬ Suggested route

═ Other roads

Tips for Drivers

Length: around 55 km (34 miles). Major roads are of a good standard, but country roads can be in poorer condition.
Places to eat: cafés and/or restaurants are found in most towns. Hammenhög has a typical Skåne inn, ideal for a lunch break. Äpplets Hus, Kivik, is worth a look.

```
0 kilometres          10
0 miles        5
```

④ Glimmingehus
The evocative 16th- century knight's manor offers exciting ghost trails and a taste of medieval cooking.

Map labels: Kristianstad, Brösarps Backar, Ravlunda, Kivik, Fågeltofta, St Olof, Rörum, Vik, Baskemölla, Smedstorp, Simrishamn, Tomelilla, Lund, Ystad, Hammenhög, Glimmingehus, Brantevik, Skillinge, Glemmingebro, Löderup, Ystad, Åles Stenar, Sandhammaren, Baltic Sea, 19, 11, 9

Heliga Trefaldighetskyrkan, a Renaissance church, Kristianstad

⑮ Kristianstad

Skåne. E22. 🚗 36,000. 🚆 🚌 🚢 ℹ️
Stora Torg, 044-13 53 35. 🎭 Sommar i
City (Jul). 🌐 kristianstad.se/turism

The Danish King Christian IV built the town of Kristianstad in the early 17th century and the original street layout with two gates can still be seen today. The town's main sight is **Heliga Trefaldighetskyrkan** (the Church of the Holy Trinity) from the same period, an excellent example of Renaissance architecture. A more recent attraction is the eco-museum **Naturum Vattenriket**, a 35-km (22-mile) stretch of wetlands on the Helgeån river. It is best seen on a guided river tour. Fishing permits can be bought at the tourist office. In 2014 Kristianstad will celebrate its 400th anniversary with a number of events around the city.

Environs

About 15 km (9 miles) to the northeast is **Bäckaskog Slott**, a former monastery dating from the 13th century, which was rented by the Swedish royal family during the 19th century. Set in beautiful parkland, the castle is now a hotel with a restaurant.

Rinkaby Kyrka lies halfway between Kristianstad and Åhus. The 13th-century church contains paintings from the 15th century depicting the seasons and farming life.

Among the most idiosyncratic objects to be seen at the castle of **Trolle-Ljungby**, 10 km (6 miles) east of Kristianstad, are the Ljungby drinking horn and pipe, which feature in a local legend. On Wednesdays and Saturdays in summer they are exhibited in a window facing the courtyard.

The park of **Wanås Slott**, 20 km (12 miles) northwest of Kristianstad, is a setting for international contemporary art.

Åhus, 18 km (11 miles) southeast of Kristianstad, is a coastal community with half-timbered houses and sandy beaches. It is renowned for its many golf courses, beach handball festival and beach soccer tournament.

🏛 **Naturum Vattenriket**
Härlövsängaleden 2. **Tel** 044-13 23 30.
Open daily. **Closed** Mon (winter) and some public hols. 🔲 🔲 🔲
👤 (some parts). 🔲 🌐 vattenriket.
kristianstad.se/naturum

🏛 **Bäckaskog Slott**
Fjälkinge, 15 km (9 miles) NE of
Kristianstad. Restaurant: **Tel** 044-532 20.

🏛 **Trolle-Ljungby**
Fjälkinge, 10 km (6 miles) NE of
Kristianstad. **Tel** 044-550 43. **Open** (park & courtyard only) Jun–Sep: Wed & Sat.

⑯ Sölvesborg

Blekinge. E22. 🚗 17,000. 🚌 🚌
ℹ️ Repslagaregatan 1, 0456-100 88.
🎭 Sweden Rock Festival (early Jun).
🌐 solvesborg.se

In the Middle Ages, Sölvesborg, on the cape of Listerlandet, was an important trading centre protected by a castle. The town has a Danish feel to it and still retains its medieval charm.

In a former granary and distillery, **Sölvesborgs Museum** traces the history of Lister. The town's oldest building is **St Nicolai Kyrka**, a church with parts dating from the 13th century.

Environs

Southeast of Sölvesborg and at the far end of the cape lies the old fishing village of **Hällevik** with its traditional wooden houses, fishing harbour, smokery and guest harbour. It also has a great little fishing museum and is well worth a visit.

Ferries run from Nogersund to the island of **Hanö** in Hanöbukten bay. It's an attractive place and a popular destination for sailors. The island served as an English naval base in the Napoleonic Wars in the early 19th century and houses a graveyard for British seamen.

🏛 **Sölvesborgs Museum**
Skeppsbrogatan. **Tel** 0721-58 15 25.
Open mid-Jun–mid-Aug: Tue–Sun; rest of the year: by appointment.

⑰ Karlshamn

Blekinge. E22. 🚗 19,000. 🚆 🚌 🚌
ℹ️ Pirgatan 2, 0454-812 03 🎭 Baltic
Festival (3rd week in Jul).
🌐 karlshamn.se/VisitKarlshamn

Founded in 1664, this town was planned as a naval base, and **Kastellet**, on the island of Frisholmen, was built to defend it. However, the naval port role went to Karlskrona (see pp192–3) and Karlshamn became a trading centre with a reputation for the production of punsch. A reconstruction of Punsch-fabriken, the factory which produced the alcoholic drink "Flaggpunsch", forms part of **Karlshamns Museum**. Next to the punsch factory is **Karlshamns Konsthall** (Art Gallery).

Kastellet on the island of Frisholmen, Karlshamn

◀ The stunning interior of St Petri Kyrka, Malmö's cathedral

Other places of interest include **Skottsbergska Gården**, a merchant's house built in 1763 where both the living quarters and tobacco shop can be seen as they were in the 18th century. **Kreativum** is a fascinating science centre that will appeal to people of all ages. **Asschierska Huset**, on the square, was Karlshamn's first town hall. The celebrated **Mörrumsån** salmon fishing river runs through the municipality.

Renovated spa pavilions at Brunnsparken in Ronneby

Environs
Around 15 km (9 miles) east of Karlshamn is **Eriksbergs Vilt- och Naturpark**, one of the largest wildlife and nature sanctuaries in Europe and home to golden eagles, sea eagles and deer.

🏛 **Karlshamns Museum**
Vinkelgatan 8. **Tel** 0454-148 68. **Open** mid-Jun–mid-Aug: Tue–Sun. 🐾 📷

🏛 **Kreativum**
Strömmavägen 28. **Tel** 0454-30 33 60. **Open** Fri–Sun; daily during school holidays. 🐾 🌐 kreativum.se

⓲ Ronneby

Blekinge. E22. 👥 19,000. 🚋 🚌 🚍
ℹ Västra Torggatan 1, 0457-61 75 70.
📷 Tosia Bonnadan Market (2nd week in Jul). 🌐 visitronneby.se

Founded in the 13th century, Ronneby did not become Swedish until 1658. Prior to that, it was the main town of Blekinge and a busy trading centre. In 1564, during the Seven Years War with the Danes, it was overrun by the army of Erik XIV and burned. About 3,000 inhabitants – the majority of the population – were slaughtered in what became known as the Ronneby Bloodbath. In the early 19th century the town gained a new lease of life thanks to the Kockums foundry and enamel works in Kallinge and the Ronneby Brunn spa.

There are a few old buildings in Bergslagen and around Brunnskällan, and the beautiful 18th-century spa park has been restored.

Environs
Just east of Ronneby is the 13th-century church **Edestads Kyrka**, which once served as a defensive fort. A remarkable 4-m (13-ft) high, 8th-century runestone, **Björketorpsstenen**, lies 7 km (4 miles) east of the town. The text inscribed on the stone is a curse.

Hjortsberga Grave Field on the Johannishus ridge contains 120 ancient burial mounds. About 12 km (7 miles) northeast of Ronneby is **Johannishus Åsar**, a nature reserve set in beautiful pasture land.

⓳ Kristianopel

Blekinge. E22. 👥 1,500. 🚌 🚍
ℹ Stortorget 2, Karlskrona, 0455-30 34 90. 🌐 kristianopel.se

Enjoying a beautiful location on a peninsula in Kalmarsund, the little fortified town of Kristianopel has become a popular summer haunt with a guest harbour and tourist facilities. It was built by the Danish King Christian IV and gained its town charter in 1600. At the Peace of Roskilde in 1658 it became Swedish.

Environs
Brömsebro lies 8 km (5 miles) north of Kristianopel, just inland from the coast. Here on the border between Blekinge and Småland is where peace with Denmark was declared in 1645, when Jämtland, Härjedalen and Gotland once more became Swedish provinces. The negotiations were held on an islet in Brömsebäcken river and a commemorative stone was raised here in 1915. At the mouth of the river are the ruins of Brömsehus, a fortress which was captured in 1436 by Swedish rebel hero Engelbrekt *(see p39)*.

Salmon Fishing in Mörrumsån

Every year the salmon fishing in the Mörrumsån river attracts enthusiasts from all over the world. Fishing here dates back to the 13th century when the king held all the rights. The river flows through a beautiful landscape from Lake Vrången in the north to the sea at Elleholm via the lakes of Helgasjön and Åsnen.

A fishing permit is required and these cost between 200 and 1,200 kr per day. During the 2003 season 1,160 salmon were caught here, the record catch weighing in at 17.98 kg (39.6 lbs). Laxens Hus (Salmon World) in Mörrum gathers together everything to do with fishing and mounts a variety of exhibitions on, for example, the animal life of the river, and the history of the sport.

Fly-fishing for salmon in Mörrumsån

⓴ Karlskrona

The naval town of Karlskrona is built over several islands in the Blekinge archipelago. Granted a town charter in 1680, it was planned by Erik Dahlbergh and is said to have been inspired by both Versailles and Rome. It centres around the two squares, Stortorget on the island of Trossö, and Amiralitetstorget. The decision to locate Sweden's main naval base in Karlskrona was taken because in winter the fleet was often ice-bound in Stockholm, and an ice-free port was needed further south. Karlskrona has a number of outstanding sights from Sweden's Age of Greatness *(see pp42–3)*. In 1998 the town was declared a UNESCO World Heritage Site on account of its naval architecture.

Fredrikskyrkan on Stortorget, designed by Tessin the Younger in Baroque style, 1744

🏛 Grevagården/Blekinge Museum

Fisktorget 2. **Tel** 0455-30 49 60. **Open** Jun–Aug: daily; rest of the year: Tue–Sun. **Closed** some public holidays. 🅿 🖂 🖉 📷 ♿
W blekingemuseum.se

Grevagården on Fisktorget is the main building of Blekinge Museum. The building dates from the early 18th century and was the home of Admiral-General Hans Wachtmeister – the café is set in what was once his kitchen and store room. The museum focuses on the history of Blekinge and Karlskrona's heyday. There is a small Baroque garden reached via a double staircase flanked by two yew trees, believed to date from 1704. Outside on

the square stands Erik Höglund's statue of the *Fisherwoman*.

🏛 Stortorget

The imposing square is said to be the largest in northern Europe. It is flanked, in the Baroque tradition, by two impressive churches, both designed by the architect Nicodemus Tessin the Younger.

Fredrikskyrkan is a large basilica consecrated in 1744, but characterized by the 17th-century taste for Baroque lines. The southern tower has 35 bells which ring three times a day. The other church, Heliga Trefaldighetskyrkan (Holy Trinity), is also known as the German Church after Admiral-General Hans Wachtmeister who inspired it and is buried in the crypt. It was completed in 1709. After a fire in 1790 the church was rebuilt with a lower dome than its predecessor.

The town hall, completed in 1798, has been rebuilt several times. Today it serves as the seat of Karlskrona district court.

Vattenborgen, the now protected water tower, was built in 1863 to supply Trossö with fresh water. It was replaced by a water tower outside the town in 1939.

🏛 Marinmuseum

Stumholmen. **Tel** 0455-359 302. **Open** Jan–Apr: Tue–Sun; May–Dec: daily. **Closed** some public hols. 🅿 🖂
🖂 🖉 📷 ♿ **W** marinmuseum.se

The fascinating naval museum, opened in 1997, stands on the harbour on Stumholmen, an island which for almost 300 years has been part of the main base of the Swedish navy. The museum was founded originally in 1752 by King Adolf Fredrik to collect and document naval objects in what was known as Modellkammaren (the Model Room).

Marinmuseum covers every imaginable aspect of maritime activity. It holds a particularly impressive collection of figureheads, weapons and uniforms. From an underwater glass corridor it is possible to see the wreck of an 18th-century ship lying on the bottom of the sea.

One of the world's smallest full-rigged ships, *Jarramas*, a training ship for naval ratings, is moored on the quay outside the museum, along with the minesweeper *Bremön* and the torpedo boat *T38*. The Sloop and Long-Boat Shed contains an exhibition of working boats and often allows visitors the opportunity to see how old wooden boats are restored.

Marinmuseum, showcase for Karlskrona's naval heritage

🏛 Gamla Örlogsvarvet

Högvakten, Amiralitetstorget 1. **Tel** 0455-30 34 90. **Open** Jun–Aug: daily. 🅿 🖂 compulsory.

The Karlskrona shipyard, founded in 1679, became over time one of the country's foremost military shipyards, a position it still holds today. Fortifications and buildings were constructed to build, equip and repair warships. Additional buildings went up

The "Old Man" Rosenbom poor-box outside Amiralitetskyrkan

on the islands of Lindholmen, Söderstjärna and Stumholmen. The only way to see this vast naval harbour and its many 18th-century buildings and workshops is to take a guided tour. Among the most interesting sights in Gamla Örlogsvarvet are the 300-m (984-ft) long Rope Walk, where the rigging for the fleet was manufactured, the Wasa Shed and Polhem Dock on Lindholmen and Five-finger Dock and the Old Mast Crane in the western part of the shipyard. It is the existence of buildings such as these,

and the fact that Karlskrona is such a well-preserved example of a late-17th-century planned naval base, that has earned the town its World Heritage Site status. Karlskrona was a model for other naval bases throughout Europe in the 18th century.

Close to the entrance to the old shipyard, Högvakten, is Amiralitetskyrkan (the Admiralty church). Consecrated in 1685, it is Sweden's largest wooden church. In front of the church is a replica of the Gubben "Old Man" Rosenbom poor-box.

Today's high-tech shipyard, Karlskronavarvet, run by Kockums, is not open to the public, but new vessels can often be seen along the quay.

▦ Kungsholm Fortress
Tel 0455-30 34 90. ▧ book via the tourist office.

Located on a tiny island in the Blekinge archipelago, this remarkable circular fortress has guarded the entrance to Karlskrona from the sea for more than 300 years. It was part of a vast complex of

fortifications that included the Drottningskär citadel, towers and powder magazines.

The magnificent circular harbour at Kungsholm Fortress

Karlskrona Town Centre

① Grevagården/Blekinge Museum
② Stortorget
③ Marinmuseum
④ Gamla Örlogsvarvet
⑤ Karlskronavarvet

0 metres 500
0 yards 500

GOTHENBURG

The people of Gothenburg have nicknamed their city "the face of Sweden". This maritime metropolis has for centuries been one of Sweden's gateways to the outside world. Historically, the Göta Älv river was the country's only outlet to the west, as can be seen by the remains of fortresses and earthworks that once protected it. Gothenburg is still Sweden's most important port and holds fast to its maritime past.

With its great harbour and seafaring traditions, it is perhaps only natural that Sweden's second largest city is also its most outward looking. Visitors are always welcome and it is not for nothing that the entertainment on offer and the atmosphere have led to Gothenburg being called "Little London".

Today's Gothenburg (Göteborg in Swedish) was preceded by four earlier towns along the Göta Älv river. These were pawns in a period of constant conflict between Sweden and Denmark. The first town was built by Dutch settlers on the island of Hisingen in the early 17th century. It was hardly established before Gustav II Adolf decided in 1619 that it should be moved to the area where the suburbs of Vallgraven and Nordstaden now stand. The inhabitants still came from Holland and the grid of canals is reminiscent of Amsterdam. Gothenburg's 17th-century incarnation was as a fortified town created by the architect and field marshal Erik Dahlbergh. The 18th century saw Gothenburg become even more cosmopolitan thanks to German, English and Scottish immigration. With the advent of steam power, the shipping industry flourished in the mid-19th century, and the city became a prominent shipbuilding centre. The shipyards have mostly gone, but Gothenburg is still a major industrial city and home of the car manufacturer Volvo.

This vibrant little metropolis of 525,000 people (famous for their particular sense of humour) is ideal for sightseeing, and is peppered with green spaces, such as the Botanical Gardens, the Garden Society of Gothenburg and the amusement park, Liseberg. It is a good starting point for excursions to the west coast islands with their pretty fishing villages and smooth rocks for bathing.

Gothenburg's Botanical Gardens, a green oasis not far from the centre of the city

◀ Aerial view of Gothenburg, Sweden's most important port

Exploring Gothenburg

A good quick way to get an overview of Gothenburg is to see the city from one of the many excellent observation points such as GötheborgsUtkiken or Sjömanstornet (part of the Maritime Museum). The central parts of the town lie south of the Göta Älv river, but it is easy to cross to the large island of Hisingen by ferry, or by car via the Götaälvbron or Älvsborgsbron bridges, or the Tingstad tunnel. Gothenburg has retained its excellent tram network that provides an ideal way to tour the town, especially on the vintage carriages of the Ringlinjen line. Paddan's white tour boats *(see p209)* operate trips along the 17th-century canals and out into the lively harbour.

Sights at a Glance

1. GötheborgsUtkiken
2. Barken Viking
3. GöteborgsOperan
4. Maritiman
5. Kronhuset
6. Gustav Adolfs Torg
7. Göteborgs Stadsmuseum
8. Domkyrkan
9. Trädgårdsföreningen
10. Ullevi
11. Röhsska Museet
12. Universeum
13. Världskulturmuseet
14. Liseberg
15. Götaplatsen
16. Skansen Kronan
17. Gamla Haga
18. Feskekôrka
19. Sjöfartsmuseet Akvariet
20. Gathenhielmska Huset
21. Slottsskogen and Natur- historiska Museet
22. Botaniska Trädgården
23. The Harbour
24. Nya Älvsborgs Fästning

Feskekôrka fish market reflecting in the water of the Rosenlund Canal

0 metres		500
0 yards		500

For keys to symbols *see back flap*

Getting To Gothenburg

The sea has always been the key to Gothenburg and ferries run daily from Norway, Denmark and Germany. Fast trains whisk travellers from Stockholm or Malmö in 3 hours. A well-developed commuter train network and express bus lines ease regional trips. The E6 along the west coast and the E20 from Stockholm meet at the Göta Älv river. Landvetter international airport is Sweden's second largest airport with direct flights to many domestic and international destinations. Gothenburg City Airport is a 20-minute drive from the city centre.

VISITORS' CHECKLIST

Practical Information

🚃 525,000. ℹ Gothenburg Tourist Information Centre, Kungsportsplatsen 2 & Nordstan, 031-368 4200. 🎬 Gothenburg Film Festival (Jan/Feb); Science Festival (spring); Gothenburg Cultural Festival (Aug); Jazz Festival (Aug); International Book Fair (end of Sep); Gothenburg Horse Show (spring); Culture Night (Oct). 🌐 goteborg.com

Transport

🚇 🚌 🚆 ✈ Landvetter 45 km (28 miles) E of the centre.

Poseidon by Milles in Götaplatsen

Central Gothenburg

Street-by-Street: Västra Nordstan

This part of Gothenburg is the pulse of the seafaring city, encapsulating almost 400 years of history. On the quayside along the Göta Älv river the maritime world is ever present, with museum ships at anchor and the constant to-ing nd fro-ing of boats and ferries. Spectacular modern buildings, such as GöteborgsOperan and GötheborgsUtkiken, contrast with the city's historic monuments. These include the East India Company building on Stora Hamnkanalen, a reminder of the Dutch influence on Gothenburg's design, and Kronhuset, the city's oldest secular building. Shoppers should head for nearby Nordstan, with its department stores and galleries.

❸ ★ GöteborgsOperan
Generous donations enabled the building of the long-awaited Opera House, which opened in 1994.

❹ ★ Maritiman
In the harbour is one of the world's largest floating ship museums. Both the destroyer *Småland*, launched 1952 (in the background), and the submarine *Nordkaparen*, 1962, can be boarded.

Ture Rinman footbridge

Key
  Suggested route

❼ Göteborgs Stadsmuseum
The former East India Company's classical 18th-century headquarters building is now the setting for Göteborgs Stadsmuseum.

❶ GöteborgsUtkiken
The top of the striped skyscraper provides an excellent view over the river and the bustling harbour below.

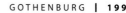

Locator Map
See map pp196–7

Lilla Bommen marina

Torsten Henrikssons footbridge

Nordstan shopping-mall

❷ ★ Barken Viking
After a lifetime on the high seas, the 1906 barque, *Viking*, lies at anchor in the harbour. It now serves as a restaurant and hotel.

❻ Gustav Adolfs Torg
"The town shall be here," pointed King Gustav II Adolf, as depicted by Bengt Erland Fogelberg's statue (1854). The anniversary of the king's death at the Battle of Lützen on 6 November 1632 is commemorated in the square every year.

Ö S T R A   H A M N G A T A N

NEDRE KVARNBERGSG

TORGGATAN

AHUS GATAN

P O S T G A T A N

GUSTAV ADOLFS TORG

N O R R A   H A M N G A T A N

Kungs-torget

0 metres   200
0 yards   200

❺ Kronhuset and Kronhusbodarna
Next to the 17th-century Kronhuset, the Kronhusbodarna sheds are occupied by craft-workers and restaurants.

GötheborgsUtkiken (the "Lipstick"), and the sailing ship *Viking*

❶ Götheborgs-Utkiken

Lilla Bommen 2. **Tel** 031-15 42 15.
🚊 5, 10. 🚌 18, 19, 25, 52, 90, 91.
Open 11am–3pm daily (Jul & Aug:
to 4pm). Access by lift every hour.
🅿️ 📷

The cheeky red and white
GötheborgsUtkiken office
building has dominated the
Lilla Bommen harbour area
since 1989. Architects Ralph
Erskine and Heikki Särg's daring
design was soon christened the
"Lipstick" by Gothenburg wits.
Standing 86 m (282 ft) above sea
level, it offers incredible views
over the harbour
and the city centre
from the top floor.

❷ Barken Viking

Gullbergskajen. **Tel** 031-63 58 00.
🚊 5, 10. 🚌 40, 42, 52, 99. **Open** daily.
Closed 22–31 Dec. 🖥️ summer.
📷 ♿ limited access.
🅆 barkenviking.com

One of the world's few preserved
four-masted barques from the
great age of sail is permanently
moored in Gothenburg. The
Viking was built in 1906 by
the Copenhagen shipyard
Burmeister & Wain. She sailed
the wheat route to Australia
and shipped guano from Chile
in South America. A fast and
beautiful vessel, she logged a
record speed of 15.5 knots in
1909. Her days as a merchant
ship ended in 1948. In 1950 she

became a training centre for
sailors and chefs.

Today, the *Viking* is an unusual
setting for an hotel and
conference centre. In summer
the 97 m (318 ft) deck becomes
a popular harbourside café,
restaurant and bar, with a very
lively, bustling atmosphere.

❸ Göteborgs-Operan

Christina Nilssons Gata. **Tel** 031-13
13 00. 🚊 5, 10. 🚌 18, 19, 25, 52,
90, 91, 114. **Open** mid Aug–Jun: in
conjunction with performances; other
times: phone for info. **Closed** 1 May,
Good Friday, 24, 25, Dec. 📷 🅿️
(Swedish and English); book in
advance. 🖥️ 📷 🏨 ♿
🅆 opera.se

The 1994 opening of the
impressive Opera House
reflected in the water of the
Göta Älv river had been eagerly
anticipated by western
Sweden's music lovers. This is
shown by the vast donation
wall listing the names of the
6,000 people who helped to
fund the new building.

The theatre is designed on a
grand scale. The octagonal
auditorium seats 1,300 people,
all able to enjoy the excellent
acoustics. The main stage
covering 500 sq m (5,380 sq ft)
is complemented by a

The striking exterior of the riverside GöteborgsOperan, the city's main venue for opera, musicals and ballet further four equally large areas for storing sets. Using advanced technology, it is possible to switch quickly between productions, thus enabling the Opera House to stage a repertoire of opera, musicals and contemporary dance.

Architect Jan Izikowitz was inspired by Gothenburg's harbourside location, the aim of his design being for the "building to be possessed by a lightness which encourages thoughts to soar like seagulls' wings over the mighty river landscape".

Gustav Adolfs Torg flanked on its north side by Börsen, built in 1859

The destroyer *Småland*, 1952, in Maritiman

❹ Maritiman

Packhusplatsen 12. **Tel** 031-10 59 50. 🚋 5, 10, 13. 🚌 18, 19, 25, 52, 86, 90, 91, 96, 114, 194, 197. **Open** Apr: Sat & Sun; May & Sep: 11am–5pm daily; Jun–Aug: 10am–6pm daily. 🌐 **maritiman.se**

As the city's new port facilities moved further out towards the sea, Gothenburg's inner harbour became denuded of ships. Fortunately, the situation was rectified in 1987 when Göteborgs Maritima Centrum was set up on the harbour. The museum, now has 13 vessels at anchor, comprising what is said to be the world's largest floating ship museum.

Vessels include the destroyer *Småland*, built in 1952 at Eriksbergs shipyard on the other side of the river, the submarine *Nordkaparen* (1962), and the monitor *Sölve* (1875), as well as lightships, fireboats and tugs.

❺ Kronhuset

Postgatan 6–8. 🚋 1, 2, 3, 4, 5, 6, 7, 9, 10, 11, 13. 🚌 16, 40, 42, 50, 52, 58, 60, 86, 90, 91, 99, 771. 🖥 📷 ♿

A grand brick building in Dutch style, Kronhuset was constructed in 1643–55 and is Gothenburg's oldest preserved secular building. This part of town was originally a storage area for the artillery. The ground floor was converted into a chamber for the parliament of 1660.

Today, the building is used regularly for popular events such as concerts and exhibitions.

Around the square are Kronhusbodarna (the Kronhus sheds), which create a pleasant setting for crafts people whose

Mid-17th-century Kronhuset, one of Gothenburg's oldest buildings

wares include pottery, glass, clocks and homemade sweets. There is also an old-fashioned country store with a café.

❻ Gustav Adolfs Torg

🚋 1, 2, 3, 4, 5, 6, 7, 9, 10, 11, 13. 🚌 16, 40, 42, 50, 52, 58, 60, 86, 90, 91, 99, 771.

Gothenburg's founder, Gustav II Adolf, gave his name to the city's central square. Since 1854 Bengt Erland Fogelberg's statue of the "hero king" has gazed imperiously over the square and Rådhuset (the Town Hall), Börsen (the Stock Exchange) and Stadshuset (the City Hall).

On 6 November, the date on which the king died at the Battle of Lützen in 1632, a special marzipan cake is made in his honor. It is topped with a piece of chocolate in the shape of the king's head.

Rådhuset, closest to Norra Hamngatan, was designed by Nicodemus Tessin the Elder and completed in 1673. It has a Functionalist extension designed in 1937 by Gunnar Asplund *(see p105)*.

Both the 18th-century **Stadshuset** and Wenngrenska Villa, located on the north side of the square, are used by the city administration. **Börsen**, designed by P J Ekman in 1849, is the city's main venue for receptions and council meetings.

Ostindiska Huset (East India House) housing Göteborgs Stadsmuseum

❼ Göteborgs Stadsmuseum

Norra Hamngatan 12. **Tel** 031-368 36 00. 🚊 1–11. 🚌 60, 86, 90.
Open 10am–5pm Tue–Sun (to 8pm Wed). **Closed** public holidays. ♿
🅿 pre-book. 🔲 ✏ ♿
🌐 stadsmuseum.goteborg.se

The City Museum is located in the Ostindiska Huset (East India House). The building, designed by Bengt Wilhelm Carlberg and Carl Hårleman, was constructed in 1747–62 as management premises, auction rooms and a warehouse for the East India Company. When trading ceased in the early 19th century the building became a natural history museum, and in 1861 the City Museum was founded.

The permanent exhibitions show the early history of Western Sweden and the importance of the Göta Älv river as a route to Europe from the Viking period onwards. Displays focus on the history of the first inhabitants of Gothenburg and the industrialization and social upheavals of the 20th century. The work of the East India Company and its trade in exotic goods such as Chinese porcelain, silk and lacquer work, is also featured.

Chinese plate in the collection of Göteborgs Stadsmuseum

❽ Domkyrkan

Västra Hamngatan. **Tel** 031-731 61 30.
🚊 1, 2, 6, 9, 11, 13. 🚌 16, 40, 60.
Open daily. ✏ pre-book. 🔲 ♿
✝ daily.

Gothenburg's cathedral, Gustavi Domkyrka, was designed by C W Carlberg in Neo-Classical style in 1815–25. It stands on the ruins of its two predecessors, which were both destroyed by fire.

In front of the cathedral in Domkyrkoplan is one of the city's preserved watering places: from the late 18th century water was transported here in hollowed-out oak logs from the well of Gustafs Källa to the south of the city.

Gustavi Domkyrka's impressive gilded altarpiece

❾ Trädgårds-föreningen

Slussgatan. **Tel** 031-365 58 58.
🚊 1–5, 7, 9–11, 13.
🚌 21, 25, 28, 29, 43, 58, 59, 60, 514.
Park: **Open** 7am–6pm daily.
🌳 ✏ 🔲 🅿 ♿
Palm House: **Tel** 031-365 58 58.
Open 10am–4pm daily.
Closed 24, 25 & 31 Dec. ✏ ♿
🌐 tradgardsforeningen.se

Gothenburg has many parks, but Trädgårdsföreningen is in a class of its own. In 1842 work began to transform a marshland south of Vallgraven into beautiful parkland for the benefit of the city's residents.

The flora of five continents are represented in the magnificent Palmhuset (Palm House) built in 1878. The building is filled with flowering camellias, giant bamboo, exotic orchids and plenty of palm trees.

Vattenhuset (the Water House) is carpeted by the twisting roots of mangrove trees and the 2-m (6-ft) wide petals of the giant water-lily.

The Rosarium is not to be missed, especially by rose lovers. It has become a leading world collection with more than 1,900 varieties.

There are cafés in the park and Trägår'n, a restaurant and nightclub which has been

The East India Company

Attracted by goods such as tea, silk and porcelain, Sweden was one of the countries which invested in trade with China in the 18th century and Gothenburg became a natural centre for this highly lucrative industry. The Swedish East India Company received its charter in 1731 and operated for 82 years, based in Ostindiska Huset *(see above)*. In total, 132 expeditions were made to China in 38 different ships. In recent years interest in the work of the Company has resulted in the building of the East Indiaman *Götheborg*. This exact replica of the ship, which sank off Nya Älvsborgs Fästning *(see p209)* on its homeward voyage 250 years ago, set out to sail the traditional trade route to Canton in 2005. Since its return in 2007, the ship has been moored in the harbour.

The East Indiaman *Wasa* at Nya Älvsborgs Fästning

Trädgårdsföreningens Palmhuset, containing plants and trees from five continents in various climatic zones

entertaining pleasure-seeking locals since the 19th century. It is now housed in a new building with a large open-air terrace for partying.

⑩ Ullevi

Skånegatan. **Tel** 031-81 10 20.
🚋 1, 3, 6. 🚌 2, 8, 60.
Open during events. ♿ 🚻

Sweden's largest arena, Ullevi, opened for the 1958 football World Cup and over the years has hosted numerous international events. Architect Fritz Jaenecke's elegant wave-shaped ellipse has been renovated and modernized several times. The arena seats 43,000 spectators for sporting events and can accommodate an audience of 75,000 for concerts.

In front of the arena, a statue has been erected in honour of the great Swedish boxer Ingemar "Ingo" Johansson (1932–2009).

⑪ Röhsska Museet

Vasagatan 37–39. **Tel** 031-61 38 50.
🚋 3, 4, 5, 7, 10. 🚌 42, 45, 49, 58, 753, 760, 764, 765. **Open** 11am–5pm Tue– Sun. **Closed** some public hols (check the website). ♿ 📷 pre-book.
🍴 🎁 ♿ 🌐 designmuseum.se

The country's leading museum of applied art and design, Röhsska Museet contains a marvellous collection of 20th-century Nordic domestic and decorative items. Other parts of the museum are devoted to European applied art, and antiquities from the ancient world, Japan and China. A mere fraction of the total of 50,000 objects can

be displayed at any one time. Specialist temporary exhibitions are also mounted.

The museum was founded with donations from financiers Wilhelm and August Röhss. It opened in 1916 as the Röhss Museum of Handicrafts in the beautiful brick building designed by architect Carl Westman.

Next to the museum is the University College for Arts and Crafts Design.

Chinese sculpture, Röhsska Museet

⑫ Universeum

Korsvägen. **Tel** 031-335 64 50. 🚋 2, 4, 5, 6, 8. 🚌 50, 52, 100, 330, 513, 753. **Open** 10am–6pm daily.
🍴 🎁 📷 ♿ 🚻
🌐 universeum.se

Along the Mölndalsån river, not far from Kungsportsavenyn, spreads an area containing several of Gothenburg's major sights and venues, including Liseberg (see p204), Ullevi and Universeum, the largest science centre in Scandinavia.

While the aim of Universeum is to stimulate the interest of

children and young people in science and technology, it provides a fun, educational experience for the entire family.

The centre was built largely with recycled or ecologically friendly materials, and solar panels on the roof ensure that the building has a low impact on the environment.

Exhibits are often interactive and include a tropical rainforest populated by snakes, frogs and spiders; a large aquarium with sharks and rays, as well as a Swedish West Coast tank filled with local sea life; and a space station where you can learn about the life of an astronaut in space.

⑬ Världskultur- museet

Södra Vägen 54. **Tel** 010-456 12 00.
🚋 2, 4, 5, 6, 8, 13. 🚌 49, 50, 52, 91, 157, 513, 761, 771. **Open** noon–5pm Tue, Thu & Fri, noon–8pm Wed, 11am– 5pm Sat & Sun (Jun–Aug: noon–5pm Tue–Fri, 11am–5pm Sat & Sun).
Closed some public hols. ♿ 🎁 🍴 📷 🚻 ♿ 🌐 varldskulturmuseet.se

Designed by the London-based architects Cécile Brisac and Edgar Gonzalez and completed in 2005, the icecube-like Världskulturmuseet is a museum of world cultures. The exhibitions, like the building, are far from traditional; they are intended to surprise, provoke and question stereotyped attitudes towards culture and subculture, and are complemented by a programme of concerts, films, dance and poetry.

Universeum, designed by Gert Wingårdh and built in 2001

Konstmuseet on Götaplatsen, the city's main square, with Carl Milles' statue of Poseidon in the foreground

⑭ Liseberg

Örgrytevägen 1. 🚋 2, 4, 5, 6, 8, 13. 🚌 50, 49, 52, 91, 513, 761, 771. **Tel** 031-400 100. **Open** last week in Apr–last week in Sep: opening times vary. Christmas opening: mid-Nov–23 Dec. 🍴 🅿 ♿ 🏠 ♿ 🅦 **liseberg.se**

The people of Gothenburg are rightly proud of their amusement park which attracts huge numbers of visitors. Apart from the latest rides, this is the place for dancing and entertainment, shows and theatre performances. It is also a beautiful green park where garden design has always played a major role.

The park's history began in the 18th century when financier Johan Anders Lamberg bought the land and built the first magnificent house, Landeriet,

Flower Girl by Gerhard Henning in Liseberg park

in 1753. He had two passions in life – gardening and his wife Lisa, after whom the new house on the hill was named, Liseberg.

The City of Gothenburg bought the site for the Gothenburg Exhibition in 1923 and founded the amusement park with the installation of an impressive wooden roller coaster. Other rides followed, attracting 140 million visitors over the past 80 years. "Balder" is said to be the best wooden roller coaster in the world. It reaches a speed of 90 km/h (56 mph) from a top height of 36 m (118 ft). This roller coaster is reminiscent of the park's first one. "Kanonen" offers another extreme experience, with its rapid acceleration, sharp loops and turns and 360-degree rotation.

⑮ Götaplatsen

🚋 4, 5. 🚌 42, 58, 158. Konstmuseet: **Tel** 031-368 35 00. **Open** 11am–6pm Tue, Thu; 11am–9pm Wed; 11am–5pm Fri–Sun. **Closed** 1 Jan, Good Friday, 1 May, Midsummer, 6 Jun, 24, 25 & 31 Dec. 🍴 🅿 🏠 ♿ 🅦 **konstmuseum.goteborg.se** Konsthallen: **Tel** 031-368 34 50. **Open** 11am–6pm Tue, Thu; 11am–8pm Wed; 11am–5pm Fri–Sun. 🍴 🅿 🏠 ♿ 🅦 **konsthallen.goteborg.se** Konserthuset: **Open** for concerts. **Tel** 031-726 53 10. Stadsteatern: **Tel** 031-708 71 00. **Open** for performances. 🅦 **stadsteatern.goteborg.se**

The focal point of the city is Götaplatsen, the square at the southwestern end of Kungsportsavenyn. Here Gothenburg's bastions of culture, Konstmuseet (the Art Museum), Konsthallen (the Art Hall), Konserthuset (the Concert Hall), Stadsteatern (the City Theatre) and Stadsbiblioteket (the City Library) sit in state. In the centre of this grand square, the water plays around Carl Milles' giant statue *Poseidon*, which has become the symbol of Gothenburg.

Götaplatsen was built for the city's 300th anniversary and the Gothenburg Exhibition in 1923, which is why many of the buildings were exhibition premises from the start. Wide steps lead up from the southeastern side of the square to **Konstmuseet**, designed by Sigfrid Ericson. It contains a rich collection of Nordic art, with key works by Carl Larsson, Ernst

Liseberg's main stage and venue for shows, bands, acrobats and more

For hotels and restaurants in this area see pp284–289 and pp294–301

Josephson and the Gothenburg Colourists. The Danish golden age, Dutch and Flemish painting and French Modernists are also represented. Pride of place is taken by Furstenbergska Galleriet, a copy of the gallery which the great patron of the arts had in his private palace in the late 19th century. The neighbouring **Konsthallen** shows temporary exhibitions. The bronze lion on the façade is by Palle Pernevi.

Konserthuset on the south-western side of the square was designed by Nils Einar Eriksson and opened in 1935. The foyer is decorated with murals by Prince Eugen (Grove of Memories) and Otte Sköld (Folk Song) as well as a large tapestry by Sven X-et Erixson (Melodies in the Square).

Stadsteatern, built in 1934, reopened in 2002 after extensive renovation to highlight the best of Carl Bergsten's elegant 1930's architecture.

Skansen Kronan fortress (1687) on guard high above Gothenburg

⓰ Skansen Kronan

Skansberget. 🚋 1, 6. 🚌 60, 80, 760, 764, 765. **Tel** 031-711 30 33. **Open** 10am–3pm Tue–Fri. **Closed** public holidays. 🎫 📷 pre-book. ♿ limited access.

Topped by a golden crown, the octagonal Skansen Kronan fortress dates from Sweden's Age of Greatness (see pp42–3). It sits enthroned on the peak of Skansberget. Like its counterpart Skansen Lejonet, near the station area, Kronan is one of the most striking survivors of Erik Dahlbergh's fortifications. It was built in 1687 to protect the city from attack from the south. During the 1850s it was used as a shelter for homeless citizens and has also been a prison.

The fortress is surrounded by Skansberget, a leafy park

Walkers and shoppers in Haga with its pleasant wooden houses

offering excellent views from the top, up steep steps.

⓱ Haga

🚋 1, 3, 6, 9, 11. 🚌 60, 80, 760, 764, 765.

The former working-class area of the city south of Vallgraven is one of the few places to experience old Gothenburg. The cobbled streets, courtyards and wooden houses of Gamla Haga are home to craftspeople and lined with small shops, cafés and restaurants.

Haga was Gothenburg's first suburb as early as the 17th century and was mainly populated by harbour workers. During the industrialization of the 19th century a shanty town grew up here and tenements filled with people thronging in from the countryside to seek work.

In the 1960s and 70s Haga was fast becoming a slum and threatened with demolition. Widespread public opposition to the plans ensured that important parts were saved and the houses renovated. Some of the landshövdingehusen ("county governor's houses") typical of the area can be seen. These were built in the 1880s,

when rules set in 1854 banning wooden houses in the centre more than two storeys high were circumvented – with the governor's approval. Providing the building had a ground floor in brick, as these do, it could have two wooden floors above and not constitute a fire risk.

⓲ Feskekôrka

Rosenlundsvägen. 🚋 1, 3, 6, 9, 11. 🚌 50, 60, 91, 80, 760, 764, 765. **Open** 10am–6pm Tue–Fri, 10am–3pm Sat. **Closed** public hols. 🍽 🚫 ♿

It is easy to see why the wits of Gothenburg nicknamed the fish market Feskekôrka (the fish church). Victor von Gegerfelt borrowed from Gothic church architecture when he designed this market hall in 1874, incorporating a steeply pitched roof and large oriel windows.

The catch from the North Sea is brought here directly, guaranteeing the freshest mackerel and the most delicious shellfish. These days there is more to the market than simply selling fish over the counter – the hall provides a colourful setting for restaurant tables at which seafood specialities can be sampled.

Feskekôrka fish market, a paradise for lovers of fish and seafood

⑲ Sjöfartsmuseet Akvariet

Karl Johansgatan 1–3. **Tel** 031-368
35 50. 🚋 3, 9 and 11. **Open** 10am–
5pm Tue–Sun (10am–8pm Wed).
Closed some public holidays. 🅿
🅲 phone for info. 🖳 📷 ♿
w sjofartsmuseum.goteborg.se

The maritime history of
Gothenburg and Bohuslän
is one of the subjects of
Sjöfartsmuseet (the Maritime
Museum). Set up in 1933, it
was funded by the Broström
shipping family and is situated
on Stigberget, high above the
Göta Älv river. The fascinating
displays also explore the
sometimes complex
relationship between man and
sea, and show how the port has
adapted to a changing world.

Those who wish to find
out more about marine life
can head to **Akvariet** (the
Aquarium), which has 25
tanks covering both Nordic
and tropical waters. Here, it is
possible to see how crabs,
starfish and sea anemones
live 40 m (130 ft) below the
surface. A touch-pool allows
visitors to come into close
contact with some creatures.

Gamla Varvsparken contains
various busts including one of
the shipbuilder F H af Chapman
(1721–1808) *(see p83)*.

Sjömanstornet tower
outside the museum is topped
by Ivar Johansson's bronze
sculpture *Woman by the Sea*,

The sculpture *Woman by the Sea* topping
the "sailors' tower"

Gathenhielmska Huset, once the home of Privateer Captain
Lars Gathenhielm

1933, in memory of the sailors
from western Sweden who
died in World War I.

⑳ Gathenhielmska Huset

Allmänna Vägen. 🚋 3, 9, 11.
Closed to the public.

The western side of the
Stigberget hill was formerly the
site of the Amiralitetsvarvet
shipyard and it was here in the
early 1700s that Privateer
Captain Lars Gathenhielm was
granted land by Karl XII. His
widow built a two-storey manor
house here in 1740. It is one of
Sweden's best examples of a
Carolian wooden house
designed to imitate stone.

Next to the house is an
open-air museum of small
wooden houses showing what
a suburb looked like in 1800.

㉑ Slottsskogen and Naturhistoriska Museet

Linnéplatsen. 🚌 42, 52, 80, 760. 🚋 1,
2, 6. Naturhistoriska museet: **Tel** 010-
441 44 00. **Open** 11am–5pm Tue–Sun.
Closed some public holidays. 🅿
🅲 phone to book. 🖳 📷 ♿
w gnm.se

Since the 1870s, Slottsskogen
has been one of the city's finest
green spaces. Criss-crossed by
paths, it features dazzling
planting, ponds, a zoo and
various activities. In spring the
azalea valley is ablaze with
colour. In 1999, what was then
the world's longest border, with
over 90,000 flowering bulbs,

was created. There
are a number of
old cottages from
western Sweden
to be seen in the
park. Areas for sport
and outdoor
activities include
Slottsskogsvallen.
The park has several
cafés and a
restaurant.

Gothenburg's
oldest museum,
**Naturhistoriska
Museet** (the
Museum of Natural History), lies
in the northern part of the park.
Dating from 1833, it moved to
Slottsskogen in 1923. Its vast
collection of more than 10
million exhibits incorporates
animals of all sizes from all
around the world, including
brightly coloured insects and
an African elephant.

The most famous of its
stuffed animals is Malmska
Valen, a blue whale measuring
more than 16 m (52 ft) long,
which was beached in
Askimviken in 1865. It was
stuffed and mounted on a
treetrunk. The upper jaw
opens, and inside the whale
there is a room with benches
and wall hangings where it is
said coffee used to be served.
Now the whale is only open for
visits on special occasions.

㉒ Botaniska Trädgården

Carl Skottsbergs Gata 22 A. **Tel** 031-
741 11 00. 🚌 58. 🚋 1, 2, 7, 8, 13.
Open 9am–sunset daily. 🅿 voluntary.
🛒 🖳 📷 ♿ **w** gotbot.se

Covering 1,750,000 sq m
(432 acres) and containing
16,000 species, Gothenburg's
Botanical Garden is one of the
largest of its kind in Europe. Just
under a fifth of the area has
been developed into gardens,
while the remainder forms a
nature reserve partly consisting
of primeval forest.

The gardens began to be
designed in 1916 and have
been expanded continually
ever since. The Rhododendron
Valley offers a rich tapestry of

◀ The beautiful *Götheborg*, a replica of an 18th-century sailing ship dazzling flowers in late spring each year.

The Rock Garden, in a former quarry, contains 5,000 alpine plants from around the world. In early summer the Japanese Glade with its scented magnolias is a delight while autumn sees an oriental riot of colour.

Large greenhouses shelter the plants from the sometimes bitter climate. The controlled environments within recreate a variety of conditions from desert to steaming rain forest. In the tropical house, bamboo and banana plants stretch more than 10 m (33 ft) up to the ceiling and there are 1,500 orchids in the most amazing colours and shapes.

Botaniska Trädgården, a blossoming oasis in the city

㉓ The Harbour

N of the centre between Götaälvbron and Älvsborgsbron bridges. **Tel** 031-60 96 60. 🚊 to Lilla Bommen. 🚢 from Lilla Bommen or Paddan sightseeing boat from Kungsportsplatsen bridge, up to 4 times an hour. 🌐 stromma.se/en/Gothenburg

Seafaring has been of immense importance to Gothenburg and the harbour and shipyard have long dominated the area along the Göta Älv river. Now the shipbuilding industry is a shadow of its former self and

Eriksbergs shipyard with Sjömanstornet and Älvsborgsbron bridge

apart from ferry traffic, the major shipping activities have moved down to the mouth of the river. Yet, although there is little loading and unloading to be seen in the centre of the city these days, three times more goods are shipped today than in the 1960s.

The inner harbour and shipyard area bordered by the imposing **Älvsborgsbron** bridge have been transformed to provide housing, offices and centres for research and education. Nevertheless, the pulse of seafaring can still be experienced either on a regular ferry from Lilla Bommen to **Eriksbergsvarvet** shipyard, or on the white, flat-bottomed **Paddan Boats** which run from Kungsportsplatsen bridge (about a 10-minute walk away) via 17th-century Vallgraven down the river to the inner harbour. The round trip takes about 50 minutes.

GöteborgsOperan is best viewed from the water (see p200), as are **Barken Viking** (see p200) and **Göteborgs Maritima Centrum** (see p201). Eriksbergs shipyard on Hisingen is the

home port of the spectacular East Indiaman *Götheborg (see p202)*, which is often out on voyages all around the world. Tours also operate around the island of Hisingen and the outer harbour, and to the Gothenburg archipelago. The **Fishing Harbour** holds an auction Tuesdays to Fridays at 6.30am.

㉔ Nya Älvsborgs Fästning

8 km (3 miles) W of the centre. **Tel** 031-60 96 70. 🚢 from Lilla Bommen. **Open** Jul–mid-Aug. 🎫 📷 ♿

In 1660 a new fortress on Kyrkogårdsholmen, at the mouth of the Göta Älv river, replaced the dilapidated, centrally located Älvsborg castle to defend Sweden's precious gateway to the North Sea. It was besieged by the Danes in 1717 and 1719, but never captured. In the late 18th century it became a prison which closed in 1869.

Today the fortress is a popular tourist destination in summer; it even has a wedding chapel.

Gothenburg's Inner Harbour

Key

🚢 Ferry and tour-boat boarding

-- Paddan sightseeing route

Frihamnen

Barken Viking

Götaälvbron

GöteborgsOperan

Eriksbergs varvet

Göteborgs Maritima Centrum

159

Göta Älv

Fiskhamnen

Sjöfartsmuseet

45

0 metres 1000
0 yards 1000

Älvsborgsbron

WESTERN GÖTALAND

Spanning four provinces – Dalsland, Bohuslän, Västergötland and Halland – this attractive and immensely diverse part of Sweden borders Norway to the west, touches on the great forests in the north and reaches to Lake Vättern in the east. Sweden's largest lake, Vänern, lies at its heart. The waters of the Kattegat and Skagerrak wash the rocky shores and sandy beaches along the coast.

Dalsland in the northwest of Western Götaland is one of Sweden's smallest provinces and is relatively unknown even among Swedes. The landscape is hilly and it is often said that the border with Norrland starts here with the mountain area of Kroppefjäll as its southwestern outpost. From the plains of agricultural Dalsland this border can be seen rearing up like a dark forest-clad wall to the west, while the blue expanse of Lake Vänern glistens to the east. The area is sparsely populated, but has a huge variety of wildlife including many species of birds and fish.

In the southwest, Dalsland borders Bohuslän, a coastal province where the smooth bare rocks are dotted with brightly-painted little wooden houses. Here fishing and the stone industry have been the backbone of the economy since the Middle Ages, but today tourism is the chief money earner; the population of many coastal communities doubles in summer. Bohuslän's main city is Gothenburg, Sweden's second largest metropolis *(see pp194–209)*.

Västergötland lies between lakes Vänern and Vättern. The area has been inhabited since ancient times and has many prehistoric remains. It was the first region in Sweden to be converted to Christianity and has an abundance of early churches. The country's first Christian king, Olof Skötkonung, is thought to have been baptised at Husaby in 1008 *(see p38)* and two of the medieval royal dynasties had their roots in Västergötland. Some claim that this was indeed the cradle of Sweden.

Halland, the coastal region south of Gothenburg, is also a summer paradise, with its long sandy beaches. There are several towns for shopping and some of southern Sweden's most interesting castles and manor houses.

Gunnebo, a wealthy merchant's 18th-century manor house near Gothenburg, now a museum

◄ Sailing past a typical West Coast settlement in Bohuslän, with fishermen's huts and boats

Exploring Western Götaland

Driving is one of the best ways to explore Western Götaland and experience Dalsand's landscape of lakes, mountain plateaus and rural flatlands, and still have time to spend on the sandy beaches of Halland in the south. Boat trips are a popular way of seeing the small islands and fishing hamlets off the coast of Bohuslän, while the scenery around lakes Vänern and Vättern can be enjoyed from aboard a ferry. Between the lakes, the great forest of Tiveden offers opportunities for hiking. The region as a whole is one in which the ancient past is always present, especially at the UNESCO World Heritage Site of Tanum, where Bronze Age people carved pictures in the rock.

The former lighthouse-keeper's cottage on the approach to Marstrand, now an exclusive summer residence

Getting Around

For drivers, two major roads cross through Western Götaland: the E20, which comes from the northeast via Örebro across the plains to Gothenburg on the west coast, and the E6, which follows the coast northwards towards Norway. Road 45 from Värmland runs south through Dalsland. There are bus and train links between the large towns and populated areas. Regular ferries operate to the majority of inhabited islands along the coast.

Key

▬▬▬ Motorway

▬▬▬ Major road

═══ Minor road

⊸⊸ Railway line

──── Minor railway

▬▬▬ International border

△ Summit

For additional map symbols *see back flap*

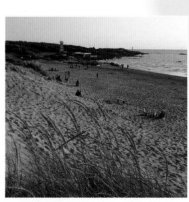

Tylösand outside Halmstad, one of the many glorious, long sandy beaches of Halland

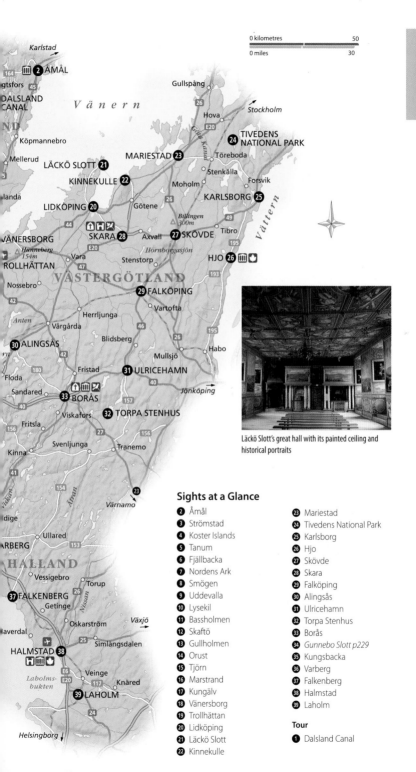

0 kilometres 50
0 miles 30

Karlstad

ÅMÅL ❷
164
45 gtsfors
DALSLAND
CANAL
ND

Gullspång
26
Hova
E20
Stockholm

Köpmannebro

TIVEDENS ❷❹
NATIONAL PARK

Mellerud
LÄCKÖ SLOTT ❷❶
MARIESTAD ❷❸
Töreboda
Stenkälla

KINNEKULLE ❷❷
Moholm
Forsvik
landa
26
KARLSBORG ❷❺

LIDKÖPING ❷⓿
Götene

VÄNERSBORG
44
SKARA ❷❽
Axvall
SKÖVDE ❷❼
Tibro
49

ROLLHÄTTAN
Hunneberg
154m
E20
Vara
Stenstorp
Hornborgasjön
HJO ❷❻
195

VÄSTERGÖTLAND
47
193

Nossebro
42
FALKÖPING ❷❾
Vartofta

Anten
Herrljunga
46

Vårgårda
Blidsberg
26
195

ALINGSÅS ❸⓿
42
Mullsjö
Habo

Floda
180
Fristad
ULRICEHAMN ❸❶

Sandared
40
Jönköping

BORÅS ❸❸
157

Viskafors
TORPA STENHUS ❸❷

Fritsla
156

Svenljunga
27
156

Kinna
Tranemo

41

154
Värnamo
23

dige
Ullared
153

RBERG

HALLAND
Vessigebro
Torup

FALKENBERG ❸❼
26
Getinge

Oskarström
Växjö

averdal
25
Simlångsdalen

HALMSTAD ❸❽
E6
E20
Veinge
117
Knäred

Labolms-
bukten
LAHOLM ❸❾
24

Helsingborg

Läckö Slott's great hall with its painted ceiling and historical portraits

Sights at a Glance

❶ A Tour on the Dalsland Canal

From Bengtsfors the Dalsland Canal carves its way south towards Köpmannebro on Lake Vänern, passing through 19 locks and dropping 45 m (148 ft) to the lake. The scenery varies from beautiful, almost untouched countryside to modern communities, from old ironworks to historic manor houses. The spectacular aqueduct at Håverud is formed from a series of steel plates joined by 33,000 rivets. Both a rail and a road bridge traverse the deep gorge. The canal was designed by Nils Ericsson in the 1860s.

One of the canal's 19 locks making navigation possible

② Baldersnäs Herrgård
The manor house stands on a promontory in Lake Laxsjö, on the Dalsland Canal. It is set in a romantic park with paths, caves and artificial islands.

① Bengtsfors
The canal trip begins or ends here. Don't miss Gammelgården open-air museum with its wooden cottages and storehouses.

③ Högsbyn Rock Carvings
Pictures of ships, people and footprints carved in stone 3,000 years ago can be reached by special boat from Håverud, or by car.

④ Håverud Aqueduct
A solution to the problem of crossing a gorge and a 9-m (30-ft) high waterfall was to build four locks and a long steel aqueduct over the waterfall, followed by another lock.

Key

▬▬ Suggested route by car

– – Route by boat

═══ Other roads

━━ Railway line

Tips for Drivers

Length: 5½ hours by boat.
Boat route: from Bengtsfors to Köpmannabro or reverse. The boat stops at several points along the way. Return by bus or train, around 1 hour.

0 kilometres   5
0 miles   3

Map labels: Årjäng, 172, Laxarby, Åmål, 164, Bengtsfors, Billingsfors, 172, Dals Långed, Bränna, Åmål, Köpmannebro, 45, Vänern, Mellerud

Hotell Skagerack on the harbourfront in Strömstad

❷ Åmål

Dalsland. Road 45. 🚆 12,000.
🚌 🚏 🚈 Karlstad. 🚢 ℹ️ Marinan,
Hamngatan 1, 0532-170 98. 🎪 Åmål
Blues Festival (2nd week in Jul).
🌐 dalsland.nu

Dalslands only town, Åmål, was founded in 1643. Thanks to its strategic location on Lake Vänern, Åmål soon became an important market place, controlling timber exports to Norway and later acting as a transit port for timber and iron to Gothenburg. After several fires in the 17th century and a major fire in 1901, a new town was built on the north side of the Åmålsån river. Little remains of the original buildings apart from a few 18th-century houses around the town park, Plantaget. The local history museum, **Åmåls Hembygdsmuseum**, whose three floors house a dentist's clinic and a flat furnished in 1920s style, can be found in Snarhögsgården. The Railway Museum is located in former engine sheds at Åmål Östra.

At **Forsbacka** on the Åmålsån river, 7 km (4 miles) from Åmål towards Bengtsfors, a mechanical hammer for producing iron bars was built at the end of the 17th century. It was used until the end of the 19th century. Today the 18th-century house at Forsbacka ironworks is a hotel and the old buildings are protected. A golf course is on the land.

🏛 **Åmåls Hembygdsmuseum**
Hamngatan 7. **Tel** 0532-158 20.
Open mid-Jun–Aug: daily. 🎪
🚻 partly.

❸ Strömstad

Bohuslän. E6. 🚆 12,000. 🚌 🚈
🚢 from Sandefjord, Norway. 🚏 from
Rygge, Norway. 🚢 ℹ️ Norra Hamnen,
0526-623 30. 🎪 Winter World Festival
(1st weekend in Mar), Strömstad
Shrimp Festival (Jul), Summer music
(Jul). 🌐 vastsverige.com

When Strömstad became Swedish in 1658 it was just a small fishing village, but by 1676 it had become a town, acting as a strategic counter to the Norwegian towns of Halden and Fredrikstad. In the mid-19th century sea-bathing became the fashion and ever since, Strömstad, with its glorious island archipelago and many hours of sunshine, has been one of Sweden's major holiday resorts.

Strömstad is a modern town and its proximity to Norway is evident from the number of Norwegian cars and boats. The Svinesund bridges between Sweden and Norway offer magnificent views.

The **Strömstads Museum** focuses on local history, while **Friluftsmuseet Fiskartorpet** is an open-air museum featuring fishermen's cottages.

The harbour with bars and shops is in the centre of the town and boats from here serve the islands, including Kosteröarna. Seal safaris operate to waters around the Ursholmarna islands south of Sydkoster. The nature reserves on Rossö and Saltö can be reached by car.

🏛 **Strömstad Museum**
Södra Hamngatan 22.
Tel 0526-102 75. **Open** Mon–Sat.
Closed public holidays.

🏛 **Friluftsmuseet Fiskartorpet**
Karlsgatan 45. **Tel** 0526-617 53.
Open summer: daily. 🖥

❹ Koster Islands

Bohuslän. 🚆 300. 🚢 from Strömstad
(about 45 mins). 🚢 ℹ️ Norra
Hamnen, Strömstad, 0526-623 30.

The islands of Koster are renowned for their beauty and their flora. Together they form a nature reserve. These are the westernmost Swedish islands to be inhabited. Sydkoster is the largest island in the group. It is greener than Nordkoster and is best explored by bike. In contrast, Nordkoster is much more barren and can easily be explored on foot.

The highlights of the Koster Islands' calendar include the Koster Chamber Music Festival in July and the lobster festival in the autumn, when visitors can sample the freshest seasonal shellfish and take part in thrilling fishing trips.

Made for sunbathing, the polished granite rocks on Nordkoster

For hotels and restaurants in this area see pp284–289 and pp294–301

❺ Tanum

Bohuslän. E6. 🅰 12,000. 🚉 🚌
ℹ Tourist Office, Tanumshede, 0525-
183 80. 🅦 **tanumturist.se**

The municipality of Tanum
has an extraordinary 525 km
(326 miles) of coastline indented
with fjords and bays. It stretches
from Gerlesborg in the south
to Resö in the north, and is
sheltered by a mass of islets and
skerries offshore. Inland, farms
nestle between rocky outcrops.

Above all, Tanum is renowned
for its Bronze Age rock carvings,
with the earliest dating from
around 1000 BC. Indeed, the
concentration of these pictorial
images and their contribution
to the understanding of Bronze
Age culture is such that they
were designated a UNESCO
World Heritage Site in 1994.
Subjects include human life,
animals, boats and weapons
carved onto smooth rock.

The largest carving, covering
200 sq m (2,150 sq ft), can be
seen at Vitlycke. **Vitlycke
Museum** is well worth a visit for
a fascinating insight into this
form of rock art. The museum
contains exhibitions and a
reconstructed Bronze Age farm.
Guided tours by night, when
carvings that are not visible by
day emerge in the light of a

Fjällbacka's painted wooden houses in the shadow of Vetteberget

torch, are especially enthralling
for any age group.

Around the region, carvings
featuring hunting scenes can
be seen at **Fossum**, east of
Tanumshede; **Tegneby** has
images of ships; and at
Asberget scenes containing
animals, ploughs and axes
can be found.

🏛 **Vitlycke Museum**
3 km (2 miles) S of Tanumshede.
Tel 0525-209 50. **Open** May–Sep.
🕒 by arrangement. 🅿 🎦 📷 🛍 👤

❻ Fjällbacka

Bohuslän. E6/road 163. 🅰 850. 🚉 to
Tanum, then bus. ℹ Torget, 0525-
321 20. 🎣 Mackerel Fishing World
Championships (last Sat in Aug).

On the coast between
Strömstad and Uddevalla lies
the picturesque village of
Fjällbacka. There has been a
settlement here since the 17th
century and like many other
villages along this coast the
community made a living from
herring fishing and seafaring.
Today, holidaymakers come for
the swimming and boating.

Attractive low-rise wooden
houses and shops line the
narrow streets, but it is the
harbour which is the heart
of the community. Fjällbacka
has a stunning location with
islands offshore and the 70-m
(230-ft) high mountain,

Bronze Age Rock Carvings

The rock carvings at Tanum represent a high point in the artistic
language of pictures and symbols used by Bronze Age people more
than 3,000 years ago. Images reflect daily life and hardships, battles
won and lost, weapons and hunting scenes. Mating scenes, fertility
symbols and the afterlife are also common. The importance of the
sea is reflected in the proliferation of ships and fishing scenes. It is
thought that the rock paintings were primarily of ritual significance,

but the depiction of animals
could have acted as a calendar
to show when various
creatures could be hunted.
Hands and feet as motifs are
thought to be associated with
a godly being too holy to have
his whole body depicted.

Rock carvings can be found
all over the world, with the
oldest dating from 20,000 BC.
Those in Sweden are younger,
since it wasn't completely free
of ice until 6,500 BC. The
carvings at Tanum date from
1000–500 BC.

Bronze Age warrior in a state of sexual
arousal, Tanum

Bust of actress Ingrid Bergman (1915–82)
in Fjällbacka

Vetteberget, creating a precipitous backdrop to the village centre and square known as Ingrid Bergmans Torg. Actress Ingrid Bergman spent many summers in Fjällbacka and after her death her name was given to the square and a bust made by Gudmar Olovson (1983). Fjällbacka is also known as the location of author Camilla Läckberg's series *"The Fjällbacka Murders"*, which has sold millions of books worldwide.

Vetteberget is divided by a huge gorge, known as Kungsklyfta, named after King Oscar II who visited Fjällbacka in 1887 and had his name carved at the entrance to the chasm. This dramatic setting was also used as a location for the film of Astrid Lindgren's children's book *Ronja Rövardotter* (Ronja the Robber's Daughter).

❼ Nordens Ark

Bohuslän. Road 17, 20 km (12 miles) N of Smögen. 🚌 **Tel** 0523-795 90. **Open** daily; hours vary, so call ahead. 🖼️ 🏠 📷 🌐 **nordensark.se**

This nature park and zoo caters specifically for endangered species. Located in Åby Säteri, it contains animals from every corner of the world, including ancient Swedish breeds such as Gotland sheep and mountain cows, Nordic wild animals such as wolves and wolverine, and

Red panda one of the many endangered species at Nordens Ark

exotic species such as the Amur leopard and a variety of parrots. Many of the creatures are part of special programmes to protect them from extinction.

To see the animals up close, follow the 3-km (2-mile) walk around the park – and bring binoculars to spot the wide variety of birds. The route takes you between the enclosures via wooden bridges and along gravel paths. Admission in the summer includes a guided tour. The breeding and quarantine areas are not open to the public.

Nordens Ark is a particularly enjoyable outing for families as there are special children's activities throughout the park. Youngsters can find out how animals adapt in relation to their

food, enemies and the environment by being active themselves, trying things out and playing – even adults find these activities entertaining.

Overnight accommodation is also available.

❽ Smögen

Bohuslän. E6/Road 174. 🔼 1,500. 🚌 from Gothenburg. 🛥️ ℹ️ Sotenäs Tourist Office, Kungshamn, 0523-66 55 50. 🎉 Herring and Shellfish Festival (3rd weekend in Jul), Tradjazz (first weekend in Aug). 🌐 **sotenasturism.se**

One of Sweden's largest fishing communities, Smögen today is a delightful holiday resort with shrimp trawlers and the daily fish auction providing popular entertainment. Commerce is particularly lively along the wooden quayside.

Ferries operate to the island of Hållö, a nature reserve south of Smögen where there is a lighthouse, **Hållö Fyr**, which has guided seafarers since 1842.

The **Sotenkanalen** links Smögen and Hunnebostrand. Built in the 1930s, the canal is 6 km (4 miles) long and a popular tourist route. **Hunnebostrand** is a typical west coast holiday destination and home to Svenska Hummerakademien (the Swedish Lobster Academy). The village's development was based on stonemasonry.

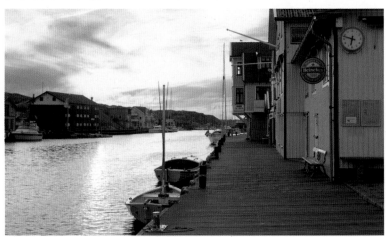

Wooden houses lining the quays of Smögen's well-protected harbour

⑨ Uddevalla

Bohuslän. E6, road 44. 🚗 36,000. 🚉
🚌 ✈ Trollhättan. 🛈 Södra Hamnen,
0522-69 84 70. 🎌 Motocross World
Championships (first weekend in Jul),
West Coast Dance Festival (mid-Jul),
Uddevallakalaset (last weekend in Jul).
🔲 **uddevalla.com**

The town of Uddevalla was
famous for shipbuilding on
a grand scale until the 1980s
when an economic crisis forced
the closure of its shipyard.
Uddevalla's history dates from
1498 when it gained its town
charter. Its strategic location
helped trade to flourish, but
also left it open to attack. It
became Swedish in the Peace
of Roskilde in 1658, as the
statues of Karl X Gustav and
Erik Dahlbergh in front of the
old town hall testify. Among
the town's attractions, the
collections at **Bohusläns
Museum** focus on the cultural
and natural heritage of the
region. The museum is situated
by the harbour, and includes
Konsthallen, a gallery for
contemporary art. **Sveriges
Sjömanshusmuseum**
concentrates on the history
of seafaring. **Bohusläns
Försvarsmuseum** (Defence
Museum) has a soldier's
cottage among its exhibits.
Uddevalla also has a pleasant
seaside promenade.

Environs
Nature lovers will enjoy the
unusual shellbanks and
museum devoted to them,
Skalbanksmuseet, in Kuröd,
outside Uddevalla.
    The old church of **Bokenäs**
is originally from the 12th
century. The tower and the

Ornate carving on the façade of Restaurang Havsbadet, Lysekil

church's restored ceiling
paintings date from the
18th century. The church is
on road 161, 23 km (14 miles)
west of Uddevalla.

🏛 Bohusläns Museum
Museigatan 1. **Tel** 0522-65 65 00.
Open daily. **Closed** some public hols.
🔲 by arrangement. 🔲 🖋 🔲

🏛 Skalbanksmuseet
5 km (3 miles) E of Uddevalla.
Tel 0522-65 65 00. **Open** Jun–Aug:
Tue–Sun. 🔲

⑩ Lysekil

Bohuslän. E6/road 162. 🚗 7,500.
🚌 from Uddevalla. 🚢 from
Fiskebäckskil. 🛈 Strandvägen 9,
0523-130 50. 🎌 Hot Bulb Engine
Festival (3rd weekend in Aug).
🔲 **lysekil.se**

When Lysekil gained its town
charter in 1903 the town was
already an established seaside
resort. Buildings in the old part
of Lysekil, Gamlestan, are more
than 200 years old. A walk along
Strandgatan reveals the charm
of this old quarter.
    The 19th-century sea-bathing
area has been beautifully
restored. There is a cold bath
house, Oscars Festsal,
and the Nordic-style
Curmanska Villas. The
rest of the town is
dominated by the
large, Neo-Gothic
granite church
dating from 1901.
    Lysekil lies at the far
end of the Stångenäset
peninsula, with
Gullmarsfjorden –
Sweden's only real
"fjord" in a Norwegian

sense – to the south and
Brofjorden to the north, and
here the sea has always played
a major role. The town's
aquarium, **Havets Hus**, is
devoted to the marine and
plant life found off the
Bohuslän coast. Around 100
different species of fish can
be viewed in their natural
habitats. There is a walk-through
aquarium and a multi-media
centre. The town's fishing
traditions can also be
experienced at the Hot Bulb
Engine Festival.

🏛 Havets Hus
Strandvägen 9. **Tel** 0523-66 81 61.
Open Feb–Dec: daily.
🔲 🔲 🔲 🔲 🔲 🔲

⑪ Bassholmen

Bohuslän. Road 161 towards
Fiskebäckskil. 🚌 to Källeviken, then
2 km (1 mile) walk and boat. 🚢 from
Uddevalla (Tue–Thu). 🔲 🛈 Södra
Hamnen, Uddevalla, 0522-69 84 70.

The nature reserve on the island
of Bassholmen, between Orust
and Skaftö, is one of the
highlights of the Bohuslän
archipelago. The landscape is
one of narrow valleys, leafy
meadows and pine forest, with
grazing horses and sheep. It is
a particularly attractive area
for walking. In the centre of
the island an old farm stands
amid parkland and trees.
    Bassholmen is also home
to a number of traditional
shipbuilder's yards, which
come under the care of the
Föreningen Allmoge Båtar, a
society which works to preserve
and renovate the traditional

Bohusläns Museum in Uddevalla with a display of old
working boats

wooden boats of Bohuslän. Many of these boats can be seen in the museum.

Every summer boating enthusiasts converge on the island for a nostalgic feast to study the craftsmanship involved in greater detail and experience the life of a boatman at the end of the 19th century.

There is a guest jetty in the former shipyard for visiting craft. In summer boats run to Bassholmen from Uddevalla.

Grundsund harbour, edged with original fishermen's huts

Skaftö from the mainland. **Fiskebäckskil** in Gullmarsfjorden is a seafaring community established at the end of the 19th century, featuring a captain's house, richly decorated wooden cottages and romantic gardens. It is also the site of Kristineberg Marine Research Station.

The village of **Grundsund** dates from the 17th century. A canal runs through it past the closely packed red fishermen's huts on the lively quayside, so typical of the west coast. The small wooden church, built in 1799, is well worth a look. Delicious fresh seafood is served in the harbourside inn.

Fiskebäckskil, a summer paradise on Skaftö in Gullmarsfjorden

⑫ Skaftö

Bohuslän. Road 161 towards Fiskebäckskil. 🚌 from Uddevalla. 🛈 Lysekil Tourist Office, 0523-130 50.

The best way to see the island of Skaftö is to walk or cycle around it. The scenery varies between fertile agricultural land, pine forests and bare hills. Skaftö's potatoes and strawberries are justifiably famous. In the centre of the island is Gunnesbo, a favourite spot for children where pony rides and a mini-zoo can be found.

In the far south on the slopes running down towards the sea lies **Rågårdsvik**, a small community overlooking the wide Ellösefjorden and the village of Ellöse, site of the internationally successful Hallberg Rassy shipyard. Rågårdsvik Pensionat provides excellent west-coast cuisine.

Between Skaftölandet and Orust are the winding, narrow Malö straits, made famous by the songs of troubadour Evert Taube, while the beautiful Snäckedjupet separates

⑬ Gullholmen

Bohuslän. 🏠 150. 🚢 from Tuvesvik, Orust. 🛈 Henåns Tourist Office, 0304-33 44 94. 🌐 **sodrabohuslan.com**

Dating from 1585, Gullholmen is one of the oldest fishing communities in Bohuslän. In the mid-19th century one of Sweden's early canning factories was set up here. Line fishing on the Dogger Bank in the North Sea produced good catches

and in 1910 Gullholmen had a fishing fleet of more than 50 cutters. As the fishing industry declined, so did the population and summer residents have taken over many of the houses. Gullholmen is a typical west-coast summer paradise.

Sights include the church, inaugurated in 1799, and the pilot's lookout which was dismantled in 1916, but is now being rebuilt. **Skepparhuset**, a late 19th-century captain's home with original interiors, is well worth a look. South of Gullhomen, as if thrown out to sea, lies the completely barren **Käringön**. The island is so bare that in the past earth for its small churchyard had to be transported from Orust. The charming tightly-packed houses are almost entirely used by summer visitors and in the season the popular guest harbour is bursting with life. A fishing cottage houses a small museum. The island can be reached by boat from Hälleviksstrand or by ferry from Tuvesvik.

Weathervane, Fiskebäckskil

🏛 Skepparhuset
Tel 0304-570 70. **Open** four weeks in summer. Contact the tourist office.

Picturesque houses by the harbour in Gullholmen

Mollösund, a typical fishing village on Orust

⑭ Orust

Bohuslän. 🗺 15,000. 🚌 from Stenungsund. 🚶 Hamntorget 18, 0304-33 44 94. 🛥 Boatyard open days (last weekend in Aug). 🖥 orust.se; 🖥 sodrabohuslan.com

One of Sweden's largest islands, Orust's fortunes over the centuries have been tied to the rise and fall of herring fishing. On the southwest coast, the village of **Mollösund** dates from the 16th century, when herring fishing was at its height. A decline in stocks brought poverty, but with the herring's reappearance in the 1750s the population increased, inns opened and refineries for making fish oil from herring developed. The bare rocks of Bohuslän are a reminder of this time; the fish oil refineries needed lots of wood and the coastline was practically deforested.

Most homes had a fisherman's hut on the harbour and even today the houses and huts are closely packed together. There is a strong smell of stockfish hanging out to dry to produce *Lutfisk* for the Swedish Christmas table.

Today Orust is a centre for the manufacture of superior leisure boats. Half the boats exported from Sweden come from here. The boatyards display their craft in the "Öppna Varv" open days.

⑮ Tjörn

Bohuslän. 🗺 15,000. 🚌 from Stenungsund. 🚶 Tjörn Tourist Office, 0304-60 10 16. 🛥 Round Tjörn Yacht Race (3rd Sat in Aug). 🖥 tjörn.se; 🖥 sodrabohuslan.com

The municipality of Tjörn comprises six inhabited islands. Fishing, boat-building and small businesses are the cornerstones of the economy and in summer the population doubles with the arrival of holidaymakers.

Opened in 1960, the **Tjörn Bridges** offer fantastic views over land and water. Tjörnbroleden, the road linking the islands of Tjörn and Orust to the mainland at Stenungsund, crosses the bridges of Stenungsöbron, Källosundsbron and Tjörnbron over Askeröfjorden. In 1980 Tjörnbron collapsed when a ship collided with it in thick fog; a new bridge opened the following year. At its northern end is an ideal site for camping with great views.

Skärhamn, on the west side of Tjörn, is the island's main town. It has a guest harbour, restaurants and hotel. Sights include **Sjöfartsmuseum** (the Seafaring Museum) and the popular **Nordiska Akvarellmuseet** (Nordic Watercolour Museum), a stunning building hosting exhibitions and courses for amateur painters.

Tjörn Bridge, 664 m (726 yd) long, and 45 m (147 ft) high

Fishing net float

Pilane Gravfält, a burial site with more than 100 Iron Age mounds, stone circles, rings and standing stones, is on northwest Tjörn. In the summer, it hosts an amazing sculpture park. Take the road towards Kyrkesund, turn left to Hällene and after 1 km (half a mile) there is a car park.

🏛 Nordiska Akvarellmuseet
Skärhamn. Södra Hamnen.
Tel 0304-60 00 80. **Open** Tue–Sun.
Closed some public holidays.
🅿 🚻 🖬 🖼 🛍 🚻

The Watercolour Museum, Tjörn, resting on piles in the water

⑯ Marstrand

Bohuslän. Road 168. 🗺 1,400. 🚌 🚢 🚆 🚶 0303-600 87 (summer); 0303 833 27 (winter). 🛥 Fortress Re-enactments, Swedish Match Cup (one week in early Jul), Marstrand Regatta (last week in Jul). 🖥 kungalv.se; 🖥 vastsverige.com

Sun, sailing and the sea are what Marstrand is all about. The little town of pastel-coloured wooden houses has its roots in the herring boom of the mid-16th century, which attracted fortune-hunters. But it really took off in the mid-19th century as a fashionable seaside resort. Marstrand built its baths and society arrived.

The town is crowned by the impressive **Carlstens Fästning**, a fortress built in 1666–73 and redesigned in the 1680s by architect Erik Dahlbergh. At one time it was a notorious prison. Tours provide a glimpse into the life and times of the fortress and its inmates in the 18th century. Plays are staged here and feasts held during the summer.

Northwards into the wide waters of Marstrandsfjorden is the rocky island of **Åstol**, almost entirely covered by characteristic white houses and fishing huts. The island can be reached by a 10-minute ferry ride from Rönnäng on Tjörn.

🏛 Carlstens Fästning
Tel 0303-602 65. **Open** daily. 🎫 🖊 📷 🕹 partly.

⑰ Kungälv

Bohuslän. E6. 👤 21,000. 🚆 to Ytterby then bus. 🚌 ✈ Landvetter. ℹ 0303-109 00. 📷 Medieval Festival (mid-Jul). 🖥 **kungalv.se**; 🖥 **vastsverige.com**

Strategically located between the Nordre Älv and Göta Älv rivers, Kungälv occupies the site of the 10th-century Viking settlement of Kongahälla. It is dominated by the ruins of **Bohus Fästning**, a fortress built by the Norwegian King Håkon Magnusson in 1308. Constructed first in wood and later in stone, the fortress was at the frontline in the constant wars between Sweden, Norway and Denmark. At the Peace of Roskilde in 1658 it became Swedish, but it went on to be besieged no less than 14 times without being captured.

In 1678, 900 Swedish defenders faced 9,000 Norwegians and 7,000 German mercenaries, but still the castle didn't fall. In the 18th century it became a prison and in 1789 all the towers were destroyed apart from the main one known as "Fars Hatt" (Father's Hat).

Red-roofed Gungälv church, situated in the market square, dates from 1679.

🏛 Bohus Fästning
Tel 0303-109 00. **Open** May–Sep: daily. **Closed** Midsummer's Eve. 🎫 📷 by arrangement.

⑱ Vänersborg

Västergötland. Road E45. 👤 4,700. 🚆 🚌 ✈ ℹ Railway Station, 0521-135 09. 📷 Christmas market (Dec). 🖥 **visittv.se**

Vänersborg is otherwise known as "Little Paris" after the poems of Birger Sjöberg (1885–1929). A statue of the local poet's muse, Frida, can be seen in the beautiful Skräckleparken on the lake shore, and a reconstruction of his home is in **Vänersborgs Museum**. Other museums focus on medical history, dolls and sport. The town was founded in 1644 and its Neo-Classical church completed in 1784.

Environs
Just over 5 km (3 miles) east of the town, the steeply-sided hills of Halleberg and Hunneberg rise up over the landscape. The hillside forests are a nature reserve featuring a large elk population, which is the focus of an annual royal hunt.

On top of Hunneberg is **Kungajaktmuseet Älgens Berg** where the "king of the forest" is presented in interactive displays. The intricacies of elk hunting are explained and visitors can try their hand at shooting an elk themselves, virtually of course.

🏛 Vänersborgs Museum
Tel 0521-600 62/26 41.40. **Open** Tue, Thu, Sat & Sun (also Wed Jul–Aug). 📷 🖊 🖥 **vanersborgsmuseum.se**

🏛 Kungajaktmuseet Älgens Berg
Hunneberg. On road 44. **Tel** 0521-27 00 40. **Open** Jan: Tue–Fri; Jun–Aug: daily; Sep–Dec & Feb–May: Tue–Sun.. **Closed** some public hols. 📷 🎫 by appointment. 📷 💻 🖊 🖥 **algensberg.com**

Staircase of locks on the Trollhättan Canal, rising 32 m (105 ft)

⑲ Trollhättan

Västergötland. Road E45. 👤 56,000. 🚆 🚌 ✈ 🚢 ℹ Innovatum, Åkersjövägen 10, 0520-135 09. 📷 Fallens Dagar (3rd weekend in Jul). 🖥 **visittv.se**

The opening of the Trollhättan Canal in 1800, linking Lake Vänern and the North Sea, marked the birth of Trollhättan as an industrial town. Today, Trollhättan successfully combines high-tech industries such as GKN with a burgeoning film industry that has earned the town its local nickname, "Trollywood".

The town's main sight is the waterfall area where four locks regulate the once wild 32-m (105-ft) high falls. In summer the sluices are opened several times a week to let the mass of water rush freely down river.

The technology centre **Innovatum Science Center** (ISC) features multi-media exhibits on the history and development of Trollhättan. From the Innovatum area, a cable car transports visitors 30 m (98 ft) above the canal to the opposite bank. A short walk leads to the Canal Museum.

🏛 Innovatum Science Center (ISC)
Åkersjövägen 10. **Tel** 0520-28 94 00. **Open** mid-Jun–mid-Aug: daily; other times: Tue–Sun. 🎫 💻 🖊 📷 🖊

Bohus Fästning, the impregnable 14th-century fortress at Kungälv

⑳ Lidköping

Västergötland. Road 44. 🏠 25,000.
🚉 🚌 🏛 ⚓ ℹ️ Gamla Rådhuset
på Nya stadens torg, 0510-200 20.
W **lackokinnekulle.se**

The town of Lidköping lies at
the heart of the area of Västergötland that is considered to be
the cradle of the Svea Kingdom.
Like so many of Sweden's
wooden towns, Lidköping
suffered a devastating fire in
1849, though some of the 17th-
century buildings around the
square of Limtorget survived.

The Lidan river divides the
town into old and new, and the
two main squares (1446 and
1671 respectively) face each
other across the water. Nya
Stadens Torg (New Town Square)
is the site of a former hunting
lodge, which the founder of
the new town, Magnus Gabriel
de la Gardie, brought here to
serve as a town hall.

Lidköping is known for the
Rörstrands Porcelain Factory and
Rörstrands Museum attracts
visitors in search of bargain dinner
services or simply to enjoy the
showpieces in the museum.

Vänermuseet with the Paleo
Geology Centre is an interactive
science museum.

Environs
Husaby, 10 km (6 miles) east of
Lidköping, encapsulates

Läckö Slott, a splendid castle on the shore of Lake Vänern

Swedish history. It was here at
Husaby well that King Olof
Skötkonung was baptised by
the English monk Sigfrid in
1008. A 12th-century church
now stands at the site.
Gösslunda Kyrka, just west
of the town, also dates from
the 12th century. Outside is a
rune stone that was originally
part of the church wall.

To the northwest of Lidköping
is **Spikens Fiskehamm,
Kållandsö**, the only active
fishing harbour on Lake Vänern,
and a lively tourist destination.

🏛 **Rörstrands Museum**
Fabriksgatan 4.
Open daily. **Closed** some public
holidays. 🖥 ♿ 📷
W **rorstrandcenter.se**

🏛 **Vänermuseet**
10 min walk from the centre. **Tel** 0510-
77 00 65. **Open** Jun–Aug: daily; Sep–
May: Tue–Sun. **Closed** some public
holidays. 🚗 📷 by arrangement.
🖥 ♿ 📷 W **vanermuseet.se**

㉑ Läckö Slott

Västergötland. 25 km (15 miles)
N of Lidköping. 🚌 from Lidköping.
Tel 0510-48 46 60. **Open** May–Sep:
times vary; see website. 🚗 📷 🖥
📷 🏠 ♿ Medieval Market (3rd
weekend in Jun). W **lackoslott.se**

Jakob de la Gardie was the first
to make his mark on Läckö Slott
after it was assigned to him in
1615. In 2001 Läckö was named
the most beautiful castle in
Sweden. It is surrounded by

water on three sides. Originally
built in the 13th century by
Bishop Brynolf Algotsson, it
became the seat of the bishops
of Skara. Count Jakob and his
son, Magnus de la Gardie,
embarked on remodelling the
castle in the 17th century. But
in 1681 Läckö was claimed by
Karl XI in his recovery of crown
lands from the nobility and its
contents were scattered.

Restoration work in the 20th
century has revealed more than
200 rooms, including the richly
decorated apartment of
Princess Marie Euphrosyne, wife
of Marcus de la Gardie, and the
King's Hall with its paintings of
the Thirty Years' War.

Läckö is the setting for art
exhibitions and summer opera
performances are held in the
courtyard. The garden is also
open to the public.

㉒ Kinnekulle

Västergötland. Road 44. ℹ️ Gamla
Rådhuset på Nya stadens torg,
Lidköping, 0510-200 20.
W **lackokinnekulle.se**

The 306-m (1,000-ft) high
plateau of Kinnekulle, known
as "the flowering mountain",
rises from the Västergötland
landscape, providing habitats
for wild flowers, deciduous
woods, pine forests, meadows
and pastures. It is topped with
bare limestone and a 20-m
(66-ft) high lookout tower.
Those not up to the climb can

Rörstrand ceramic stove, now in the
porcelain factory museum

◀ The famous colourful boathouses in the harbour of Smögen

enjoy the views from the restaurant at Högkullen. Limestone has been quarried here since the 12th century. In summer demonstrations at the remaining quarry show how the work used to be carried out.

The area is peppered with ancient Stone Age and Bronze Age sites.

Forshems Kyrka, just to the east, dates from the 12th century and is known for its stone reliefs. The churchyard of the 12th-century church at **Kinne-Vedum**, 2 km (1 mile) north of Götene, has several lily stones, typical of this area.

㉓ Mariestad

Västergötland. E20. 🗺 15,000. 🚊 🚌 🛥 Lidköping. ⬛ 🛆 🛈 Kyrkogatan 2, 0501-75 58 50. 🛥 Göta Canal Swim (4th week in Jul). 🕸 **vastsverige.com**

Duke Karl founded the pretty town of Mariestad in 1583, naming it after his wife, Maria of Pfalz. He built the cathedral and lavishly decorated it in the Baroque style. It is well worth exploring the interesting little streets surrounding the cathedral, as these are lined with buildings from the 18th and 19th centuries.

In 1660 Mariestad became the county town of Skaraborg. The former royal manor of Marieholm, on an island where the River Tidan flows into Lake Vänern, was the governor's residence. It now houses **Vadsmo Museum** and **Mariestads Industrimuseum** (Industrial Museum).

Mariestad's location on Lake Vänern and the River Tidan makes it an idyllic summer town. The Göta Canal (see pp150–51) runs through it and

Kanalmuseet (the Canal Museum) is located in Sjötorp just north of the town.

Those keen on rural life should head for **Klockarbolet** in Odensåker, a reconstructed village dating from the 17th and 18th centuries.

🏛 **Vadsbo Museum and Mariestads Industrimuseum**
Marieholm. **Tel** 0501-75 58 30. **Open** Wed; other days by appointment. 🚻 🚻 🖥 🚻 🖥 ♿

🏛 **Kanalmuseet**
Sjötorp, off road Rv 26. **Tel** 0141-20 20 50. **Open** Jun–Aug: daily. 🚻

㉔ Tivedens National Park

Västergötland. Road 49. 🚌 from Karlsborg. 🛈 Karlsborgs Tourist Office, 0505-173 50.

On the border between Närke and Västergötland lies Tiveden National Park, an untouched area of rugged wilderness. It was established in 1983 to protect the remaining primeval forest and lakes, of which Fagertärn is the original habitat of the large red water-lily (see p25).

The area is very hilly and demanding for walkers. There is a visitor centre at Stenkälla with information on trails, parking and things to see inside the park.

Giant Ice Age boulders, some up to 10 m (33 ft) high, litter the forest around **Trollkyrka**, the hill east of the road by the visitor centre. The mountain's name is thought to be derived from the fact that the site was used by local people who came here to worship after the ban in 1726 on holding religious services outside churches.

Karlsborgs Fästning, a 19th-century wartime hideaway

㉕ Karlsborg

Västergötland. Road 49. 🗺 7,000. 🚌 🛆 🛈 Karlsborgs Tourist Office, Storgatan 65, 0505-173 50. Fortress: **Tel** 0505-173 50. **Open** call for opening hours. 🚻 🖥 🚻 🕸 **karlsborgsturism.se**

In 1819 King Karl XIV Johan decided that a fortress should be built at Vanäs on the shore of Lake Vättern. It was named Karlsborg and was to act as an emergency capital in the event of war; a place of safety for the royal family, the national bank and the government. The 90 years it took to build meant that by the time it was finally finished the fortress was out of date and it never had any real significance. Today, however, it is a major tourist attraction. The "town" enclosed within the 5-km (3-mile) long walls is best viewed on one of the hour-long guided adventure tours that run daily in the summer. Action fans can watch *Fästningsäventyret*, an adventure depicting life in the fortress in the 1860s complete with stunt men and special effects.

Outside the fortress, the Göta Canal wends its way towards Lake Vänern, passing **Forsviks Bruk**, which offers an interesting glimpse into Sweden's industrial heritage, with a blacksmith's forge, sawmill and working flour mill.

🏛 **Forsviks Bruk**
8 km (5 miles) north of the centre. **Tel** 010-441 43 65. **Open** Jun–Aug: daily. 🚻 🕸 **forsviksbruk.se**

Marieholm, the former governor's residence in Mariestad

Hjo's wooden buildings, awarded the Europa Nostra medal in 1990

㉖ Hjo

Västergötland. Road 193/194.
🚗 6,000. 🚌 to Skövde then bus.
🚢 🚌 🛈 Floragatan 1, 0503-352 55.
🎭 Craft Fair (2nd weekend in Jul),
Round Vättern cycle race (3rd
weekend in Jun). 🖥 hjo.se

Mention Hjo and Swedes
immediately think of the
exquisite little wooden houses
dating from the end of the
19th century with their ornately
carved verandas. Hjo is a
delightful town to visit. On
the shore of Lake Vättern is
Stadsparken, a park created
when Hjo Spa was founded in
the late 19th century. Villa Svea,
one of the former spa buildings
in the park, houses **Hjo
Stadsmuseum** (the Town
Museum). It is worth a look for
its remarkable calendar clock
Hjouret, and recreated rooms
from the heyday of the spa. The
park also contains Fjärilsmuseum
(the Butterfly Museum) and
Vätternakvarium, an aquarium.

Just like the town, the harbour
has medieval origins, but the
present one was built in the
mid-19th century after the
construction of the Göta Canal.
In summer, the *Lok-Hjo-Motivet*
train takes guided tours (daily
except Monday) through the
town starting from the harbour.
The steamer *S/S Trafik* (1892)
runs Sunday tours to Visingö,
and jazz cruises to Vadstena
across the lake.

The Hjoån river valley,
stretching from Lake Vättern
to Mullsjön lake 4 km (2.5 miles)
west of Hjo has several
spectacular waterfalls.

🏛 **Hjo Stadsmuseum**
Villa Svea, Stadsparken. **Tel** 0503-352
55. **Open** May–Aug. ♿ partly.

㉗ Skövde

Västergötland. Road 48/49. 🚗 33,000
🚗 🚌 🛈 Sandtorget, 0500-44 66 88.
🎭 Food Festival (last weekend in
Aug), Skövde Film Festival (Nov).
🖥 skovde.se

Skövde is situated between the
two largest lakes in Sweden:
Vänern and Vättern. According
to local folklore, it became a
trading centre in the 12th century, when pilgrims came here
to honour Sweden's first female
saint – St Elin, or Helena. Skövde
has been destroyed by fire on
several occasions; the last time
was in 1759. The only building
that survived was a single 17th-
century house, **Helénsstugan**,
which today is part of Skövde
Stadsmuseum (Town Museum).
The museum also holds
exhibitions in the main
museum building in Norrmalm.

Kulturhuset, designed by
Hans-Erland Heineman in 1964,
houses the library, an
art gallery,
a cinema and a theatre
that often hosts shows
featuring popular
Swedish musicians
and comedians.

The town has
a bustling city
centre with many
independent shops
and several large malls.

Environs
Rising to the west of
Skövde is the 300-m
(984-ft) high **Billingen**
plateau, with views
stretching as far as Lake
Vättern. The area is a
popular recreation spot,
with everything from
hiking and mountain-
bike trails to canoe

rentals, an outdoor swimming
pool and a small fishing lake. In
winter there is a ski slope and
cross-country ski trails.

West of Skövde, on road 49,
is the 12th-century church
Våmbs Kyrka. The church was
restored to its original
appearance in the 1940s. On
the same road, slightly nearer
to Skövde, is **Varnhems
Klosterkyrka**, a 13th-century
three-aisle basilica.

🏛 **Helénsstugan**
Helénsparken, Skövde Stadsmuseum.
Tel 0500-49 80 69. **Open** summer. 🎭
🕐 by arrangement.

🏛 **Kulturhuset**
Trädgårdsgatan. **Tel** 0500-44 66 88
(tourist office). 🎭 💻 🖥

㉘ Skara

Västergötland. E20. 🚗 11,000. 🚌
🛈 Biblioteksgatan 3, 0511-325 80.
🎭 Naturum Crane Dance (end Mar–
Apr). 🖥 skara.se/turism

Traditionally an important seat of
learning and a bishopric, Skara is
one of Sweden's oldest towns.
The 11th-century cathedral lies
at its heart, surrounded by a
network of streets following a
pattern set out in the Middle
Ages. On Stora Torget stands
Krönikebrunnen, a well which on
its exterior chronicles important
events in the history of Skara and

The nave of Skara's Gothic cathedral, founded in the
12th century

of Sweden. Stadsparken is the site of **Västergötlands Museum** with its local history collection, and Fornbyn, an open-air museum complete with cottages showing how people lived in the past.

Environs
Axvall, 8 km (5 miles) from Skara on road 49, is the location of **Skara Sommarland**, the largest amusement park in Scandinavia, with a water park, go-kart track, campsite and holiday cottages.

Around 20 km (12 miles) east of Skara, Lake **Hornborgasjön** is a popular resting place for birds; every year, in March and April, dancing cranes gather here in their thousands. There is an observation tower and two information centres.

🏠 **Skara Sommarland**
Axvall, road 49 towards Skövde.
Tel 010 708 80 00. **Open** Jun–Aug
(times vary). 🧒 🆆 **sommarland.se**

🦅 **Hornborgasjön**
Naturum Hornborgasjön, road 189.
Tel 010-224 50 10. **Open** daily in
season. 🆆 **hornborga.com**

㉙ Falköping

Västergötland. Road 46. 🚗 15,000. 🚌
ℹ️ Trädgårdsgatan 27, 0515-88 70 50.
🆆 **falkoping.nu**

Between the hills of Mösseberget and Ålleberg lies the old town of Falköping. Of particular interest are the 12th-century church, St Olofs Kyrka, the medieval wooden houses and the town square, Stora Torget, with Ivar Tengbom's statue *Venus Rising from the Waves* (1931). **Falbygdens Museum** describes the local history.

Environs
Ekornavallen, 15 km (9 miles) north of Falköping, is an important historic burial site from the Stone, Iron and Bronze Ages.

Dalénmuseet in Stenstorp uses sound-and-light shows to illustrate the life and work of the 1912 Swedish Nobel laureate Gustaf Dalén, who invented the AGA oven and was an innovator

in the the field of lighting technology.

Gökhems Kyrka, west of the town, is a small Romanesque apse church without a tower. It dates from the early 12th century. Inside, limestone paintings depict *The Creation*.

Gudhems Klosterruin and **Klostermuseum** north of the town are the ruins of a convent founded in 1160. Today it is a museum. **Karleby**, to the east, is one of three villages along a road which probably existed in the Stone Age. Each farm had its burial site and there are 13 passage tumuli here, including one with a burial chamber 17 m (56 ft) long.

🏛️ **Falbygdens Museum**
St Olofsgatan 23. **Tel** 0515-88 50 50.
Open Tue–Fri & Sun. **Closed** some public holidays.

🏛️ **Dalénmuseet**
Stenstorp, 10 km (6 miles) N of centre.
Tel 0500-45 71 65. **Open** Mar–Sep:
Tue–Sun, Jul also Mon; Oct: Sat & Sun.
Closed Dec–Feb, Midsummer Eve. 🧒
🆆 **dalenmuseet.se**

㉚ Alingsås

Västergötland. E20. 🚗 25,000. 🚌 🚆
ℹ️ Estrad, Bryggaregatan 2, 0322-61
62 00. 🥔 Potato Festival (3rd weekend
in Jun), Ljus i Alingsås (Oct).
🆆 **alingsas.se**

Jonas Alströmer and the textile industry have, between them, left their mark on Alingsås. In the early 18th century,

Skulls of Stone Age inhabitants from the Falköping area in Falbygdens Museum

Ahlströmer founded his textile factory and on the proceeds he built **Nolhaga Slott**, a manor which today has a zoo and bird park.

Alingsås Kulturhus contains Alingsås Museum, an art gallery and library, and organizes regular events.

Environs
Gräfsnäs Slottsruin and Park is a ruined castle and park on Lake Anten, 20 km (12 miles) north of Alingsås. An exhibition describes its history. On the road towards Gothenburg lies **Nääs Slott**, a 17th-century castle with an impressive 19th-century interior. Here, the handicraft tradition of western Sweden is cultivated through events and exhibitions. The Midsummer celebrations here are fantastic.

🏛️ **Alingsås Kulturhus**
Södra Ringgatan 3. **Tel** 0322-61 65 98.
Open hours vary. **Closed** some public
holidays. 🧒 (free on Fri). ♿

🏛️ **Nääs Slott**
Floda, E20, 30 km (19 miles) N of
Gothenburg. **Tel** 0302-318 39.
Open winter: Mon–Fri; summer: daily.
📷 🍴 🖥️ ✏️ 🏠 🆆 **naas.se**

Nolhaga Slott, home of the textile magnate Jonas Ahlströmer, 1727

Ulricehamn Town Hall, 1799, located at the market square

❶ Ulricehamn

Västergötland. Road 40. 🚗 9,000. 🚌 🚆 𝑖 Järnvägsgatan 2b, 0321-59 59 59. 🅦 **ulricehamns turistbyra.se**

The town of Ulricehamn occupies a beautiful setting on Lake Åsunden in an area rich in historic monuments. Originally known as Bogesund, there has been a settlement here since the 14th century. The old coaching road across Västergötland to Halland ran through the town along Storgatan, the main street.

Textile enterprises dominate the local economy and in Gällstad the knitwear shops south of the town are open daily.

Boat trips on the **M/S Sylvia** leave Ulricehamn and sail to Fästeredssund, or even further south to Hofsnäs, where it is possible to rent a bike for the return trip. There are also themed trips available, including one that takes in several of the mansions around the lake.

Environs
Bystad, a farmstead 30 km (19 miles) south of Ulricehamn, has one of Sweden's oldest wolf traps, a pit measuring about 5 m (16 ft) in diameter and more than 3.5 m (11 ft) deep.

Along the road between Ulricehamn and Mullsjö lies **Näs Gård**. The manor's six historic red-painted buildings date from the 17th, 18th and 19th centuries and now form a regional cultural centre and art gallery. Concerts and other cultural events are held here.

Södra Vings Kyrka is a medieval gem of a church, dating in part from the 12th century. The artistic decoration is unusually lavish and includes 15th-century limestone paintings in the nave. The stately lectern was carved in Rococo style in 1748.

🚢 M/S Sylvia
For information and bookings, contact the Tourist Office. **Tel** 0321-59 59 59. 🅦 **rederiasunden.se**

❷ Torpa Stenhus

Västergötland. 30 km (19 miles) SE of Borås. **Tel** 033-28 13 24. **Open** May–mid-Sep: Sat–Sun (mid-Jun–mid-Aug: daily). 🎫 🅖 Eng 11am. 🖥 🅦 torpastenhus.se

Standing on a promontory at the southern end of Lake Åsunden is the medieval castle Torpa Stenhus. It belonged to the Stenbock family and from the 14th–mid-17th century was an important stronghold for defence against the Danes. In summer, Torpa Slottsteater stages a series of theatrical performances in a splendid outdoor setting.

Painting of Saturn at Torpa Stenhus

❸ Borås

Västergötland. Road 40. 🚗 105,000. ✈ 🚆 🚌 𝑖 Sven Eriksonsplatsen 3, 033-35 70 90. 🎭 Culture Night (first week in May), Harvest Festival (first week in Sep). 🅦 **boras.com**

In 1620 King Gustav II Adolf decided that the textile pedlars of the Knallebygden area should have a town of their own and Borås was founded. Textile factories still line the Viskan river, which winds through the town, although the industry has lost ground in recent years.

Borås is a green town with beautiful parks: Stadsparken in the centre is popular, as is Ramnaparken where the open-air Borås Museum is located. Also in the town centre is **Borås Djurpark**, a zoo with more than 80 species from all corners of the world. Large enclosures and attractive grounds make this zoo a pleasant family park.

Environs
On the road between Borås and Alingsås lies **Hedareds Kapell**, Sweden's only preserved stave church. Apart from its windows and shingled roof, the little, wooden 16th-century church remains as it was when it was built, complete with original 16th-century paintings.

Textilmuseet (the Textile Museum of Sweden), formerly housed in a late-19th-century spinning shed, has moved into the Textile Fashion Center in Simonsland. Its collection ranges from displays on industrial history to future textiles via art and design.

🦓 Borås Djurpark
Boråsparken, bus line 1 or 150 from Södra Torget. **Tel** 033-35 32 70. **Open** May–mid-Sep: daily; Oct & Apr: Sat & Sun; some school holidays. daily. 🎫 🖥 🅖 🅦 boraszoo.se

🏛 Textilmuseet
Kvarteret Simonsland. **Tel** 033-35 89 50. **Open** call ahead. 🎫 🅖 by arrangement. 🖥 🅖 🅦 boras.se/textilmuseet

Pink flamingo, one of the many exotic species at Borås Djurpark

❸④ Gunnebo Slott

In the 1780s, John Hall, one of the richest men in Sweden at the time, commissioned city architect Carl Wilhelm Carlberg of Gothenburg to design a summer villa and park at Gunnebo. On completion in 1796, Carlberg had created one of the most beautiful and stylistically pure examples of Neo-Classical Swedish architecture. Hall is said to have paid the bill with 38 barrels of gold, but that included everything: the interiors, servants' quarters, orangery, park, kitchen gardens and greenhouse. An adjoining farm made the estate virtually self-sufficient.

VISITORS' CHECKLIST

Practical Information
15 km (9 miles) SE of Gothenburg. E6/E20, then Gunnebogatan. **Tel** 031-334 16 00. Mansion: **Open** (tours only) see website for times. **Closed** 1 Jan, 24, 25 & 31 Dec. 🅿 ♿ book ahead in Dec. 🛍 🎁 ℹ 🖂 Garden: **Open** daily. 📷 mid-Jul–mid-Aug: Sun & public hols 2pm. ♿ 🌐 **gunneboslott.se**

Transport
🚉 Mölndal Station 🚌

The Hall
Three magnificent French windows let in the sunlight, which is reflected on the beautiful parquet floor.

Oval vestibule

Northern Façade
Ionian columns frame the sheltered terrace which opens onto the garden with its neatly clipped trees.

The frieze on the southern gable is made from lead painted to imitate marble.

The staircase leads to the park with its parterres and gravel paths.

The entrance is through the cellar, the starting point for tours.

Ceramic Stoves
The interior design, including exquisite ceramic stoves, is by Carlberg who adopted the light Gustavian style which pervades the entire house.

Park and Gardens
The French-inspired formal garden surrounding the house was also designed by Carlberg, as was the English park, which makes an ideal setting for a walk.

Varberg Fästning, a fortress on the shores of the Kattegat housing a local history museum

㉟ Kungsbacka

Halland. E6/E20. 🚗 17,000. 🚉 🚌
ℹ️ Storgatan 15, 0300-83 45 95.
🎵 Kungsbacka Chamber Music Festival (first weekend in Aug).
🌐 **kungsbacka.se**

Although Kungsbacka was an important trading centre in the 13th century, almost nothing remains of the old wooden town. All but two of the houses were destroyed in a devastating fire in 1846. The two survivors are the red cottage in Norra Torggatan and the mayor's house at Östergatan 10. The pretty pastel-painted wooden houses that replaced the old at the end of the 19th century can be seen around the square. Today, Kungsbacka is almost a southern suburb of Gothenburg.

Environs
Around 10 km (6 miles) outside Kungsbacka at Rydet is **Mårtagården**, a typical 18th-century sea captain's house.

Tjolöholms Slott, one of Sweden's more unusual buildings, lies 15 km (9 miles) south of Kungsbacka. This magnificent English Tudor-style mansion was built for a Scottish merchant and completed in 1904. It contained state-of-the-art features such as vacuum cleaners, showers and hot-air

Tjolöholms Slott, an eccentric English Tudor-style mansion with Art Nouveau interiors

heating. The house is surrounded by lovely parkland.

🏠 **Tjolöholms Slott**
10 km (6 miles) S of the centre, E6/E20 to Fjärås exit, then road 939. **Tel** 0300-40 46 00. **Open** Mar–May & Sep–Nov: Sat & Sun; mid-Jun–Aug: daily. Park **Open** daily. 📷 🌐 **tjoloholm.se**

㊱ Varberg

Halland. E6/E20. 🚗 25,000. 🚉 🚌
🚢 from Grenå. ℹ️ Brunnsparken, 0340-868 00. 🌐 **visitvarberg.se**

The coastal town of Varberg has, since the 19th century, been famous for its bathing, whether the cold curative baths fashionable of the period or swimming from the rocks and sandy beaches. The town was founded in the 13th century, but little from that time remains after several fires.

The harbour area is worth a look and, in particular, **Kallbadhuset**, the renovated cold bath house in Moorish style with separate sections for men and women. The oriental touch is repeated in **Societetshuset**, built in the 1880s when the town's popularity as a spa was at its height. Today it houses a restaurant, pub and disco, playground and mini-golf. On summer evenings concerts are held on the stage in the park.

Guarding the approach from the sea is the mighty Varbergs Fästning. Most of the fortress was built in the 17th century with parts dating from the 13th century. Today it houses a museum, **Hallands Kulturhistoriska Museum**, focusing on

the history of Halland. The museum's biggest attraction is the 14th-century Bocksten Man whose body was discovered in a bog still dressed in a complete outfit from the Middle Ages. The notorious bullet which killed King Karl XII in 1718 is also on show. An outpost of the museum is Båtmuseet, the boat museum in Galtabäck, 10 km (6 miles) south of Varberg, displaying traditional boats and models.

🏛️ **Hallands Kulturhistoriska Museum**
Varbergs Fästning. **Tel** 0340-828 30.
Open daily. 📷 📷 by arrangement.
🌐 **hkm.varberg.se**

㊲ Falkenberg

Halland. E6/E20. 🚗 19,000. 🚉 🚌
ℹ️ Holgersgatan 11, 0346-88 61 00.
🎵 Song festival (first week in Jul).
🌐 **visitfalkenberg.se**

A town with medieval roots, Falkenberg stands at the mouth of the River Ätran. The oldest areas of the town still have their wooden buildings, including St Laurentii Kyrka (St Laurence's church), parts of which date from the 14th century.

The pottery **Törngrens Krukmakeri** (1789) is still in operation, run by the seventh generation of potters.

Falkenbergs Museum is housed in a half-timbered granary at Söderbron. The grain dryer is a lofty landmark in the old town. The museum features a faithful reproduction of an apartment from the 1950s and the café has a working jukebox.

Falkenberg has several interesting smaller museums, including **Falkenbergs Hembygdsmuseum** (Rural

Museum) in St Lars Kyrkogata, a rural museum with a section on salmon fishing. The **Fotomuseet Olympia** in Sandgatan is housed in the town's first cinema (1912) and displays cameras and photos.

Environs

North of the town is **Morups Tånge**, known for its lighthouse built in the mid-19th century. The beach below is a nature reserve, a wetland area of international interest and a home for waders.

Törngrens Krukmakeri
Krukmakaregatan 4. **Tel** 0346-103 54. **Open** daily. Nygatan 34 (Mon–Sat).

Falkenbergs Museum
Skepparesträtet 2. **Tel** 0346-88 61 25. **Open** Sep–May: Tue–Thu & Sat; Jun–Aug: Tue–Sun.

Fly-fishing in the salmon-rich River Ätran in Falkenberg

❸❽ Halmstad

Halland. E6/E20. 90,000. from Grenå. *i* Tourist Office, Fattighuset, Köpmansgatan 20, 035-12 02 00. Street Theatre Festival (Aug). **halmstad.se**

At the point where the River Nissan flows into Laholmsbukten bay lies Halmstad. In the Middle Ages it was the largest town on the west coast. Today, the medieval inner city with its half-timbered architecture is classified as being of national interest. Kirsten Munk's house on Storgatan is an exceptional 17th-century building in green-glazed Dutch brick. Local craftsmen can be seen at work in **Fattighuset**, Lilla Torg, a former poorhouse dated 1859.

Several modern artists have left their mark on the town and Carl Milles' fountain *Europa and the Bull* in Stora Torg and Picasso's

The former training ship *Najaden* against a backdrop of Halmstad Slott

Woman's Head, which stands between the bridges over the river Nissan, are easily encountered on a stroll.

Halmstad Slott, a 17th-century castle, was built by the Danish King Christian IV. The former training ship *Najaden*, moored on the quayside in front of the castle, is undergoing renovation until at least 2016.

Hallands Konstmuseum (the County Museum) has a wide collection of art and cultural history.

Environs

Äventyrslandet, 9 km (5.5 miles) west of Halmstad, is a fun destination for children, with its water park, funfair, dinosaur park and circus show. To the north, the popular summer resorts of Tylösand, Haverdal and Frösakull spread out along the coast. **Simlångsdalen**, around 20 km (12 miles) from Halmstad on road 25, has several natural attractions including Danska Fall in the River Assman, a 36-m (118-ft) high waterfall.

Fattighuset
Lilla Torg. **Tel** 035-21 15 15. **Open** Mon–Sat.

Hallands Konstmuseum
Tollsgatan. **Tel** 035-16 23 00. **Open** Tue–Sun. **hallandskonstmuseum.se**

Äventyrslandet
Gamla Tylösandsvägen 1. free, from Halmstad. **Tel** 035-10 84 60. **Open** Jun–Aug: daily. **aventyrslandet.se**

❸❾ Laholm

Halland. Road 24. 6,000. *i* Teckningsmuseet, Hästtorget, 0430-154 50. Waterfall Day (2nd Sun in Aug), Salmon Festival (mid-Sep).

Halland's oldest and smallest town, Laholm is primarily associated with the long sandy beaches around the bay of Laholmsbukten. Mellbystrand, on the bay 6 km (4 miles) to the west of the town, throngs with holidaymakers in summer. The River Lagan also attracts visitors for the salmon fishing.

Laholm itself is characterized by its winding streets and low houses, reminiscent of Danish rule before 1645. Of the buildings around the square, the 200-year-old **Rådhuset** (Town Hall) is particularly beautiful. On the western gable there is an automaton symbolizing the meeting in Laholm in 1278 between the Swedish King Magnus Ladulås and Danish King Erik Klipping.

The renovated old fire station, with a beautiful view over the Lagan, houses the tourist office, as well as Teckningsmuseet, a museum of drawings with large, airy galleries.

Laholm's tidy rows of houses bearing the hallmarks of the town's Danish past

WESTERN SVEALAND

Värmland, Närke and Dalarna, with their rich rural heritage, colourful folk costumes, red-painted wooden houses and pastoral scenes, attracted visitors long before the onset of tourism. Stretching from the flatlands of Närke to the mountains of Dalarna, this region is known for its annual ski race and Midsummer festivities, as well as its industrial heritage based on mining and forestry.

Large expanses of water dominate all three provinces. Southern Värmland encompasses the huge Lake Vänern, which is also the end of the line for the arterial Klarälven river. The beautiful Fryken lakes provided inspiration for one of the province's well-known authors, Selma Lagerlöf *(see p237)*. Her home, Mårbacka, was in this region where so many of her adventures are set. There is plenty of scope for outdoor activities in Värmland, including boating, canoeing, rafting on the Klarälven river and fishing. The forests have exciting trails where walkers are unlucky if they don't see an elk, and on wildlife safaris there is even the chance of glimpsing one of the big four predators – bear, wolf, lynx or wolverine.

Närke, one of Sweden's smallest provinces, is sandwiched between two large lakes, Hjälmaren and Vättern. The centre of the province is dominated by the fertile Närke flatlands, encircled by forest, including the once infamous haunt of bandits, Tiveden, in the south. Örebro, Western Svealand's largest metropolis and Närke's county town, has all the charm of a small town.

Dalarna has the beautiful Siljan lake and the Dalälven river with its arms stretching into the mountains. The province offers more contrasts than most – from the gentle farmland around Siljan to the mountainous north. Every March, these are linked by the Vasaloppet race *(see p249)*, when tens of thousands of skiers head from Sälen down to Mora. Midsummer celebrations on Siljan are emblematic of Dalarna. Villages compete to see who has the most stylish maypole, the most accomplished musicians and the best folk dancers.

Rustic interior of Gammelgården in Mora, Dalarna

◀ Swedes in traditional costume performing a folk dance in the Dalarna region

Exploring Western Svealand

Fertile agricultural land spreads out around the major lakes, Vänern, Vättern, Hjälmaren and Siljan, and along the river valleys, giving way to a predominantly forested landscape. The region provides ample opportunities for nature lovers, with its abundance of wildlife, and for anglers, who will easily find a good catch. The mountains in Dalarna are the setting for some of the country's most popular ski resorts, walking trails and national parks. Motorists have many attractive small roads to choose from, while the Fryksdalsbanan and Inlandsbanan railway lines guarantee spectacular sights from the train window and leisurely boat trips provide glorious views from the water.

Author and Nobel laureate Selma Lagerlöf's Mårbacka, one of Värmland's many stately homes

Getting Around

Passing through Örebro and Karlstad, the E18 motorway crossing from Stockholm to Oslo is the main artery for traffic to this region. Travelling up into Värmland and Dalarna, the roads follow the river valleys, where the local population is also concentrated. Rail links are good to the southern parts of the provinces, but the northern areas can only be reached by car or bus. Between towns and popular tourist areas the bus services are quite frequent, but they can be patchy in rural areas. In summer, boats ply the major lakes of Vänern, Hjälmaren and Siljan.

Key

▬▬▬ Motorway
▬▬ Major road
══ Minor road
┅┅ Main railway
── Minor railway
▬▬▬ International border
△ Summit

For additional map symbols see back flap

0 kilometres 50

0 miles 30

The 16th-century Ornässtugan (in foreground), one of the places associated with Gustav Vasa's adventures in Dalarna

Engelbrekt, champion of liberty, in Örebro, by C G Qvarnström, 1866

Sights at a Glance

2 Arvika
3 Borgviks Bruk
4 Värmlandsnäs
5 Karlstad
6 Hagfors
7 Filipstad
8 Karlskoga
9 Askersund
10 Örebro pp242–3
11 Ludvika
12 Hedemora
13 Borlänge
14 Sundborn
15 Falun
16 Leksand
17 Rättvik
18 Mora
19 Orsa
20 Sälen
21 Idre and Särna

Tour

1 Around the Fryken Lakes

❶ A Tour around the Fryken Lakes

Author Selma Lagerlöf called the Fryken lakes the "smiling leaves", and it is the natural surroundings, the glittering waters, the flowering meadows and the dark forests on the horizon that strike visitors most. The author's spirit is a constant presence, and no more so than at the Rottneros estate, which is Ekeby in *Gösta Berling's Saga*, and the author's home, Mårbacka, across the water. The best ways to experience the lakes are aboard the vintage steamer *Freja af Fryken*, or by bicycle or car from Sunne, the main centre of the area.

View across Övre Fryken from Tossebergsklätten

② Sunne
The regional centre of the Fryksdal valley, Sunne is beautifully situated on the water between Övre Fryken and Mellanfryken. Heritage centres and a host of events in summer, including the Fryksdal Dance, reflect the area's rich folk traditions.

① Sahlströmska Gården
The home of artist siblings Sahlström in Utterbyn features mementoes of some of the early 20th century's most colourful Swedish artists.

④ Mårbacka
Nobel laureate Selma Lagerlöf's home has been kept just as it was on her death in 1940. Exhibitions linked to the author's work are held in the summer.

③ Rottneros
The estate has magnificent gardens and a large sculpture collection. For children, there is Nils Holgersson's Adventure Park.

Key

▬ Suggested route

═ Other roads

— Fryksdalsbanan railway line

⑤ S/S Freja av Fryken
In 1896, the queen of the Fryken lakes capsized; 98 years later she was salvaged from the lake bed and now sails from the port of Kil, powered by her original 1868 engine.

Tips for Drivers

Length: 75 km (47 miles) by road.
Stopping-off point: Tosseberg, 20 km (12 miles) north of Sunne on the road to Torsby.
Other routes: train, Kil–Torsby on Fryksdalsbanan, "Sweden's most beautiful railway". Boat trips: S/S Freja av Fryken (Tel: 0567-167 70).

0 kilometres 8

0 miles 5

❷ Arvika

Värmland. Road 61. 🚗 26,000.
🚌 🚲 ✈ 🚢 Storgatan 22,
0570-817 90. 🎪 Gammelvala (late
Jul), Arvika Hamnfest (early Aug).
W visitarvika.se

The people of Värmland are
known for their wit and ability
to tell funny stories, particularly
in Jösse, where Arvika is the
main town. It is situated on a
hill above the bay of Kyrkviken,
which is linked to the lake of
Glafsfjorden by a narrow strait.

Arvika Fordonsmuseum,
centrally located next to the
fire station, has an exciting
collection of veteran vehicles,
including hundreds of cars,
motorcycles and carriages.

The area has long been
home to craftworkers and
artists, as can be seen in the
Rackstadmuseet in Taserud just
outside the town. This is where
sculptor Christian Eriksson set
up his studio, Oppstuhage,
in the mid-1890s. For many
years it was a magnet for
artists attracted by the pristine
Värmland countryside, such as
the painter Gustaf Fjaestad,
renowned for his winter scenes.

Klässbols Linneväveri, 20 km
(12 miles) south of Arvika, is the
Nordic region's only damask
weaving mill and a rewarding
destination for those who
want to see how the linen
tablecloths for the Nobel Prize
banquets, or fabric for the
Royal Family, are made.

A 1903 Humber in Arvika Fordonsmuseum

🏛 **Arvika Fordonsmuseum**
Thermiavägen 2. **Tel** 0570-803 90.
Open daily. Group bookings: by
appointment. 🚗 🅿 🚻 🏠 ♿

🏛 **Rackstadmuseet**
Taserud. **Tel** 0570 809 90. **Open** Jun–
Aug: daily; Sep–May: Tue–Sun.
Closed some public hols. 🚗 🅿 🏠
W rackstadmuseet.se

🚌 **Klässbols Linneväveri**
Damastvägen 5. 20 km (16 miles)
S of Arvika. **Tel** 0570-46 01 85.
Open Oct– Apr: Mon–Fri & Sat;
May–Sep: daily. 🅿 only pre-booked.
🅿 🏠 ♿ **W** klassbols.se

❸ Borgviks Bruk

Värmland. 35 km (22 miles) W of
Karlstad. Road 45. 🚗 400. 🚌 Borgvik
Byggnadsvård: **Tel** 072-216 55 18.
Open Jun–Aug.

The ironworks in Borgvik
operated from 1600 to 1925.
The foundry ruins and works
buildings along with the striking
manor and 18th-century

church make Borgvik one
of the leading monuments
to a bygone industrial age in
Värmland. Near Västra Smedbyn
is **von Echstedtska Gården**.
This impressive 1760s' Carolian
manor is known for its murals.
Even the privy has burlesque
and, to say the least,
educational paintings.

🚌 **von Echstedtska Gården**
Västra Smedbyn. 20 km (12 miles) NW
of Säffle. **Tel** 0533-630 74. **Open** May–
Sep. 🚗 🅿 only pre-booked. 🅿 🏠

❹ Värmlandsnäs

Värmland. 5 km (2 miles) S of Säffle.

Jutting out into Lake Vänern
is a large peninsula noted for
its excellent agricultural land
and the medieval churches of
Botilsäter and **Millesvik**.

From the southernmost tip
in Ekenäs it is possible to head
out to **Lurö**, Sweden's largest
inland archipelago. This is the
ideal spot to enjoy countryside
well off the beaten track. The
boat trip to the main island of
Lurö takes an hour.

Perfect bathing spots along the shore
at Värmlandsnäs

Selma Lagerlof

In 1909, Selma Lagerlöf (1858–1940) became the first woman to
receive the Nobel prize for literature. And despite the passing of
a century since she wrote her first masterpiece, interest in the

Selma Lagerlöf, sculpture by
Carl Eldh, Rottneros

author's captivating adventures continues
unabated. Numerous film and TV versions
of her works have been produced,
including *The Treasure, Thy Soul Shall Bear
Witness!, The Emperor of Portugallia* and
Jerusalem. When she made her debut in
1891 with the imaginative novel *Gösta
Berling's Saga*, she put the Värmland
countryside around the Fryken lakes and
the family estate of Mårbacka on the
literary map. Even more remarkable was
the success of *The Wonderful Adventures
of Nils*. The tale of the tiny boy's epic
journey with wild geese was translated
around the world.

The Almen quarter, a heritage centre in Karlstad on the Klarälven river

❺ Karlstad

Värmland. E18. 🚗 69,000. 🚆 🚌 ➤
🛈 Västra Torggatan 26, 054-540 24
70. 🎿 Swedish Rally (1st weekend in
Feb), Putte i Parken music festival (Jul).
🌐 destinationkarlstad.se

The phrase *"Sola i Karlsta"* (Enjoy
the sun in Karlstad) has been
used to attract visitors to the
Värmland metropolis. Yet this is
no sunnier a place than any
other in the province. It was, in
fact, a jovial hostess at the town's
inn who brought sunshine into
people's lives in the early 1800s
– her statue now stands outside
the Stadshotell. Karlstad was
built on the delta formed by the
Klarälven river before it flows
into Lake Vänern, and was a
market town in medieval times.
It received its charter in 1584
along with its name from the
then king, Karl IX.

Karlstad has been devastated
by fire on many occasions, most
recently in 1865. The Almen
quarter on Västra Älvgrenen is a
heritage centre comprising
traditional wooden houses which
survived the blaze. Another
survivor was the bishop's palace,
built in 1781. The cathedral was
less fortunate, having to have its
exterior rebuilt along with its
tower. Parts of the early
18th-century interior were
preserved. A well-known feature
of the town is the 12-arched
Östra Bron bridge, built in 1811.
A good insight into Värmland's
history and folk culture can be
gained at **Värmlands Museum**
down by the river. **Sandgrund
Lars Lerin** is an art gallery
devoted to Lars Lerin, one of

Sweden's most famous artists.
The beautifully situated **Alsters
Herrgård**, 8 km (5 miles) east of
Karlstad, is the birthplace of
poet Gustaf Fröding in 1860.
The manor is a memorial to him
and other local poets.

The open-air museum
in **Mariebergsskogen**
has several historic
buildings, including a
sauna and smoking
hut built by Finnish
immigrants. In the
grounds lies Värmlands
Naturum, featuring
the flora and fauna
of the province.

Gustaf Fröding
(1860–1911)

🏛 Värmlands Museum
Sandgrundsudden. 400 m (440 yd)
N of the centre. **Tel** 054-701 19 00.
Open daily. 🚫 🍴 📷 ⚒ 📹 ♿

🏛 Sandgrund Lars Lerin
V. Torgg. 28. **Tel** 054-10 07 80. **Open**
Tue–Sun. 📹 🌐 sandgrund.org

🏛 Alsters Herrgård
8 km (5 miles) E of Karlstad. **Tel** 054-
540 23 50. **Open** May–Aug: daily;
Sep: weekends only. 🚫 🍴 📹 📷

❻ Hagfors

Värmland. Road 62. 🚗 6,500. 🚌
🛈 Folkets Väg 1, 0563-187 50.
🎿 Swedish Rally (early Feb), Klar-Hålja
Festival (early Jul), Klarälvsmässan Fair
(3rd week in Aug).

In the heart of Värmland on the
Klarälven river lies Hagfors,
which has long been a centre
for the steel and forestry
industries. Today, steel is still
manufactured in Uddeholm
just to the west of the town.

Hagfors is a good starting
point for trips up the Klarälven
valley and out into the forest.
Various places upriver offer raft
and small boat launch areas,
providing the opportunity to
spend a few relaxing days drifting at 1–2 knots, watching the
world go by. **Ekshärad**, 20 km
(12 miles) north of Hagfors, has
a red shingled church
built in 1686 with
superb views of the
river. The churchyard
is known for around
300 iron crosses with
"leaves" which play
in the wind.

Southwest of the
town is Uddeholm, a
small village with an
original 1940s mill
that now houses a
museum and art gallery,
Stjärnsfors Kvarn. Visitors can
enjoy a ride on an inspection
trolley from the mill to Hagfors,
a 6-km (3.5-mile) round trip.

🏛 Stjärnsfors Kwarn
Uddeholm. **Tel** 0563-234 00. **Open**
Jun–Aug: daily; other times: by appt.
For trolley rides, call 0563-187 50.

Alsters Herrgård, near Karlstad, birthplace of poet Gustaf Fröding

❼ Filipstad

Värmland. Road 63. 🚗 6,500. 🏠 🚌
ℹ️ Viktoriagatan 8, 0590-613 54.
🎪 Oxhälja Market (1st Sat in Sep).

Karl IX founded Filipstad in 1611, naming it after his son Karl Filip. Mining, ironworking and blacksmithing were the mainstay of the town, but today it is known for a very different type of industry – it is home to the world's largest crispbread bakery, which bakes the famous Wasabröd. A bread museum is combined with the bakery – both are open from Monday to Saturday.

Two of the town's great sons have contrasting memorials. A life-size sculpture by K G Bejemark of the popular poet and songwriter Nils Ferlin (1898– 1961) in top hat and tails has been placed on a park bench. Next to Daglösen lake stands inventor John Ericsson's imposing mausoleum. He was a locomotive and warship pioneer and inventor of the screw propeller. Two *Monitor*-type cannons stand next to the monument.

John Ericsson grew up along with his equally illustrious brother Nils in the mining community of **Långban**, 20 km (12 miles) north of Filipstad. Here an entire community built around iron has been preserved,

Alfred Nobel's laboratory in the Nobelmuseet, as it was when he died

including a foundry, gaming house and pithead buildings. Mineral hunters investigating the slag heaps of Långban have unearthed an exceptionally diverse collection of no less than 312 minerals.

🏛 Långban

20 km (12 miles) N of Filipstad.
Tel 0590-221 81. **Open** mid-Jun–mid-Aug: daily. 🎫 📷 🚻 🅿

Statue of the poet Nils Ferlin on his park bench in Filipstad

The Inventor John Ericsson

The multi-talented Swedish-American inventor John Ericsson (1803–89) was born in Långban, Värmland, where his father was mine captain. At the age of 13, he was employed in the construction of the Göta Canal (*see p150*), together with his brother, Nils (1802–70), the father of the Swedish railway. He wrestled with the development of a steam engine and in his early twenties went to England to exploit his invention. He constructed a groundbreaking engine

John Ericsson's mausoleum

(1829) which, in the locomotive *Novelty*, took part in the Manchester-Liverpool race and was narrowly beaten by George Stephenson's *Rocket*. In the USA, Ericsson designed the frigate *Princeton*, and fitted his newly created screw propeller. In competition, the ship claimed victory over the fastest paddle-steamer of the day, the *Great Western*. Ericsson's ultimate triumph came in the American Civil War with the design of the armour-plated warship *Monitor*, with a rotating cannon tower. She overcame the Southern States' *Merrimac* in 1862.

❽ Karlskoga

Värmland. E18. 🚗 29,000. 🚌 ℹ️
Kyrkbacken 9, 0586-614 74. 🎪 Swed-ish Touring Car Championship (end May & mid-Aug). 🌐 **karlskoga.se**

Iron ore has been mined and processed in this area since the 13th century, but it was not until Alfred Nobel (*see p75*) bought the Bofors ironworks and cannon factory in 1894 that the foundation was laid for Karlskoga's expansion. During the 20th century, Bofors grew to become one of the world's leading arms manufacturers.

The **Nobelmuseet** in Björkborns manor, Nobel's last home, shows developments at Bofors and offers an insight into the life of the inventor. Nobel's laboratory is just as he left it when he died. The stable where he kept his Russian stallions is now an industrial museum displaying the history of the ironworks.

Karlskoga's only preserved blast furnace can be found at **Granbergsdals Hytta**, 10 km (6 miles) north of the town.

At the end of the Ice Age water poured out from a lake at **Sveafallen** near Degerfors, 15 km (9 miles) south of Karlskoga. The landscape it created can be seen in the Domedagsdalen (Doomsday valley) and from walking trails through the nature reserve.

Kristinehamn is an idyllic town 25 km (16 miles) west of Karlskoga. Its claim to fame is Picasso's 15-m (50-ft) high sculpture of a Native American head to the south of the town.

🏛 Nobelmuseet

2 km (1 mile) N of the centre.
Tel 0586-834 94. **Open** Tue–Sun (Jun–Aug: daily). **Closed** some public hols.
🎫 📷 (Swedish and English). 🅿

Stjärnsunds Slott, home of Gustaf, the 19th-century "singing prince"

❾ Askersund

Närke. 🖼 4,000. 🚗 🚌 🛈 Rådhuset, 0583-810 88. 🎷 Trad Jazz Festival (2nd week in Jun), Golf Week (2nd week in Jul), All Car and Bike Meet (end of Jul). 🌐 **askersund.se**

On the north shore of Lake Vättern lies Askersund, the main town of southern Närke, offering easy access to the forests of Tiveden and islands on the lake. Askersund received a mention in a Papal letter dated 1314. A devastating fire struck the town in 1776, but many wooden buildings constructed since then have been preserved.

The brick-built church, **Landskyrkan**, designed by Jean de la Vallé in 1670, survived the fire. It is one of the most splendid religious buildings from Sweden's Age of Greatness (*see pp42–3*), with its magnificent Baroque pulpit and altar-piece. The Oxenstierna-Soopska chapel designed by Erik Dahlbergh contains a tin sarcophagus.

Environs

Lake Vättern's northern archipelago comprises around 50 islands, most of which are a nature reserve. The islands can be reached by boat from Askersund. Plying the route is the *S/S Motala Express*, which entered service in 1895 and is known as "the prisoner of Vättern" as she is too large to leave the lake via the Göta Canal.

Stjernsunds Slott 4 km (2 miles) south of Askersund was the home of the "singing prince" Gustaf (1827–52), the song-writing son of Oscar I. It was so lavishly decorated that today

it is considered to contain Sweden's finest mid-19th-century interiors.

🏛 **Stjernsunds Slott**
4 km (2 miles) S of Askersund. **Tel** 0583-100 04. House **Open** 15 May–31 Aug: daily; other times: by appt. 🎟 📷 oblig. 🌳 Park **Open** daily.

❿ Örebro

See pp242–3.

⓫ Ludvika

Dalarna. Road 50. 🖼 14,000. 🚗 🚌 ✈ 🛈 Bergslagsgatan 10, 0771-62 62 62. 🎷 Dan Andersson Week (last week in Jul), Dragon Boat Festival (May/Jun), Ludvika Festival (1st week in Jul). 🌐 **visitsodradalarna.se**

The western part of Bergslagen has foundries, mines and mining magnates' estates around every corner. The industry has also left its mark on the main town, Ludvika. **Ludvika Gammelgård och Gruvmuseum** offers a good impression of mining as it was in bygone times as does the surrounding countryside.

Environs

For many years Grängesberg, 16 km (10 miles) southwest of Ludvika, was central Sweden's

largest iron ore mine. It was closed in 1989. Ore deposits extended beneath the settlement, and in places buildings had to be abandoned to allow mining to continue. The ore was taken by railway to Oxelösund on the Baltic coast.

Grängesbergs Lokmuseum (the Locomotive Museum) contains the world's only operational steam turbine locomotive.

Skattlösberg 35 km (22 miles) northwest of Ludvika, is where Dan Andersson, "poet of the forests", was born in 1888. It is typical of the villages created by immigrant Finns in the 17th and 18th centuries. **Luossa-stugan**, where Andersson used to write, is now a memorial to the much loved poet.

🏛 **Ludvika Gammelgård och Gruvmuseum**
Ludvika. **Tel** 0240-100 19. **Open** 16 Jun–17 Aug: daily; 1–15 Jun & 18–31 Aug: Mon–Fri. 🎟 📷 🖥

🏛 **Grängesbergs Lokmuseum**
Grängesberg. **Tel** 0240-207 35. **Open** mid-Jun–mid-Aug: daily. **Closed** Midsummer's Eve. 🎟 📷 🖥 🏧

🏛 **Luossa-stugan**
Skattlösberg. **Open** Jun–Aug: daily. 🎟 📷

⓬ Hedemora

Dalarna. Road 70. 🖼 16,000. 🚗 🚌 🛈 Railway station, 0225-343 48. 🎷 Hedemora Market (mid-May).

This small Dalarna town is the oldest in the province with a charter dating from 1446. The 13th-century church and the pharmacy built in 1779 are among the few buildings which survived a major fire in 1849. Another survivor is **Theaterladan** from the 1820s.

Hedemora, Dalarna's oldest town, granted a town charter in 1459

It was built by a theatre-loving merchant above a granary. Performances take place here in the spirit of the early 19th century and the grain has made way for a museum.

Environs
Husbyringen, north of Hedemora, is the location for a 60-km (37-mile) circular tour, taking in the countryside and local culture. There are mining centres en route and Kloster has the ruins of an abbey. The star feature is Stjärnsund's 18th-century mining settlement, where the father of Swedish mechanics, Christopher Polhem, worked.
Polhemsmuseet exhibits the work of this inventive genius, including the Stjärnsund clock and ingenious Polhem lock.

Theaterladan
Gussarvsgatan 10. **Tel** 0225-210 64. **Open** times vary. phone for tour. teaterladanhedemora.se

Polhemsmuseet
Stjärnsund, 15 km (9 miles) S of Hedemora. **Tel** 0225-803 05. **Open** times vary. pre-book.

Carl Larssongården, a place of pilgrimage for interior designers

Environs
Stora Tuna, 4 km (2 miles) southeast of Borlänge, is the traditional centre of the flatlands. The medieval church was built at the end of the 15th century with the aim of becoming Dalarna's cathedral, but the province never became a diocese. Its treasures include a 15th-century crucifix.

Christopher Polhem (1661–1751)

At **Ornässtugan**, it is said that in the 16th century the future king, Gustav Vasa, fled from Danish knights via the privy.

Jussi Björlingmuseet
Borganäsvägen 25. **Tel** 0243-742 40. **Open** Sep–May: Tue–Fri; Jun–Aug: daily. **Closed** some public holidays.

Ornässtugan
8 km (5 miles) NE of Borlänge. **Tel** 0243-22 30 72. **Open** May: pre-book; Jun–Aug: daily. obligatory.

⓮ Sundborn
Dalarna. 12 km (7 miles) NE of Falun. 800. 023-600 53.

In the village of Sundborn is **Carl Larssongården**, Lilla Hyttnäs, home of the artist Carl Larsson (1853–1919). The well-preserved interior contains wooden furniture, traditional Swedish textiles and influences from the Arts and Crafts movement and Art Nouveau. Sundborn's shingled wooden church, built in 1755, features paintings by Larsson (1905) and the graveyard contains the artist's family plot.

Nearby, **Stora Hyttnäs** manor is a complete home from the early 20th century with a textile collection and garden.

Carl Larssongården
Tel 023-600 53. **Open** Jan–Sep: daily; other times: by appt. **Closed** public holidays. obligatory. limited access. carllarsson.se

Stora Hyttnäs
Tel 073-550 62 25. storahyttnas.se

⓭ Borlänge
Dalarna. Road 50/E16. 49,000. Sveagatan 1, 0771-62 62 62. Dalecarlia Cup (early Jul). visitsodradalarna.se

Dalarna's second largest town, Borlänge came to prominence in the 1870s when the Domnarvets Jernverk ironworks was established and several railway lines came together here. But it only received its town charter in 1944. In recent years it has gained a university college to add to its iron and paper industries.
Jussi Björlingmuseet celebrates the town's greatest son, the internationally renowned tenor Jussi Björling (1911–60). All his recordings can be enjoyed here.

Carl and Karin Larsson

Through his book *A Home* (1899), the interior design of artist Carl Larsson and particularly his wife, Karin, as expressed in their house in Sundborn, attracted attention worldwide. The couple had lived around Europe before settling with their children in a wooden farmhouse in Sundborn. Here they were able to develop their ideas for home interiors, producing a decorative scheme in traditional rural Swedish style using rustic furniture, home-woven textiles and colourful country patterns combined with a touch of the Arts and Crafts and Art Nouveau movements. This was in strong contrast to the stifled, bourgeois tastes which prevailed at the end of the 19th century. The joy and happiness in the Larsson home can be traced in every brushstroke and line of his book illustrations, which perhaps explains why Carl and Karin's Swedish idyll continues to inspire interior designers (*see pp30–31*).

Karin and Kersti by Carl Larsson

⑩ Örebro

There has been a town on this site for 750 years, but in 1854 a major fire destroyed the centre of Örebro. This gave scope for a new, more spacious layout on both sides of the Svartån river and elegant buildings coupled with the castle and St Nicolai Kyrka created a particularly fine townscape. A local newspaper described it as "a magnificent 19th-century salon, extravagantly furnished with buildings which proclaim growth and success". But there is also a greener side to Örebro with the promenade that follows the Svartån river to the delights of Wadköping and Karlslund. The river can be explored on foot, by bicycle or in a rowing boat. The free salmon fishing should not be missed.

Örebro Slott on the Svartån river, now the county governor's residence

🏰 Örebro Slott

Kansligatan. **Tel** 019-21 21 21.
Open daily. ☑ obligatory. ▣ 🔲 ☑
🔲 limited access. Northwest Tower:
Open Sat & Sun (daily in the summer).
📷 ☑ obligatory. ☑ **orebroslott.se**

Örebro Slott has dominated the town since Örebro received its charter in the 13th century. In 1347, King Magnus Eriksson gathered the great and the good at Örebro House, as the castle was then called, to adopt a common law for Sweden. At the end of the 16th century, King Karl IX remodelled the castle to create a Renaissance palace. Today's appearance, however, with its mighty round towers, is the result of major rebuilding in the 1890s.

The castle has been the scene of a number of historical events, including the adoption of the first Swedish Parliament Act in 1617 and the election of the French Marshal Jean-Baptiste Bernadotte as heir to the Swedish throne in 1810. Now it is the official residence of the county governor and also houses a small tourist information point. An exhibition

in the Northwest Tower highlights the castle's history.

🏛 Örebro Läns Museum

Engelbrektsgatan 3. **Tel** 019-602 87 00.
Open daily. **Closed** public holidays.
📷 phone to book. ▣ 🔲 ☑ **olm.se**

With its roots in the 1850s, the county museum is Sweden's oldest, although the main collection of more than 100,000 objects from across the county is on show in a 1960s' building in Slottsparken. A permanent exhibition focuses on farming since the Stone Age. The museum's most valuable artifacts, including the Viking silver from Eketorp *(see p161)*, are housed in the Treasury.

🏛 Rådhuset

Stora Torget. **Closed** to the public.
Built in 1858–63, the magnificent Neo-Gothic Town Hall was something of a showpiece in its time. King Karl XV didn't think the castle-like building befitted a provincial town, calling it: "…sparkling wine not weak beer!" Today only a fraction of Örebro's

administration fits into the Town Hall, although it remains the seat of the Municipal Executive Board. When the clock chimes (at 12:03 and 18:03pm, and at 9:03pm in the summer), automatons from Örebro's history appear, such as reformer Olaus Petri *(see p63)*.

⛪ St Nicolai Kyrka

Nikolaigatan 8. **Tel** 019-20 95 30.
Open daily. 📷 phone for info.
🔲 🔲 Sun.

The church on Stortorget has origins from the 13th century, but has been restyled many times. The north and south entrances are from the original church and were carved from Närke limestone. The rest is an example of English-inspired Neo-Gothic style, with the tower added at the end of the 19th century.

🌳 Stadsparken

Floragatan 1. **Tel** 019-21 10 00.
Open daily.
Voted Sweden's most beautiful city park, this green area boasts a series of themed gardens, including a rose garden, a magnolia garden and a herb garden. There is also a theatre and a children's island featuring its own railway and a petting zoo.

🏛 Wadköping

On the Svartån river, 1 km (half a mile) from the centre. **Tel** Tourist Office, 019-21 21 21. **Open** Tue–Sun. ▣ 📷
🔲 ☑ **orebro.se/wadkoping**

The beautiful promenade along the Svartån river through Stadsparken leads to the idyllic

Wadköping, an open-air museum with traditional wooden houses

wooden houses of Wadköping. This is a cultural centre to which old buildings have been moved to make way for the modern town. It is a vibrant community with craftworkers and small shops, and many people live here.

The oldest building is the early 16th-century Kungsstugan (King's Cabin), named after its use by the then Duke Karl on his visits to Örebro in the 1580s. His bedchamber has murals painted by his personal artist.

Other buildings include Hamiltonska Huset (1844), moved here from the south of the town, where it was the grandest building of its era, and Cajsa Warg's Hus (17th century), the childhood home of the well-known cookery writer Casja Warg. In summer there are concerts and theatre performances.

🏛 Svampen

Dalbygatan 3. **Tel** 019-611 37 35. **Open** daily. 🅿 🖥 🚹 ♿ 🔗 **svampen.nu**

The mushroom-shaped water tower, which offers a superb view of the town, the flatlands of Närke and Lake Hjälmaren, has become a symbol of Örebro. Since its opening in 1958,

8 million visitors have enjoyed the panorama from a height of 55 m (180 ft). Its construction has set something of a trend – there is a copy in Riyadh in Saudi Arabia.

The tower contains the science centre **Aqua Nova**, where the public has the opportunity to conduct practical experiments with water in all its forms.

🏛 Karlslunds Herrgård

5 km (3 miles) W of Örebro. Diedens Allé 11. **Tel** 019-27 07 88. **Closed** to the public.

Owned by Örebro town, the royal estate of Karlslunds Herregård dates from the 16th century and brings together nature and culture in perfect harmony. The Gustavian manor house, built in 1804–09, incorporates wings from the 18th century.

Karlslunds Herrgård's Gustavian manor house dating from 1804–09

VISITORS' CHECKLIST

Practical Information
Närke. 🗺 140,000. 🛈 Örebro-kompaniet, Olof Palmes Torg, 019-21 21 21. 🎭 Hjalmars Revue (spring, autumn), Craft Fair (Apr, Dec), Cheese and Wine Fair (Apr, Oct), Crayfish Fishing on Svartån (Aug), O Helga Natt concert (mid-Dec), Christmas Markets in Wad-köping (Dec). 🔗 **visitorebro.se**

Transport
✈ 12 km (7 miles) W of Örebro, E18. 🚍 🚌

The estate was once a self-sufficient community with around 80 buildings, including Carlslunds Kraftstation, built in 1897, which is the country's oldest working power station.

🏊 Gustavsvik

Gustavsviksvägen 11. **Tel** 019-19 69 10. **Open** see the website. 🔗 **gustavsvik.se**

A leisure complex with several pools (including a paddling pool for young kids), a golf course and camping facilities, Gustavsvik draws a large number of visitors every year.

Orebro Town Centre

① Örebro Slott
② Örebro Läns Museum
③ Rådhuset
④ St Nicolai Kyrka
⑤ Stadsparken
⑥ Wadköping

The huge Stora Stöten (Great Pit) in the old Falu copper mine outside Falun

⑮ Falun

Dalarna. Road 50/E16. 🏠 37,000. 🚊
🚌 ✈ ℹ️ Ttotzgatan 10–12, 0771-62
62 62. 🎭 Old World Christmas Market
at Falu Gruva (2nd Sun in Dec).
w visitsodradalarna.se

It goes without saying that
Falun still has a colourful
impact on Sweden. Wooden
buildings painted in the
distinctive Falun Rödfärg
(Falun Red) can be seen
everywhere. The paint has been
made since the 17th century
from powdered ore containing
ferrous sulphate from the **Falu
Gruva** (Falun copper mine), on
the back of which the town was
founded. Falu Gruva was the
country's treasure chest – at its
peak, two-thirds of the world's
copper was mined here. The
entire area, including Stora
Stöten (the Great Pit, formed by a
collapse in 1687), Falun's
historic buildings and industrial
remains, and outlying
settlements, was
designated a UNESCO World
Heritage Site in 2001.

   Dalarnas Museum gives a
broad insight into the cultural
history of Dalarna with
extensive collections of folk
costumes, local paintings
and traditional craftwork.

🏛 **Falu Gruva**
1 km (half a mile) S of the centre.
Tel 023-78 20 30. **Open** daily (hours
vary). **Closed** 1 Jan, Good Friday,
Midsummer, 24 & 25 Dec. 🎭 🛈 daily
(Swedish and English). 🖥 🚫 🏠 ♿
above ground only. **w** falugruva.se

🏛 **Dalarnas Museum**
Tel 023-76 55 00. **Open** daily. **Closed**
1 Jan, Good Friday, Midsummer's Eve,
Midsummer Day, 24, 25 & 31 Dec. 🎭
🛈 🖥 ♿ **w** dalarnasmuseum.se

⑯ Leksand

Dalarna. Road 70. 🏠 16,000. 🚊 🚌
ℹ️ Kyrkallén 8, 0248-79 72 00.
🎭 Music by Siljan Lake (1st week in
Jul), Rowing race in church boats (1st
Sun Jul). **w** siljan.se

The landscape around Siljan lake
is especially beautiful, but the
Leksand area is the most striking.
One of the best times to see the
lake is during the annual rowing
race in church boats in early July.

   Another event worth seeing is
Himlaspelet, one of Sweden's
oldest rural pageants. First
performed in 1941, Rune
Lindström's play about a path
which leads to heaven depicts
the witch trials of the 1670s.

   The onion dome of Leksand's
18th-century Baroque church
can be seen from far and wide.
Parts of the church date from
the 13th century.

Environs
**Karlfeldtsgården – Sångs i
Sjugare** was the summer retreat
of author and Nobel prize-winner
Erik Axel Karlfeldt (1864–1931). It
lies on Opplimen lake just north

The folk sculpture *Dalecarlian Couple*
in Leksand

of Leksand. Here it is possible to
follow in the footsteps of the
author's heroine, who came
wandering over the meadows
of Sjugare. Also worth a visit is
the garden on the poet's estate.

   Younger visitors to Leksand
will be attracted by **Äventyret
Sommarland**, comprising three
amusement parks on the banks
of Siljan lake: Waterland,
Motorland and Summerland.

   Insjön, 8 km (5 miles) south of
Leksand was the birthplace in
1899 of the Swedish mail order
business run by Åhlén & Holms.
The mail order tradition lives on
with Clas Ohlson, whose store
attracts so many DIY enthusiasts
that Insjön has become Dalarna's
most visited tourist destination.

🏛 **Karlfeldtsgården –
Sångs i Sjugare**
7 km (4 miles) N of the centre. Road
Rv 70. **Tel** 0247-600 28. **Open** May–
Sep: Tue, Thu & Sat; other times: by
appointment. 🎭

🎢 **Äventyret Sommarland**
Tel 0247-139 39. **Open** mid-Jun–mid-
Aug: daily. **Closed** Midsummer's Eve.
🎭 📷 🖥 🚫 **w** sommarland.nu

⑰ Rättvik

Dalarna. Road 70. 🏠 4,500. 🚊 🚌
ℹ️ Riksvägen 40, 0711-62 62 62.
🎭 Music on Siljan Lake (Jul), Classic
Car Week (late Jul). **w** siljan.se

No one can fail to notice Rättvik's
landmark, Långbryggan pier.
After docking at the pier on the
M/S Gustaf Wasa, passengers
have a 628-m (690-yd) walk to
reach the mainland. The pier with
all its fine carpentry was built in
1895 to allow steam boats to
moor near the shallow shore.

Rättvik also has a medieval church, beautifully situated on a promontory surrounded by former church stables – the oldest dating from the 1470s.

Environs
A search for older Dalarna buildings, rural communities and paintings will be rewarded at **Gammelstan** in Norrboda, 35 km (22 miles) north of Rättvik. The village street is lined with old buildings, some of which date back to the 17th century.

Tällberg, 12 km (7 miles) south on the shore of Lake Siljan, has many preserved timber houses in the classic Dalarna style. It is also known for its top-class hotels and guest houses, including the renowned Åkerblads *(see p291)* with its excellent restaurant. At the top of the village, Holens Gammelgård features workshops selling traditional handicrafts.

At **Dalhalla**, 7 km (4 miles) north of Rättvik, a limestone quarry has been converted into an auditorium. The quarry forms an amphitheatre with unique acoustics which have been praised by the world's top opera singers. Concerts are held in summer, and Dalhalla can also be toured in the day. The area was formed 360 million years ago when a meteor landed here, creating a crater which encompasses the whole of the Siljan region.

Bedroom in Zorngården, Anders Zorn's home and studio

Dalhalla
7 km (4 miles) NW of the centre. Road 70. **Tel** 0248-79 79 50. **Open** for performances and tours. **dalhalla.se**

⑱ Mora

Dalarna. Road 70. 🚆 11,000. 🚌 Siljan Tourism Mora, Strandgatan 14, 0248-79 72 00. 🎿 Winter Festival (Feb), Vasaloppet Ski Race (1st Sun in Mar). **siljan.se**

The municipality of Mora and the town itself – beautifully situated between Orsasjön and Siljan lakes – offers a wide range

of attractions. Mora is particularly associated with King Gustav Vasa (1496–1560) and artist Anders Zorn (1860–1920). Gustav Vasa's travels in Dalarna in 1520 to mobilize local men against the Danish occupation have left many traces. Near Mora, the Utmeland monument (1860) shows several romanticized paintings chronicling Gustav's adventures. It was built over the cellar where he is said to have hidden from Danish scouts. The annual Vasaloppet ski race *(see p249)* is another memorial to the king. At the finishing line in Mora stands Anders Zorn's statue of Gustav Vasa and the nearby **Vasaloppsmuseet** recounts the history of the famous ski race and has a permanent exhibition.

Zorn's statue of Gustav Vasa in Mora

Anders Zorn became known internationally not least for his portraits of plump, naked local women. He was genuinely interested in peasant culture and an ardent collector of local handicrafts. In **Zorngården**, which he built himself, he revelled in a world of National Romanticism. On the estate there are a number of older buildings which have been moved here, such as the 12th-century bakehouse which was used as a studio. The nearby Zornmuseet displays Zorn's own art and private collections.

Environs
Nusnäs, 8 km (5 miles) south of Mora, is where the national symbol of Sweden, the Dala horse, is manufactured. Originally a 19th-century toy,

the horses are carved with a knife and colourfully decorated. It is possible to watch them being made on weekdays.

On the island of **Sollerön** on Lake Siljan is the boatyard where the traditional church boats used on church outings and rowing races between the lakeside villages are made. There is also a pretty church dating from 1785.

Tomteland in Gesunda is the home of Father Christmas and his workshop, which is busy all summer making presents for children. The huge park offers various activities, including the witch's school – for youngsters who want to learn about magic and how to help friends and protect the environment.

Vasaloppsmuseet
Vasaloppets Hus. **Tel** 0250-392 00. **Open** Mon–Fri; mid-Jun–mid-Aug: daily. **Closed** some public holidays. by appt. **vasaloppet.se**

Zorngården
Vasagatan 36. **Tel** 0250-59 23 10. **Open** daily. **Closed** Good Friday, 24 & 25 Dec. **zorn.se**

Tomteland
Gesunda. 12 km (7.5 miles) S of Mora. **Tel** 0250-287 70. **Open** varies, phone for info. **santaworld.se**

A giant-sized Dala horse, manufactured in Nusnäs

Horse-riding in Dalafjällen, one of the many outdoor activities on offer

⑲ Orsa

Dalarna. Road Rv 45. 🏔 5,000. 🚌 ℹ️ Dalagatan 1, 0248-79 72 00. 🎭 Orsayran Music Festival (Weds in Jul). 🌐 siljan.se

The Orsa region extends from the gentle agricultural landscape around Lake Orsasjön to the desolate lands of Finnmark in the north.

In the past many of the local inhabitants made grindstones as a sideline, a skill which can now be studied at **Slipstens-museet** in Mässbacken, 12 km (7 miles) northeast of Orsa.

In this part of Sweden animals are still taken to the mountains for summer grazing. Around Djurberga, Fryksås and Hallberg it is possible to see how dairymaids used to live, far from their villages, churning butter and making cheese from the milk of hornless mountain cattle and goats.

In **Våmhus**, on the western side of Orsasjön, two crafts are practised which in the past were a major source of income locally: basket weaving and making jewellery out of hair. The women used to walk as far afield as St Petersburg in Russia, and Germany, to sell their work.

Orsa Grönklitt, 14 km (9 miles) north of Orsa, is the main area for outdoor activities. At Orsa Björnpark (Orsa Bear Park) special paths and ramps allow a close-up view of the bears, wolves, lynx and wolverine which live here in large enclosures.

🏛 **Slipstensmuseet**
Mässbacken. **Tel** 0250-55 02 55. **Open** summer. 🎭 📷 pre-book. 📱 ✏️

🗺 Orsa Grönklitt
Grönklitt. 15 km (9 miles) NW of Orsa. ℹ️ 0250-462 00. **Open** daily. 📱 ✏️ 🏠 ♿ 🌐 orsagronklitt.se

⑳ Sälen

Dalarna. Road 71. 🏔 1,200. 🚌 ℹ️ Centrumhuset, 0280-187 00. 🎭 Snowboarding World Cup, Speed Skiing World Cup (May), Vasaloppet Ski Race (1st Sun in Mar).

Like the majority of Dalarna's mountains, Transtrandsfjällen, with Sälen at their heart, are rounded and undulating and less dramatic than the those further to the north. The highest peak, Östra Granfjället, is 949 m (3,114 ft) above sea level. However, the terrain is excellent for both downhill and cross-country skiing and this, combined with its relative proximity to Sweden's cities, has made the area one of the country's leading destinations for winter sports enthusiasts.

Whether it's black runs for advanced skiers, velodrome curves, spines or jumps for snowboarders, or family slopes for children, there is plenty to choose from in Sälen. Around 200 km (124 miles) of trails are marked for cross-country skiers and summer hikers alike.

Sälen is the starting point of the 90-km (56-mile) Vasaloppet ski race to Mora.

㉑ Idre and Särna

Dalarna. Road 70. 🏔 1,500. 🚌 ℹ️ Framgårdsvägen 1, Idre; Högenvägen 2, Särna; 0771-99 88 00. 🎭 Mountain Orienteering (4th week in Jun), Mountain Festival (2nd week in Jul), Festival Week (3rd week in Jul). 🌐 visitidre.se

Northernmost Dalarna, with the towns of Idre and Särna, belonged to Norway until 1644 and the local dialects still sound Norwegian. This is a mountainous region, with impressive views. In the Nipfjället mountains it is possible to drive up to a height of 1,000 m (3,280 ft) for a good view of Städjan, a peak 1,131 m (3,710 ft) high. The STF mountain station at **Grövelsjön** on Långfjället, to the north, is an ideal starting point for mountain tours.

Idrefjäll is a year-round mountain resort with excellent slopes and lifts. It offers geat skiing in winter and a range of activities in the summer. Särna has a beautiful wooden church dating from the late 17th century and the rural museum of Buskgården.

Fulufjället National Park contains Sweden's highest waterfall, Njupeskär, with a drop of 90 m (295 ft). The effects of a violent storm in August 1997 can still be seen at Göljån, where 400 mm (16 in) of rain fell in 24 hours. Streams became torrents and fallen trees dammed the water, ploughing wide furrows through the forest.

The distinctive peak of Städjan in the Nipfjället mountains

◀ Aerial view of a picturesque city on the banks of Siljan, Dalarna

The Vasaloppet Ski Race

The world's longest and oldest ski race was first held in 1922 when 122 competitors skied the 90 km (56 miles) from Sälen to Mora. Today more than 15,000 skiers take on the challenge on the first Sunday in March. The race also includes spin-off events such as *TjejVasan* (for women, 30 km/18 miles) and *HalvVasan* (half-course, 45 km/28 miles). A staff of 3,000 support the skiers by providing blueberry soup, ski waxing and blister plasters. And all because in 1520 Gustav Vasa could not get the men of Dalarna to rise up against the Danes. Disheartened, he fled on skis from the Danish troops towards Norway, but when the local men heard about the Stockholm Bloodbath *(see p64)*, they changed their minds and their two best skiers raced to intercept their future king near Sälen.

In summer, a hiking trail follows the course from Berga in Sälen to the finish at Zorn's statue of Gustav Vasa in Mora.

Berga, just south of the village of Sälen, is the starting point for the more than 15,000 skiers who are let loose in the early dawn in several stages, top skiers first.

Evertsberg lies halfway between Sälen and Mora. Here, as in many places along the route, the competitors fortify themselves with blueberry soup. Those only skiing half the race can leave the track at this point.

The first steep hills are succeeded by flat marshland.

VÄSTERDALÄLVEN

Sälen
Smågan
11 km (7 miles)
Berga
Transtrand
Mångsbodarna
24 km (15 miles)
VÄNAN
Risberg
35 km (22 miles)
Evertsberg
47 km (29 miles)
ÖSTERDALÄLVEN
Oxberg
61 km (38 miles)
Hökberg
70 km (43 miles)
Mora
90 km (56 miles)
Eldris
80 km (50 miles)

0 kilometres   20
0 miles   10

The First Vasaloppet

At Christmas 1520 Gustav Vasa fled on skis from Mora towards Norway to escape Danish troops. At Lima, near Sälen, local men caught up with him and persuaded the future king to turn back. Since 1922 almost 750,000 skiers have repeated the achievement, albeit skiing in the opposite direction.

Mora marks the end of the race. The winning time is usually just over four hours, but some entrants can take ten hours. The text on the finishing line reads: "In the footsteps of our forefathers for the victories of tomorrow."

SOUTHERN NORRLAND

The six provinces of Southern Norrland cover almost a quarter of the country. The character shifts noticeably from the coast with its industry and fishing to the farming communities up along the river valleys, then westwards through forests to the mountains of Härjedalen and Jämtland. Natural resources such as timber and waterpower have had a visible impact on the region.

In the Middle Ages, the southeasterly province of Gästrikland belonged to Svealand and its gently rolling landscape is more akin to that of neighbouring Uppland than Norrland. An offshoot of the Bergslagen mining district extends into this area and ironworking formed the basis of today's manufacturing industry. The trading port of Gävle has long been a gateway to Norrland.

The pass between Kölberget and Digerberget in the province of Hälsingland is another gateway to the north, beyond which the mountainous Norrland landscape becomes more evident. Huge wooden mansions stand proud with their ornate porches and exquisitely decorated interiors. These houses are evidence of the successful trade in the green gold of the local forests in a landscape of which 80 per cent is covered with productive woodland. Exploitation of

the forests had an even bigger impact on the provinces of Medelpad and Ångermanland. At the end of the 19th century, the timber barons of Sundsvall and Ådalen had made themselves a fortune. Today, processing wood into pulp and paper is still a key industry. The smell of sulphur can be quite striking – as is the herring dish *surströmming* (fermented Baltic herrings), best sampled by those who dare at one of the fishing villages along the High Coast, a UNESCO World Heritage Site *(see p260)*.

The provinces of Jämtland and Härjedalen only became part of Sweden in 1645. There is often talk of the "Republic of Jämtland" among diehard locals who seek self-rule. The mountains stretch out to the west, attracting visitors both to the ski resorts and to the upland areas where the wildlife and countryside can still be enjoyed undisturbed.

A reindeer herd round-up for division according to owner, by use of lassos and ear tags

◀ Spectacular winter landscape, Härjedalen

Exploring Southern Norrland

In this region of immense contrasts, the coastal provinces of Gästrikland and Hälsingland are home to a colourful rural culture enlivened with traditional folk music and dancing. The High Coast, with its dramatic island archipelago accessible by bridges and ferries, is Ångermanland's contribution to UNESCO's list of World Heritage Sites. Inland, the mountainous provinces of Jämtland and Härjedalen offer wide open spaces for skiing and hiking.

One of the best ways to experience Norrland's varied landscape is to start from the coast and follow one of the river valleys which cut across the country. As the roads wind up-river, they pass through dense forests and on up into the mountains.

The heather and rushing streams of Helag, with the mountain of Helagsfjället in the distance

Getting Around

The E4 along the coast and the E14 from Sundsvall across the country to Trondheim in Norway are the main arteries for motorists. The inland roads running north-south are of a generally good standard. The roads east-west tend to follow the courses of the rivers. The main railway line runs north-south. Along the coast, the railway goes as far north as Härnösand before heading inland. The Jämtland mountains can be reached by train, but in Härjedalen transport is by car or bus. The Inlandsbanan railway operates in summer. Air travel is an option and the range of domestic flights is good.

Key

▬▬▬ Motorway
▬▬▬ Major road
═══ Minor road
▬▪▬ Main railway
──── Minor railway
▬▬▬ International border
△ Summit

For additional map symbols *see back flap*

Storjorm
Kvarnbergsvattnet
Gäddede
Fågelberg

Sösfjöfjället
1246m

340

336

Kallsjön
Lillhol

JÄMTLAN

Tännforsen
Åreskutan
1420m

Trondheim
Handöl
E14
17
16
Järpen
Krokom
Häggen

STORLIEN
ÅRE

Storsjön

ÖSTERSUND

Helagsfjället
1797m
Myrviken
Brur

THE HÄRJEDALEN MOUNTAINS

E45

Röros
Mittådalen
Ljungan
Svens

18

Funäsdalen

Tännäs
Vemdalen
Råt
Rogen
Hede

HÄRJEDALEN

311
Ytterhogd
Lofsdalen
Duvberg

SVEG **19**

Lillhärdal

Lillhamra

Mora

A wooden mansion in Arbro, Hälsingland, typical of the area's traditional architecture

Nämforsen Falls and one of Europe's largest rock carving sites *(see p259)*

0 kilometres	50
0 miles	30

Boathouses in Norrfällsviken on the High Coast in Ångermanland *(see pp260–61)*

Sights at a Glance

1. Dalälven Delta
2. Gävle
3. Sandviken
4. Söderhamn
5. Bollnäs
6. Hudiksvall
7. Ljusdal
8. Ljungadalen
9. Sundsvall
10. Härnösand
11. Ådalen
12. Örnsköldsvik
13. *The High Coast pp260–61*
14. Indalsälven
15. Östersund
16. Åre
17. Storlien
18. *The Härjedalen Mountains pp264–5*
19. Sveg

The Dalälven delta, one of the top ten fishing spots in Sweden

❶ Dalälven Delta

Gästrikland, Uppland. 🛈 Gysinge Tourist Office, 0291-210 00. 🎣 Weir Day in Älvkarleby (first Sun before Midsummer).

Before the mighty Dalälven river empties into the bay at Gävle, it forms an expansive delta with hundreds of small islands. The flora and fauna are abundant and the area offers some of the best sport fishing in Sweden.

Least affected by forestry and farming is the area around Färnebofjärden, part of which was declared a national park in 1998. The birdlife is incredibly diverse, with more than 100 breeding species, including several different endangered woodpeckers and owls.

A good place to start exploring the area is Gysinge on road Rv 67, 38 km (24 miles) south of Gävle. The falls between Färnebofjärden and Hedesundafjärden attracted ironworking here at the end of the 17th century. The well-preserved industrial community has a main street dating from the 1770s and a magnificent manor from 1840. Gysinge is also home to **Dalälvarnas Flottnings-museum**, which shows just how important the river once was for timber transportation.

Another important feature of the Dalälven river is hydroelectric power, which manifests itself in **Älvkarleby**, further down-river. The imposing power station, built in 1915, is an attraction in itself, but the most impressive sight is when the water is released at full-flow on Weir Day. Älvkarleby attracts many anglers, who annually land as much as 20 tonnes of salmon and sea trout.

In **Österfärnebo**, Koversta rural heritage centre is an 18th-century village, offering an insight into local rural life.

🏛 Dalälvarnas Flottningsmuseum

Gysinge Bruk. **Tel** 0291-210 00. **Open** mid-May–mid-Aug: daily. 🐾 ♿

❷ Gävle

Gästrikland. 🚹 96,000. 🚃 🚌 🛈 Drottninggatan 22, 026-17 71 17. 🖥 visitgavle.se

Gästrikland's main town has been the gateway to Norrland since the Middle Ages. The mouth of the Gävleån river made an ideal port and traders set up base here to conduct business in the north. The harbourside warehouses along Skeppsbron bear witness to this. Gävle remains one of Sweden's larger ports, although operations have moved further out into the bay. A fire in 1869 destroyed the buildings north of the river, with the exception of the town hall built in 1790 and **Heliga Trefaldighetskyrkan**,

a three-aisle Baroque church dating from 1654. As a result, Gävle has attractive 19th-century buildings and broad tree-lined esplanades as protection against fires. The jewel is the splendid theatre on Rådhusesplanaden, built in 1878. The city park, **Boulog-nerskogen**, which features Carl Milles's famous sculpture, *Five Playing Geniuses,* is the most popular of Gävle's parks.

South of the Gävleån river lies **Gävle Slott**, Sweden's northernmost royal fortification, dating from the 16th century. This is also the location of the old town, "Gamla Gefle", with fine streets of wooden houses from the 18th century which have attracted many artists and craftsmen. **Joe Hill Gården** on N Bergsgatan, the birthplace of the Swedish-American union agitator, is now a museum. Other museums include **Länsmuseet Gävleborg** with extensive collections relating to the history of Gästrikland.

Sveriges Järnvägsmuseum offers a delightful selection of old locomotives and carriages, from mining titans to neat little narrow-gauge carriages.

The oldest Swedish locomotive (1855) in Sveriges Järnvägsmuseum

Fängelsemuseet is a small but fascinating museum housed in 17th-century prison cells. It gives an insight into prison life at the time.

Furuviksparken attracts families who come to enjoy its Nordic and exotic animals, and live performances, and to swim in a beautiful setting.

🏛 **Länsmuseet Gävleborg**
S. Strandgatan 20. **Tel** 026-65 56 00.
Open Tue–Sun. **Closed** public holidays. 🚻 💻 🅿
🌐 lansmuseetgavleborg.se

🏛 **Sveriges Järnvägsmuseum**
Rälsgatan 1. **Tel** 010-123 21 00.
Open Jun–Aug: daily; Sep–May: Tue–Sun. **Closed** public holidays.
🚻 💻 🅿 ♿

🏛 **Fängelsemuseet**
Hamiltongatan 1. **Tel** 026-65 44 30.
Open Wed–Sun. **Closed** public holidays. 🚻 🌐 fangelsemuseet.se

🎡 **Furuviksparken**
10 km (6 miles) E of the centre. Road Rv 76. 🚌 **Tel** 010-123 21 00. **Open** end May–Aug: daily. 🚻 💻 🍴 ♿

❸ Sandviken

Gästrikland. 🏔 23,000. 🚉 🚌
ℹ Folkets Hus, Köpmangatan 5–7, 026-24 13 80. 🎭 Bangen Jazz Festival (end Jun), Chamber Music Festival (end Jul). 🌐 gastrikland.com

The town of Sandviken grew up with the establishment of an ironworks on the shore of Storsjön lake in 1860. The new railway line to Gävle was one of the factors in its location. Using the groundbreaking Bessemer production process, Sandviken soon gained a reputation for its steel. In the 1920s it began making stainless steel and by the 1940s it was the world's leading producer of steel for tools and drill bits.

Environs
Evidence of Sandviken's ironworking roots can be seen in Högbo. Today the community is a centre for recreation and adventure sports. Located nearby in Kungsgården is **Rosenlöfs Tryckerimuseum**, which has a still-functioning printing press from the 1890s.

Opposite Sandviken, on the southern shores of Storsjön, lies the medieval church of **Årsunda**, with paintings by the master Eghil. Just south of the church is a Viking burial ground, which inspired the Årsunda Viking centre, offering activities with a Viking slant.

🏛 **Rosenlöfs Tryckerimuseum**
Kungsgården, 10 km (6 miles) W of Sandviken. **Tel** 0290-376 18.
Open Jun–Aug: Sat & Sun; Jul: Tue–Sun. **Closed** Midsummer. 🚻 🍴 🅿

❹ Söderhamn

Hälsingland. 🏔 13,000. 🚉 🚌
ℹ Köpmangatan 11, 0270-753 53.
🎭 Family fun evenings at Östra Berget (Thu in Jul), Herring Games (mid-Aug).

Sweden's ambitions for power and the need for armaments lead to the foundation of Söderhamn in 1620. Hälsingland's weapon makers were brought together from around the region to work in the town. The gun and rifle-making factory, built in 1748, now houses the town museum, **Söderhamns Stadsmuseum**.

Russian attacks in 1721 and four disastrous fires have meant that the only remaining building of significance is **Ulrika Eleonora Kyrka**. The red cruciform church was designed by Tessin the Younger in 1693. The upside of

Part of an old furnace in the town of Sandviken, famous for its steel production

the fires is that a series of parks now creates a green patchwork around the city. Söderhamn's landmark is the **Oscarsborg** tower, which rises proudly on Östra Berget. Anyone braving the 125 steps is rewarded with a breathtaking view of the town and archipelago.

Today Söderhamn is a thriving coastal community that offers great opportunities for swimming, boating and fishing.

Environs
The 10 km (6 miles) of the Söderhamnsfjärden inlet were lined with 11 steam-powered sawmills during the industrial boom of the late 19th century. The industrial museum in Ljusne and **Bergviks Industrimuseum** tell the story. Modern technology is on display at **Söderhamns/F15 Flygmuseum**, which exhibits military aircraft.

The 13th-century church **Tronö Kyrka**, 17 km (11 miles) northwest of Söderhamn, complete with walls, gates and bell tower, is unusually redolent of the Middle Ages. The arch-bishop and Nobel prize-winner Nathan Söderblom (1866–1931) was born in the rectory, which now houses his memorabilia.

🏛 **Söderhamns Stadsmuseum**
Oxtorgsgatan 5. **Tel** 0270-157 91.
Open by appt or for exhibitions.

🏛 **Bergviks Industrimuseum**
15 km (9 miles) west of the centre.
Tel 0270-42 44 65. **Open** by appointment. 🐾 voluntary. 🍴

🏛 **Söderhamns/F15 Flygmuseum**
Flygstaden, 4 km (2 miles) east of the centre. **Tel** 0270-142 84. **Open** Jun–Aug: daily; Sep–May: Sun-Tue.
🚻 🍴 by appointment. ♿

Oscarsborg lookout tower, offering a superb view of Söderhamn

Kämpen rural heritage centre at a 16th-century farm in Bollnäs

❺ Bollnäs

Hälsingland. 🏛 13,000. 🚊 🚌
ℹ Kulturhuset, Odengatan 17b,
0278-258 80. 🎭 Bollnäs Stadsfest
(1st weekend in Jul). 🌐 bollnas.se/
turism

Located in the heart of
Hälsingland's rich farming land,
Bollnäs is the gateway to the
valleys of the Voxnan and
Ljusnan rivers. The town itself
has a semi-modern centre, with
some wooden mansions. The
church, built in the 1460s,
contains ornate medieval
sculpture work. The
Classical-style **Bollnäs
Museum** (1929) is worth
a visit, as is the
Kulturhuset next
door, which has a
room devoted to
Onbacken, an Iron
Age settlement just a
stone's throw away.
Also worth visiting is **Kämpen**
rural heritage centre, a
16th-century farm displaying a
wealth of local culture.

Environs
Hälsingland was a major flax-
growing area in the 1700s, and
local landowners displayed their
wealth in lavishly decorated
wooden mansions (see p24).
These farmhouses are now a
designated UNESCO World
Heritage Site. Some of Hälsingland's finest estates and farms
can be seen around Alfta, about
20 km (12 miles) into the
Voxnadalen valley. Alfta rural
heritage centre, **Löka**, in
Gundbo, comprises three farm
buildings, some with beautiful
murals. **Hansers** farm has wall
hangings from the 15th century.
In **Arbrå**, 16 km (10 miles)

north of Bollnäs, there is an
18th-century wooden mansion
(Träslottet) on the Hans-
Andersgården estate where
journalist Willy Maria Lundberg
(b.1909) created a centre for the
preservation of old buildings. As
well as being an attraction in its
own right, the manor also has
exhibitions and specialist
gardens. In summer, the tourist
office runs guided tours of
Hälsingland's farms
and manor houses.
　　　Växbo, east of
　　Bollnäs, has the only
　　　flax-spinning works
　　　in Sweden, which
　　produces and sells
　　items such as tablecloths
　　and napkins.

Log-floater by Per
Nilsson Öst (1972)

🏛 **Bollnäs Museum**
Odengatan 17. **Tel** 0278-
253 26. **Open** during exhibitions Tue–Sun. 📷 ♿

❻ Hudiksvall

Hälsingland. 🏛 17,000. 🚊 🚌 ⛴
ℹ Storgatan 33, 0650-191 00.
🎭 Delsbo Festival (1st Sun Jul).
🌐 hudiksvall.se

Fishing, seafaring and trade
have been the mainstay of
Hudiksvall throughout its

400-year history. In the late
19th century the timber
industry boomed and the
town became known for its
high living, giving rise to the
phrase "Happy Hudik".
　　Despite attacks by Russian
forces in the 18th century and
numerous fires, a number of
older buildings remain, giving
the town charm and character.
The Sundskanal in the centre,
a canal linking Lillfjärden and
Hudiksvallsfjärden inlets, is
lined with red huts and
merchants' warehouses from
the mid-19th century.
　　East of the inlet is Fiskarstan
(Fishermen's Town), with its
partly-preserved wooden
houses from the early 19th
century. Along Hamngatan
there are several fine old
merchants' yards featuring the
elegant wood-panelled
architecture of the time. They
have terraces on the waterside
and shops on the parallel street
of Storgatan. An example is
the **Bruns Gård** pharmacy,
which has an ornate pharmacy
entrance on Storgatan and a
winged house on the terraces
of Hamngatan.
　　Dominating the skyline is
St Jakobs Kyrka, a church
built in the 17th and 18th
centuries, although its onion
dome dates from 1888.
　　Hälsinglands Museum, in
an imposing former bank
building, provides a good
picture of the colourful
history of the area.

Environs
Hudiksvall municipality covers
a large area of northern
Hälsingland, including **Delsbo**
and the beautiful Dellensjö
lakes to the west. South of

Picturesque warehouses and quay on Sundskanalen in Hudiksvall

Torpsjön, a typical lake on the mighty Ljungan river, with Fränsta Kyrka on its shore

the town is **Iggesund**, with its 400 years of ironworking history, and **Enånger**, where the 15th-century church contains exquisite medieval ceiling paintings by Andreas Erici and wooden sculptures by master sculptor Håkon Gullesson.

🏛 Hälsinglands Museum
Storgatan 31. **Tel** 0650-196 01.
Open Mon–Sat. **Closed** public holidays & eves of public holidays.
🎧 by appointment. 📷 📷 ♿

❼ Ljusdal

Hälsingland. 🚃 🚌 ❼ Stations-gatan 2, Järvsö, 0651-403 06.
W ljusdal.se

In the heart of northwest Hälsingland on the Ljusnan river is Ljusdal. Settlers have long been attracted to this fertile valley and their history is explored in **Ljusdalsbygdens Museum**. Christianity came early to the area; parts of the church of **St Olovs Kyrka** are 12th-century.

Environs
Opportunities for fishing and walking present themselves at every turn around this area. From **Lassekrog**, 40 km (25 miles) upstream from Ljusdal, those who dare can run the rapids on the Ljusnan river. Lassekrog has been an inn since the 17th century. Here, author Albert Viksten's forest camp is a monument to the foresters of old.
South of Ljusdal, at **Järvsö**, wildlife from the north, including predators such as bear, wolf, wolverine and lynx and their prey, can be seen at **Järvzoo Djurpark** and the

adjacent Rovdjurscentret (Predator Centre). Järvsö village itself is known for having Sweden's largest provincial church; when it was completed in 1838 it had space for 2,400 parishioners. Also here is **Järvsö Bergscykel Park**, which offers downhill mountain biking facilities. On the opposite bank lies **Stenegård**, a 19th-century trading post, now a centre for arts and crafts, with a theatre in the wooden barn.

🏛 Ljusdalsbygdens Museum
Museivägen 5, Ljusdal. **Tel** 0651-71 65. **Open** Tue–Sat. **Closed** public holidays. 🎧 by appointment. 📷

🐾 Järvzoo Djurpark
1 km (half a mile) south of Järvsö centre. **Tel** 0651-411 25. **Open** daily.
🐾 🎧 by appointment. 📷

🐾 Järvso Bergscykel Park
Anders Persvägen 29, Ljusdal.
Tel 0651-76 91 92. **Open** Jun–Sep: daily. **W** jarvsobergscykelpark.se

Ljusdalsbygdens Museum, in a wooden Hälsingland building

❽ Ljungadalen

Medelpad. E14. ❼ Sundsvalls Tourist Office, 060-658 58 00.

The 350-km (220-mile) Ljungan river rises at Helagsfjällen mountain and flows into the Gulf of Bothnia just south of the town of Sundsvall. In Medelpad, the river forms an often wide valley with a series of lakes. The E14 follows long stretches of the river, offering spectacular views. The great Norrland forests loom on the horizon and the river was an important timber route.
Stöde Kyrkby on Stödesjön lake, 40 km (25 miles) west of Sundsvall, has a long history, which is illustrated at the Huberget rural heritage centre. The church was built in the 1750s, but contains medieval artifacts from an older, now demolished church.
Borgsjö, 40 km (25 miles) further upriver, has a fine Rococo church built in 1768, with a superb wooden bell tower from 1782. Next to the church is Borgsjö rural heritage centre featuring Jämtkrogen Inn, which was relocated here from the Jämtland border.
Ånge, a railway junction 100 km (60 miles) west of Sundsvall, is an ideal starting point for exploring the area. To the west, the countryside of Haverö spreads out around the Havern and Holmsjön lakes, which are good for canoeing.
Haverö Strömmar is an 8-km (5-mile) stretch of at times wild rapids with three streams where former dams, mills and fishing huts have been preserved.
Alby, just off route 83, has a restored eel house showing a fishing method used in the 16th century.

The carefully restored Hotell Knaust's marble staircase

❾ Sundsvall

Medelpad. 🚗 50,000. 🚆 🚌 ✈️
Midlanda. 🚢 ℹ️ Stora Torget, 060-
658 58 00. 🎭 Sundsvall Street Festival
(1st or 2nd weekend Jul), Dragonboat
Festival (1st week in Aug), Selånger
market (2nd weekend in Aug).
🌐 visitsundsvall.se

The view from Norra and Södra
Stadsberget hills shows
Sundsvall sandwiched between
the mouths of the Ljungan and
Indalsälven rivers. The sheltered
inlets attracted traders to this
spot in the 6th century, as
can be seen from the Högom
burial ground near Selånger.
Alongside Selånger's
12th-century church lay
St Olofs Hamn, the starting
point for trading missions
and pilgrimages to
Norway's Nidaros
(Trondheim).
   Sundsvall was
founded in 1624.
It took off in the
mid-1800s with
the advent of the
steam-powered
sawmill. Sweden's first such
sawmill was built in 1849 in
Tunadal; when the industry was
at its height there were 19
sawmills on the island of Alnön
alone. In 1888, fire destroyed
large parts of the town centre.
The railway station survived, and
the attractive wooden building
is now a casino. A grand "stone
town" rose from the ashes. In

Statues on the roof of Sundsvall
town hall

Stora Torget stands the statue of
the founder King Gustav II Adolf.
The square is flanked by the
Town Hall and the **Hirschska
Huset** with its extravagant
pinnacles and towers. A notable
building on Storgatan is the
newly renovated **Hotell Knaust**,
built in 1890, with its superb
marble staircase. The cultural
centre, Kulturmagasinet, near
the harbour, contains the town
library and **Sundsvalls Museum**.
On Norra Stadsberget lies
Sundsvalls Stadspark, which
has a collection of buildings
from Medelpad, as well as
animal enclosures and lookout
towers. Södra Stadsberget's
outdoor recreation centre has
adventure trails for children.

Environs
Linked to
Sundsvall by
the Alnöbron
bridge, **Alnön**
has many
monuments
to the timber
industry. The
13th-century church is
interesting for its wooden
interior and medieval paintings
and sculptures, and the fishing
village of **Spikarna** is well
worth a visit.
   Around 26 km (16 miles)
southeast of Sundsvall lies
Galtström, Medelpad's first
ironworks, built in 1695. The
works have been restored.

🏛 **Sundsvalls Museum**
Kulturmagasinet. **Tel** 060-19 18 00.
Open daily. **Closed** Easter Mon,
Whit Mon, Midsummer's Eve.
🔲 by appointment. 🔲 🔲 🔲 ♿

🏛 **Sundsvalls Stadspark**
Norra Stadsberget. **Tel** 060-15 40 00.
Open daily. **Closed** eves of public
holidays. 🔲 (by Stadsparken). 🔲 by
appointment. 🔲 🔲 🔲 ♿

❿ Härnösand

Ångermanland. 🚗 18,000. 🚆 🚌 ⛴
ℹ️ Stora Torget, 0611-204 50.
🎭 Midsummer celebrations at
Murberget, Härnösandskalaset (Jul),
Park Festival (2nd–3rd week in Jul).

The county town of western
Norrland has a proud history.
It received its town charter
from Johan III in 1585, became
diocesan capital in 1647 and
had an upper secondary
school by 1650.
   Härnösand's rich history,
combined with the fact that,
in contrast to other Norrland
coastal towns, it was spared
major fires for almost 300 years,
makes it an interesting place to
stroll around. The Russians
plundered Härnösand in 1721. A
new wooden town replaced the
old and charming districts such
as Östanbäcken and Norrstan
still remain. Standing out among
the many public buildings are
the town hall from the 1790s
on Stora Torget, the old upper
secondary school and the
county governor's residence.
   At Murbergets Frilustmuseum,
which is part of **Länsmuseet
Västernorrland**, 18th-century
buildings have been preserved,
including the town hall built
in 1727. This large open-air
museum also reflects farming
culture, with crofts and farms,
a blacksmith's and sawmill,
and a Norrland church village.
   Skeppsbron fills with yachts in
July when the town's maritime
history is celebrated at the
Härnösandskalaset festival.

🏛 **Länsmuseet Västernorrland**
Murberget. **Tel** 0611-886 00. **Open**
Tue–Sun (mid-Jun–mid-Aug: daily).
Closed 1 Jan, Easter, 1 May, 24, 25, 31
Dec. 🔲 by appointment. 🔲 🔲 ♿
🌐 murberget.se

⑪ Ådalen

Ångermanland. Road 90. 🚌 from Örnsköldsvik. 🅸 Kramfors Tourist Office, 0612-800 00. 🎿 Kramfors Town Festival (weekend before Midsummer).

As the forestry industry flourished, Ådalen, the river valley leading to Junsele, became a hotbed of trade unionism and earned the nickname "Red Ådalen". In 1931, the year of the Great Depression, a most unlikely event occurred: the military shot indiscriminately into a peaceful strikers' march in Lunde, killing five people. Lenny Clarhäll's powerful sculpture depicting the drama stands beside Sandöbron bridge.

Already in the mid-18th century, Livonian Christoffer Kramm set up a water-powered sawmill on the site which in 1947 became the town of Kramfors. Cargo ships were able to navigate 50 km (31 miles) up the river and the lower valley became a magnet for the forestry industry. The line of factories is now almost entirely gone. Further up river, however, there are numerous power stations – the Faxälven tributary is home to 36 alone. Particularly worth visiting is **Nämforsen**, where in summer visitors can view the large power station and occasionally see the mighty waterfall burst into life. The islands in the falls are an outstanding site for rock carvings. From 4000–2500 BC, hunters carved out over 2,500 figures.

One of the many rock carvings in Nämforsen from around 4000 BC

⑫ Örnsköldsvik

Ångermanland. 🚆 to Sundsvall or Mellansel, then bus/taxi. 🚌 ✈ ⛴ 🅸 Lasarettsgatan 5, 0660-881 00. 🎿 Harbour Festival (1st weekend in Jul), Dragonboat Festival (mid-Aug). 🌐 ornskoldsvik.se/turism

Nolaskogs is one of the names by which this part of northern Ångermanland is known. It means "north of the forest" – the wild frontier forest of Skule (see p260).

Its main town, Örnsköldsvik, or Ö-vik as it is often called, was founded in 1842. Unusually for the time, it was named after a non-royal figure, the county governor Per Abraham Örnsköld. There are good views of the town from Varvsberget and from the top of the ski-jumping tower on Paradiskullen. Many of the town's older buildings have been lost to modern developments. A few exceptions include the delightful town hall which,

Arken, designed by architect Per Eddi Byggstam, 1991

thankfully for Ö-vik's remarkably large artists' colony, was saved as an exhibition space. The beautifully restored junior secondary school houses **Örnsköldsviks Museum**, which displays the history of Nolaskogs.

Attractive new architecture can be seen in the development of the inner harbour, where **Arken** – a centre for offices, university buildings and a library – forms an exciting backdrop. One of its glass-roofed courtyards houses the **Hans Hedbergs Museum** dedicated to the Swedish sculptor (see p30).

Environs

Next to an excavation site in **Gene fornby**, 5 km (3 miles) south of the town, a 6th-century farm has been reconstructed, where people come to live and work as they did in the Iron Age.

The most striking medieval church in the area is the octagonal **Själevads Kyrka** from 1880, which was voted Sweden's most beautiful church in a nationwide poll.

🏛 **Örnsköldsviks Museum**
Läroverksgatan 1. **Tel** 0660-886 01. **Open** Midsummer–Aug: daily; other times: Tue–Sat. **Closed** public holidays. ☐ 📷

🏛 **Arken**
Strandgatan 21. **Tel** 0660-785 00. Public areas: **Open** daily. **Hans** Hedbergs Museum: **Open** ring Tourist Office 0660-881 00 for info. **Closed** public holidays. ☐ 🚫

Surströmming, a Fishy Delicacy

The coast of Southern Norrland has a speciality which many Swedes, not only the people of Norrland, consider to be the ultimate delicacy, although the majority probably detest it. This treat is fermented herring, known as *surströmming*, which, after around eight weeks of fermenting, is canned. When the can is opened it produces what is, to say the least, a characteristic aroma, which aficionados consider absolutely divine. The fishing villages along the High Coast (see pp260–61), such as Ulvöhamn, are the centre of production, and a market is now opening up as far afield as Japan. The fermented herring is eaten reverentially, almost ritually, in early autumn, accompanied by small almond-shaped potatoes and chopped onion. It is best washed down with copious amounts of beer and schnapps.

Can of Surströmming

⑬ The High Coast

Sweden's spectacular high coast is best experienced on a light summer evening, when the wooded hills are reflected in the calm waters of the bays, or on the quay in Ulvöhamn during the *surströmming* season *(see p259)*, when the peculiar speciality of fermented herring is enjoyed with flat bread, tiny potatoes and schnapps. A boat is ideal for getting around, but the Höga-kustenbron bridge provides easy access and ferries sail regularly from several ports. The dramatic landscape is the main attraction. Declared a UNESCO World Heritage Site in 2000, it is the result of the land rising 300 m (984 ft) since the ice receded around 9,600 years ago. At that time Skuleberget hill, north of Docksta, was a tiny island.

Skuleskogens National Park
Watched over by Skuleberget hill, the park covers 30 sq km (12 sq miles) of wilderness, with walking trails through magical ancient forest and over the clifftops along the coast.

Ullångersfjärden
Motorists on the E4 rejoin the Gulf of Bothnia at Ullångersfjärden bay which, with its high, sheer cliffs, is almost fjord-like.

Nordingrå
"Fair Nordingrå" was a tourist destination long before the term High Coast was coined. Beautiful roads lined with steep hills pass through stunning scenery.

Högakustenbron
Since 1997, the 1,800-m (6,000-ft) bridge, suspended on 180-m (600-ft) high pylons, has offered travellers breathtaking views. There is a tourist information point in the hotel on the north side of the bridge.

For hotels and restaurants in this area see pp284–289 and pp294–301

VISITORS' CHECKLIST

Practical Information
Ångermanland. E4. *i* Örnsköldsvik Tourist Office, 0660-881
00. Kramfors Tourist Office, 0612-
800 00. Härnösands Turistbyrå,
0611 204 50. Skule National Park
Skule Naturum, 0613-70 02 00.
Skule Song Festival (1st weekend in Jul). **hogakusten.com**

Transport
from Örnsköldsvik.

Skagsudde

The High Coast walking
trail stretches 127 km
(79 miles) from the mouth
of the Ångermanälven
to Örnsköldsvik.

• Köpmanholmen

Trysunda

Trysunda
One of the best-preserved villages,
Trysunda has a richly decorated,
17th-century fishermen's chapel.
Part of the island is a nature reserve.

N. Ulvön

Hjältön

Ulvöhamn

Gulf of Bothnia

S. Ulvön

Ilom • Norrfällsviken

Omnefjärden

Ulvöhamn
This is the spiritual
home of the herring
speciality, *surströmming*.
Norrland's largest fishing
fleet made its home in
the sheltered harbour
lying between Norra and
Södra Ulvön. The chapel
dates from 1622.

• Bönhamn

0 kilometres   10
0 miles   5

Högbonden
The 100-year-old lighthouse
on the island of Högbonden
warned shipping of the rocky
coastline. Today it is a youth
hostel, reached by boat from
Bönhamn, the most authentic
fishing village on the
mainland, and the place to
savour local specialities such
as fresh river salmon, whitefish
and, of course, *surströmming*.

Key

■ Major road

═ Minor road

-- Ferry route

- - High Coast walking trail

National Park

Nature Reserve

For additional map symbols *see back flap*

Thai monument in Utanede, commemorating the King of Siam's royal visit in 1897

⓮ Indalsälven

Jämtland/Medelpad. Road 86. 🚆 to Sundsvall, then bus. 🛈 Ragunda Tourist Office, 0696-68 10 90. 🎪 Vildhussen Festival (1st and 2nd weeks in Jul). 🌐 **ragundadalen.se**

The 430-km (270-mile) long Indalsälven river rises in the mountains of Norway and flows into Klingerfjärden, north of Sundsvall. The lower stretch of the river from Ragunda in Jämtland includes **Döda Fallet** (the Dead Falls) caused by a disastrous attempt by Vildhussen *(see box)* to control the river in 1796.

Döda Fallet is now a nature reserve where it is possible to walk around the rocky landscape and see the giant basins carved out by stones in the falls. An extraordinary revolving open-air theatre has been created next to the falls, with a stand for an audience of 420. A stage in the round is set against breathtaking natural scenery.

Utanede features an exotic Thai pavilion, the **King Chulalongkorn Memorial**, erected in memory of the King of Siam's trip along the river in 1897 as a guest of King Oscar II. The decorative elements of the golden pavilion were built by Thai craftsmen and seven million parts were shipped to Sweden and assembled. The interior holds a life-sized bronze statue of the king.

Among the churches along the river, **Lidens Kyrka**, dating from 1510, has the most attractive location (road 86, 37 km/23 miles northwest of Sundsvall) and contains medieval sculptures, with a Madonna from the 13th century. Vildhussen is buried in the cemetery here.

Bergeforsen on the coast is the last of the river's many power stations. There is an aquarium where Baltic fish such as salmon, sea trout and eel are raised.

🏯 **King Chulalongkorn Memorial** Utanede. Road 86, 7 km (4 miles) south of Bispgården. **Tel** 0696-68 10 90. **Open** mid-May–mid-Sep: daily. 🅿️ 🚻 daily. ♿ some facilities. 🌐 **thaipaviljongen.se**

Vildhussen and the Dead Falls

A drama which was to have a lasting impact unfolded on 6 June 1796 in Ragunda on the Indalsälven river. Magnus Huss, known as Vildhussen (Wild Huss), a merchant in Sundsvall, had been building a log flume to bypass the 38-m (125-ft) high Storforsen waterfall when an unusually high spring flood put pressure on the lake above the falls. The log flume burst and the river forged a new route, emptying the 27-km (17-mile) long lake in just four hours and sending so much soil and debris downstream that it formed Sweden's largest delta at the river mouth. The Storforsen waterfall had become Döda Fallet (the Dead Falls). Local people were sceptical of Huss's scheme from the start and despite the now navigable river and fertile land on the old lake bed, discontent brewed. A year later Huss died when his boat capsized. Rumour has it that the oars had been hidden and his boat pushed out into the fast-flowing river.

Döda Fallet, Vildhussen's creation

⓯ Östersund

Jämtland. 🚇 44,000. 🚌 🚆 ✈ 🛈 Rådhusgatan 44, 063-14 40 01. 🎪 Storsjöyran Festival (last weekend in Jul), Arnljot Games (Jul). 🌐 **visitostersund.se**

Established on the shores of Storsjön lake in 1786, the county town of Östersund lies opposite Jämtland's ancient centre of Frösön. Before coming under Norwegian rule in 1178, the people of Jämtland had ruled themselves and would be happy to do so again if the Republic of Jämtland movement had its way. In a fairly lighthearted manner, the movement protects local culture – the highpoint is the Storsjöyran Festival in July.

The county museum, **Jamtli**, with its Historieland feature, offers an exciting picture of life around Storsjön. This time machine transports visitors to scenes from the 18th and 19th centuries, where history can be felt, heard and even tasted. The museum's showpiece are the oldest preserved Viking *Överhogdal* tapestries.

A short bridge leads to the rolling, green island of Frösön. Its eastern parts are more like a part of town, but the views across Storsjön to the peak of Oviksfjällen inspired the composer Wilhelm Peterson-Berger to create his distinctive home, **Sommarhagen**, in 1914. The house is now a museum and the rich interior with decorative paintings by Paul Jonze is something of a companion to Carl Larsson's Sundborn *(see p244)*. Every summer *Arnljot*, Peterson-Berger's drama about

Old stone fireplace in Jamtli Museum, Östersund

the Viking from 11th-century Frösö, is performed in a field a short distance away.

The 12th-century **Frösö Kyrka** is one of Sweden's most popular churches in which to get married. **Frösö Zoo** has 700 animal species from around the world.

Environs

Storsjön lake is best explored on a steamer, such as the 1875 *S/S Thomeé*, Sweden's oldest steamer still in regular use. Many enthusiasts try to spot the elusive Storsjö Monster, the so-called sister of Scotland's Loch Ness monster.

Brunflo, 15 km (9 miles) south of Östersund, has an 18th-century church with a 12th-century lookout tower.

🏛 Jamtli

Museiplan. **Tel** 063-15 01 10. **Open** mid-Jun–Aug: daily; Sep–mid-Jun: Tue–Sun. **Closed** 24, 25, 31 Dec. 🎨 🍴 summer. ▢ ✏ 🏠 🎁

🏠 Sommarhagen

Frösön, 9 km (6 miles from the centre). **Tel** 063-430 41. **Open** end Jun–end Aug: daily; other times by arrangement. 🎨 🍴 by appointment. ▢ 🎁

🐾 Frösö Zoo

3 km (2 miles) south of the centre. **Tel** 063-430 41. **Open** mid-Jun–mid-Aug: daily. 🎨 ▢ 🍴 🎁 ♿

⓰ Åre

Jämtland. E14. 🏔 1,000. 🚌 🚆 ✈ Östersund. 🔎 St Olofs Väg, 0647-177 20. 🎿 Alpine World Cup (Feb), St Olavsloppet (end Jun), Åre Bike Festival (1st wk in Jul), Tour of Jamtland (early Aug). 🌐 are360.com

Åreskutan is Sweden's most visited mountain peak. The cable car lifts passengers from the village of Åre to within 150 m (490 ft) of the summit at 1,420 m (4,658 ft). At this altitude, the skiing season lasts into June. Facilities are plentiful in what has become Sweden's leading ski destination. There are 40 lifts and 100 pistes, some of which are the longest and steepest in the country. Hotels and

The 1,700-m (5,600-ft) high Syl, just over a day's walk south of Storlien

conference centres rise up into the sky. This is in contrast to how the resort looked at the end of the 19th century with hotels such as Åregården and the Grand. Still here is the Bergbanan run, which has attracted tobogganists of all ages. Prominent visitors have included Winston Churchill, who came for the excellent flyfishing and to hunt elk. Today's range of activities includes scooter safaris, dog sledding, paraskiing, ice-climbing, surfing rapids and mountain biking on Åreskutan.

Environs

The **Tännforsen** waterfall, 20 km (12 miles) west of Åre, is one of the most impressive in Jämtland, with a drop of 37 m (120 ft).

Njarka Sameläger, on an island on Häggsjön lake, has a Sami camp where visitors can learn how to lasso, or taste delicacies such as reindeer heart. On Åreskutan's eastern spur, 10 km (6 miles) from Åre, lies **Fröå Gruva**, where copper was mined from 1752 to 1916. The countryside is beautiful to wander through, with buildings from various eras. At **Huså Bruk**, another centre for copper mining further to the north, is Huså Herrgård, a manor built in 1838.

Skiers resting at a hut on Åreskutan, Sweden's top ski resort

⓱ Storlien

Jämtland. E14. 🚌 🚆 ✈ Östersund. 🔎 SP Livs & Bensin petrol station, Vintergatan 25, 0647-700 20. 🌐 storlienturistbyra.se

The arrival of the railway in Trondheim in the 1880s opened up new opportunities for Storlien, which is located near the border with Norway. It is only 60 km (37 miles) to the Trondheim Fjord, and the broad pass between Stenfjället and Skurdalshöjden allows mild Atlantic winds to sweep through. The healthy air attracted spa guests to a mountain sanatorium, and with the dawn of the 20th century tourists began arriving.

Today, Storlien is a classic ski resort for both cross-country and downhill. It is also a starting point for walks in the Jämtland mountains, such as via the STF stations of Blåhammaren, Storulvån, Sylarna and Vålådalen. The mountains can also be reached from Enafors on the E14 and by train.

Popular with birdwatchers, nearby **Ånnsjön** lake has a bird station and sanctuary. **Handöl**, on the western shore, has been a site for soapstone mining since the late Middle Ages. It was also where the surviving Carolean forces gathered in 1799 after Carl Gustaf Armfelt's catastrophic retreat from Norway. The Carolean monument on the waterfront is a memorial to the 3,700 men who froze to death in the mountains. Today accommodation and better equipment have prompted more and more people to take up the challenge of completing the 75-km (47-mile) long Carolean March.

⑱ The Härjedalen Mountains

The tree line in Härjedalen is at 900 m (2,950 ft) and even in the forested lowlands in the east there are mountains with bare summits such as Sånfjället and Vemdalsfjällen. But the mightiest mountains loom large in the west towards Norway and the province of Jämtland, with Helagsfjället the highest peak at 1,797 m (5,900 ft). Funäsdalen is the local hub, from where in summer Sweden's highest road runs via the Sami village of Mittådalen and the plateau of Flatruet to Ljungdalen. There are many opportunities for ski-touring and downhill skiing, fishing in summer and hiking along the southern part of the Kungsleden trail.

Helags
STF *(see p312)* has a mountain station at the base of Helagsfjället, Sweden's highest peak south of the Arctic Circle.

Ramundberget
In the summer, this popular winter sports venue, known for its early snowfalls, is a good starting point for mountain hikes to Helags, Ljungdalen and Fjällnäs.

Funäsdalen
This lively town in the Härjedalen mountains has the award-winning Härjedalens Fjällmuseum, which shows how the Sami and upland farmers survived the challenges of past times.

Røros (Norway)

Fjällnäs

Tänndalen

84

84

Ljungda[len]

②

Mittådalen

Bruksvallarna

Tännäs

①

311

Högvålen

Idre

Rogen
The nature reserve around Härjedalen's largest lake system has unusual flora and fauna. It is great for canoeing. The Sami village of Ruvhten offers ice-fishing for grayling and char.

KEY

① **Visit a musk ox sanctuary** and see musk oxen in their natural habitat. Guided tours start at Tännäs Fishing Centre.

② **The road** over the Flatruet Plateau is only open in summer.

③ **Parts of the Sånfjället** mountain in the forest were declared a national park in 1909, partly to protect the bear population. Wolves, lynx and wolverine also live here.

Reindeer Pastures
The Sami villages of Mittådalen and Ruvhten (Tännäs) have summer pastures in the western mountains. The winter pastures stretch as far as the forests of Sveg and into Dalarna.

VISITORS' CHECKLIST

Practical Information
Härjedalen. Road 84. **i** Lofsdalen, 0680-412 33. Funäsdalen 0684-155 80. Vemdalen, 0684-301 80. Tännäs Fishing Centre: **Tel** 0684 242 00 🏠 Funäsdalen Mountain Market (Wed). **W** herjedalen.se

Transport
🚂 to Ljusdal or Östersund, then bus. 🚌 from Stockholm and Gothenburg. ✈ Sveg or Östersund.

Vemdalsfjällen
This skiers' paradise has a joint lift system for the main resorts: Vemdalskalet, Björnrike, Klövsjö and Storhågna, as well as great facilities for cross-country skiing.

Klövsjö 🎿

Vemdalskalet 🎿
→ *Storhågna*
Ånge
•**Vemdalen**
315
Hede
84
Björnrike 🎿
Sveg

kärsjövålen 🎿

3

84

Sveg

🎿 **Lofsdalen**

Sveg

Key
▰▰▰ Major road
▭▭▭ Minor road
– – Walking trail

0 kilometres   20
0 miles   10

⑲ Sveg

Härjedalen. 🏔 2,700. 🚂 Inlandsbanan (summer), or to Mora or Ljusdal then bus. 🚌 ✈ **i** Ljusnegatan 1, 0680-125 05. 🐻 Bear Festival (Jul).

Härjedalen's central town is Sveg, the gateway to the mountains. The municipality of the same name covers an area larger than many counties, and with just 11,000 inhabitants it has a population density of less than one person per sq km. Forest stretches in every direction. Winding waterways provide opportunities for fishing, canoeing and beaver safaris. The nearest mountain for skiing is a 30-minute drive away.

Around Sveg, small villages such as Duvberg, Ytterberg, Överberg and Äggen are well-preserved, with 18th-century features. **Gammel-Remsgården**, 15 km (9 miles) north of Sveg, is a typical early-18th-century Härjedalen manor house with richly decorated interiors. About 15 km (9 miles) east of Sveg lies the village of **Älvros**, whose church has a beautifully painted bell tower.

Lillhärdal, 30 km (19 miles) south of Sveg, is said to have been founded in the 9th century by the Viking Härjulf Hornbrytare. Bildhöst has one of the last working crofts, complete with cattle and milkmaids, while Hamre Skans is a timbered fortification from the 18th century.

Älvros church near Sveg, with a free-standing, painted bell tower

For additional map symbols *see back flap*

NORTHERN NORRLAND

Stretching from the populated Baltic coast through wild forests and marshes to the open expanses of the mountains, Northern Norrland is a vast, almost untouched region. The biting chill and eternal darkness of the long northern winter are compensated for by summer's midnight sun, when nature seizes its short window of opportunity to flourish and the reindeer are moved to new pastures.

The three provinces of Västerbotten, Norrbotten and Lappland make up Sweden's most northerly region. Västerbotten, on the Gulf of Bothnia, is the most southerly. Its coast and river valleys had booming settlements for many centuries. But today commercial activity is concentrated in towns such as Umeå, with its university and youthful population, and Skellefteå, known as the "Town of Gold" because of its proximity to two of Europe's largest gold deposits. Inland, the wilderness takes hold with vast tracts of forest and marsh. After a journey between Lycksele and Sorsele, Carl von Linné wrote: "A priest could never make Hell sound worse than this." But with modern transport, today's traveller can look forward to outdoor adventures and wildlife in this unspoilt landscape.

North of Västerbotten, Norrbotten's coastline harbours features of rural culture such as the church village in Gammelstad, a UNESCO World Heritage Site. The Norrbotten archipelago is renowned for being the sunniest place in the country and its beach resorts lure holiday-makers. The border with Finland lies along the Torne river, and here the phrase "two countries, one people" is the most applicable.

Lappland borders Norway in the west and Finland in the northeast, but for the Sami (Lapp) people their land extends beyond official boundaries, across the mountains and forests and down to the coast, where their thriving culture of reindeer herding, hunting and fishing prevail. Known as Laponia, this area is also a UNESCO World Heritage Site. National parks such as Sarek protect the alpine landscape with its glaciers and waterfalls. The main towns of Kiruna and Gällivare in northern Lappland owe their existence to the mining industry.

Dog sledding in Jukkasjärvi, Lapland

◀ The amazing spectacle of the Northern Lights over the frozen forests near Kiruna

Exploring Northern Norrland

An area covering more than one-third of Sweden cannot be
explored in a hurry. And things are not made easier by the large
areas of wilderness north of the Arctic Circle without roads, in
Europe's most sparsely populated region. Despite their northerly
latitude, the coastal areas combine a captivating archipelago
landscape with rich cultural sights. Spectacular roads lead up
into the mountains with romantic names such as "Saga Vägen"
(the Saga Highway) and "Blå Vägen" (the Blue Highway). Skiers
are tempted by the record-length season, while for hikers, the
northernmost section of the 440-km (275-mile) long Kungsleden
trail *(see p278)* between Abisko and Hemavan crosses the
mountainous UNESCO World Heritage Site of Laponia.

Lake Saggat seen from the Kvikkjokk road in
northwestern Lappland

Getting Around

Flying is the most comfortable means of
transport. Around a dozen airports offer
scheduled flights. Only a few trains travel on
the Vännäs–Luleå line and the Malmbanan
line running Luleå–Kiruna–Riksgränsen. The
Inlandsbanan line through Lappland from
Gällivare provides a summer tourist route.
The major roads E4, E10 and E12 (the Blue
Highway) are of a high standard, but road
conditions are variable elsewhere. Bus
services between the main towns are usually
good, but almost non-existent in the wilder
areas. Ferries operate across some mountain
lakes in summer, saving time for hikers.

Narvik
Riksgränsen
Kebnekaise 2111m
Stora Sjöfallet National Park
Vakkotavare
Padjelanta National Park
Sarektjåkkå 2090m
Sareks National Park
THE KUNGSLEDEN TRAIL
18
Kvikkjokk
Bodø
Pieskehaure
Arctic Circle
Vaulatjårro 1365m
Tjeggelvas
Mo i Rana
Jakkvik
Raker 1375m
Hornavan
ARJEPLOG 17
95
Ammarnäs
Uddjaure
Hemavan
Tärnaby
363
Storåvan
Storvindeln
Slagnäs
Ajaureforsen
Sorsele
Gardiken
LAPPLAND
45
Sandsele
370
Dikanäs
Storuman
Klimpfjäll
Storuman
E12
Björksele
Malgomaj
Vilhelmina
Lycksele
45
Dorotea
365
Österstund
Åsele
92
Fredrika
90

Key

▬▬▬ Major road

═══ Minor road

▬▬▬ Main railway

▬▬▬ Minor railway

▬▬▬ International border

0 kilometres   100

0 miles   50

For additional map symbols *see back flap*

Storehouse on stilts in Geunja Sami tourist village, Lappland

Fly fishing in Vindelälven, one of Europe's last untouched rivers

Sights at a Glance

1. Umeå
2. Holmöarna
3. Blå Vägen
4. Lövånger
5. Skellefteå
6. Boliden
7. Piteå
8. Storforsen
9. Luleå
10. Boden
11. Kalix
12. Tornedalen
13. Kiruna
14. Gällivare
15. Jokkmokk
16. Arvidsjaur
17. Arjeplog
18. The Kungsleden Trail
   pp278–9

Late afternoon in Umeå city, on the banks of the Ume river

❶ Umeå

Västerbotten. 🚗 110,000. 🚌 🚆 ✈ 🚢 from Vasa, Finland. ℹ️ Renmarkstorget 15, 090-16 16 16. 🎷 Jazzfestival (4th week in Oct), Film Festival (2nd weekend in Sep). 🌐 **visitumea.se**

With 3,000 birch trees lining the streets, it is not surprising that Umeå is known as "The City of Birches". After a major fire in 1888, a new city was built with broad, tree-lined esplanades and parks to prevent fires spreading. Post-fire buildings of interest include the **Scharinska villa** on Storgatan, designed by Ragnar Östberg, and **Moritska Gården**, Umeå's grandest residence for a local timber baron. The city's Neo-Gothic church was completed in 1894.

Umeå dates back to the 16th century. An important trading and administrative centre, it became a county town in 1622. The opening of a university in 1965 prompted an expansion that transformed Umeå into a city – Norrland's only one. With 40,000 students and lecturers, it is very much a young persons' place (average age 38). The splendid **Bildmuseet**, on the

Arts Campus, is a great showcase for international contemporary art and design.

In Gammlia, a 10-minute walk from the centre, the **Västerbottens Museum** focuses on the history of Umeå and Västerbotten. It includes Svenska Skidmuseet, which covers the history of skiing, and the fishing and maritime museum Fiske-och Sjöfartsmuseet. In the summer, the open-air museum **Gammlia Friluftsmuseum** shows off its historic farm buildings, complete with pets, and there are activities for children.

Umeå is the European Capital of Culture for 2014, which has sparked a construction boom and many cultural events.

🏛 **Bildmuseet**
Umeå Arts Campus, Östra Strandgatan 26. **Tel** 090-786 52 27. **Open** Tue–Sun. **Closed** Midsummer's Eve, 24 & 31 Dec. 🎫 by appt; **Tel** 090-786 74 00. 🌐 **bildmuseet.umu.se**

🏛 **Västerbottens Museum**
Gammlia. **Tel** 090-16 39 00/49. 🚌 **Open** Tue–Sun (mid-May–mid-Aug: daily). **Closed** 24, 31 Dec. 🖥 🎫 ♿ Gammlia Friluftsmuseum: **Open** mid-May–mid-Aug: daily. ♿ 🌐 **vbm.se**

❷ Holmöarna

Västerbotten. 🚗 90. 🚢 to Norrfjärden 30 km (19 miles) N of Umeå, then ferry. ℹ️ Umeå Tourist Office, 090-16 16 16. 🎷 Seajazz Festival (2nd weekend in July).

A 45-minute free ferry trip from Norrfjärden leads to the Holmö archipelago. There are four main islands – Holmön, Grossgrundet, Angesön and Holmögadd – and several smaller ones. The majority of the group forms part of Sweden's largest archipelago nature reserve. It is an area of exciting geological formations and extensive fields of rubble stones. The forest and shorelines provide habitats for 130 species of birds and a variety of flora.

The islands have been inhabited since the 14th century and **Holmöns Båtmuseum** focuses on the lives of the local fishermen, seal hunters and farmers.

The archipelago is ideal for cycling, bathing and fishing.

🏛 **Holmöns Båtmuseum**
At the ferry quay. **Tel** 090-552 20 (summer). **Open** mid-Jun–mid-Aug: daily. 🎫 🖥 🌐 **holmons batmuseum.se**

Encountering a reindeer on the Blue Highway

❸ Blå Vägen

Västerbotten, Lappland. E12. 🚌 ℹ️ Renmarkstorget 15, Umeå, 090-16 16 16.

From Lake Onega in Russia to Träna on Norway's Atlantic coast, the Blå Vägen (Blue Highway, E12) stretches 1,700 km (1,050 miles). The Swedish section follows the Umeälven river from Umeå through the towns of Lycksele, Storuman and Hemavan.

Sweden's 200-Year Peace

Sweden has enjoyed almost 200 years of peace. The last battles on Swedish soil took place in Sävar and Ratan north of Umeå in August 1809. Russian troops had been plundering the coast and a Swedish expeditionary force landed at the port of Ratan to attack the Russians from the rear. The troops marched south towards Sävar and clashed with the Russians on 19 August. The Swedes were defeated and withdrew to Ratan, where another battle was fought the next day. This time the Swedish troops stood their ground, but 1,000 men died in the conflict. A memorial in Sävar honours the fallen. As a result of the war, Finland was lost to Russia.

Infantryman, model, 1807

Klabböle, near Umeå, is the site of the river's first power station, built in 1899. It now houses the museum of **Umeå Energicentrum**, which is well worth a visit. There is something for everyone here, and children enjoy the "Playing with Energy" exhibit and trying to balance on logs like a log driver.

At **Vännäs**, 26 km (16 miles) from Umeå, the unspoilt Vindelälven river joins the Umeälven, and a detour can be made to the mighty **Mårdsele falls** to ride the rapids or fish for salmon, salmon trout and grayling.

Lycksele, the only town in southern Lappland, lies 123 km (76 miles) from Umeå. The local zoo, **Lycksele Djurpark**, specializes in Nordic wildlife.

🏛 Umeå Energicentrum
10 km (6 miles) W of Umeå.
Tel 090-16 03 74 (090 16 00 00 in winter). **Open** 2nd week in Jun–3rd week in Aug: daily. 🎫 💻

🐾 Lycksele Djurpark
Brännbergsvägen. **Tel** 0950-163 63.
Open 3rd week in May–Aug: daily.
🐾 🎫 💻 ⌀ 🏠 ♿
w lyckseledjurpark.com

❹ Lövånger

Västerbotten. E4. 🗺 2,400. 🚌
i Lövångers Kyrkstad, 0913-103 95.

The church village at Lövånger is one of the largest in the country with 117 cabins. It dates from the Middle Ages, although the oldest surviving cabin is from 1746. The village was built to accommodate churchgoers from remote outlying areas during church festivals. A number of cabins have been converted into hotel rooms. The 16th-century granite church of St Anne is decorated with medieval sculptures.

Sockenmuseet, just north of the church, illustrates how the people of Lövånger lived in the 19th century.

🏛 Sockenmuseet
Tel 0913-100 40. **Open** daily in summer (call for opening times). 🎫

The church village in Lövånger with accommodation for churchgoers

❺ Skellefteå

Västerbotten. E4. 🗺 35,000.
🚆 to Bastuträsk, then bus. 🚌 ✈
i Nygatan 49, 0910-45 25 00.
🎭 Skellefteå Festival (4th weekend in Jun); Woodstock Music Festival (Jul).
w destinationskelleftea.se

Northern Västerbotten had to wait until 1845 for its first town, but there had long been a marketplace alongside Skellefteå church. In order to accommodate the large congregation, a Neo-Classical cruciform church was built in 1800 on the site of a 15th-century church. Worshippers came from far afield, staying in Bonnstan, Skellefteå's church village built in the mid-19th century.

It was with the boom in the mining industry in the 1920s that Skellefteå's development took off, fuelled by the huge smelting plant at the mouth of the Skellefteälven river.

The town's green lung is the Nordanå Centrum of Culture, a park on the northern bank of the river. It houses an art gallery, **Skellefteå Museum** and historic buildings.

🏛 Skellefteå Museum
1.5 km (1 mile) W of the centre. **Tel** 0910-73 55 10. **Open** Tue–Sun. **Closed** some public hols. 🐾 💻 ⌀ 🏠 ♿

❻ Boliden

Västerbotten. E4/road 95. 🚌 ✈
Skellefteå, then bus. **i** Skellefteå Tourist Office, 0910-45 25 00. 🎭
Geology Festival (end Aug/early Sep).

The Kingdom of Gold is the name given to Skellefteå's ore field which, with Boliden at its heart, stretches from Bottenviken through northern Västerbotten towards the mountains of Lappland. Europe's two largest gold deposits are mined here, in addition to zinc, copper, silver and tungsten.

Bergrum Boliden, in the old mining office, traces the history of the formation of the sulphide ores more than 4,600 million years ago to their extraction today.

In World War II, the world's longest cable car system was constructed to transport the ore 96 km (60 miles) from the mines in Kristineberg. It is possible to travel along a 13-km (8-mile) long stretch from Örträsk to Mensträsk, swinging over the beautiful countryside at a sedate 10 km/h (6 mph).

🏛 Bergrum Boliden
1 km (half a mile) NW of the centre.
Tel 0910-58 00 60. **Open** Jun–Aug: daily. **Closed** Midsummer. 🐾 🎫
💻 🏠 ♿

The Kristineberg cable car system, once used to transport ore

Piteå's sandy beach, and Sweden's best chance of sun

⑦ Piteå

Norrbotten. E4. 🚗 42,000. 🚉
🛫 Luleå. 🚌 🚢 *i* Bryggargatan 14,
0911-933 90. 🎿 Piteå Summer
Games/International Midnight Sun
Football Tournament (end of Jun),
Piteå Dances and Smiles Festival (last
week Jul). **W** visitpitea.se

Originally located next to Öjebyn,
Piteå was moved after a fire to
the mouth of the Piteälven river.
The new town was burned by
the Russians in 1721 and rebuilt.
Picturesque wooden buildings
from the 19th century can be
found on the square of Rådhustorget, where the attractive Town
Hall dates from 1830. But it is the
coast that is the main draw. The
"Nordic Riviera" offers sandy
beaches and Sweden's best
chance of sun. If the weather
turns, there is an indoor fun pool.
   Öjebyn has a well-preserved
15th-century church and village.

Environs
Jävre, off the E4 south of Piteå,
has traces of Norrbotten's first
settlers from the Bronze Age. The
archaeology trail takes in graves,
sacrificial stones and labyrinths.

⑧ Storforsen

Norrbotten. 80 km (50 miles) NW of
Piteå, road 374. 🚌 *i* Älvsbyn Tourist
Office, 0929-108 60. **Open** Jun–Aug:
daily. 🅿 **W** digitalvisit.alvsbyn.se

Europe's mightiest untamed
stretch of whitewater can be
found on the Piteälven river, 40
km (25 miles) north of Älvsbyn.
The rapids drop 82 m (270 ft)
over 5 km (3 miles), at speeds of
over 800 cubic metres (176,000
gallons) per second. Efforts to

channel the rapids into a single
course created Döda Fallet (Dead
Falls), where giant basins can be
seen. Log floating has ceased,
but a visit to the **Skogs- och
Flottningsmuseet** will reveal how
things looked when Storforsen's
huge log jams were formed.

🏛 **Skogs- och Flottningsmuseet**
Storforsen. **Tel** 0929-17 00. **Open** May–
Aug: daily. 🅿 🍴 obligatory. 💻 🖊

Storforsen in the Piteälven river, a vast
expanse of whitewater rapids

⑨ Luleå

Norrbotten. E4. 🚗 45,000. 🛫 🚉 🚌
🚢 *i* Kulturens Hus, 0920-45 70 00.
🎿 Luleå Harbour Festival (mid-Jul).
W visitlulea.se

The county town of Luleå is
surrounded by water as the
Luleälven river flows into
glittering bays with a lush
archipelago beyond. A good
harbour was the reason for the
town's location here in the
mid-17th century, when
the original site upstream
became too shallow.
   The church village, **Gammelstads Kyrkstad**, and its church,
Nederluleå Kyrka, form a unique
monument to the old trading

centre and are a designated
UNESCO World Heritage Site.
The 15th-century granite
building with its perimeter wall
is upper Norrland's largest
medieval church. The white
steeple towers over a group of
408 small red cabins. This is
where churchgoers from
remote villages would
stay overnight and stable
their horses. The church's star
vaulting is decorated with
paintings from the Albert Pictor
school of the 1480s. The
magnificent altar-screen from
Antwerp dates from 1520.
   The cathedral in the new Luleå
was built in 1893. **Norrbottens
Museum** concentrates on the
history of Luleå and Norrbotten.
   The ore-loading harbour and
SSAB's steelworks are the
cornerstones of Luleå. They also
influence the science museum,
Teknikens Hus, where technical
experiments can be attempted,
such as drilling in a mine and
launching a space rocket.

Environs
Luleå archipelago, comprising
more than 1,300 islands and
islets, is a favourite place for
boat owners. Ferries provide
access to places of interest,
such as the fishing villages on
Kluntarna and Brändöskär.

🏠 **Gammelstads Kyrkstad**
10 km (6 miles) NW of the centre.
🚌 **Tel** 0920-45 70 10. **Open** 2nd
week in Jun–mid-Aug: daily; other
times: Tue–Thu. 🅿 🍴 🖊 🏠 ♿

🏛 **Norrbottens Museum**
Storgatan 2. **Tel** 0920-24 35 02.
Open Tue–Sun (Jun–Aug: daily).
Closed some public holidays.
🖥 💻 ♿

🏛 **Teknikens Hus**
University district, 5 km (3 miles)
N of the centre. **Tel** 0920-49 22 01.
Open Tue–Sun. 🅿 💻 🖊 🏠 ♿

Norrbottens Museum with a Sami summer
tent and hut

⑩ Boden

Norrbotten. 35 km NW of Luleå, Road 97. 🚌 🚆 Kallax. 🚐 ℹ️ Kungsgatan 40, 0921-624 10. 🎪 Boden Alive Festival (early Jul), Harvest Festival (Aug). 🌐 **experienceboden.nu**

Its strategic location on the Luleälven river, at the intersection of two main train lines, has made Boden a centre for Sweden's northerly defences. It became the country's largest garrison town at the beginning of the last century and countless young men from across the country have completed their military service here. Five artillery forts circled the town. The nuclear bunker deep in the rock was top secret until only a few years ago. Now **Rödbergsfortet** is a national monument open to the public who can experience life in the fort and even stay in rooms carved out of the rock.

The central Björknäs area is also worth a visit for its open-air heated swimming pool and to see historic Norrbotten farms.

About 3 km (2 miles) north of the centre, a Wild West ranch has been built which offers a taste of pioneering life in the 19th century.

Cannon from Boden fort

🏛 Rödbergsfortet

5 km (3 miles) W of the centre. **Tel** 070-266 31 62. **Open** 3rd week in Jun–1st week in Aug; other times by appointment. 🅿️ 🎒 💻 ♿ limited access.

⑪ Kalix

Norrbotten. E4, 50 km (31 miles) W of Haparanda. 🚌 🚐 🚆 Kallax. ♿ ℹ️ Strandgatan 10, 0923-129 79. 🎪 Grayling Day (end Jul), National River Festival (mid-Aug). 🌐 **kalix.se**

The Kalix area to the north of the Gulf of Bothnia has been inhabited since Stone Age times. **Nederkalix** became a parish in the 15th century, but its church has had a turbulent history, with devastating fires and plundering by the Russians.

Kalixälven river, one of Europe's few entirely unregulated large rivers

During the 1809 war, it served as a stable for Russian horses. Englundsgården Cultural Heritage Centre is a good example of Norrland's beautiful wooden architecture.

Environs

The **Kalixälven** is one of Sweden's few unregulated rivers, ensuring good catches of salmon trout and salmon. The archipelago offers pike and whitefish and the opportunity for seine fishing. Of the islands which can be reached by tour boat, Malören has a timber chapel dating from 1769, an old lighthouse and a pilot station.

⑫ Tornedalen

Norrbotten. Road 99. 🚐 ℹ️ Haparanda-Tornio Tourist Office, 0922-120 10. 🎪 Pajala Market (end Jun), Whitefish Festival in Kukkola (last weekend in Jul).

The Torne river and its tributary, Muonio, form the border with Finland, but culturally the areas along both shores are united. Place names are in Finnish, and many of the inhabitants speak a local form of Finnish.

Haparanda, at the mouth of the river, was created as a border town when Torneå became part of Finland in the peace treaty of 1809. A bridge links the sister towns and they share a tourist office.

The disproportionately large train station, which has both normal and Russian wider gauge tracks, is a legacy from its time as a Russian border town.

Fishing is an important part of life on the Torne. Whitefish has been caught in the Kukkola rapids 15 km (9 miles) upstream since the 13th century, using large nets fixed to piers. The best fishing is to be had in late July, when the whitefish festival is held.

Övertorneå, 70 km (43 miles) north of Haparanda, is a fertile horticultural area. The long light summer nights help berries, fruit and vegetables to develop an exceptional flavour. There is a church dating from the 17th century and a good view from the top of the mountain, Luppioberget, where Father Christmas is said to live.

Pajala is the centre of northern Tornedalen. The area is popular for fishing and wilderness camps and it is possible to shoot the rapids on the Torne and Tärendö rivers. The latter is a 50-km (31-mile) long natural link between the Torne and Kalix rivers. **Laestadius Pörte** and museum attract Laestadian Lutherans on a pilgrimage to the simple cabin of the revivalist preacher and botanist Lars Levi Laestadius (1800–61).

🏛 Laestadius Pörte

Pajala. **Tel** 0981-202 05. **Open** May–Aug: daily. 🅿️ 🎒 💻

Octagonal church in Övertorneå, the Tornedalen valley's main town

Strikingly shaped church in Kiruna, inspired by a Sami hut

⑬ Kiruna

Lappland. E10. 🗺 19,000. 🚗 🚌 ✈
🛈 Kiruna Lapland Tourist Office, Folkets Hus, Lars Janssonsgatan 17, 0980-188 80. 🎿 Snow Festival (last weekend in Jan), Kiruna Festival (4th weekend in Jun). 🌐 **kirunalapland.se**

In terms of area, Kiruna is one of the world's largest municipalities. It is the site of Sweden's highest mountain, Kebnekaise, 2,014 m (6,607 ft), from where, on a clear day, one can see one-eleventh of the country. For 50 days in summer the sun never sets, and for 20 winter days it never rises. But even in the dark and cold, the people make the best of things. In January they hold a snow festival with exciting activities such as a scooter jump show, kick-sled racing and reindeer racing. Kiruna is also one of the best places in the world to see the Northern Lights.

Kiruna's development is due largely to the local iron ore deposits. In 1899 the first ore train rolled out from the mine on the newly laid railway line to Luleå. Ten years later, Kiruna had grown to a town of 7,000 inhabitants. Older buildings include the church, a gift of the mining company LKAB in 1912, whose shape was inspired by a Sami hut, and which is richly decorated by artists of the time, including Prince Eugen, Christian Eriksson and Ossian Elgström.

The Kirunavaara mine is open for guided tours. **LKAB Visitor Centre** lies 540 m (1,772 ft) below ground and paints a vivid picture of mining in the region.

With work in the Kirunavaara mine causing dangerous subsidence, both Kiruna and the town of Malmberget are gradually being moved to a safer location.

Environs
The space centre **Esrange**, 40 km (25 miles) east of Kiruna has, since the first rocket was launched in 1966, been a vital link in the European space programme.

The former Sami village of **Jukkasjärvi**, 17 km (11 miles) east of Kiruna, has Lappland's oldest church, dating from 1607. It houses Bror Hjorth's altar-screen in wood depicting the charismatic 19th-century preacher Lars Levi Laestadius' missionary work among the Sami and Swedish pioneers.

Jukkasjärvi is renowned for **ICEHOTEL**, first created in 1992. In mid-November each year, a team of builders constructs a hotel with ice blocks and snow. Drinks are served in the cool Icebar and guests sleep on ice beds, wrapped in furs, even though it is -40°C outside. As spring arrives, the structure slowly thaws. During the summer, guided tours take in the process involved in making the ice blocks used to construct the hotel and show how the blocks are stored until work begins on the next hotel.

Altar-screen by Bror Hjorth, Jukkasjärvi church

ICEHOTEL also offers summer activities such as whitewater rafting, cross-country cycling, fishing and ice-sculpting.

Kiruna's vast mountain landscape is traversed by the **Kungsleden** trail (see p278).

🏛 **LKAB Visitor Centre**
Tel 0980-188 80 for bookings. **Open** daily. 🅿 🚻 🌐 **kirunalapland.se**

🏨 **ICEHOTEL Jukkasjärvi**
17 km (10 miles) E of Kiruna. 🚌 from Kiruna. **Tel** 0980-668 00. **Open** Dec–Apr & Jun–Aug. 🅿 🚻 🚗 🌐
see also where to Stay p289.

⑭ Gällivare

Lappland. E10. 🗺 8,500. ✈ 🚗 🚌
🛈 Storgatan 16, 0970-166 60. 🎿 Winter Market (mid-Mar), Laponia Festival (1st weekend in Jul). 🌐 **gellivarelapland.se**

The twin communities of Gällivare and Malmberget grew rapidly from the late-19th century as the mining industry developed. But there was a settlement here long before that time: a chapel was built for the Sami in the 17th century and the Sami church on the Vassaraälven river opened in 1751. The arrival of the railway in 1888 sparked an iron ore rush which can be relived at **Kåkstan** in Malmberget and experienced from 1,000 m (3,280 ft) down in the LKAB iron ore mine. **LKAB's Gruvmuseum** focuses on 250 years of mining history.

Icebar in the ICEHOTEL, Jukkasjärvi, a creation of ice and snow

◀ Autumn in the Rapa Valley, in Sarek National Park, Lappland

The Gällivare municipality stretches to the Norwegian border, covering parts of the Laponia UNESCO World Heritage Site *(see p279)*. The Dundret nature reserve offers a number of good cross-country skiing facilities.

⓯ Jokkmokk

Lappland. Road 97 & 45. 🖼 3,500. 🚌 🚂 **ℹ** Stortorget 4, 0971-222 50. 🎿 Jokkmokk Market (1st Thu–Sat Feb), Music week in Saltoluokta (end Jun). **W** turism.jokkmokk.se

The town of Jokkmokk is best-known for its winter market. For a few days in February, snow, darkness and cold give way to light, warmth and sparkling colours, when more than 30,000 people arrive to browse among the 500 market stalls and join in the festivities. The annual reindeer race through the town often causes chaos, but things are even faster at the reindeer race on the frozen Lake Talvatissjön.

The life of the Sami and the pioneering Swedish settlers is depicted in **Ájtte, Svenskt Fjäll- och Samemuseum**. Unfortunately in 1972 the Sami church built in 1753 burned down. The exterior of the new church replicates the original, but it has a modern interior.

Environs
The municipality includes the magnificent national parks of Padjelanta, Sarek, Stora Sjöfallet and a section of Muddus, which is part of the Laponia UNESCO World Heritage Site *(see p279)*.

Porjus, 40 km (25 miles) north of Jokkmokk, was Sweden's first major hydroelectric power station (1910–15). Its story is related in **Porjus Expo** which has a power station museum 50 m (164 ft) underground.

In Vuollerim, 43 km (26 miles) south of Jokkmokk, Stone Age settlements have been uncovered on the Stora Luleälv river. The museum **Vuollerim 6000 År** gives visitors the chance to experience Stone Age life.

Muddus National Park, part of the Laponia UNESCO World Heritage Site

🏛 **Ájtte, Svenskt Fjäll- och Samemuseum**
Kyrkogatan 3. **Tel** 0971-170 70. **Open** Jun–Aug: daily; other times: Mon–Fri. 🏚 🖊 🏠 🚻 **W** ajtte.com

🏛 **Porjus Expo**
Porjus. 40 km (25 miles) N of Jokkmokk, road 45. **Tel** 0973-776 00. **Open** Jun–Aug; other times by appointment. 🏚 🖊

🏛 **Vuollerim 6000 År**
Vuollerim. 42 km (26 miles) SW of Jokkmokk, road 97. **Tel** 0976-101 65. **Open** Jun–Aug: daily. 🏚 🖊 🏠 🚻
W vuollerim6000.se

⓰ Arvidsjaur

Lappland. Road 94 & 45. 🖼 4,700. 🚌 to Jörn, then bus. 🚐 ✈ **ℹ** Östra Skolgatan 18C, 0960-175 00. 🎿 A-smällen (1st weekend in Jul), Sami Festival (last weekend in Aug). **W** arvidsjaur.se

This community in central Lapland was founded in the early 17th century when King Karl IX set up a church here to bring Christianity to the Sami. **Arvidsjaur's Sami church village** contains 80 huts and cabins from the 18th century.

Located in Glommersträsk, a small village southeast of Arvidsjaur, is **Hängengården**, a homestead dating from the

Traditional huts and log cabins in Arvidsjaur's 18th-century Sami church village

1800s. It is now a museum with 12 old buildings and around 3,000 items of interest.

In the summer a steam train operates on the Inlandsbanan line to the **Rallarmuseet** in Moskosel, which tells of the pioneers who built the railway.

🏛 **Rallarmuseet**
Moskosel, 40 km (25 miles) N of Arvidsjaur, road Rv 45. **Tel** 0960-175 00. **Open** mid-Jun–mid-Aug: daily. 🖥 🚻 limited access.

🏛 **Hängengården**
Glommersträsk, 45 km (28 miles) SE of Arvidsjaur, road Rv 95. **Tel** 0960-202 91. **Open** early Jun–mid-Aug: call for opening times. 🖥

⓱ Arjeplog

Lappland. Road 95. 🖼 3,100. ✈ Arvidsjaur. 🚐 **ℹ** Torget 1, 0961-145 20. 🎿 Marknan (1st week in Mar), Sami Culture Week (1st week in Oct). **W** polcirkeln.nu

On the "Silver Road" between Hornavan and Uddjaur lies Arjeplog, home to the **Silvermuseet**. It was created by the "Lappland doctor" Einar Wallquist, whose home Doktorsgården is open to the public in July. In addition to 16th-century Sami silverwork, the museum looks at the life of the Sami and the pioneering incomers.

The area has much to offer hunting and fishing enthusiasts.

🏛 **Silvermuseeet**
Torget. **Tel** Tourist Office, 0961-145 20. **Open** Jun–mid-Aug: daily; other times: Mon–Sat. 🏚 🖊 🏠 🚻 limited access.

⓲ The Kungsleden Trail

The best way to experience the magnificence of the Swedish mountains is to hike along a few stages of the Kungsleden Trail. In 1900, the Swedish tourism organisation, Svenska Turistföreningen (STF), drew up plans for a network of marked walking trails and huts for overnight stays through the mountains from Lappland south to Grövelsjön lake in Dalarna. Today, the 440-km (275-mile) long stretch between Abisko mountain station on the Malmbanan railway line in the north and Hemavan in southern Lappland forms the Kungsleden Trail. The simple huts have given way to mountain stations and rest cabins which offer hikers shelter in bad weather and overnight accommodation. Some also have a ferry service to help people on their way.

Mountain walkers on the well-marked Kungsleden Trail

Sarek
Perhaps the most spectacular of Sweden's national parks, Sarek has 200 lofty peaks, more than 100 glaciers, wild waterfalls and valleys such as Rapadalen. It is home to elk, lynx and wolverine.

Ammarnäs
The village is located in the Vindelfjällen nature reserve, created in 1976 and known for its fauna. Its 200 inhabitants mostly live off tourism and reindeer herding.

Hemavan is the final point for the Kungsleden Trail's northern section. With the ski town of Tärnaby close by, it is a mecca for alpine skiers.

Key

- ‒ ‒ Kungsleden Trail
- – – Other walking trails
- ▨ Major road
- ▨ Minor road
- — Railway line
- ⌂ Mountain stations and cabins

Padjelanta National Park
Vaisa
Kutjaure
K
Låddejåkkå
Araslu
Staloluokta
Tuottar
Sårjåsjaure · Staddajåkkå
Tarraluop
Sämmarla
Vaimok
Pieskehaure · Tarreka

Vuonatjvike
Jäl
Pieljekaise
Bäverholmen · Adolfström
Dalovardo
Sjnjultie
Vitnjul
Rävfallsstugan
95

Skidbäcksstugan
Tärnasjö
Viterskalet · Serve
Syter · Ammarnäs
Aigert
Hemavan
363
Tärnaby
E12

Övre Umaj
E12

0 kilometres 30
0 miles 20

Riksgränsen
is the last station on the Malmbanan line and a skier's paradise with lifts often operating until as late as Midsummer.

VISITORS' CHECKLIST

Practical Information
Lappland. E12 to Hemavan, E10 to Kiruna and Abisko. 🅸 Kiruna Tourist Office, 0980-188 80, Abisko Tourist Station, 0980-402 00, Tärnaby Tourist Office, 0954-104 50. 🚗 guided tours in some parts. 🆆 stfturist.se

Transport
✈ Storuman or Kiruna, then bus. 🚌 to Kiruna and Abisko. 🚗

Nikkaluokta is the end of the road. It is a 19-km (12-mile) walk to the STF mountain station at Kebnekaise; 7 km (4 miles) can be cut by catching the lake ferry.

Abisko
Thanks to the E10 and its own train station, the STF tourist facility at Torneträsk in Abisko national park is a natural starting point for mountain walkers.

Kebnekaise
Topping the Kebnekaise massif is Sweden's highest peak at 2,016 m (6,614 ft). Below the summit, the STF station in Ladtjodalen, 690 m (2,264 ft), is a good starting point for tackling the range.

Laponia World Heritage Site

The mountainous region of Lappland was designated a UNESCO World Heritage Site in 1996. Laponia has been home to the Sami since prehistoric times and provides the ideal conditions for their traditional nomadic reindeer herding, governed by the seasons. It is also Europe's largest single wilderness area, home to brown bears and alpine flora, as well as being geologically important. These factors contributed to its inclusion on unesco's list. The region includes the four national parks Padjelanta, Sarek, Stora Sjöfallet and Muddus, as well as the wetlands of Sjaunja with their rich birdlife.

Sjaunja National Park's extensive wetlands

Stora Sjöfallet
This area is impressive for the mountains and glaciers of Akka and the primeval pine forests, but the waterfall is dry due to hydro-electric schemes.

TRAVELLERS' NEEDS

WHERE TO STAY

Sweden has a wide variety of hotels and guesthouses to suit all tastes and budgets – from small family-run establishments to historic manor houses and large luxury hotels. In addition, there are more than 400 youth hostels that offer great value and comfort. There are also several bed-and-breakfast (B&Bs) options, often advertised with a *RUM* (room) sign by the roadside. In the mountains, ski resorts offer both hotels and small huts to rent. Cottages are also plentiful elsewhere in Sweden, sometimes on or near campsites. Pages 284–9 have details of places to stay throughout the country, covering everything from cosy B&Bs to designer hotels.

Lobby of the pleasant Clarion Hotel Wisby in Visby, Gotland *(see p286)*

Choosing a Hotel

Staying in well-appointed hotels in prime locations can be costly, but there are also plenty of budget options to choose from. Among the cheaper alternatives are youth hostels, or *Vandrarhem*, most of which are of a high standard. Another good option is a self-catering cottage, the ideal family accommodation at a reasonable price.

Larger hotels cater mainly to business travellers. They are often busy during the week but offer discounted weekend rates.

It is advisable to book a room well in advance, particularly in cities during the week. Hotels in Stockholm tend to be busy in summer and when events or trade fairs are on. To find out when the busiest times are likely to be, check the **Stockholm Visitors Board**'s events calendar online.

How to Book

It is very easy to make hotel reservations online. If you are looking for a room in Stockholm, the Stockholm Visitors Board offers a booking service. Another good site is **Visit Sweden**, which lists all kinds of accommodation and also provides an online booking service. Most travel websites will offer deals when you book your hotel and flight together.

Hotel Chains

International and Nordic hotel chains are well represented in towns across Sweden. Some chains are taking over and renovating older hotels, keeping the classic features while modernizing the facilities. City hotels cater mainly to business travellers but often offer good deals off-season and at weekends. All establishments offer central booking facilities, either by phone or online.

Elite Hotels has centrally located hotels in Swedish towns, often in classic buildings. **First Hotels** is a Nordic chain with an environment-friendly ethos and 61 hotels across the country. **Historic Hotels of Sweden** has 12 charming properties, including castles and manor houses, while **Nordic Choice Hotels** has hotels

The spectacular ICEBAR at ICEHOTEL in Jukkasjärvi *(see p289)*

across Sweden in six categories: Comfort, Quality Hotels, Quality Resorts, Clarion, Clarion Collection and Nordic Hotels & Resorts. **Radisson Blu** has a number of large hotels at the higher end of the price range in several Swedish cities, and **Best Western**, an international chain, has over 60 properties across the country. **Rica Hotels** can be found in the main cities and on the West Coast, while **Scandic Hotels** is the leading chain in the Nordic region, with more than 70 hotels across Sweden.

Prices and Payment

Prices in the hotel listings that follow are for a standard double room, including service and VAT. However, most hotels offer discounted rooms at weekends and in low season. For cheaper hotels this means a price reduction of 100–300 Kr per night, for medium-priced hotels around 500 Kr and for top hotels up to 1,000 Kr.

Most hotels accept major credit cards. Larger hotels will also change foreign currency, though the easiest and cheapest way of changing money is using a bureau de change *(see p322)*.

Youth Hostels

There are more than 400 youth hostels in Sweden; most are affiliated to the **Svenska Turistföreningen (STF)**. Their flagship property is the *af Chapman* in Stockholm *(see p83)* – floating proof that a youth hostel can be just as spectacular as a top-class hotel. **Sveriges Vandrarhem i Förening (SVIF)** has around

Scandinavian design at its best in the lobby of the Sheraton Stockholm Hotel *(see p284)*

180 youth hostels throughout the country. Both STF and SVIF are members of the International Youth Hostel Federation (IYHF). It is possible to book online on both the STF and SVIF websites.

The standard of youth hostels in Sweden is generally high, and they are popular with people of all ages. Expect to pay around 300 Kr per person in a double room and 150 Kr in a larger room or dormitory, with a discount of around 50 Kr for STF members. Prices usually exclude breakfast and bed-linen hire. Be aware that many youth hostels close in winter.

Bed & Breakfasts

A B&B can be a good alternative to a hotel or youth hostel. There is usually a reasonable range of B&Bs in large towns and close to major roads. They offer a choice of single or double rooms or an apartment; breakfast, bed linen and towels are usually provided. Expect to pay 300–500 Kr per person per night

at a town B&B; an apartment will cost from around 600 Kr per night. In the capital, rooms can be booked through **Bed & Breakfast Service Stockholm** for a small fee.

Cottages and Camping

Sweden's *allemansrätten* – right to roam – allows for the freedom to camp in forests and on open land, though not in view of houses on private land. Staying at a campsite will, however, ensure a more comfortable stay, with better facilities and often cottages to rent. Visit the **Sveriges Camping-och Stugföretagares Riksorganisation (SCR)** website for details. Campsites are graded on a scale of one to five stars.

Recommended Hotels

The hotels in this book have been carefully selected and are among the best in the country. A wide variety of accommodation options are covered, from classic hotels that have retained their historical aspects, to boutique hotels focusing on modern Scandinavian design, or unique places that have a greater emphasis on sustainability.

Entries labelled as DK Choice draw attention to establishments that are exceptional in some way. They may be set in beautiful surroundings, in a historic building, or in a more unusual location, such as on a boat, offer excellent service, have stunning interiors and rooms, a superb on-site restaurant, or a great spa. Whatever the reason, you will have a memorable stay.

The unmistakable Den Röda Båten, a hostel docked at Södermalm *(see p285)*

Where to Stay

Stockholm

Gamla Stan

First Hotel Reisen ⊗⊗
Historic **Map** 3 C3
Skeppsbron 12, 111 30
Tel 08-22 32 60
ⓦ firsthotels.com
Splendid location overlooking
Stockholm's waterfront. Some
rooms have saunas and Jacuzzis.

Hotel Sven Vintappare ⊗⊗
Historic **Map** 3 B3
Sven Vintappares Gränd 3, 117 27
Tel 08-22 41 40
ⓦ hotelsvenvintappare.se
Located in a house built in 1607,
this hotel has seven rooms, all
decorated in Gustavian style.

Lord Nelson Hotel ⊗⊗
Historic **Map** 3 B3
Västerlånggatan 22, 111 29
Tel 08-506 401 20
ⓦ lordnelsonhotel.se
At just under 6-m (20-ft) wide,
Sweden's narrowest hotel is a
friendly, family-run affair.

Rica Hotel Gamla Stan ⊗⊗
Historic **Map** 3 B4
Lilla Nygatan 25, 111 28
Tel 08-723 72 50
ⓦ rica.se/gamlastan
In a 17th-century building, this
hotel combines features period
decor with modern amenities.

City

Clarion Hotel Sign ⊗⊗
Design Hotel **Map** 1 B4
Östra Järnvägsgatan 35, 101 26
Tel 08-676 98 00
ⓦ clarionsign.com
Stockholm's largest hotel has
more than 500 rooms. Each
floor's decor is dedicated to a
different Scandinavian designer.

Comfort Hotel Stockholm ⊗⊗
Design Hotel **Map** 1 B4
Kungsbron 1, 111 22
Tel 08-56 62 22 00
ⓦ nordicchoicehotels.com
Close to the World Trade Center,
this hotel has an atmosphere of
understated elegance.

Hotel Rival ⊗⊗
Design Hotel **Map** 3 A5
Mariatorget 3, 118 91
Tel 08-545 789 00
ⓦ rival.se
Sweden's first boutique hotel is
owned by former ABBA member
Benny Andersson. Comfortable
rooms, cocktail bar and bistro.

Nordic Light Hotel ⊗⊗
Design Hotel **Map** 1 B4
Vasaplan 7, 101 37
Tel 08-50 56 30 00
ⓦ nordiclighthotel.se
"Mood rooms" for all the senses,
brunch buffet and DJ sessions.

Nordic Sea Hotel ⊗⊗
Design Hotel **Map** 1 B4
Vasaplan 4, 111 20
Tel 08-50 56 30 00
ⓦ nordicseahotel.se
Nordic Light's sister hotel has
comfortable rooms and is home
to the Stockholm Ice Bar.

**Radisson Blu Royal
Viking Hotel** ⊗⊗
Modern **Map** 1 C5
Vasagatan 1, 101 24
Tel 08-50 65 40 00
ⓦ radissonblu.com
Offers free Wi-Fi, a health centre
and pool, and a fish restaurant.

**Radisson Blu
Waterfront Hotel** ⊗⊗
Design Hotel **Map** 1 C5
Nils Ericsons Plan 4, 111 64
Tel 08-50 50 60 00
ⓦ radissonblu.com
Pet-friendly hotel with great views
over the city and Lake Mälaren.

Sheraton Stockholm Hotel ⊗⊗
Luxury **Map** 1 C5
Tegelbacken 6, 101 23
Tel 08-412 34 00
ⓦ sheratonstockholm.com
Beautifully appointed rooms, many
with views across Gamla Stan.

Story Hotel ⊗⊗
Design Hotel **Map** 2 D4
Riddargatan 6, 114 35
Tel 08-54 50 39 40
ⓦ storyhotels.com
Bohemian-chic with great art and
a graffiti decorated garden.

Blasieholmen & Skeppsholmen

Af Chapman & Skeppsholmen ⊗
Unusual **Map** 4 E3
Flaggmansvägen 8, 111 49
Tel 08-463 22 66
ⓦ stfchapman.com
The *Af Chapman*, a well-known
city landmark, is now a hostel
with private rooms, disabled
access and on-site cafeteria.

Hotel Skeppsholmen ⊗⊗
Design Hotel **Map** 4 E3
Gröna Gången 1, 111 86
Tel 08-407 23 00
ⓦ hotelskeppsholmen.com

Located in a historic building,
this boutique hotel is modern
and stylish on the inside.

Berns Hotel ⊗⊗⊗
Luxury **Map** 2 D4
Näckströmsgatan 8, 111 47
Tel 08-56 63 22 00
ⓦ berns.se
Stockholm's grand old dame of
luxury, with a majestic restaurant.

Grand Hôtel Stockholm ⊗⊗⊗
Luxury **Map** 3 C1
Södra Blasieholmshamnen 8, 103 27
Tel 08-679 35 00
ⓦ grandhotel.se
Five-star hotel near the Royal
Palace. Fine-dining options and
the Nordic Spa & Fitness Centre.

Hotel Lydmar ⊗⊗⊗
Luxury **Map** 3 C1
Södra Blasieholmshamnen 2, 103 24
Tel 08-22 31 60
ⓦ lydmar.com
Classic luxury and comfort, with
free Wi-Fi, movies and breakfast.

Further Afield

ARLANDA: Jumbo Stay ⊗
Budget
Jumbovägen 4, 190 47
Tel 08-59 36 04 00
ⓦ jumbostay.se
A surprising airport hotel,
offering rooms inside a
decommissioned jumbo jet.

The lounge and bar at Jumbo Stay, a unique
budget option near Arlanda airport

Stately exterior of Djurgården's Scandic Hotel Hasselbacken

DJURGÅRDEN: Scandic Hotel
Hasselbacken ⊕⊕
Historic
Hazeliusbacken 20, 100 55
Tel *08-51 73 43 00*
🅦 scandichotels.com
Ideal for families, there is a colourful playroom, kids activities and special rates for family rooms.

ÖSTERMALM:
Mornington Hotel ⊕⊕
Modern
Nybrogatan 53, 102 44
Tel *08-50 73 30 00*
🅦 mornington.se
Four-star hotel featuring a library, restaurant and health club.

SÖDERMALM: Den Röda Båten ⊕
Design Hotel
*Södermälarstrand 6,
Kajplats 10, 118 20*
Tel *08-644 43 85*
🅦 theredboat.com
A hotel and hostel spread over two colourful ships.

DK Choice

**SÖDERMALM: Långholmen
Hotel & Vandrarhem** ⊕
Historic
Långholmsmuren 20, 117 33
Tel *08-720 85 00*
🅦 langholmen.com
A totally unique accommodation experience, this former prison has been converted into a three-star hotel and a youth hostel. The rooms, or cells, have been completely renovated but maintain features such as heavy secure doors. The establishment also has a bar and an inn, both serve food as well as drinks.

SÖDERMALM: Tre Små Rum ⊕
Cosy
Högbergsgatan 81, 118 54
Tel *08-641 23 71*
🅦 tresmarum.se
This is a tranquil place to stay, with organic breakfasts included in the price of the room.

Eastern Svealand

ESKILSTUNA:
Sundbyholms Slott ⊕⊕
Luxury
Sundbyholms Slott, 635 08
Tel *016-42 84 00*
🅦 sundbyholms-slott.se
This romantic castle with lake views offers fabulous afternoon teas and murder mystery dinners.

KATRINEHOLM:
Dufweholms Herrgård ⊕⊕
Historic
Herrgårdsvägen 16, 641 92
Tel *0150-754 00*
🅦 dufweholm.se
A carefully restored manor with a spa, relaxation centre and library.

NORRTÄLJE:
Pensionat Granparken ⊕⊕
Historic
Gjuterivägen 10, 761 40
Tel *0176-103 54*
🅦 pensionatgranparken.se
A laid-back hotel in an early 19th-century villa. Beautiful garden.

NYKÖPING: Clarion Collection
Hotel Kompaniet ⊕⊕
Historic
Folkungavägen 1, 611 34
Tel *0155-28 80 20*
🅦 clarionhotel.com
In a former furniture factory, this hotel has modern facilities.

SIGTUNA: Stadshotell ⊕⊕
Luxury
Stora Nygatan 3, 193 30
Tel *08-59 25 01 00*
🅦 sigtunastadshotell.se
Sweden's smallest five-star hotel opened in 1909. King Gustav V stayed here once.

TROSA: Bomans Hotell ⊕⊕
Design Hotel
Hamnen, 619 30
Tel *0156-525 00*
🅦 bomans.se
All the rooms are individually decorated, you can choose from

a range of style such as Manolo Blahnik, Le Dolce Vita and Larsson.

UPPSALA: Clarion Hotel Gillet ⊕⊕
Modern
Dragarbrunnsgatan 23, 753 20
Tel *018-68 18 00*
🅦 clarionhotelgillet.com
Well-appointed rooms and a popular restaurant and bar..

DK Choice

VÄSTERÅS: Utter Inn ⊕⊕
Design Hotel
*Västeråsfjärden, Lake Mälaren,
721 87*
Tel *021-39 01 00*
🅦 visitvasteras.se
One of the more unsuual places to stay, this small, picturesque red hut on Lake Mälaren can be reached by boat from Östra Hamnen. Created by artist Mikael Genberg, there are great panoramic views from the platform the hut rests on. There is one bedroom, which is submerged in the lake, while the hut contains a small kitchen. Open Apr–Oct.

Eastern Götaland

BORGHOLM: Halltorps
Gästgiveri ⊕⊕
Historic
Landsvägen Halltorp 105, 387 92
Tel *0485-850 00*
🅦 halltorpsgastgiveri.se
A 17th-century manor house with well-equipped rooms, a spa, open fires and wine tastings.

GRÄNNA: Hotel Amalias Hus ⊕⊕
Historic
Brahegatan 2, 563 32
Tel *0390-413 23*
🅦 amaliashus.se
This romantic 18th-century house features individually designed rooms, each with its own story.

JÖNKÖPING: Elite Stora
Hotellet ⊕⊕
Historic
Hotellplan, 553 20
Tel *036-10 00 00*
🅦 elite.se
Scenically located on Lake Vättern. Comfortable rooms and an on-site gastropub, The Bishop's Arms.

KALMAR: Calmar Stadshotell ⊕⊕
Historic
Stortorget 14, 392 32
Tel *0480-49 69 00*
🅦 profilhotels.com
A modern hotel in a historic building with a restaurant, pub and free Wi-Fi. Buffet breakfast.

DK Choice

**KOSTA: Kosta Boda
Art Hotel** ⊛⊛
Design Hotel
Stora vägen 75, 360 52
Tel *0478-348 30*
W kostabodaarthotel.com
This quirky hotel in the heart
of the Kingdom of Crystal
naturally has a strong emphasis
on glass decorative touches,
which can be seen throughout.
Guests also enjoy spa facilities, a
restaurant and a spectacular
Glass Bar, which is worth a visit
just for its gorgeous design.

**LINKÖPING: Scandic
Frimurarehotellet** ⊛⊛
Modern
St. Larsgatan 14, 582 24
Tel *013-495 30 00*
W scandichotels.se
Rooms have Nordic decor, and
there's free Wi-Fi and a gym.

**NORRKÖPING: Elite Grand
Hotel** ⊛⊛
Historic
Tyska Torget 2, 600 41
Tel *011-36 41 00*
W elite.se
A centrally located spa hotel, with
modern rooms and a restaurant.

SKILLINGARYD: Villa Vilan ⊛
Budget
Galtås, 568 92
Tel *0370-741 31*
W villa-vilan.com
B&B with Jacuzzi and sauna,
located close to nature.

SKRUV: Grimsnäs Herrgård ⊛
Historic
Grimsnäs Herrgård, 360 53
Tel *0478-204 00*
W grimsnas.se
Environmentally friendly B&B/
hostel in a pleasant manor house
tucked away in a deep oak forest.

**VADSTENA: Vadstena
Klosterhotel** ⊛⊛
Historic
Lasarettsgatan 5, 592 30
Tel *0143-315 30*
W klosterhotel.se
This former royal-palace-turned-
monastery-turned-hotel features
fabulous decor.

**VÄXJÖ: Clarion Collection
Hotel Cardinal** ⊛⊛
Modern
Backgatan 10, 352 30
Tel *0470-72 28 00*
W clarionhotel.com
All modern amenities, such as
high-speed Wi-Fi, a sauna and
complimentary organic breakfast.

Entrance to the Kosta Boda Art Hotel in the
Kingdom of Crystal

**VETLANDA: Best Western
Vetlanda Stadshotell** ⊛
Modern
Stortorget 5, 574 32
Tel *0383-120 90*
W vetlandastadshotell.net
International chain hotel with
comfortable rooms, good
restaurant and a weekend disco.

VIMMERBY: Hotel Carl IX ⊛⊛
Family-Friendly
Sevedegatan 37, 598 37
Tel *0492-125 15*
W hotellcarl9.se
Centrally located hotel with four
different room types, as well as
apartments. A great place to stay
in summer.

Gotland

**BURGSVIK: Pensionat
Holmhällar** ⊛
Budget
Vamlingbo Austre 980, 623 31
Tel *0498-49 80 30*
W holmhallar.se
Tranquil B&B near a 3-km (2-mile)
stretch of beach. Breakfast buffet,
lunch and dinner options.

**KLINTEHAMN: Pensionat
Warfsholm** ⊛
Room With a View
Klinte Varvsholm 612, 623 76
Tel *0498-24 00 10*
W warfsholm.se
This charming villa is scenically
perched right by the sea. The
top tower has been turned into
a mini-suite.

**LJUGARN: Kalkpatronsgården
Borgvik Pensionat** ⊛
Family-Friendly
Katthammarsvik, 623 69
Tel *0498-520 87*
W borgvik.com
Rooms and apartments, as well
as cottages with sea views and
a restaurant.

VISBY: Clarion Hotel Wisby ⊛⊛
Historic
Strandgatan 6, 621 24
Tel *0498-25 75 00*
W clarionwisby.se
Parts of this hotel in a former
warehouse date from the 1300s.

VISBY: Hotell St. Clemens ⊛⊛
Historic
Smedjegatan 3, 621 55
Tel *0498-21 90 00*
W clemenshotell.se
Five buildings connected via two
picturesque gardens.

Southern Götaland

BÅSTAD: Hotel Skansen ⊛⊛
Historic
Kyrkogatan 2, 269 33
Tel *0431-55 81 00*
W hotelskansen.se
Well-equipped rooms, buffet
breakfast and a traditional spa.

DK Choice

GLUMSLÖV: Örenäs Slott ⊛⊛
Luxury
Örenäs Slott, 261 63
Tel *0418-45 11 00*
W orenasslott.com
Skåne is the heartland of
Swedish fine dining and this
hotel is known for its excellent
food. A stay here guarantees a
gastronomic experience amid
luxurious surroundings. Rooms
are individually decorated and a
pool is available in summer.
Golf and champagne weekend
packages are available.

**HELSINGBORG: Elite Hotel
Mollberg** ⊛⊛
Historic
Stortorget 18, 251 14
Tel *042-37 37 00*
W elite.se/eng/node/172
Sweden's oldest hotel, dating to
the 14th century, has great views.

KARLSKRONA: Hotell Siesta ⊛⊛
Design Hotel
Borgmästaregatan 5, 371 31
Tel *0455-801 80*
W hotellsiesta.com
This Spanish-themed hotel has
a sauna and outdoor spa, as well
as a popular evening buffet.

**KRISTIANSTAD: First Hotel
Christian IV** ⊛⊛
Historic
Västra Boulevarden 15, 291 31
Tel *044-20 38 50*
W firsthotels.com
Modern hotel in former bank,
with spacious rooms.

LANDSKRONA:
Hotel Öresund ⊗⊗
Historic
Selma Lagerlöfs väg 4, 261 31
Tel *0418-47 40 00*
🅦 hoteloresund.se
The building dates from the
18th century but the rooms are
modern and spacious.

LUND: Grand Hotel ⊗⊗⊗
Luxury
Bantorget 1, 221 04
Tel *046-280 61 00*
🅦 grandilund.se
Rooms are decorated in Jugend
style at this hotel dating from
1899. Two restaurants and a deli.

MALMÖ: Moment Hotel ⊗
Budget
Norra Vallgatan 54, 211 22
Tel *040-23 50 40*
🅦 momenthotels.com
Small but comfortable rooms
with Wi-Fi and flat-screen TVs.

MALMÖ: Hotel Mäster Johan ⊗⊗
Modern
Mäster Johansgatan 13, 211 21
Tel *040-664 64 00*
🅦 masterjohan.com
Tastefully furnished business
rooms or suites, with a gym and
sauna on site. Bike hire available.

SKANÖR: Hotell Gässlingen ⊗⊗
Historic
Rådhustorget 6, 239 30
Tel *040-45 91 00*
🅦 hotelgasslingen.com
A member of the Historic Hotels
of Sweden, the Gässlingen has a
Thai-Swedish spa, Jacuzzi, sauna
and outdoor pool.

YSTAD: Sekelgården ⊗⊗⊗
Boutique
Långgatan 18, 271 23
Tel *0411-739 00*
🅦 sekelgarden.se
Romantic hotel located in an old
townhouse. Family-run and full
of old-world charm.

Gothenburg

CENTRE: Barken Viking ⊗⊗
Historic
Lilla Bommens Torg 10, 411 04
Tel *031-63 58 00*
🅦 barkenviking.com
Stay aboard a three-star ship in
Gothenburg's harbour.

CENTRE: Best Western
Hôtel Eggers ⊗⊗
Luxury
Drottningtorget, 411 03
Tel *031-333 44 40*
🅦 hoteleggers.se
Old-world charm including chan-
deliers, antique rugs and tapestries.

DK Choice

CENTRE: Clarion
Hotel Post ⊗⊗
Design Hotel
Drottningtorget 10, 411 03
Tel *031-61 90 00*
🅦 clarionpost.com
Housed inside the former post
office building, this hotel looks
spectacular. Guests are greeted
by a dazzling crystal reception
desk, and the public areas are
equally striking. Additional
features include a roof-top pool,
bar area and sun terrace, a spa
and two restaurants.

CENTRE: Elite Park Avenue
Hotel ⊗⊗
Modern
Kungsportsavenyn 36-38, 400 15
Tel *031-727 10 00*
🅦 elite.se
Four-star hotel with restaurant,
café and gym. Rooms have a
range of CDs and DVDs.

CENTRE: Scandic Opalen ⊗⊗
Modern
Engelbrektsgatan 73, 412 52
Tel *031-751 53 00*
🅦 scandichotels.com

Sauna, gym, Jacuzzi, parking and
free Wi-Fi are available at this hotel.
Rooms have parquet flooring.

FURTHER AFIELD: Radisson
Blu Riverside Hotel ⊗⊗
Modern
Lindholmspiren 4, 417 56
Tel *031-383 40 00*
🅦 radissonblu.com/riverside
hotel-gothenburg
Elegant rooms and a fantastic
fitness complex with gorgeous
views of the harbour.

Western Götaland

DALS LÅNGED: Baldersnäs
Herrgård ⊗⊗
Historic
Baldersnäs 22, 660 10
Tel *0531-412 13*
🅦 baldersnas.com
Classic Swedish mansion set on a
lakeside peninsula in the middle
of a nature reserve. Great views.

FALKÖPING: Nästegården B&B ⊗
Budget
Sätuna, Nästegården, 521 94
Tel *0500-49 20 26*
🅦 nastegarden.se
Near Hornborga Lake. Period
rooms and a pleasant garden.

FJÄLLBACKA: Stora Hotellet
Bryggan ⊗⊗
Historic
Ingrid Bergmans Torg, 457 40
Tel *0525-310 60*
🅦 storahotellet-fjallbacka.se
Charming rooms, some with
a nautical theme, in this hotel
located on the pier.

HALMSTAD: Best Western Plus
Grand Hotel ⊗⊗
Historic
Stationsgatan 44, 302 45
Tel *035-280 81 00*
🅦 grandhotel.nu
Opened in 1905, this hotel has
attractive, colourful rooms with
black-and-white bathrooms.

LIDKÖPING: Stadt Lidköping ⊗⊗
Historic
Gamla Stadens Torg 1, 531 32
Tel *0510-220 85*
🅦 stadtlidkoping.se
Lakeside hotel with a restaurant,
pub and conference rooms.

MARIESTAD: Hotell Vänerport ⊗⊗
Budget
Hamngatan 32, 542 30
Tel *0501-77 111*
🅦 vanerport.se
Individually decorated rooms
with great attention to detail.
Breakfast buffet.

Beautifully lit and spacious sauna at Gothenburg's Scandic Opalen

For more information on types of hotels *see page 283*

**MARSTRAND: Marstrands
Havshotell** ⓦⓦ
Modern
Varvskajen 2, 442 66
Tel *0303-24 02 00*
ⓦ marstrands.se
Seaside hotel offering a variety of
spa and sports package deals.

**SMÖGEN: Hotell Smögens
Hafvsbad** ⓦ
Historic
Hotellgatan 26, 456 51
Tel *0523-66 84 50*
ⓦ smogenshafvsbad.se
Popular when it opened in
1900, this spa hotel is now
a year-round resort.

STRÖMSTAD: Laholmen ⓦⓦ
Modern
Laholmen, 452 30
Tel *0526-197 00*
ⓦ laholmen.se
Great for business and holiday
guests. Conference facilities, bar
and nightclub.

DK Choice

TJÖRN: Salt & Sill ⓦⓦ
Unusual
Danmark, 471 51 Klädesholmen
Tel *0304-67 34 80*
ⓦ saltosill.se
Sweden's first floating hotel is
located in a peaceful, traditional
herring fishing village. The 23
rooms have been designed in
modern Nordic style. A restaurant with outdoor seating in the
summer serves fine Swedish
cuisine. Also has the world's
fastest floating sauna boat!

TROLLHÄTTAN: Albert Hotell ⓦⓦ
Historic
Strömsbergsvägen 2, 461 57
Tel *0520-129 90*
ⓦ alberthotell.com
A four-star hotel housed in a villa
dating from 1857, complete with
a resident ghost. Great dining.

View from the slopes of the spectacular
Hotel Fjällgården in Åre

**VARBERG: Best Western Varbergs
Stadshotell & Asia Spa** ⓦⓦ
Historic
Kungsgatan 24-26, 432 41
Tel *0340-69 01 00*
ⓦ varbergsstadshotell.com
Pleasant hotel in an old building
with a spa. Spectacular sea views.

VÄDERÖARNA: Värdshus ⓦ
Historic
Ramnö, Norra Väderöarna, 457 40
Tel *0525-320 01*
ⓦ vaderoarna.com
This rustic hotel's prices include
accommodation, sauna and boat
transfer from Fjällbacka.

**VÄNERSBORG: Quality Hotel
Vänersborg** ⓦ
Modern
Nabbensbergsvägen 2, 462 40
Tel *0521-57 57 20*
ⓦ qualityvanersborg.se
Facilities here include conference
rooms, gym and spa treatments.

Western Svealand

DK Choice

**ARVIKA: Spahotell Scandic
Arvika** ⓦ
Historic
Torggatan 9, 671 31
Tel *0570-197 10*
ⓦ scandichotels.se
Quietly elegant spa hotel
housed in one of Arvika's oldest
buildings. The excellent spa is
adult's only, children aged 15
or over are admitted only with
a parent or guardian.

BORLÄNGE: First Hotel Brage ⓦⓦ
Modern
Stationsgatan 1–3, 784 33
Tel *0243-21 76 60*
ⓦ firsthotels.com
Pleasant hotel with two restaurants
and a weekend nightclub.

**FALUN: Clarion Collection
Hotel Bergmästaren** ⓦⓦ
Modern
Bergsskolegränd 7, 791 12
Tel *023-70 17 00*
ⓦ clarionhotel.com
Pet-friendly hotel with sauna, hot
tub and organic breakfasts.

**KARLSTAD: Elite Stadshotellet
Karlstad** ⓦⓦ
Historic
Kungsgatan 22, 651 08
Tel *054-29 30 00*
ⓦ elite.se
Stay in individually decorated
rooms at this beautiful riverside

hotel. There is a cosy pub and
restaurant on the premises.

**MORA: Best Western
Mora Hotell & Spa** ⓦⓦ
Historic
Strandgatan 12, 792 30
Tel *0250-59 26 50*
ⓦ morahotell.se
Housed in a 19th-century
building overlooking Lake Siljan.
Steam room, pool and sauna.

ÖREBRO: Elite Stora Hotellet ⓦⓦ
Historic
Drottninggatan 1, 701 45
Tel *019-15 69 00*
ⓦ elite.se
Grand old building in a scenic
riverside location. Bar, sauna
and parking.

**RÄTTVIK: Dala Wärdshus Hotell
Gärdebygården** ⓦ
Budget
*Hol Daniels väg, Hantverksbyn,
795 36*
Tel *0248-302 50*
ⓦ dalawardshus.se
Peaceful hotel on the lake, with
a private beach. Summer only.

**SUNNE: Quality Hotel
Selma Lagerlöf** ⓦⓦ
Modern
Ekebyvägen 1, 686 35
Tel *0565-68 88 00*
ⓦ selmahotel.se
Pleasant lakeside hotel with good
conference and meeting facilities,
as well as a nightclub.

TÄLLBERG: Åkerblads ⓦⓦ
Historic
Sjögattu 2, 793 70
Tel *0247-508 00*
ⓦ akerblads.se
Beautifully furnished hotel with
a spa, restaurant and impressive
wine cellar. Some parts date back
to the 15th century.

Southern Norrland

DK Choice

ÅRE: Hotell Fjällgården ⓦⓦ
Ski Lodge
Fjällgårdsvägen 35, 830 13
Tel *0647-145 00*
ⓦ fjallgarden.se
Dating from 1910, this hotel
offers fantastic views, sauna,
spa and tasty cuisine right
on the slopes. There is also
a mountain funicular link to
the city. In summer there's
mountain biking, ziplining, elk
safaris and white-water rafting.

**HÄRNÖSAND: First Hotel
Stadt** ⊗⊗
Modern
Skeppsbron 9, 871 30
Tel *0611-55 44 40*
🅦 firsthotels.com
Harbour-side hotel with sea
views and conference facilities.

**HIGH COAST: STF Vandrarhem
Köpmanholmen** ⊗
Budget
Köpmansholmsvägen 2, 893 40
Tel *0660-22 34 96*
🅦 svenskaturistforeningen.se
This quayside hostel offers single,
double and dormitory rooms.

**HIGH COAST: Hotell Höga
Kusten** ⊗⊗
Design Hotel
Hornöberget, 872 94 Sandöverken
Tel *0613-72 22 79*
🅦 hotellhoga-kusten.se
Twenty-eight artistically decorated
rooms. Meditation path and pool.

**HUDIKSVALL:
First Hotel Statt** ⊗⊗
Historic
Storgatan 36, 824 22
Tel *0650-150 60*
🅦 firsthotels.com
Beautifully restored 19th-century
building with a spa, gym and pool.

**ÖRNSKÖLDSVIK: First Hotel
Statt** ⊗⊗
Historic
Lasarettsgatan 2, 891 21
Tel *0660-26 55 90*
🅦 firsthotels.com
The building dates from 1913, but
the rooms are modern and
functional. Breakfast included.

**ÖSTERSUND: Best Western
Hotel Gamla Teatern** ⊗⊗
Historic
Thoméegränd 20, 831 34
Tel *063-51 16 00*
🅦 gamlateatern.se
All modern facilities in this hotel
housed in a converted theatre.

**STORLIEN: Storliens
Högfjällshotell** ⊗⊗
Ski Resort
Geijerbacken 10, 830 19
Tel *647 701 70*
🅦 sportstyle.se/storlien
One of Scandinavia's largest
hotels. Enjoy the roaring open
fires, indoor pool and sauna.

SUNDSVALL: Gaffelbyn ⊗
Budget
Norra Stadsberget, 856 40
Tel *060-61 21 19*
🅦 gaffelbyn.se
Good hostel with kitchen facilities.
Some rooms have en-suite
bathrooms. Free parking.

Comfortable seating in the lobby of the Scandic Ferrum, Kiruna

SVEG: Lilla Hotellet ⊗
Budget
Älvgatan 8, 842 32
Tel *0680-102 84*
🅦 lillahotellet.se
Comfortable rooms with discounts
for longer stays. Buffet breakfast.

Northern Norrland

**ABISKO: STF Abisko
Turiststation** ⊗
Mountain Resort
Abisko Turiststation, 981 07
Tel *0980-402 00*
🅦 svenskaturistforeningen.se
Located above the Arctic Circle
amid pristine scenery. Great for
winter skiing and summer hiking.

**HAPARANDA: Haparanda
Stadshotell** ⊗⊗
Historic
Torget 7, 953 31
Tel *0922-614 90*
🅦 haparandastadshotell.se
A pet-friendly hotel with rooms
dating back to 1900, conference
facilities and a nightclub.

HARADS: Tree Hotel ⊗⊗⊗
Design Hotel
Edeforsväg 2A, 960 24
Tel *0928-104 03*
🅦 treehotel.se
Six spectacularly designed tree
rooms and a sauna in the forest
of Harads. Fantastic views.

DK Choice

**JUKKASJÄRVI:
ICEHOTEL** ⊗⊗⊗
Design Hotel
Marknadsvägen 63, 981 91
Tel *0980-668 00*
🅦 icehotel.com
ICEHOTEL is rebuilt every year
with different room designs.
Delicious Arctic cuisine can
be sampled in the restaurant
(see p301). Northern Lights
excursions can be arranged.

KIRUNA: Scandic Ferrum ⊗⊗
Modern
Lars Janssonsgatan 15, 981 31
Tel *0980-39 86 00*
🅦 scandichotels.com
Child-friendly hotel with non-
smoking rooms. Facilities include
a sauna and gym. Free Wi-Fi and
complimentary breakfast.

LULEÅ: Elite Stadshotellet ⊗⊗
Historic
Storgatan 15, 972 32
Tel *0920-27 40 00*
🅦 elite.se
A unique and stylish hotel with
a renowned restaurant and
gastropub on site.

PITEÅ: Piteå Stadshotell ⊗⊗
Historic
Olof Palmes Gata 1, 941 33
Tel *0911-23 40 00*
🅦 piteastadshotell.com
Four-star hotel with top dining
and business facilities.

**RIKSGRÄNSEN: Hotell
Riksgränsen** ⊗⊗
Ski Resort
Riksgränsvägen 15, 981 94
Tel *0980-641 00*
🅦 riksgransen.se
Sweden's northernmost ski hotel.
Excellent skiing and spa facilities.

**SKELLEFTEÅ: Skellefteå
Stadshotell** ⊗⊗
Design Hotel
Stationsgatan 8, 931 31
Tel *0910-71 10 60*
🅦 skellefteastadshotell.se
Four-star city hotel dating to
the middle of the 19th century.
Renovated, comfortable rooms,
with free Wi-Fi and flat-screen TVs.

**UMEÅ: Clarion Collection
Hotel Uman** ⊗⊗
Historic
Storgatan 52, 903 26
Tel *090-12 72 20*
🅦 clarionhotel.com
Pleasant old-fashioned hotel
that is very pet-friendly. Organic
breakfasts and afternoon tea.

For more information on types of hotels *see page 283*

WHERE TO EAT AND DRINK

The Swedish culinary scene is constantly evolving, and the traditional *husmanskost* (home fare) in particular is enjoying a creative renaissance with a new generation of award-winning chefs. Several restaurants in the country have been awarded Michelin stars, and many of the top chefs run their own establishments. International influences are often combined to create innovative and delicious dishes often referred to as "crossover", or modern Swedish, cuisine. Traditional Swedish dishes are frequently served at lunchtime and are excellent value for money. There are also plenty of fast-food outlets, Chinese restaurants, pizzerias and kebab houses offering inexpensive food. Hot-dog stands, providing filling snacks, can be found practically everywhere.

Where to Eat

A wide range of restaurants can be found in Sweden's major cities; however, there are also a number of good places to eat in smaller towns and in the countryside, where many historic manor-house hotels have excellent restaurants. Larger department stores and shopping malls, as well as most museums, have decent restaurants or cafés. Open sandwiches with a variety of fillings can be bought at cafés and cake shops, which often serve inexpensive hot dishes at lunchtime as well. Larger towns often have market halls with excellent eateries, but they are not open in the evenings. Along the coast and inland there are many establishments that open only in the summer.

Many restaurants and cafés offer outdoor seating areas in the summer. In fine weather, eateries can also be spotted in parks and green areas, such as Djurgården in Stockholm and Kungsportsavenyn in Gothenburg.

Types of Restaurant

Trendy restaurants can be very crowded and noisy, so if you are looking for somewhere quieter with a pleasant atmosphere, it may be best to choose an established restaurant. Sweden offers an excellent range of cuisines and there are many specialist eateries serving international dishes or modern Swedish cooking.

Irrespective of quality, most restaurants charge roughly the same prices, but if you are looking for something cheaper, there are plenty of budget options. If you have a sweet tooth, you should visit one of the country's many cafés or traditional cake shops, with their delicious Danish pastries, cakes, cinnamon buns and gateaux. An increasing number of bars have also opened up, often attached to restaurants in the cities and to hotels in the countryside.

The dress code is usually informal, even at the more elegant restaurants. Ties are very rarely required, though shorts are not acceptable. Many restaurants do not allow guests to take outdoor clothing into the dining room.

Smoking is banned in all bars and restaurants in Sweden.

Opening Times

The majority of restaurants open for lunch at 11:30am and close around 10pm. Dinner is served from 6pm or even earlier. Many establishments are closed on Sundays or Mondays. Smaller restaurants may close for their annual holiday in July or during the winter months.

Prices for lunch are often reasonable, even at the more elegant establishments. *Dagens lunch* (lunch of the day) is generally not served after 2pm, even if the restaurant is open in the afternoon.

Restaurants with music, entertainment or a nightclub usually serve dinner until late. Hot-dog kiosks and pizzerias remain open till late, sometimes even round the clock.

Vegetarian Food

Interest in vegetarian food is growing in Sweden, and excellent vegetarian cuisine is now served at most restaurants. There are also many completely vegetarian and vegan eateries in the major cities.

Booking a Table

Reservations are recommended for evening meals. However, many places do not accept bookings for lunch; if you want to be sure of a table at midday,

The dimly lit and cosy dining space at Villa Sjötorp in Ljungskile *(see p299)*

The unique decor of Pontus!, one of Stockholm's best fine-dining restaurants *(see p294)*

it is best to arrive before 11:30am or after 1pm, by which time most of the lunchtime clientele will have left.

Children

Children are welcome in most restaurants, except those eateries that are open only in the evenings and have a nightclub. Kids will usually be offered a special children's menu or half-portions from the standard menu. Most restaurants provide highchairs.

Prices

Generally, hot dishes are priced from about 100 Kr; at expensive or award-winning restaurants, the average price of a main course is closer to 200 Kr.

Lunch prices are around 70–80 Kr, often including a non-alcoholic drink and coffee. However, the price of beer, wine and other alcoholic drinks varies considerably. The more expensive the restaurant, the higher the price of wine. The house wine is usually the cheapest, with a bottle costing from 150 Kr. Beer is cheaper in pubs than it is restaurants. Tap water is free of charge, and Sweden's drinking water is of excellent quality.

Tips are always included in the price, but if you want to reward particularly good service, you can round up the bill. Leaving your coat in a manned cloakroom costs about 10 Kr per item. Credit cards are accepted in virtually every restaurant.

Reading the Menu

Dinner at a Swedish restaurant usually includes a *förrätt* (starter), *varmrätt* (hot main course) and *efterrätt* (dessert). Most places offer one or more fixed-price meals, with a choice of two or three dishes at a lower price than the à la carte menu. It is perfectly acceptable to have just a starter or main course. At lunchtime most people order only one course. Some high-end restaurants may have dessert or cheese trolleys. Many restaurants have menus in English; if not, the waiters and waitresses are usually familiar with English and will be happy to explain the choices available.

Some restaurants serve a typical Swedish *smörgåsbord*, mostly on Sundays *(see p292)*. On the coast they often specialize in fish or shellfish buffets. During December, a *Julbord* is usually available. This is similar to the usual *smörgåsbord*, but with a lavish buffet of traditional seasonal dishes. You can eat as much as you like at a fixed price, but drinks are not included.

What to Drink

Wine and beer are the normal accompaniments to a meal, as well as water. The wine list often features wine from countries outside Europe, along with a cheaper house wine.

Beer is graded into three classes, with Class I being the weakest. *Husmanskost* (home cooking) is usually washed down with beer, sometimes accompanied by one of many different-flavoured schnapps. Pubs and restaurants usually offer a wide selection of beers, often with one or more on draught.

Spirits and wines are more expensive in restaurants in Sweden than in most other countries; this is because of the high duty on alcohol and Systembolaget *(see p319)*, the state alcohol-monopoly chain.

Recommended Restaurants

The restaurants on the following pages have been carefully selected to give a cross-section of options in every region: you will find everything from fine dining and traditional restaurants to modern Swedish, international cuisine and bistro fare.

The fine-dining options include some of the best restaurants in Sweden, often located in historic, atmospheric and scenic places. Traditional restaurants have a strong emphasis on Swedish home cooking and classic ingredients, and are frequently found in rural locations. Modern Swedish cuisine combines local ingredients and international flavours. The international and bistro options serve mostly global favourites at reasonable prices. Many of the restaurants listed use organic local produce whenever possible.

The DK Choice entries highlight exceptional establishments that offer more than just excellent food.

Elegantly served dish at Mälmo's Salt & Brygga *(see p298)*

The Flavours of Sweden

Thanks to strict regulations, Sweden is one of most unpolluted countries in Europe and produces some of the purest food. Salmon can be caught in the heart of Stockholm, zander and herring are fished from the nearby coastal waters and the lakes and rivers are full of crayfish and other delicacies. Fish is a staple, but other gastronomic treats are also on offer. Wild game, such as grouse, reindeer and elk, is abundant in autumn and winter. The forests are full of berries and mushrooms, and the rich pastures produce superlative dairy produce, including several fine cheeses.

Fresh dill

Fresh anchovies on offer at Östermalmshallen food market

A traditional *smörgåsbord* will start with a selection of different herring appetizers, followed by a variety of cold dishes such as hard-boiled eggs, meat pies and salads. Then a number of hot dishes are served, including such offerings as meatballs, fried potatoes and Jansson's Temptation (a gratin of potatoes, onions, anchovies and cream). Finally an array of desserts will be placed on the table. Diners help themselves, changing their plates between courses.

Some Swedes will prepare a *smörgåsbord* as a good way of using left-overs. Inventive cooks often improvise a very simple version when unexpected guests arrive, using larder staples, such as eggs, slices of cheese and cooked meats, and

The Smörgåsbord

The *smörgåsbord* made its first appearance on Swedish tables sometime in the 18th century, when it consisted of a spread of hot and cold hors d'oeuvres that would be served as a prelude to a grand lunch or dinner. All this was washed down with ice-cold "schnapps" (vodka). Gradually, however, it has grown into a full-scale meal.

Beetroot & orange salad

Cucumber salad

Rye crispbread

Pickled herring

Egg with lumpfish roe

Cheese

Pork liver pâté

Pickled herring

Lingonberry tartlets

Selection of items typically found on a cold *smörgåsbord*

Local Dishes and Specialities

A typical Swedish breakfast often includes yoghurt or *filmjölk* (a type of soured milk yoghurt) with cereal. Many Swedes, however, prefer a more savoury start to the day and cheese, ham and even liver paté may be on offer. Bread spread with *kaviar* (a cod's roe paste) is also eaten at breakfast. For lunch, most people reach for something quick and simple to prepare. Salad, perhaps served with a seafood, ham or vegetable quiche, is common and pasta is popular too. As well as the main meals, a break for coffee and pastries, known as *fika*, is taken at any time of the day. This strong Swedish tradition is a sociable event as much as an occasion to eat. In the evening, families usually get together for the main meal of the day - dinner, a more elaborate, but still homely, affair.

Lingonberries

Gravad Lax, a salmon fillet, marinated for two days in sugar, salt and dill, is served with a creamy mustard sauce.

A colourful vegetable stall at Hötorget market

Sweden's Dining "Revolution"

The turn of the 21st century has witnessed a renaissance of gourmet cooking in Sweden, with people now visiting Stockholm for its food as well as its culture. Traditional dishes, made with the finest – usually organic – ingredients are being given an original, modern twist. Instead of simple meatballs with lingonberries, chefs are increasingly offering delights such as *foie gras* with a spiced mixed berry and apple chutney and turning cheap staples, such as pig's offal, into magnificent, melt-in-the-mouth mousses.

WHAT TO DRINK

Beer Along with vodka, beer is the most popular drink to accompany a *smörgåsbord*. Until recently, little was on offer other than insipid lagers, but a recent beer-making revival has made styles from dark porters to pale ales available, including some interesting fruit beers.

Vodka About 60 types of "schnapps", each flavoured with different herbs and spices, are made in Sweden.

Punsch This sweet arak spirit is often taken with coffee or served hot with pea soup.

Wine A huge variety of fine wines are imported, but are usually very expensive.

tinned or pickled fish. During the Christmas season, many Stockholm restaurants serve a special *smörgåsbord*, known as a Julbord, which will include dishes using nearly every part of the pig, such as various hams, trotters and a special brawn called *sylta*, made from the head.

Rustic Fare

The Swedes are very good at using cheap cuts to prepare delicious dishes. Seasoning is usually kept simple with salt, pepper and fresh dill. Such homely fare, known as *husmanskost*, is central to the Swedish diet and regularly features on the menus of many Stockholm restaurants. One favourite is yellow pea soup, traditionally served on Thursdays, accompanied by sausages or lightly salted meat

and mustard. This is generally followed by pancakes with jam, washed down with hot *punsch*. Other popular dishes include *pytt i panna* (a hash of meat, onions and potatoes) and meatballs served with lingonberry jam.

A selection of fine fish from Sweden's pristine coastal waters

Jansson's Temptation is a dish of layered potato, pickled sprats and onion with cream, baked until golden.

Meatballs made from beef or pork are drenched in a rich meaty sauce and served with lingonberries.

Apple cake is a delicious buttery dessert traditionally served piping hot with cold vanilla sauce.

Where to Eat and Drink

Stockholm
Gamla Stan

Bistro & Grill Ruby ⓦⓦ
Bistro **Map** 3 C3
Österlånggatan 14, 111 31
Tel *08-20 60 15* **Closed** *Sun (bistro)*
This establishment in the heart
of Gamla Stan is the place for
charcoal-grilled beef, pork and
lamb. Weekend brunch from noon.

Den Gyldene Freden ⓦⓦ
Traditional **Map** 3 C4
Österlånggatan 51, 111 31
Tel *08-24 97 60* **Closed** *Sun*
Serving typical Swedish dishes
since 1722. Enjoy pikeperch,
Swedish meatballs and other
classics in a beautiful setting.

Mr French ⓦⓦ
Fine Dining **Map** 3 C3
Tullhus 2, Skeppsbron, 111 30
Tel *08-20 20 95*
One of Stockholm's top chefs
is at the helm of this restaurant.
The menu is inspired by classic
French brasserie fare and features
grills and the freshest seafood.

Pontus! ⓦⓦ
Fine Dining **Map** 3 C3
Brunnsgatan 1, 111 30
Tel *08-545 273 00* **Closed** *Sun*
Lunch and dinner menus are
devised by Swedish master chef
Pontus Frithiof. From burgers to
foie gras, dishes here are a careful
balance of rustic and luxurious.

Frantzén ⓦⓦⓦ
Fine Dining **Map** 3 B3
Lilla Nygatan 21, 111 28
Tel *08-20 85 80* **Closed** *Sun & Mon*
An elegant addition to
Stockholm's culinary scene, this
establishment has appeared on
the World's 50 Best Restaurants
list. Try the 17-course taster menu.

City

Ett litet hak ⓦⓦ
Traditional **Map** 2 E4
Grev Turegatan 15, 114 46
Tel *08-660 13 09* **Closed** *Sun*
Ett litet hak, meaning "a small
hangout", serves rustic Swedish
dishes, including Arctic char,
cured salmon and fish stew. Ask
for a table outside when the
weather is good and enjoy
people watching with your meal.

Fredsgatan 12 ⓦⓦ
Fine Dining **Map** 3 A1
Fredsgatan 12, 111 52
Tel *08-248 052* **Closed** *Sun*
This Michelin-starred restaurant
offers a large menu created
with the finest ingredients. The
pheasant, oysters and clams
are especially recommended.

Nalen ⓦⓦ
Traditional **Map** 2 D3
Regeringsgatan 74, 111 39
Tel *08-505 292 00* **Closed** *Sun*
Located inside one of the best-
known nightspots in Sweden,
Nalen places the emphasis firmly
on simple, traditional Swedish
food. A bar, nightclub and concert
hall are also on the premises.

Sturehof ⓦⓦ
Modern Swedish **Map** 2 D4
Sturegallerian 42, Stureplan 2, 114 46
Tel *08-440 57 30*
Boasting an illustrious history as
one of Stockholm's first fish and
seafood restaurants, Sturehof now
serves the freshest daily catches
and other Swedish produce.

Price Guide
Prices are for a three-course meal for
one, half a bottle of house wine and
other charges such as service and cover.
ⓦ **under 450 Kr**
ⓦⓦ **450–1,000 Kr**
ⓦⓦⓦ **over 1,000 Kr**

DK Choice

Operakällaren ⓦⓦⓦ
Fine Dining **Map** 3 B1
Operahuset, Karl XII:s Torg, 111 86
Tel *08-676 58 00*
Closed *Sun & Mon*
One of Sweden's historic culinary
institutions, Operakällaren
(meaning "Opera Cellar") got
its name as early as 1787,
when it was located in the cellar
underneath the Opera House.
The magnificent surroundings
complement the exquisite
dining experience. Also on the
premises are Café Opera, the
Opera Bar, the Terrace and
the tiny Bakfickan bar.

Blasieholmen & Skeppsholmen

Mathias Dahlgren Matsalen ⓦⓦⓦ
Fine Dining **Map** 3 C1
Södra Blasieholmshamnen 6, 111 48
Tel *08-679 35 84* **Closed** *Sun & Mon*
The restaurant of the Grand Hôtel
Stockholm is suitably impressive
and serves modern Swedish
gourmet food. The Matbaren
bistro is also in the hotel and
is open at lunchtime too.

Further Afield

DJURGÅRDEN:
Rosendals Trädgårdscafe ⓦ
Traditional
Rosendalsterrassen 12, 115 21
Tel *08-545 812 70* **Closed** *Sun &
Mon in winter*
Set in a pleasant garden, this café
serves excellent seasonal lunches,
including sandwiches and hot
meals, at affordable prices.

DJURGÅRDEN: Wärdshuset
Ulla Winbladh ⓦⓦ
Traditional
Rosendalsvägen 8, 115 21
Tel *08-534 897 01*
This former bakery dating from
1897 serves rustic Swedish
home cooking prepared with
the freshest, seasonal ingredients.
There is indoor as well as terrace
seating, and a wide selection of
fine wines.

Beautifully lit dining hall at Den Gyldene Freden, a traditional Swedish restaurant

GÅRDET: Dell'Attore
Italian
Skeppargatan 60, 114 59
Tel *08-442 61 18*
Popular with locals, Dell'Attore is a great place to enjoy authentic Italian pizzas. Book ahead to avoid waiting.

KUNGSHOLMEN: La Famiglia
Italian
Alströmergatan 45, 112 47
Tel *08-650 63 10* **Closed** *Sun & Mon in Jul*
Family-friendly restaurant serving classic Italian pasta dishes, fish and regional specialities cooked on a wood-fire grill. Good desserts.

KUNGSHOLMEN: Mäster Anders
Modern Swedish
Pipersgatan 1, 112 24
Tel *08-654 20 01*
The charcoal grill offers a mix of meat and fish dishes. Try the grilled Arctic char.

NORRTULL: Stallmästaregården
Fine Dining
Norrtull, 113 47
Tel *08-610 13 00*
An old-fashioned inn in a scenic location overlooking Brunnsviken Bay. Classic Swedish dishes have an emphasis on organic and local produce. Delicious desserts.

DK Choice

ÖSTERMALM: Östermalm Saluhall
Traditional
Östermalms Torg, 114 39
Tel *08-553 404 40* **Closed** *Sun*
Stockholm's delightful indoor food hall, housed in a beautiful late 19th-century building, has eight eateries to choose from, including seafood restaurants, sandwich bars, coffee shops and bistros. Particularly popular is Gerda's Fish and Seafood Restaurant, serving up the latest catch. There is also a market that sells fresh produce. Open only in the daytime.

ÖSTERMALM: Esperanto
Fusion
Kungstensgatan 2, 114 25
Tel *08-696 23 23* **Closed** *Sun–Tue*
This elegant restaurant offers a menu that expertly mixes Swedish-style dishes with Japanese ingredients. The menu changes seasonally but sample dishes include wild river salmon with chilled *dashi*.

Range of international wines on display at the luxurious Gondolen in Södermalm

ÖSTERMALM: Teatergrillen
Modern Swedish
Nybrogatan 3, 114 34
Tel *08-545 035 65* **Closed** *Sun*
The menu at this fine restaurant has an obvious French twist. Try their famous *Biff Rydberg*, a delicious beef and potatoe dish, or the *entrecôte* served from the *Silvervagnen* trolley.

SOLNA: Ulriksdals Wärdshus
Traditional
Ulriksdals Slottspark, 170 79 Solna
Tel *08-85 08 15* **Closed** *Mon*
This beautiful inn serves typical rustic Swedish cuisine and is particularly renowned for its *smörgåsbord* and the Christmas equivalent, *julbord*.

SÖDERMALM: Nytorget Deli
Modern Swedish
Nytorget 4, 116 40
Tel *08-599 091 80*
This popular place is a mix of restaurant, food hall, deli and bakery. Shop and eat all under one roof.

SÖDERMALM: Roxy
Modern Swedish
Nytorget 6, 116 40
Tel *08-640 96 55*
Swedish food with Spanish, Italian and French influences prepared using organic produce. Weekend brunch from noon.

SÖDERMALM: Gondolen
Fine Dining
Stadsgården 6, 116 45
Tel *08-641 70 90* **Closed** *Sun*
Dangling 33-m (108-ft) above water, Gondolen is one of the city's most unique restaurants. Enjoy spectacular views and delicious gourmet food.

SÖDERMALM: Nyagatan
Traditional
Skånegatan 84, 116 37
Tel *08-644 48 84*
The food here is prepared with organic produce and accompanied by delicious home-baked breads. Cooking classes and other events.

SÖDERMALM: Pelikan
Traditional
Blekingegatan 40, 116 62
Tel *08-556 090 90*
Swedish *husmanskost*, or home-cooking, at its finest. Meatballs, herring, crayfish and local beers.

SÖDERMALM: Sjögräs
Fine Dining
Timmermansgatan 24, 118 55
Tel *08-84 12 00* **Closed** *Sun*
French cuisine with Swedish influences, and a different *plat du jour* (dish of the day) every day. The rum bar downstairs boasts the widest selection of rums in northern Europe.

VASASTAN: Stockholms Matvarufabrik
Modern Swedish
Idungatan 12, 113 45
Tel *08-32 07 04* **Closed** *Sun*
Housed inside an old food processing plant, this place offers a good mix of meat, fish and vegetarian dishes made with classic Swedish ingredients.

VASASTAN: Storstad
Fine Dining
Odengatan 41, 113 51
Tel *08-673 38 00* **Closed** *Sun*
This spacious family-run restaurant located in a traditional Vasastan building serves creative Swedish cuisine.

VASASTAN: Värdshuset Clas på Hörnet
Fine Dining
Surbrunnsgatan 20, 113 48
Tel *08-16 51 36* **Closed** *Sun*
Housed in a quaint inn that first opened its doors in 1731, this restaurant offers classic Swedish dishes created with international touches. Weekly lunch specials.

Eastern Svealand

JÖNÅKER: Wreta Gestgifveri
Modern Swedish
Wreta Gestgifveri, 611 90 Ålberga
Tel *0155-720 22*
A mix of Swedish and international dishes, along with great dessert options are available. There is an outdoor dining area in summer and a pleasant garden.

For more information on types of restaurants *see page 291*

Lavish bar at the Asian-American restaurant Jay Fu in Uppsala

NYKÖPING: Mickes Skafferi ⓦⓦ
Modern Swedish
Västra Storgatan 29, 611 32
Tel *0155-26 99 50* **Closed** *Sun*
"Micke's Pantry" offers plenty
of Swedish fare with interesting
Mediterranean influences, such
as the rack of lamb with beets
and mushroom gnocchi.

DK Choice

**TROSA: Bomans Hotel
& Restaurang** ⓦⓦ
Traditional
Östra Hamnplan 1, 619 30
Tel *0156-525 00* **Closed** *Sun*
This well-loved family-run
restaurant offers a small but
quality menu. You'll find
traditional Swedish cuisine with
an emphasis on food-and-wine
pairings. Try the delicious beef
with truffle, green beans and
red-wine sauce. There is an
excellent selection of Swedish
and international beers.

UPPSALA: Jay Fu ⓦⓦ
Asian-American
Saluhallen, St Eriks Torg 8, 753 10
Tel *018-15 01 51* **Closed** *Sun*
Known as an "Amasian
steakhouse", this restaurant
naturally serves fabulous steaks,
along with crispy tempura, pork
chops and fresh burgers, all
accompanied by a wide selection
of beers and international wines.

**UPPSALA:
Restaurang Lingon** ⓦⓦ
Fine Dining
Svartbäcksgatan 30, 753 32
Tel *018-10 12 24*
Old-fashioned food traditions
meet modern, creative culinary
styles at this classic Swedish
restaurant located inside a
wooden house. There is outdoor
seating in the summer.

UPPSALA: Villa Anna ⓦⓦ
Modern Swedish
Odinslund 3, 753 10
Tel *018-580 20 00* **Closed** *Sun*
Award-winning chefs concoct
innovative culinary delights
based on traditional Swedish
recipes. The focus is on locally
sourced organic ingredients.

UTÖ: Utö Värdshus ⓦⓦ
Fine Dining
Gruvbryggan, 130 56
Tel *08-504 20 300*
A former mining office has been
turned into a pleasant inn and
restaurant. There is à la carte
dining and alfresco seating in
the summer months.

VÄSTERÅS: Frank ⓦⓦ
Bistro
Stora Torget 3, 722 15
Tel *021-13 65 00* **Closed** *Sun & Mon*
A busy and lively place where the
menu changes depending on the
seasons, the ingredients available
and even the chefs' moods. Try
the four-course "surprise menu".

Eastern Götaland

**JÖNKÖPING: Den
Småländska Kolonin** ⓦⓦ
Modern Swedish
Kyrkogatan 4, 553 16
Tel *036-71 22 22* **Closed** *Sun*
An exciting restaurant offering
some unusual dishes such as
chocolate terrine with Jerusalem
artichoke ice cream. The lunchtime menu changes daily, and
there is a bar upstairs.

KALMAR: Gröna Stugan ⓦⓦ
Fine Dining
Larmgatan 1, 392 32
Tel *0480-158 58*
A former coffee house known as
the Green Barn in the 1920s, this

cosy green wooden cottage now
offers gourmet Swedish cuisine.
Daily fixed-price lunch menus,
as well as buffets for groups.

**LINKÖPING:
Stångs Magasin** ⓦⓦ
Modern Swedish
Södra Stånggatan 1, 582 73
Tel *013-31 21 00* **Closed** *Sun*
Located in an old warehouse.
There are à la carte and tasting
menus to choose from, as well as
a strong wine list. The emphasis
is on good-quality and locally
sourced organic produce.

**MOTALA: Bryggeriet
Rock 'n' Roll Bar** ⓦ
American
Prästgatan 3, 591 30
Tel *0141-23 39 13* **Closed** *Sun–Tue*
This informal bar and restaurant
serves great burgers, fries, nachos
and *burritos*. There is also a good
selection of beers and whiskeys.

NORRKÖPING: Pappa Grappa ⓦ
Italian
*Gamla Rådstugugatan 26–28,
602 24*
Tel *011-18 00 14*
Traditional Italian trattoria serving
quality *antipasti*, as well as pasta,
meat and fish dishes. A pizzeria
on the same premises offers
reasonably priced fare.

ÖLAND: Kvarn Krogen ⓦ
Pizzeria
*Eketorpsvägen 1, 386 63,
Degerhamn*
Tel *0485-66 11 40* **Closed** *Mon*
This restaurant, housed in a
quaint windmill, serves several
kinds of pizza and an à la carte
menu. Extremely family-friendly,
with a special children's menu.

DK Choice

**ÖLAND: Guntorps
Herrgård** ⓦⓦ
Fine Dining
*Gunstorpsgatan, 387 36,
Borgholm*
Tel *0485-130 00* **Closed** *Sun
in winter*
Housed in a traditional white-
painted manor house in a
pleasant setting, Guntorps
Herrgård offers some of Öland's
finest cuisine, made using
seasonal and locally sourced
ingredients. The menu changes
weekly according to produce
supply and has included baked
fallow deer fillet and smoked
pork belly salad. Choose
between the three- and five-
course dinners. There is also a
lovely spa and accommodation.

VÄSTERVIK: Saltmagasinet ⊛⊛
Modern Swedish
Kulbacken, 593 38
Tel *0490-189 35*
This place is widely regarded as one of the country's best restaurants for its use of organic produce and strict environmental policies. There is an expert sommelier on hand, as well as a bakery and patisserie.

VIMMERBY: Brygghuset ⊛⊛
International
Åbrovägen 13, 598 40
Tel *0492-753 80* **Closed** *Sun*
A gastropub serving fish and chips, burgers and more. There are lunch and dinner menus, a salad bar and a special children's menu. Good selection of drinks to choose from, including beers and whiskeys.

Gotland

**VISBY: Hamnplan 5
Restaurang & Nattklubb** ⊛
International
Hamnplan 5, 621 57
Tel *0498-21 07 10* **Closed** *Sun–Thu*
Multi-cuisine restaurant and nightclub serving pasta dishes, Tex-Mex fare and Swedish specialities. Happy hours and live entertainment are also on offer.

VISBY: 50 Kvadrat ⊛⊛⊛
Fine Dining
S:t Hansgatan 15, 621 56
Tel *0498-27 83 80* **Closed** *Nov & Dec*
Said to be one of Sweden's finest restaurants. Choose from four- to eight-course sample menus that use the best of Gotland's seasonal produce. Expect sophisticated, impressive cuisine

Beautifully prepared seared fresh tuna with wasabi and soy at Pumphuset, Landskrona

VISBY: Bakfickan ⊛⊛
Traditional
Stora Torget 1, 621 56
Tel *0498-27 18 07*
This picturesque Visby haunt features seasonal rustic cooking, including fresh fish and seafood. Signature dishes include smoked prawns and fish soup.

VISBY: Friheten Restaurang ⊛⊛
Bistro
Strandgatan 6, 621 43
Tel *0498-24 99 07* **Closed** *Sun*
Pleasant 17th-century taverna. Varied menu of traditional Swedish fare, as well as a few international favourites.

Southern Götaland

ÅHUS: Handelsbaren ⊛⊛
Modern Swedish
Åvägen 4, 296 38
Tel *044-24 73 30* **Closed** *Winter*
Soak in some of the best views in Åhus from this charming restaurant in a red wooden villa by the sea. Great seafood.

**BILLEBERGA: Farbror
Elofs Skafferi** ⊛⊛
Modern Swedish
Kvarngården 1, 260 21
Tel *0418-43 11 77* **Closed** *Mon*
The menu features hints of Tuscan and Provençal cuisine, using herbs from the restaurant's own garden. Seating is either inside an old barn or out in the courtyard.

**BRANTEVIK: Branteviks
Bykrog** ⊛⊛
Fine Dining
Mästergränd 2, 272 38
Tel *0414-220 69* **Closed** *Mon & Tue*
This village taverna specializes in French gourmet dining and offers excellent food-and-wine pairings. Cookery courses are also available.

BRÖSARP: Brösarps Gästgifveri ⊛
Modern Swedish
Albovägen 21, 273 50
Tel *0414-736 80*
Romantic inn painted a traditional red. On the menu are local delicacies, including wild boar. On Sundays, try the herring buffet.

GENARP: Häckeberga Slott ⊛⊛
Traditional
Häckeberga Slott, 247 98
Tel *040-48 04 40* **Closed** *Sun*
Culinary delights in a castle setting. There is a breakfast buffet, as well as lunch and dinner menus. Try the Swedish herring, goose and local cheeses.

Beautiful interiors of Vimmerby's Brygghuset, featuring a fantastic bar

HELSINGBORG: Gastro ⊛⊛⊛
Fine Dining
Södra Storgatan 11–13, 252 23
Tel *042-24 34 70* **Closed** *Mon & Tue*
One of Skåne's finest restaurants, Gastro offers seasonal tasting menus, a children's menu, different wine lists and cooking classes. There is also a cheaper sister bistro next door.

KARLSKRONA: 2 Rum & Kök ⊛⊛
Modern Swedish
Södra Smedjegatan 3, 371 31
Tel *0455-104 22* **Closed** *Sun*
"Two Rooms & Kitchen" serves modern and traditional dishes prepared with flair. Their "North to South" menu showcases food from all across Sweden.

KRISTIANSTAD: Bar-B-Ko ⊛⊛
Bistro
Tivoligatan 4, 291 53
Tel *044-21 33 55* **Closed** *Sun*
As the name suggests, Bar-B-Ko specializes in all things grilled. Although the meat is first-rate, delicious fish and vegetarian options also appear on the menu.

**KRISTIANSTAD:
Tomarp Gårdshotell** ⊛⊛
Modern Swedish
Helmershusvägen 218, 291 94
Tel *044-931 18* **Closed** *Sun*
A pleasant country hotel and restaurant offering daily lunches, afternoon tea and tapas in the summer. Reserve in advance.

LANDSKRONA: Pumphuset ⊛⊛
Traditional
Nedre Gatan 97, 261 61
Tel *0418-131 30* **Closed** *Mon*
A restored and redesigned old pumping station with fantastic views. Tasty traditional Swedish dishes include herring, Arctic char and sausages.

For more information on types of restaurants *see page 291*

Classy decor at Bastard Mat & Vin, one of Malmö's trendiest restaurants

LUND: Gattostretto ◎◎
Italian
Kattesund 6A, 222 23
Tel *046-32 07 77* **Closed** *Sun*
You could spend all day here: coffee and cake mid-morning, a pasta dish for lunch, delicious ice cream in the afternoon and an extensive dinner menu.

MALMÖ: Bastard Mat & Vin ◎
European
Mäster Johansgatan 11, 211 21
Tel *040-12 13 18* **Closed** *Sun & Mon*
Arguably the trendiest place in Malmö, Bastard prepares each dish using organic and local produce whenever possible. Craft beers and organic wines.

MALMÖ: Grand Öl & Mat ◎◎
Bistro
Monbijougatan 17, 211 53
Tel *040-12 63 13* **Closed** *Sun–Tue evenings, Sat lunch; lunch Jun–mid-Jul; mid-Jul–mid-Aug*
This is what you get when you combine a posh hotel with a noisy beer hall. Enjoy great food in a convivial atmosphere.

DK Choice

MALMÖ: Salt & Brygga ◎◎
Traditional
Sundspromenaden 7, 211 16
Tel *040-611 59 40* **Closed** *Sun; mid-Dec–early Feb*
Considered one of the best organic restaurants in Sweden, Salt & Brygga relies on local produce and fish from sustainable sources, as well as Fairtrade coffee. Using the finest ingredients from Skåne, it re-creates traditional Swedish cuisine with exciting and innovative influences. Homemade bread and a large salad buffet are included in all lunchtime meals. Great sea views.

MALMÖ: Årstiderna ◎◎◎
Fine Dining
*Kockska Huset,
Frans Suellsgatan 3, 211 22*
Tel *040-23 09 10* **Closed** *Sun*
"The Seasons" combines the best of Swedish and international cuisines in an intimate setting. There is also a vegetarian menu and a good wine list.

MÖLLE: Maritime ◎◎
Fine Dining
Bökebolsvägen 11, 263 77
Tel *042-36 22 30* **Closed** *Sun*
Feast on gourmet seafood and enjoy lovely harbour views at this restaurant in the Grand Hôtel Mölle. Well-stocked wine cellar.

SKANÖR: Skanörs Fiskrögeri ◎◎
Traditional
Skanörs hamn, 239 21
Tel *040-47 40 50* **Closed** *Mon (Apr, May & Sep); Oct–Mar*
This old-fashioned rögeri (smokery) is located in an area that has a long fish-smoking history. Not surprisingly it specializes in smoked, marinated and grilled fish and seafood.

TRELLEBORG: Idala Gård ◎◎
International
Idalavägen 335, 231 91
Tel *0410-33 13 13* **Closed** *Sat lunch, Sun evening*
Swedish cooking with a good dose of Italian cuisine thrown in. Great Italian cheeses, olives, cold cuts and salads, and delicious pizza on Thursday nights.

DK Choice

VIKEN: Vikens Hamnkrog ◎◎◎
Fine Dining
Bÿösa Backen 6, 260 40
Tel *042-23 73 03* **Closed** *Mon–Thu evenings*
The "Harbour Inn" is a pleasant restaurant in a serene village on the southern Swedish coast. Diners can choose from a great selection of seafood and fish, dishes include rack of lamb with baked artichoke, fish soup with dill *aioli* and grilled trout with *beurre blanc* sauce. The cosy bar does an "after-work" buffet, and self-catering accommodation is available.

YSTAD: Bryggeriet Restaurant & Pub ◎
Modern Swedish
Långgatan 20, 271 43
Tel *0411-699 99* **Closed** *Sun–Tue*
Pleasant restaurant and pub with its own micro-brewery, in a rustic setting. Daily lunchtime specials, as well as pub and grill menus. Try their unique do-it-yourself Black Rock Grill.

Gothenburg

CENTRE: Restaurang Trädgår'n ◎
Modern Swedish
Nya Allén 11, 411 38
Tel *031-10 20 80* **Closed** *Sun*
This popular, stylish restaurant is known for its weekend brunch. The à la carte menu offers a good range of dishes from steak to fish and pasta. There's also a nightclub on the premises.

CENTRE: Familjen ◎◎
Traditional
Arkivgatan 7, 411 34
Tel *031-20 79 79*
A friendly and welcoming place from the team behind Kock & Vin *(see below)*. There is a champagne and oyster happy hour on Friday and Saturday evenings.

CENTRE: Heaven 23 ◎◎
International
Mässans gata 24, 412 51
Tel *031-750 88 05*
Located on the 23rd floor of the Hotel Gothia Towers and offering spectacular views over the city, this restaurant serves modern seasonal food. Its signature dish is the king size shrimp sandwich. Large range of Austrian wines.

CENTRE: Kock & Vin ◎◎
Fine Dining
Viktoriagatan 12, 411 25
Tel *031-701 79 79* **Closed** *Sun*
This Michelin-starred restaurant is considered one of Sweden's best. Exciting tasting menus change seasonally, and there is also modern Swedish food à la carte. Great food-and-drink pairings.

Modern seating arrangement at Malmö's Salt & Brygga

CENTRE: Restaurang Gabriel ⊛⊛
Fine Dining
Feskekôrka, Rosenlundsgatan, 411 20
Tel *031-13 90 51* **Closed** *Sun & Mon*
A gourmet seafood restaurant located inside Feskekôrka (Fish Church), the city's indoor fish market. The shellfish buffet is stocked with the freshest catch of the day. Open lunchtime only.

CENTRE: Smaka ⊛⊛
Traditional
Vasaplatsen 3, 411 26
Tel *031-13 22 47*
Rustic Swedish home cooking in a pleasant red-brick building. Good selection of beers and outdoor seating in summer.

DK Choice

CENTRE: Fiskekrogen ⊛⊛⊛
Fine Dining
Lilla Torget 1, 411 18
Tel *031-10 10 05* **Closed** *Sun*
One of the best fish and seafood restaurants in the country, Fiskekrogen has been serving up the tastiest catches since 1977. There are set menus, as well as a seafood buffet and a variety of fish dishes to choose from. The impressive setting makes it a perfect place for a romantic dinner. Extensive and impressive wine list.

CENTRE: Restaurang Fond ⊛⊛⊛
Traditional
Götaplatsen, 412 56
Tel *031-81 25 80* **Closed** *Sun*
The emphasis here is on seasonal, locally sourced food and Nordic flavours. Try the sampler menu, paired with a choice of wines.

FURTHER AFIELD: Sjömagasinet ⊛⊛⊛
Fine Dining
Klippans Kulturreservat, Adolf Edelsvärds gata 5, 414 51
Tel *031-775 59 20* **Closed** *Sun*
Set within a red wooden house right by the sea. There is a special seafood menu and a lunch menu that changes daily. There are cookery classes inside the old smithy.

Western Götaland

HALMSTAD: Restaurang Akvarell ⊛⊛⊛
Fine Dining
Tylöhusvägen 1, Tylösand, 301 16
Tel *035-305 01* **Closed** *Sun & Mon; Jan & Feb*
One of Sweden's best restaurants, with tasting menus, an extensive wine list and great views.

Beautiful white exterior of Villa Sjötorp, one of Ljungskile's best fine-dining places

KARLSBORG: Idas Brygga ⊛⊛
Modern Swedish
Skepparegatan 9, 546 32
Tel *0505-131 22* **Closed** *Sun evening*
Historic hotel and restaurant by the Göta Canal. High-quality cooking with locally sourced ingredients and international influences. Lunchtime buffet.

LJUNGSKILE: Villa Sjötorp ⊛⊛
Fine Dining
Sjötorpsvägen 5, 459 33
Tel *0522-201 74*
Set in a beautiful white villa by the sea, this restaurant has a large garden and outdoor terrace seating. The exceptional seasonal menus use local, organic produce. Extensive wine list.

MARIESTAD: Sill & Dynamit ⊛⊛
Traditional
Gästhamnen, Hamngatan 19, 542 30
Tel *0501-141 80* **Closed** *Sun evening*
The menu at this restaurant reflects the lakes, forests and farmlands in the surrounding area. Great fish entrées and good food-and-wine pairings.

MARSTRAND: Restaurang Grand Tenan ⊛⊛⊛
Fine Dining
Rådhusgatan 2, 442 67
Tel *0303-603 22*
The restaurant of the Grand Hotel offers elegant dining in a pretty setting. The signature dish, crayfish *au gratin*, is a must-try. Excellent Christmas buffet.

MELLBYSTRAND: Strandhotellet Mellbystrand ⊛
Traditional
Kustvägen 39, 312 60
Tel *0430-250 19*
Built in 1927, Strandhotellet used to be a favourite society hangout. Its restaurant, noted for its fine cuisine, offers delicious lunches. Dinner service only in the summer.

DK Choice

STRÖMSTAD: Rökeriet i Strömstad ⊛⊛
Traditional
Torskholmen, 452 31
Tel *0526-148 60* **Closed** *Sun & Mon*
This family-run traditional smokery on the waterfront relies on local producers and is part of the international Slow Food movement. Old-style wood-fired ovens are used to smoke the delicious fish and seafood dishes on the menu. There is also a fish and seafood shop on the premises.

SYDKOSTER: Kosters Trädgårdar ⊛⊛
Fine Dining
Kosters Trädgårdar, 452 05
Tel *0526-205 99* **Closed** *Sep–May*
Wonderful restaurant and garden using its own organic produce in many dishes. Try the summertime buffet, with lots of fresh greens.

VÄNERSBORG: Restaurang Teatergränd ⊛
Modern Swedish
Kungsgatan 13, 462 33
Tel *0521-644 60* **Closed** *Sun & Mon*
In addition to the à la carte menu, there are early dinner specials and Friday buffet dinners.

Western Svealand

ARVIKA: Barbord ⊛⊛
Modern Swedish
Hantverksmagasinet, Spårgatan 1, 671 30
Tel *0570-133 30* **Closed** *Sun–Tue*
Lovely harbour restaurant with a terrace on the lakefront. On the menu are tasty Swedish dishes with international touches. Great cocktails and weekend brunch.

For more information on types of restaurants *see page 291*

DK Choice

BOGEN: Värdshuset Tvällen ⓦⓦ
Traditional
Tvällen, Bogen, 670 35
Gunnarskog
Tel *0570-77 30 24* **Closed** *Mon (year-round) & Tue (Aug–Jun)*
This back-of-beyond rustic inn by a lake in a deep forest is well worth the trek. On the menu is traditional Swedish home-cooking, especially game dishes – moose, reindeer, wild boar – accompanied by wild mushrooms or fresh berries. A lovely treat for the palate.

The snow-covered ornate gate marking the entrance to Östersund's Take Mikado

FALUN: Kopparhatten Café & Kök ⓦ
Bistro
Stigaregatan 2–4, 791 60
Tel *023-191 69* **Closed** *Sun–Tue evenings*
Guests can choose from a tapas bar, an à la carte menu and a lunchtime buffet at this Falun favourite. Coffee and cake are served all day.

KARLSTAD: Blå Kök & Bar ⓦⓦ
Modern Swedish
Kungsgatan 14, 652 24
Tel *054-10 18 15* **Closed** *Sun and lunch in summer*
Trendy restaurant serving up fine Swedish cuisine with plenty of creative touches. There are daily lunchtime and dinner specials.

KRISTINEHAMN: Mastmagasinet ⓦ
Modern Swedish
Södra Hamngatan 5, 681 31
Tel *0550-803 40* **Closed** *Sun*
Housed in an old wooden warehouse on Lake Vänern, painted a traditional red. There is plenty of variety on the menu, including potato cakes, pea soup and salmon pie.

ÖREBRO: Slottskällaren ⓦⓦ
Fine Dining
Drottninggatan 1, 701 45
Tel *019-15 69 60* **Closed** *Sun; Mon evening.*
Located in a rustic cellar dating back to the 1300s. In summer, diners can eat on the outdoor terrace overlooking the river.

RÄTTVIK: Jöns Andersgården ⓦⓦ
Swedish-Italian
Bygatan 16, 795 35
Tel *0248-130 15* **Closed** *Mon–Wed; Oct–Feb*
Savour regional Dalecarlian cuisine with strong Italian influences in this picturesque 16th-century farmhouse.

SÄLEN: Gammelgården ⓦⓦ
Traditional
Sälfjället 1, 780 67
Tel *0280-877 00*
This ski lodge with cosy, intimate surroundings and open fires serves an à la carte menu of traditional Swedish fare. It also has a "waffle cottage" that uses a 100-year-old waffle recipe.

TÖCKFORS: Waterside Restaurant ⓦⓦ
Mediterranean
Bögatan 1, 670 10
Tel *0573-299 99* **Closed** *Mon; mid-Dec–mid-Feb*
The Waterside enjoys a scenic location along the Dalsland Canal. There's a lunch menu and à la carte options in the evening.

Southern Norrland

ÅRE: Villa Tottebo ⓦⓦ
Modern Swedish
Parkvägen 1, 830 13
Tel *0647-506 20*
This traditional hunting lodge dating from 1897 serves rustic dishes with a modern twist. Try the local cheeses, Swedish air-dried ham and game meatballs.

BJÄSTA: Näske Krog ⓦⓦ
Traditional
Norum, 893 91
Tel *0660-22 82 38*
Closed *mid-Dec–Apr*
Restaurant and café on the picturesque High Coast. Along with the traditional fare there are some international dishes on the menu too..

GÄVLE: Restaurang Matildas ⓦⓦ
Fine Dining
Timmermansgatan 23, 802 52
Tel *026-62 53 49* **Closed** *Sun & Mon*
Family-run restaurant offering fresh food of a high quality. A

classic Swedish menu includes dishes made with locally sourced seasonal and organic produce.

HIGH COAST: Restaurang Skutskepparn ⓦⓦ
Traditional
Barsta 270, 870 30 Nordingrå
Tel *0613-230 90* **Closed** *Winter*
Summertime restaurant in an old fishing village. On the menu are fresh fish and home-made mashed potatoes. Their popular pub evenings feature troubadours.

ÖSTERSUND: Innefickan Restaurant & bar ⓦⓦ
Fine Dining
Postgränd 11, 830 31
Tel *063-12 90 99* **Closed** *Sun & Mon*
Centrally located, with a focus on local produce and unusual combinations, such as black pepper reindeer with cassis.

DK Choice

ÖSTERSUND: Take Mikado ⓦⓦⓦ
Japanese
Infanterigatan 12, 831 32
Tel *063-209 08*
Closed *Mon & Mon*
Possibly the finest Japanese restaurant in Sweden, Take Mikado tempts with traditional cuisine prepared by head chef Tsukasa Takeuchi. There is fresh tofu, *shabu-shabu*, sashimi, tempura and miso soups on the menu. Dishes and tables need to be booked three days in advance.

STORLIEN: Restaurang Flamman ⓦⓦ
Modern Swedish
Vintergatan 46, 830 19
Tel *0647-700 10*
Closed *Mon, Tue, Thu*
Housed in a wooden building dating from the1930s. The varied

menu ranges from modern Swedish classics to wood-fired pizzas. A good budget option.

SUNDSVALL: Brandstation Bar & Matsalar ⊗⊗
Modern Swedish
Köpmangatan 29, 851 11
Tel *060-12 39 36* **Closed** *Sun*
"The Fire Station" describes itself as a "Norrland meat and beer bar", and it lives up to that claim with its menu of modern classics with Italian and French influences. Excellent reindeer dishes.

SUNDSVALL: Sundsvalls Stadshus ⊗⊗
Fine Dining
Stora Torget, 852 30
Tel *060-12 92 60* **Closed** *Sun*
Classic Swedish cuisine with a Mediterranean twist is served in the old Florentine town hall. Outdoor terrace seating in summer.

VEMHÅN: Vålkojan ⊗⊗
Traditional
Vålkojan 615, 840 91
Tel *0684-320 41*
Traditional restaurant, café and bar in a scenic riverside location. Choose between fine Swedish home-cooked dishes, open sandwiches and delicious waffles.

Northern Norrland

BODEN: Norrigården Restaurang & Konferens ⊗⊗
Traditional
Kyrkkläppen 3, 961 64
Tel *0921-103 51* **Closed** *Sat & Sun*
An 18th-century manor house with quaint wooden beams and a cosy atmosphere in a picturesque location. Lunchtime and evening menus. Excellent waffles.

BORGAFJÄLL: Hotell Borgafjäll & Spa ⊗⊗
Fine Dining/Bistro
Hotell Borgafjäll, 917 04
Tel *0942-421 00* **Closed** *Oct, Nov, May & Jun*
Choose between three- and six-course dinner menus featuring local delicacies, including regional cheeses. Good wine list.

GAMMELSTAD: Margaretas Värdshus
Traditional
Lulevägen 2, 954 33
Tel *0920-25 42 90*
An old-world inn with a strong focus on gastronomy, especially traditional Lapland cuisine. Cosy and convivial atmosphere.

JOKKMOKK: Hotel Jokkmokk ⊗⊗
Traditional
Solgatan 45, 962 31
Tel *0971-777 00*
Guests can savour traditional Lapland cuisine while enjoying fantastic views of Lake Talvatis. Plenty of reindeer and elk dishes.

DK Choice

JUKKASJÄRVI: ICEHOTEL Restaurant ⊗⊗⊗
Modern Swedish
Marknadsvägen 63, 981 91
Tel *0980-668 00*
Enjoy modern European cuisine with influences from Lapland at this award-winning restaurant. Food made with ingredients sourced from the lakes, rivers and mountains in the area are served on beautiful ice plates; the cocktails at the bar are also served in signature ice glasses made with water from the nearby Torne River.

KIRUNA: Restaurang Reenstierna ⊗
International
Scandic Hotel Ferrum, Lars Janssonsgatan 15, 981 31
Tel *0980-39 86 00*
Offers gorgeous views over Kebnekaise, Sweden's highest mountain. The menu features standard dishes, including pasta and hamburgers.

LULEÅ: Restaurang Ripan ⊗
Modern Swedish
Varvsgatan 39, 972 32
Tel *0920-168 68*
Classic Swedish fare, as well as international options such as a wide selection of pizzas. Popular with locals, the lunch buffet includes traditional food, homemade bread and a salad bar.

LULEÅ: Tallkotten Restaurang ⊗⊗
Italian
Storgatan 15, 972 32
Tel *0920-27 40 20* **Closed** *Sun; Jul*
High-quality classic Italian food served in large, light and airy premises. Choose from a range of pizzas, pasta dishes, omelettes and other main courses.

SKELLEFTEÅ: Nordanågården ⊗⊗
Fine Dining
Nordanå, 931 21
Tel *0910-533 50*
Charming old inn built in 1868. Inexpensive lunchtime buffet and popular Sunday buffet with cold cuts, salads and seafood.

TÄRNABY: Virisen ⊗
Traditional
Virisen 105, 920 64
Tel *0940-860 13 or 070-274 41 88*
The place to try Lapland cuisine, including ptarmigan, Arctic char, mushrooms and berries. Open for breakfast, lunch and dinner, but book in advance.

UMEÅ: Viktoria ⊗⊗
Fine Dining
"Blå Huset", Vasagatan 11, 903 29
Tel *090-71 11 15* **Closed** *Sun*
Popular restaurant serving the freshest local food. The adjacent bar, Soffan, offers an express lunch on weekdays; in summer there is a simpler menu for alfresco dining.

VILHELMINA: Hotell Wilhelmina ⊗⊗
Bistro
Volgsjövägen 16, 912 34
Tel *0940-554 20*
This restaurant in a pleasant mountain hotel offers Swedish and international cuisine. Children's menu available.

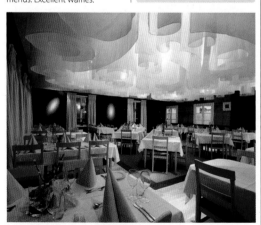
Spectacularly decorated interior of ICEHOTEL Restaurant

For more information on types of restaurants *see page 291*

SHOPPING IN SWEDEN

Sweden is worth visiting for the shopping alone. In all Swedish towns, and even in the big cities, the shops are within easy walking distance of each other. The city centres offer a good range of small, trendy boutiques for fashion and interiors, shops for antiques and curios, luxury international designer outlets and well-stocked department stores. Cameras, mobile phones, furs, children's clothing, toys and Swedish glass and designer goods are cheaper in Sweden than in many other countries. Those looking for a typical Swedish souvenir could buy a Dala horse or a proper Swedish schnapps glass from one of the factories in the Kingdom of Crystal. Although Lapland is a long way north, Sami handicrafts can be bought in most craft shops, including knives with carved bone handles and silverwork. Leather and fur goods are also good value.

Opening Times

Most shops usually open at 10am and close at 6pm, although many in Stockholm city centre remain open until 7pm. Most shops are open until 2pm on Saturdays, while the major department stores stay open until 5pm. Large stores, shopping malls and some city-centre shops are open on Sundays. Market halls are closed on Sundays and public holidays. Many larger supermarkets are open daily until 8pm.

Payment

All the major credit cards and traveller's cheques are accepted at most Swedish shops. You may be asked for proof of identity. Some larger shops also accept euros *(see p322)*. Goods can be exchanged if you produce the receipt. Purchases can be made on a sale-or-return basis if this is noted on the receipt.

Value Added Tax

Value added tax ("MOMS" in Swedish) is charged on all items except daily newspapers. The VAT rate is 25 per cent; but only 12 per cent on food and 6 per cent on books. VAT is always included in the total price.

Tax-Free Shopping

Residents of countries outside the European Union are entitled to a refund of the VAT paid on their purchases. Look for the "Tax-free shopping" sign in shop windows. Keep your receipts and on departure from the EU go to the Global Refund office at the airport or ferry terminal to obtain a 15–18 per cent refund.

Sale-time at an elegant shoe shop in Stockholm

Sales

Twice a year Sweden's shops and department stores have sales with reduced prices on clothing, shoes and other fashion goods. Sales are indicated by the *rea* sign. The year's first sales period starts after Christmas and continues throughout January. The second sales period lasts from late June to the end of July.

Shopping Centres and Department Stores

The best-known Swedish superstore internationally is **IKEA**, which has 18 outlets across the country from Haparanda in the north to Malmö in the south, and has become a popular tourist attraction in its own right. It sells not only furniture, but everything else for the home. The textiles section is particularly good, as well as the kitchenware and china departments.

NK, Stockholm's most exclusive department store

IKEA's home furnishings stores can be found in many parts of Sweden

Another well-known store is the fashion house **H&M** (Hennes & Mauritz), which has branches in many towns. It stocks the latest fashions at low prices. H&M has its own designers and makes clothing for women, men, teenagers and children. The shops also sell accessories, underwear, perfume and cosmetics.

NK (Nordiska Kompaniet) in Stockholm and Gothenburg is Sweden's leading department store, in which many well-known names in fashion and cosmetics have their own outlets. NK is a practical choice for those in a hurry. It stocks everything from Swedish-designed products, jewellery, handicrafts and souvenirs to cameras, films, books and CDs.

Åhléns, which has stores in many towns and cities, offers most items at good prices.

Opened in the 19th century, but thoroughly modern, **PUB** is a haven for fashionistas. Almost every large town has its own

Åfors glassworks store, Kingdom of Crystal, Småland *(see pp156–7)*

shopping centre or mall with a standard range of stores such as H&M, Lindex, Kappahl, Twilfit and Dressmann (clothing), Guldfynd (jewellery), Cervera (glass and china), Hemtex (textiles), Elgiganten (cameras, stereos, TVs) and Teknik-magasinet (electronics).

In Stockholm, **Gallerian** on Hamngatan is the largest mall and the prices are lower than in the elegant **Sturegallerian** near Stureplan with its many trendy boutiques.

Nordstan, off Brunnsparken in Gothenburg, is a mall with department stores such as Åhléns and specialist shops.

HansaCompagniet in central Malmö is a modern shopping centre.

A few examples of the larger shopping centres around the country include **Kungspassagen** in Umeå, **Forumgallerian** in Uppsala and **Krämaren** in Örebro.

Most towns have local markets selling flowers, fruit, vegetables and sometimes also handicrafts. Smaller places only have an outdoor market once a week, but in Hötorget in Stockholm, trading carries on every day except Sundays.

Wines and Spirits

The only shops selling alcohol in Sweden are run by Systembolaget, the state monopoly chain. They are open Mon–Fri 10am–6pm and Sat 10am–2pm (except public holiday weekends). The minimum age for buying alcohol at Systembolaget shops is 20 and staff are entitled to ask for proof of age *(see also p319)*.

DIRECTORY

Shopping Centres & Department Stores

Åhléns
Klarabergsgatan 50, Stockholm.
Map 1 C4. **Tel** 08-676 60 00.
W ahlens.se

Forumgallerian
Bredgränd 6, Uppsala.
Map see p135.
W forumgallerian.se

Gallerian
Hamngatan 37, Stockholm.
Map 2 D4. **Tel** 08-533 373 00.
W gallerian.se

HansaCompagniet
Stora Nygatan, Malmö.
Map see p183. **Tel** 040-770 00.
W hansamalmo.se

H&M
Hamngatan 22, Stockholm.
Map 2 D4. **Tel** 08-524 635 30.
W hm.com/se

IKEA
Kungens Kurva, Stockholm.
Tel 0775-700 500.

Kompassen
Kungsgatan 58–60, Gothenburg.
Map see p196. W kompassen.se

Krämaren
Drottninggatan 29, Örebro.
Map see p243. **Tel** 019-760 92 40.
W kramaren.se

Kungspassagen
Skolgatan 62, Umeå.
W forvandlingen.se

NK
Östra Hamngatan 42, Gothenburg.
Tel 031-710 10 00. W nk.se

NK
Hamngatan 18–20, Stockholm.
Map 2 D4. **Tel** 08-762 80 00.
W nk.se

Nordstan
Brunnsparken, Gothenburg.
Map see p196. **Tel** 031-700 86 60.
W nordstan.se

PUB
Drottninggatan 63, Stockholm.
Map 3 A1. W pub.se

Sturegallerian
Grev Turegatan 9 A, Stockholm.
Map 2 D4. **Tel** 08-611 46 06.
W sturegallerian.se

Triangeln Köpcentrum
Södra Förstadsgatan 41, Malmö.
Map see p183. **Tel** 040-23 02 06.

What to Buy in Sweden

The Dala wooden horse must be the most typical Swedish souvenir. But it is facing strong competition from the elk, which has become a symbol for a nation with vast tracts of unspoilt countryside. The Swedes love the great outdoors, so there are plenty of shops selling top-class sporting equipment. Swedish glass and crystal are renowned around the world. Orrefors and Kosta Boda are just two of several glassworks producing both classic and modern glassware. Educational toys in natural materials are a Swedish speciality and so are clogs, which can be found in most shoe shops.

Hand-painted clogs

Handicrafts & Design

Modern Swedish design is a familiar concept worldwide, even for simple everyday items (see pp30–31). Handicrafts have a long tradition in Sweden and contemporary designers often use old crafts such as wrought-iron work, weaving, pottery and woodcarving.

Dala Horse and Cockerel
Originally the brightly painted Dala horses and cockerels were toys carved from left-over fragments of wood. Later the horse became a national symbol, now sold in many variants.

Swedish Glass
Hand-blown sets are made in Småland's glassworks, as well as artistic crystal creations and objects for daily use.

Cheese slicer and knife by Michael Björnstierna

Nobel glass carafe from Orrefors by Gunnar Cyrén

Traditional schnapps glasses

Tray with design by Josef Frank, Svenskt Tenn

Objects for the Home
The larger department stores often commission well-known designers for porcelain, glass, textiles and household items which make highly desirable gifts.

Mama, a humorous clothes hanger

Crux rug by Pia Wallén

Children's Toys
Colourful wooden toys from Brio are worldwide favourites. Educational picture books, games and puzzles are all excellent gifts for children.

Outdoor Gear

Many Swedes enjoy outdoor pursuits such as fishing, hunting, sailing, golf, camping and all types of winter sports, so there are plenty of well-equipped sports shops around. Unique items include Sami handicrafts beautifully made from reindeer horn or skin.

Hand Knits

Caps and gloves with attractive designs, known as *lovikka*, are made from a special wool which gives good protection in cold or wet conditions.

Drinking vessel in carved wood

Reindeer Skin Rucksack

Rucksacks have always been popular in Sweden. This exclusive leather model is made in Lapland.

Spinning Reel and Lures

ABU-Garcia makes top-quality fishing tackle, perfect for Sweden's long coastline, countless lakes and rivers with their rich and varied fishing.

Sami Handicrafts

A hunting knife with a sheath of reindeer horn, or a *kåsa*, a drinking vessel carved in birch, are not only attractive, but useful when out walking in the wild.

Swedish Delicacies

Among the many Swedish goodies are preserves made from wild berries, such as lingonberries (served with meatballs or pancakes) and cloudberries (delicious with whipped cream). Ginger biscuits are for Christmas while crispbread is great year-round, especially with herring.

Lingonberry preserve

Cloudberry jam

Pickled Herring

Pickled herring should be enjoyed with new potatoes cooked with dill, chopped chives and sour cream. Versions flavoured with mustard, dill or other herbs or spices are also available.

Swedish schnapps gift-pack miniatures

"Raspberry boat" candy

Salt liquorice

Crispbread

Ginger biscuits

Where to Shop in Sweden

Clothing from all the well-known international fashion houses can be found in Stockholm, Malmö and Gothenburg. If you want something rather different, it is worth seeking out the creations of younger Swedish fashion designers. Swedish interior design is famous for its clean lines, functionalism and the use of pale wood, and the country is a paradise for anyone interested in design. Handicrafts are of a high quality. Leisurewear and sports goods offer excellent value for money.

Fashion

Stockholm's top places for fashion are in the "golden triangle" bounded by Stureplan, Nybroplan and Norrmalmstorg. Clothing at more moderate prices can be bought in department stores and shopping centres across the country. **GeKås** in Ullared and **Knalleland** in Borås have become popular attractions due to their low prices and large number of stores and factory outlets, not least in the "mail-order town" of Borås, with its weaving and textile traditions.

If you are looking for Swedish designers, **NK** in Stockholm and Gothenburg (see p303) has a good selection of clothing created by younger designers as well as mainstream Swedish brands. Classic men's clothing of high quality is designed by Oscar Jacobsson, while Stenström shirts are sold in department stores and the more elegant menswear boutiques. **Björn Borg** has his own shops selling men's and women's clothing and under-wear, perfume and accessories. The designer **Filippa K** produces smart clothing for fashionable women and men.

Design and Interior Decoration

Stockholm, Gothenburg and Malmö have a number of interior decoration shops selling the products of young designers and well-known artists. To see the latest on offer, it is worth visiting **DesignTorget**, which has stores in all three cities' displaying designers' work. Stockholm's **R.O.O.M** in the PUB department store and **Asplund**

in Östermalm, and **Norrgavel** in Stockholm, Gothenburg, Malmö, Umeå, Uppsala and Lammhult are just a few of the shops with the most up-to-the-minute selection of products. **Svenskt Tenn** is Stockholm's oldest shop for interiors, with both new and classic designs. **Nordiska Galleriet** in Stockholm has exclusive modern furniture and decorative items, while **Blås & Knåda** on Hornsgatan displays and sells the largest selection of contemporary Swedish ceramics and glass, both objects of art and items for everyday use. **Nordiska Kristall** on Kungsgatan has a wide choice of Swedish glassware, which can also be found in department stores.

Music and Multimedia

Många Swedish pop bands now have an international reputation. Exciting new talents continue to find their way into the charts, and the latest products can often be bought in the large record shops before they become available outside Sweden. Apart from pop and rock, Sweden has a long folk-music tradition, as well as many jazz musicians and opera singers.

Sport and Leisure

The Swedes devote a lot of time to outdoor sports and activities. With shops all over the country, **Naturkompaniet** and **Peak Performance** have an exclusive selection of sportswear and equipment. **Stadium** and **Intersport** have a varied choice of sports clothing and equipment at attractive prices and are also nationwide. Good

equipment and exclusive clothing for hunting and fishing can be bought at **Walter Borg** in central Stockholm. **Löplabbet** countrywide specializes in running and jogging.

Souvenirs and Handicrafts

Schnapps glasses, silver jewellery, hand-painted clogs, Sami crafts, hand-knitted garments, candles, Christmas decorations and wrought-iron products can all be bought in department stores and shops specialising in Swedish handicrafts.

At Skansen open-air museum in Stockholm, visitors can shop for handicrafts in attractive little houses.

Nusnäs in Dalarna is the place to buy the original Dala horse, which can be found at **Nils Olsson Hemslöjd AB**.

Yllet in Visby sells hand-spun wool, woollen garments and sheepskin goods.

Markets

Små local markets can be found almost everywhere, but a few have become so big that they have attracted international attention.

Jokkmokk's winter market (1st Thu–Sat in Feb) is a major Sami market. Skänninge market (1st Wed–Thu in Aug) is a classic affair dating back to the Middle Ages. The Kivik market (mid-Jul) is like an amusement park. Michaelmas markets are held in central Sweden in autumn.

The bustling flea market in Vårberg Centrum, Stockholm, is the place to find a bargain every day of the week. Entrance fee Sat–Sun, free on other days.

Glass and China

Most department stores and gift shops sell glass from Swedish manufacturers. Visitors to the Kingdom of Crystal in Småland have a choice of no fewer than 13 glassworks within a radius of a few miles (see pp156–7). At **Orrefors Kosta Boda Glasbruk**, there are bargains to be had among the everyday glassware and the studio glass. **Reijmyre** in Östergötland is also popular among bargain-hunters. For porcelain, the factory shop at **Rörstrand** offers value for money.

Swedish Delicacies

The capital has three market halls – **Östermalmshallen, Hötorgshallen** and **Söderhallarna** – which are a joy to just wander around.

Salmon, bleak roe, smoked eel and smoked reindeer meat are all delicious culinary souvenirs. Lund's **Saluhall** and Gothenburg's **Briggen** are also pleasant market halls offering mouth-watering Swedish delicacies.

On the west coast, seafood is a must and whether you are after prawns, crab or autumn's black gold, lobster, it is best purchased at the harbourside when the boats come in. In the

north, game of various kinds is the big attraction and you can often find smoked reindeer and reindeer heart in grocery stores, along with fermented Baltic herring and Norrland cloudberry jam.

Swedish crispbread is another delicacy and the bakery in Leksand has a factory shop. Traditional red and white striped candy rock originates from Gränna, which has a large number of shops selling rock.

DIRECTORY

Fashion

Björn Borg
Sergelgatan 12,
Stockholm. **Map** 1 C4.
Tel 08-21 70 40.
W bjornborg.com

Charlotte Göteborg
Drottninggatan 28,
Gothenburg. **Map** see
p196. **Tel** 031-701 75 40.
W charlottegoteborg.se

Dunderdon
Stuk, Södra Larmgatan 16,
Gothenburg.
Map see p196.

Filippa K
Grev Turegatan 18,
Stockholm. **Map** 2 D4.
W filippa-k.com

Ge-Kås i Ullared
Danska Vägen, Falkenberg.
Tel 0346-375 00.
W gekas.se

Knalleland
Bergslenagatan 45, Borås.
Tel 033-14 03 35.

MQ
Södra Tullgatan 3, Malmö.
Tel 040-12 01 31.
Strömpilsplatsen 9–15,
Umeå. **Tel** 090-786 36 80.
W mq.se

Olsén Mode
Södergatan 21, Malmö.
Map see p183.
Tel 040-12 10 50.

Design and Interiors

Asplund
Sibyllegatan 31,
Stockholm. **Map** 2 E3.
Tel 08-662 52 84.
W asplund.org

Blås & Knåda
Hornsgatan 26,
Stockholm. **Map** 3 A5.
Tel 08-642 77 67.
W blasknada.se

DesignTorget
Kulturhuset, Sergels Torg
3, Stockholm. **Map** 1 C4.
Tel 08–21 91 50.

Södra Vallgatan 3, Malmö.
Tel 040-30 70 82.

Vallgatan 14, Gothenburg.
Map see p196.
Tel 031-774 00 17.
W designtorget.se

Establish
Humlegårdsgatan 14,
Stockholm. **Map** 2 E3.
Tel 08-545 853 40.

Nordiska Galleriet
Nybrogatan 11,
Stockholm. **Map** 2 E4.
Tel 08-442 83 60.
W nordiskagalleriet.se

Nordiska Kristall
Kungsgatan 9,
Stockholm. **Map** 2 E4.
Tel 08-10 43 72.

Norrgavel
Birger Jarlsgatan 27,
Stockholm. **Map** 2 D3.
Tel 08-545 220 50.

Engelbrektsgatan 20,
Malmö. **Map** see p183.
Tel 040-12 22 46.
W norrgavel.se

R.O.O.M
PUB, Hötorget,
Stockholm. **Map** 1 C4.
Tel 08-692 50 00.

Svenskt Tenn
Strandvägen 5,
Stockholm. **Map** 2 E4.
Tel 08-670 16 00.
W svensktenn.se

Music

Bengans Skivbutik
Stigbergstorget 1,
Gothenburg.
Tel 031-14 33 00.
W bengans.se

Sport and Leisure

Intersport
Björnvägen 1, Umeå.
Tel 090-70 63 50.

Löplabbet
Djäknegatan 2, Malmö.
Tel 040-12 35 70.

Naturkompaniet
Kungsgatan 4A,
Stockholm.
Map 2 D4.
Tel 08-723 15 81.

Peak Performance
Biblioteksgatan 18,
Stockholm.
Map 2 D4.
Tel 08-611 34 00.

Södergatan 9, Malmö.
Map see p183.
Tel 040-97 02 20.

Stadium
Fredsgatan 8, Gothenburg.
Map see p196.
Tel 031-711 06 09.
W stadium.se

Walter Borg
Kungsgatan 57B,
Stockholm. **Map** 1 C4.
Tel 08-14 38 65.
W walterborg.se

Souvenirs and Handicrafts

Nils Olsson Hemslöjd AB
Edåkersvägen 17, Nusnäs.
Tel 0250-372 00.

Svensk Hemslöjd
Norrlandsgatan 20,
Stockholm. **Map** 2 D4.
Tel 08-23 21 15.

Yllet
St Hansgatan 19, Visby.
Tel 0498-21 40 43.

Glass and China

Orrefors Kosta Boda Glasbruk
Kosta. **Tel** 0478-345 00.
Orrefors. **Tel** 0478-345 29.
W kostaboda.se
W orrefors.se

Reijmyre
Rejmyre. **Tel** 011-871 84.
W reijmyre.se

Rörstrand (littala)
Lidköping.
Tel 0510-250 80.

Gustavsberg.
Tel 08-570 356 55.
W rorstrand.se
W iittala.com

Swedish Delicacies

Briggen
Nordhemsgatan 28,
Gothenburg.

Hötorgshallen
Hötorget, Stockholm.
Map 1 C4.

Östermalmshallen
Östermalmstorg,
Stockholm. **Map** 2 E4.

Saluhall
Lund.
W lundssaluhall.se

Söderhallarna
Medborgarplatsen,
Södermalm, Stockholm.

ENTERTAINMENT IN SWEDEN

The range of cultural events and entertainment in Sweden is large and richly varied. The whole spectrum is covered from outdoor celebrations to mark local customs to top international acts performing in giant arenas. The seasons have an effect on what's on: large city theatres tend to close during the summer and launch their new programmes of plays, opera and dance in late August or early September. Meanwhile, summer reviews, popular comedies and local historical plays are staged across the country.

In parks, palace gardens and amusement parks, summer is a particularly eventful time, with artists of every imaginable kind putting on a performance. Added to that are the countless markets, festivals covering film, jazz, music, food, theatre, folklore, and much more besides. Winter brings ski races and skating, indoor fairs and Christmas markets. Nightlife continues all year. There are excellent nightclubs and casinos in the major cities. Jazz clubs and pubs offer a wide range of live music to suit all tastes.

Sources of Information

A reliable source of information is **Visit Sweden**'s official tourist and events guide on the Internet. This provides listings for everything from music and sport to seasonal events such as Medieval Week in Visby or the Vasaloppet ski race in Dalarna. The site has links to the websites of Stockholm, Gothenburg and Malmö, but also has details of events across the country.

Daily newspapers and free local papers are an excellent source for regional events such as concerts, theatre performances and nightclubs. The tourist information offices and most hotels also have listings and can often help with advice and booking tickets.

Booking Tickets

Tickets for most events can usually be bought at the box office of the theatre or sports arena in question, but to ensure admission it may be more practical to book in advance, with the help either of the hotel or a tourist information office. Another alternative is to use a booking agency, such as **ticnet.se**, which allows you to purchase tickets to stage shows, concerts and sports events online. At **Box-office** in Stockholm, tickets can be purchased over the counter for various events in Sweden and beyond, and tickets ordered via the event organizer can be collected. Many tickets are also sold via ticket service outlets across the country.

Major Arenas and Cultural Centres

In addition to the long-established, traditional theatres, many towns and cities have built multipurpose cultural

Dalhalla's music stage *(see p245)* in a dramatic quarry near Rättvik

complexes offering a wide spectrum of public events. Often such centres are home to the local theatre company and orchestra.

The major entertainment and event arenas, such as **Ericsson Globen** and the **Friends Arena** in Stockholm, the **Malmö Arena** in Malmö and **Scandinavium** in Gothenburg, have a huge audience capacity. International rock and pop concerts, charity galas and major sporting events are usually held at these enormous venues.

In the summer, the large outdoor stages, for example at Skansen and Gröna Lund in Stockholm, Liseberg in Gothenburg and Dalhalla, between Rättvik and Mora, attract a wide range of jazz, folk and classical artists alike.

Theatre

Sweden has almost 500 theatres spread across the country. Many are town or county theatres, but there are also private theatres with long traditions and small park and amateur theatres.

Sea of people at the Philharmonic's annual outdoor concert, Stockholm

Sweden's national theatre is **Kungliga Dramatiska Teatern** *(see p77)*, which has six stages. It regularly mounts international and Swedish classics, including Shakespeare and Strindberg, as well as modern foreign and Swedish works.

Lighter plays and musicals are often performed at **ChinaTeatern** in Stockholm and **Lorensbergsteatern** in Gothenburg. Venues such as **Konsertteatern** in Sundsvall and **Göta Lejon** in Stockholm often stage performances suitable for children and families.

GöteborgsOperan, with a wide repertoire of opera and musicals

Classical Music, Dance and Opera

World-class music can be heard at **Berwaldhallen** in Stockholm, the home of Sveriges Radios Symfoniorkester and the Radiokören choir, considered one of the internationally leading a cappella ensembles. **Konserthuset** *(see p74)* is the base for the Royal Stockholm Philharmonic Orchestra. The season runs from August to May.

Konserthuset in Gothenburg is home to Göteborgs Symfoniker. Norrköping has the **Louis De Geer konsert & kongress** venue and Folkets Park in Sundsvall has **Tonhallen**, one of Sweden's best concert halls.

Classical opera and ballet of the highest quality can be seen at **Kungliga Operan** *(see p72)*. Every season at least three major ballets delight packed houses. This venue also stages traditional performances of most operas in their original language. During the summer, popular opera performances are held at **Drottningholms Slottsteater** *(see p115)*. All the

operas staged here are from the 18th century, with an orchestra of the period.

The spectacular modern **GöteborgsOperan** *(see p200)* is an exciting, internationally renowned venue for opera, ballet and musicals. Norrlandsoperan in Umeå and Malmö Opera och Musikteater are two of the country's other major venues for opera and ballet.

Dansens Hus in Stockholm, which has taken over the National Theatre's former venue, often hosts top-name dance companies from Sweden and abroad.

Folk Music

Swedish folk music is enjoying a resurgence in popularity. Skansen in Stockholm *(see p98)* is the prime venue, where musicians and folk dancing troupes perform regularly at traditional events. However, there are local folk groups and regional clubs covering practically every corner of the country. The easiest way of finding out where and how to enjoy Swedish folk music is to check at the local tourist information office or in the local press.

There are a few permanent venues for folk music: **Folkmusikhuset** in Stockholm, **Folkmusikkaféet** in Gothenburg and **Folkmusikens Hus** in Rättvik are just some

of the places offering a wide programme of performances and information about forthcoming events.

Church Music

Many churches in the cities hold organ recitals at lunchtime, for example Jacobs Kyrka in Stockholm *(see p72)*, where visitors can take a breather in a tranquil setting. Storkyrkan *(see p63)* also holds concerts on Saturday and Sunday afternoons in the spring and autumn. The cathedrals of Uppsala Domkyrka *(see p134)* and Västerås Domkyrka *(see p142)* stage organ recitals every Saturday. Many churches also have a concert programme, particularly in conjunction with major religious festivals.

Rock and Pop

The largest of the rock and pop venues are Ericsson Globen and the Friends Arena in Stockholm, the Malmö Arena in Malmö and Scandinavium in Gothenburg. These attract top international artists, along with the many successful Swedish bands. **Cirkus** in Stockholm is a well-established venue for music and theatre in a beautiful old setting. More modern rock venues include **Münchenbryggeriet** in Stockholm, **Kulturbolaget** in Malmö and **Trädgår'n** in Gothenburg. Around the country there are smaller theatres, students' unions and clubs where groups and artists perform.

Sundsvalls Teater, an ambitious, go-ahead regional theatre

Concert in the ruins of Bohus Castle in Kungälv

Jazz Clubs

Jazz has enjoyed a renaissance in recent years and the range on offer increases annually. One venue of repute is **Fasching** in Stockholm, with performances almost daily. Another jazz haunt in the capital is **Stampen**, which attracts a rather more mature audience. Gothenburg has **Nefertiti** and across the country there are jazz clubs holding concerts once a month or so.

Jazz cruises have become popular in the summer. The Stockholm archipelago is plied by *S/S Blidösund*. Cruises are also organized elsewhere in the country, for instance across Lake Vättern and the Åland Sea, on the Dalälven river and out into the Gothenburg archipelago.

Music Pubs

Swedish pub culture has changed enormously and it is becoming increasingly common to follow the Continental pattern of slipping into a bar or pub for a while after work, having a beer and listening to music.

Many pubs have introduced live music – some have folk singers performing on a regular basis, while others have a DJ. The best way of being sure to hear live music is to scan the local press entertainment (*nöjen*) pages.

In Stockholm, the Irish pub **The Dubliner** offers live Irish music. The popular **Engelen** bar has live music several days a week. Gothenburg's finest pubs include **Sticky Fingers** and Jameson's pub, and Helsingborg has its own English pub, Charles Dickens, where the clientele can enjoy karaoke, live music, singers, bands and various other forms of entertainment.

There are a number of traditional English and Irish-style pubs spread across the country, usually offering a wide range of beer and spirits and serving a selection of bar snacks.

Nightclubs, Casinos and Shows

Generally speaking, nightclubs hold traditional disco nights on Friday and Saturday. During the rest of the week the venue is usually hired by various clubs focusing on different styles of music. Almost all the larger towns and cities have one or two nightclubs, but the quality varies, as does the music on offer. In Stockholm, the majority and the best of the capital's nightclubs are located around Stureplan. At the rear of the Opera House is **Café Opera**, Stockholm's longest-established nightclub, with an international style. The crowd is usually quite mixed – young, trendy types and older, smartly-dressed folks. **Sturecompagniet** is a large club on several floors. At street level there is also a rock bar. Swedish celebrities and visiting foreign stars mingle at top celeb hangout **Spy Bar**, but it can be difficult to get in on certain nights. Other well-known nightclubs include **Crown** in Malmö and **Gutekällaren** in Visby.

A relative newcomer to the entertainment scene is the state-run casino chain **Casino Cosmopol**, which to date has opened branches in Stockholm, Gothenburg, Malmö and Sundsvall.

A combination of good food and top-flight entertainment is on offer at **Hamburger Börs** in Stockholm, with its shows featuring the best Swedish artists. **Wallmans Salonger**, which can be found in Stockholm and Helsingborg (summer) and Sälen and Åre (winter), offers musical entertainment with dinner served by waiters and waitresses who are, in fact, professional performers.

In Gothenburg, **Rondo** is a classic show venue.

Festivals

Countless festivals large and small are organized all across Sweden in the summer. Almost every town has its own festival, some with a specific focus, such as folk, jazz or rock.

Among the most renowned of the local festivals are Göteborgs kulturkalas in Gothenburg, Storsjöyran in Östersund and Gatufesten in Sundsvall.

There are numerous music festivals, often attracting huge audiences. Some famous music festivals include the Sweden

A traditional folk music festival in Tällberg on Lake Siljan in Dalarna

Rock Festival in Sölvesborg, the Gotland Chamber Music Festival in Visby, the Stockholm Jazz Festival and the Umeå International Jazz Festival.

The best-known film festivals in Sweden are the **Göteborg International Film Festival** (Jan/Feb) and the **Stockholm International Film Festival**

(Nov); however, several other cities and towns across the country hold their own film festivals with a different focus, such as Umeå (Sep).

DIRECTORY

Sources of Information

Visit Sweden
Tel 08- 789 10 00.
W visit-sweden.com

Booking Tickets

Box-office
Kungsgatan 38,
Stockholm.
Tel 08-10 88 00.
W boxoffice.se

Ticnet
Tel 077-170 70 70.
W ticnet.se

Arenas, Cultural Centres

Ericsson Globen
Globentorget 2, Stockholm.
Tel 077-131 00 00.

Friends Arena
169 79 Solna, Stockholm.
Tel 08-502 535 00.
W friendsarena.se

Malmö Arena
Arenagatan 15, Malmö.
Tel 0775-78 00 00.

Scandinavium
Valhallagatan 1,
Gothenburg.
Tel 031-81 10 20.

Theatre

China Teatern
Berzelii Park, Stockholm.
Tel 08-562 892 00.

Göta Lejon
Götgatan 55, Stockholm.
Tel 08-505 290 00.

Konsertteatern
Köpmangatan 11, Sundsvall. Tel 060-61 32 62.

Kungliga Dramatiska Teatern
Nybroplan, Stockholm.
Tel 08-667 06 80.

Lorensbergsteatern
Lorensbergsparken,
Gothenburg.
Tel 031-708 62 00.

Classical Music, Dance, Opera

Berwaldhallen
Dag Hammarskjölds Väg 3,
Stockholm.
Tel 08-784 18 00.

Dansens Hus
Barnhusgatan 12–14,
Stockholm. Map 1 C3.
Tel 08-508 990 90.
W dansenshus.se

Drottningholms Slottsteater
Drottningholms Slott,
Lovön, W of Stockholm.
Tel 08-556 931 00.

GöteborgsOperan
Christina Nilssons Gata,
Gothenburg.
Tel 031-13 13 00.

Konserthuset
Götaplatsen, Gothenburg.
Tel 031-726 53 00.

Konserthuset
Hötorget, Stockholm.
Map 1 C4.
Tel 08-786 02 00.

Kungliga Operan
Gustav Adolfs Torg,
Stockholm. Map 2 D5.
Tel 08-791 43 00.

Louis De Geer konsert & kongress
Dalsgatan 15, Norrköping.
Tel 011-15 50 30.
W louisdegeer.com

Tonhallen
Universitetsallén 22, Sundsvall. Tel 060-19 88 00.

Folk Music

Folkmusikens Hus
Dalagatan 7, Rättvik.
Tel 0248-79 70 50.

Folkmusikhuset
Skeppsholmsgården,
Stockholm. Map 2 E5.
Tel 072-875 74 46.

Folkmusikkaféet
Allégården, Gothenburg.
W folkmusikkafeet.net

Rock and Pop

Cirkus
Djurgårdsslätten,
Stockholm.
Tel 08-660 10 20.

Kulturbolaget
Bergsgatan 18, Malmö.
Tel 040-30 20 11.

Münchenbryggeriet
Torkel Knutssonsg 2,
Stockholm.
Tel 08-658 20 00.
W m-b.se

Trädgår'n
Nya Allén, Gothenburg.
Tel 031-10 20 80.

Jazz Clubs

Fasching
Kungsgatan 63,
Stockholm. Map 1 B4.
Tel 08-534 829 60.

Nefertiti
Hvitfeldtsplatsen 6,
Gothenburg.
Tel 031-711 15 33.

Stampen
Stora Nygatan 5,
Stockholm. Map 3 B4.
Tel 08-20 57 93.

Music Pubs

Engelen
Kornhamnstorg 59 B,
Stockholm. Map 3 B4.
Tel 0771-13 01 60.

Sticky Fingers
Kaserntorget 7,
Gothenburg.
Tel 031-701 00 17.

The Dubliner
Holländargatan 1,
Stockholm. Map 1 C3.
Tel 08-679 77 07.

Nightclubs, Casinos, Shows

Café Opera
Operahuset, Stockholm.
Map 3 B1.
Tel 08-676 58 07.

Casino Cosmopol
Kungsgatan 65,
Stockholm. Map 1 B4.
Tel 08-781 88 00.

Packhusplatsen 7,
Gothenburg.
Tel 020-219 219.

Slottsgatan 33, Malmö.
Tel 040-664 18 00.

Casinoparken 1, Sundsvall.
Tel 020-219 219.

Crown
Amiralsgatan 23, Malmö.
Tel 040-611 80 88.

Gutekällaren
Stora Torget, Visby.
Tel 0498-21 00 43.

Hamburger Börs
Jakobsgatan 6,
Stockholm. Map 2 D5.
Tel 08-787 85 00.

Rondo
Örgrytevägen 5, Gothenburg. Tel 031-40 01 00.

Spy Bar
Birger Jarlsgatan 20,
Stockholm. Map 2 D3.
Tel 08-545 076 00.

Sturecompagniet
Sturegatan 4,
Stockholm. Map 2 D3.
Tel 08-545 076 70.

Wallmans Salonger
Teatergatan 3,
Stockholm. Map 2 E5.
Tel 08-505 560 00.

Bollbrogatan 6,
Helsingborg.
Tel 08-505 560 00.

Festivals

Göteborg International Film Festival
Tel 031-339 30 00.
W giff.se

Stockholm International Film Festival
Tel 08 677 50 00.
W stockholm filmfestival.se

SPORTS AND OUTDOOR ACTIVITIES

Sweden has countryside in abundance and the *"allemannsrätt"* (Right of Public Access) makes it accessible in a way rarely found elsewhere in the world. An active outdoor life is a staple of the Swedish lifestyle. Constantly rising demand for outdoor activities has led to an increasing range of trails for hiking, canoeing and cycling, and the construction of hundreds of new ski lifts, golf courses and guest harbours. There has also been a boom in adventure sports – from challenging hikes in remote mountain regions and sea kayaking in the outer archipelagos to competing in the long-distance Vasaloppet skiing race, the Vansbrosimningen swimming race, the Lidingöloppet cross-country race and the Vätternrundan cycling race, which together make up what is known as the "Swedish Classic". More leisurely pursuits include horse riding and fishing.

General Information

In addition to the tourist information offices, there are a number of organizations to assist outdoors enthusiasts. The state-run **Naturvårdsverket** has an excellent website, which also provides useful information about Sweden's 28 national parks. **Friluftsfrämjandet** is a 100-year-old voluntary organization – the backbone of outdoor life for its many activities and operations.

Hiking Trails

Although it is possible to pitch a tent almost anywhere, it is often more practical to follow one of the many well-tended hiking trails. There are numerous lowland trails, such as the Skåneleden, which runs south to north through Skåne. Mountain trails proliferate, the best of which is the renowned Kungsleden stretching 450 km (280 miles) (see pp278–9).

Maps of the trails usually provide information about stopping-off points, attractions, accommodation and services along the way.

The most popular mountain areas have marked trails for day trips and longer hikes with overnight accommodation in huts and at mountain stations. For more than 100 years, **Svenska Turistföreningen (STF)** has been the main provider of services in the mountains in summer and winter.

The mountain trails mainly run through road-free land. There are STF mountain stations at strategic locations from Abisko in Lapland to Grövelsjön in Dalarna. Although out in the wilds, these are relatively easy to access and make an excellent starting point for hiking tours in the mountains. The stations have hotel-standard accommodation, restaurants, self-catering kitchens, shops and equipment hire.

Walking with poles, a popular form of exercise

Along the trails, there are simple huts in which to stay, with a self-catering kitchen and in some cases provisions for sale. Space cannot be booked in advance, but everyone usually gets a roof over their head. In the summer, STF has special hosts to help with tips and advice.

The trails crossing the high mountains can be extremely demanding for the uninitiated. It is important not to be too ambitious and to have appropriate equipment.

Whatever the time of year, the weather changes quickly, so keep up to date with the forecast, which is usually posted at stations and huts. The summer season for mountain hiking is from about mid-June to mid-September.

Endurance Tests

Competitions for elite athletes and fitness enthusiasts alike have become increasingly popular in Sweden, attracting thousands of participants of

A hiker en route to the Sylarna mountain station, Jämtland

One of STF's many huts across the mountains

all levels. Some enter the "Swedish Classic", in which over one year competitors ski the Vasaloppet *(see p249)* or Engelbrektsloppet (60 km/37 miles), cycle the Vätternrundan (300 km/190 miles), swim the Vansbrosimningen (3 km/2 miles) and run the Lidingöloppet (30 km/ 19 miles). Other events include the Stockholm Marathon *(see p33)* and the O-ringen in orienteering.

Swimming

There are generally no restrictions for anyone wanting to take a dip in lakes, rivers and the sea. However, there is no need to take any risks as there are thousands of public bathing areas where the water quality is checked by the health authorities. Even in the north, there are plenty of opportunities to swim, for example at Pite Havsbad, where the sunny beaches are known as "The Nordic Riviera" *(see p272)*. In many places, the

natural bathing spots are supplemented by water parks and fun pools offering all kinds of watery activities, such as at Skara Sommarland *(see p227)* and Sydpoolen in Södertälje.

Generally, water quality is high in Sweden and even in the cities it is sometimes possible to swim from rocks and beaches. Långholmen in central Stockholm is a favourite spot for a dip. In hot summers, however, poisonous algae sometimes blooms along the coast, so take advice locally on whether swimming is advisable.

Indoor pools are a popular choice. Stockholm has the historic Centralbadet and Sturebadet among others.

The spa and bathing culture has a long tradition in Sweden, particularly in places such as Loka Brunn *(see p143)*, with its modern facilities.

Cycling

Pedal power is a great way to experience towns and

countryside alike. The bicycle has enjoyed something of a renaissance in Sweden and Stockholm in particular has invested heavily in cycle paths and special cycle routes.

Cycling holidays have long been popular on islands with little traffic such as Öland and Gotland. However, there are now cycle trails following minor roads and disused railway lines, often marked by green cycle-trail signs. A wide range of cycling packages is available and there are plenty of places to hire bicycles, tandems and trailers.

There are 30 or so regional cycle trails around the country, which require one or more stopovers to complete the distance. They can often be combined with the extensive Sverigeleden national trail which runs 2,590 km (1,600 miles) from Helsingborg in the south to Karesuando in the far north. The trail is well-signposted and special maps are available.

On the easier routes, 97 per cent of which are paved, those who have the time for a really long cycling holiday can experience Sweden's ever-changing landscape. Information about cycling trails is available from **Svenska Cykelsällskapet**.

Another option for those who fancy pedalling is to take a trolley trip on several railway tracks across the country where rail traffic has ceased.

A cycling trip on Visingsö in Lake Vättern, offering easy routes, fascinating sights and beautiful countryside

Trekkers heading for Storsylen in the Jämtland mountains

Winter Activities

It is no surprise that Swedish skiers have dominated the World Cup at times, both in downhill and cross-country skiing. In winter, much of the country is covered in snow and there is some great skiing to be had.

There is an extensive network of cross-country skiing trails, many of which are floodlit, a necessity during the long dark evenings. It is also possible to ski on snow-covered golf courses or on iced-over lakes and the frozen waters of the archipelagos. The ice is also ideal for skating, an enjoyable experience on a sunny winter's day. Check the safety information first, as things can quickly turn serious if the ice cracks.

Sweden has hundreds of lifts for downhill skiers, which are listed on the website for the skiing organization **SLAO**. **Skistar** deal with reservations for Sweden's two largest ski resorts: Åre, 600 km (370 miles) north of Stockholm, and Sälen, just over 400 km (250 miles) north of the capital. Most people on mountain holidays stay in self-catering cottages or apartments. Accommodation must be booked well in advance, particularly during the high season, and usually for complete weeks (Sun–Sun), weekends (Thu–Sun) or short weeks (Sun–Thu). It is easiest to buy lift passes and hire skis or snowboards at the resort.

Golf

Swedish golfers have achieved major successes in recent years, particularly in the ladies' events, with Anna Nordqvist leading the way. This golfing phenomenon is partly due to the ambitious junior programme supported by many of the country's golf clubs. Under the umbrella of the **Svenska Golfförbundet**, there are more than 400 golf courses, an extremely high figure in relation to the population size. Although the climate in parts of the country may be considered unsuitable for golf, the courses offer high quality during the summer. Almost all courses are open to guest players, but

demand is great and it can be difficult to find a suitable teeing-off time in high season at many clubs. Green fees vary from 150 kr on basic courses to more than 500 kr at exclusive city clubs. You must be a member of a golf club to play as a guest on a Swedish course.

Horse Riding

Horse riding is a popular sport in Sweden, and there are almost 1,000 riding clubs. There is a wide range of riding available, from trips for beginners on Icelandic ponies to mountain trekking for those with experience. The tourist offices can provide local contacts.

Trekking on Icelandic ponies

Boating, Canoeing, White-Water Rafting

The long coastline, inviting archipelagos and numerous lakes make exploring the country by water particularly rewarding. There are almost 500 classified guest harbours offering good facilities for sailors. The classification is administered by **Svenska Kryssarklubben**, which is also a good source of information about natural harbours and boating in general. All types of craft from simple rowing boats to large motor boats and yachts can be hired from marinas around the country. **Maringuiden** offers a wealth of useful information.

Although there are no specific requirements for sailing smaller boats, you will need basic knowledge of boating even for a day trip. As a rule,

Snowboarding and skiing are popular in the Swedish mountains

documented qualifications equivalent to the Swedish skipper's certificate *"förarintyg"* are required for taking out larger boats.

There are great opportunities for canoeing, with almost 20,000 km (12,500 miles) of trails on inland waters and around the archipelagos. The website for **Kanotleder i Sverige** lists 400 tours in Canadian canoes and kayaks, along with canoeing centres and rental sites across the country. For more advanced canoeists, there are plenty of opportunities to try sea kayaks in the outer archipelagos and white-water canoeing on the Norrland rivers. White-water rides are also possible, heading down the rapids in large rubber rafts or up on jetskis.

Hunting and Fishing

Sweden has more than 300,000 hunters and during the elk hunting season some forest villages are packed. Around 100,000 elks are shot every year. As a guest of land owners and hunting teams, foreign hunters can take part in small game and elk hunts. However, in the latter case, a special elk shooting test is required as well as a hunting permit. Taking your own weapon requires a great deal of bureaucracy, so hiring a weapon is recommended. Details about conditions, hunting times and hunt organizers are available from **Svenska Jägareförbundet**.

A third of all Swedes go fishing at least once a year, and no wonder with access to the

Rod fishing, often free along Sweden's lengthy coastline

most extensive fishing waters in Europe. There are more than 200 species of saltwater fish on the west coast, some of which also venture into the brackish water of the Baltic Sea. Added to this are around 40 species of freshwater fish in the lakes and rivers.

Rod fishing in coastal waters is often free. In other waters, the necessary fishing permit can be purchased locally. The **Sveafiskekortet** permit is a nationwide option offered by Sveaskog, which administers the national forests and land covering a fifth of the country. Sweden's leading and most traditional salmon fishing waters in Blekinge's Mörrum *(see p191)* are also state-owned.

Salmon and sea trout can even be fished in the heart of Stockholm, where Strömmen has unusually clean water for a city of a million people.

Fishing trips by boat are offered widely. **Sportfiskarna** provides information about sport fishing.

DIRECTORY

General Information

Friluftsfrämjandet
Tel 08-447 44 40.
🔲 friluftsframjandet.se

Naturvårdsverket
Tel 08-698 10 00.
🔲 naturvardsverket.se

Svenska Turistföreningen (STF)
Tel 08-463 21 00.
🔲 svenskaturistforeningen.se

Cycling

Svenska Cykelsällskapet
Sweden's cycle trails.
🔲 svenska-cykelsallskapet.se

Winter Activities

Skistar
Central reservations for ski resorts of Sälen, Vemdalen and Åre.
🔲 skistar.com

SLAO
Swedish ski lifts.
slao@slao.se

Golf

Svenska Golfförbundet
Tel 08-622 1500.
🔲 sgf.golf.se

Boating, Canoeing

Kanotleder i Sverige
Canoe trails and canoe hire.
🔲 kanot.com

Maringuiden
info@maringuiden.se

Svenska Kryssarklubben
Tel 08-448 2880.
info@sxk.se

Hunting, Fishing

Sportfiskarna
Tel 08-410 806 00.
info@sportfiskarna.se

Sveafiskekortet
info@sveaskog.se

Svenska Jägarförbundet
Tel 077-183 03 00.
🔲 jagareforbundet.se

Experiencing the Swedish countryside by canoe

SURVIVAL
GUIDE

PRACTICAL INFORMATION

Sweden is a country of huge distances – it is as far from Malmö in the south to Treriksröset in the north as it is from Malmö to Rome. So, it is worth planning any trip in advance. The local tourist offices publish useful information on the Internet. All types of accommodation from luxury hotels to bed-and-breakfasts can be booked online. Once you have arrived in Sweden, there are more than 300 authorized tourist information offices nationwide which can provide help. The towns all have modern facilities for the traveller, including banking services and emergency medical care, and the public telephone system is first-class. Customs and border controls now apply mainly to travellers from countries outside the EU. For EU citizens and Norwegians, the entry procedure is relatively straightforward.

Tourist Information

Sweden has a number of tourist offices abroad, run by **Visit Sweden**. An overview of what's on offer for tourists and links to all the local tourist offices can be found at www.visit-sweden.com.

Another general website is **Arrival Guides**, where visitors can find information on regional tourism organizations and obtain detailed information about accommodation, eating out, attractions and events. Brochures and travel tips can also be requested by e-mail or phone.

In addition to the 300 official tourist information offices, information points open in summer, often attached to larger attractions. Offices with the blue and yellow "i" sign usually offer a broader service than those with the green and white "i".

The hub of Stockholm's tourist information is the **Stockholm Tourist Center**.

Visas and Customs

Citizens of virtually all countries can enter Sweden as tourists without a visa. Norwegians and visitors from European countries which have signed the Schengen agreement do not, in principle, need a passport. However, all airlines require passports for passengers flying from countries outside the Nordic region, so it is always wise to carry your passport. Always check the latest entry requirements with the Swedish embassy in your country before leaving.

Different customs regulations apply to travellers from the European Union (EU) and those from other countries. Citizens of EU countries can take an unlimited amount of alcohol and tobacco products into Sweden without having to pay tax, provided they are for personal use. Citizens from non-EU countries can take in 1 litre of spirits or 2 litres of fortified wine, including sparkling wine, 4 litres of wine, 16 litres of beer, 200 cigarettes, or 100 cigarillos, or 50 cigars or 250 g tobacco. But they can only take in goods up to a value of 3,000 Kr in addition to normal travel-related items. To import alcohol, you must be 20 years old, and for tobacco, 18.

Items such as milk, cheese, butter, eggs and potatoes may not be taken into Sweden by private individuals from non-EU countries. Norwegians and EU citizens may only take in a maximum of 15 kg (33 lb) of fish. Visitors from some other countries are permitted to bring in 1 kg (2.2 lb) of fish, but sometimes a certificate from a recognized exporter is required.

Dogs and cats from EU countries can be taken into Sweden, providing they have a veterinary certificate from the animal's home country. The animal must also have an identification marking, as well as an import permit issued by the Swedish Board of Agriculture (available from Swedish embassies).

Tax-free sales in Sweden are permitted only for travellers with a final destination outside the EU.

Tullverket provides up-to-date information in several languages by telephone and on its website.

Opening Hours and Admission Prices

Most museums and major sights are open between 10am and 6pm all year, and they often have longer opening hours in the summer. Many museums close on Mondays. Some have extended opening hours one evening in the week. Admission to a number of state-run museums is free of charge. Admission charges for other museums can be as high as 150 Kr. There is usually

Tourist information office, Stockholm

◀ Spectacular Northern Lights display in Lapland

a discounted price for children, students and senior citizens. In many places, churches are only open for services, although some have opening hours for visitors.

Stockholm and other cities have special discount cards for tourists. They can be purchased from tourist information offices and many hotels and are valid for one or more days. A family card is usually also available. The card gives free travel on public transport, free or discounted admission to museums and other attractions and events, and may also offer discounts at restaurants and shops.

Discos and nightclubs generally charge an entrance fee of 60– 120 kr. Tickets for the theatre, concerts and sporting events can be bought locally, in the cities at special ticket offices, or online at Ticnet (www.ticnet.se).

Travellers with Special Needs

In Sweden, public areas have to be accessible for physically or visually disabled people, as well as those suffering from allergies. Sweden is a long away ahead of many other countries in this respect. Wheelchair ramps and spacious toilets for disabled people are fitted in all new buildings.

Disabled car drivers with a disability permit from their home country can park in special areas.

In Stockholm, the Tunnelbana underground network and local trains are adapted for disabled passengers. Buses "kneel" at bus stops to give a reasonable height for passengers to get on or off. Visitors from abroad can obtain information in English

The GöteborgPass, giving free admission to museums

before their stay from **DHR** by telephone or via the Internet. Brochures with information about facilities for disabled visitors at theatres, cinemas, museums and libraries are available from tourist information offices.

Etiquette

Bans on smoking are increasingly common throughout Sweden. Smoking is generally not permitted in public places, including all local transport and queues at bus stops and railway stations. Restaurants and bars are also smoke free.

The Swedes queue patiently, but guard their place jealously. They are usually friendly and pleased to help foreign tourists. The use of first names is the norm and a friendly *"Hej!"* is the common greeting.

Casual clothing is acceptable almost everywhere, including restaurants, particularly in the summer.

Service is always included in restaurant prices, but it is usual to round up the bill by up to 10 per cent for good service.

The logo of Systembolaget, the state-owned liquor store

Alcohol

Swedish policy towards alcohol is restrictive. Wines and spirits can be bought only in the relatively few shops of the state monopoly **Systembolaget**. They are open Monday–Friday 10am–6pm, and Saturday 10am– 2pm. The minimum age for buying alcohol in these shops is 20, and young people may be asked to produce proof of their age. In restaurants, the minimum age for buying alcohol is 18. Most restaurants and pubs stop selling alcohol at 1am, but some bars stay open till 5am. With a maximum

permitted blood alcohol level of only 0.2 per mil, drinking is effectively banned for car drivers.

The Swedish custom of *"skåling"* confounds many visitors. To *"skål"*, look the person in the eye, raise your glass, drink, then repeat the eye contact before putting down your glass. If the glasses are full of schnapps, then Swedes like to sing their special schnapps songs.

Personal Security and Health

Sweden is a safe destination compared with most countries in the world. You needn't worry about natural disasters such as earthquakes or hurricanes. Crime does occur, with some cities suffering more than others, but this is rarely a concern for tourists. However, it is important to lock the car and hide valuables when parked. Look out for pickpockets in the summer and avoid the empty, commercial parts of city centres late at night. Sweden has a well-developed network of emergency services which travellers can call on. Rescue services and hospital emergency clinics are highly efficient.

Policeman   Guard

Police car

Protecting Property

Although Sweden is a comparatively safe place, tourists can still run into trouble at times. Especially in the summer months, the many popular events attract bag-snatchers and pickpockets. In the cities and in crowded public areas visitors should be particularly careful to keep an eye on their property, especially handbags and cameras. Avoid using unmanned cloakrooms at restaurants and museums.

Valuables and personal documents should always be locked in the hotel safe. It is equally important not to leave any valuables in your car; ideally, choose a hotel with its own parking facilities.

There is no need to carry large amounts of cash. All major credit and debit cards are accepted in virtually all shops and restaurants, and cash machines are common, at least in larger places. When taking out cash, watch out for conmen who may offer to help, but are actually after your money or card.

Personal Safety

The Swedish police are generally extremely helpful and speak good English. Police patrolling on foot or in cars are a routine sight in the cities, and mounted police are often in evidence at special events. In the suburbs, however, police can be thin on the ground. Out in the country, the police presence is low. Not all towns have evening and night police patrols and even fewer have open police stations. In many places, uniformed security guards have taken over the function of the police. They are a common feature in department stores, at train and Tunnelbana stations and as car patrols.

Stockholm, Gothenburg and Malmö are safe to stroll around on foot. Stockholm's Tunnelbana (underground railway) is efficient and comfortable, as well as being safe at most times. CCTV security systems are installed at some stations, squares, department stores and shops.

Beware the strict rules regarding alcohol, drugs and some medications when driving. A driver is guilty of drunk driving with a blood alcohol level of only 0.2 per mil and gross drunk driving (from 1.0 per mil) is punishable by imprisonment. The possession of drugs is illegal.

Breaking traffic rules, particularly speed limits, may lead to hefty fines.

For some years it has been illegal to buy sexual services in Sweden so it is the buyer, not the prostitute, who is prosecuted. Street prostitutes are now a very rare sight in the inner cities.

Lost Property

Lost or stolen property should be reported to the nearest police station. A police report will be needed for any insurance claim. In addition to the police lost property offices (Polisens Hittegodsexpedition), large towns and cities have lost property offices (Hittegodsavdelning) at railway stations, bus stations and airports. They are often only

Mounted police

open during the day and not all of them will give information over the phone. There is usually a good chance of recovering lost goods.

Visitors from abroad should contact their embassy or consulate if they lose their passport.

Emergencies

The emergency telephone number for police, fire or ambulance is **112**. It can be dialled free of charge from all public telephones, but should be used only in emergencies.

Healthcare

No special vaccinations are needed to visit Sweden. Medical assistance is available across the country from doctors and district nurses at the local medical centre open surgeries.

There are duty clinics in the evenings and at weekends, but you must make an appointment by phone. Many hospitals have accident and emergency departments, some of which are privately run. Patients should not report to emergency clinics with minor ailments. First, contact the healthcare information service **Sjukvårdsrådgivningen** for instructions in English. Its staff have up-to-date knowledge about the current situation in the city's hospitals and can assign patients to a suitable hospital or duty doctor. Particularly during the holiday period, it is always advisable to use this central information service, to avoid unnecessarily long waiting times. For severe toothache, patients can usually receive the help of a local dentist

and larger places have special duty dentists.

Citizens of other EU and EEA countries are entitled to emergency medical care at the same low rate as Swedes if they produce a European Health Insurance (EHIC) card and a valid passport or other form of identification. More extensive treatment costs extra so it is advisable to take out separate medical insurance covering specialist care, hospital expenses and repatriation before travelling.

Medicines

In Sweden, prescription medicines are sold only at pharmacies. Medicines for minor ailments are available without a prescription, and these are also sold over the counter at supermarkets and petrol stations. However, many medicines which are available over the counter abroad require a prescription in Sweden. There is also a risk that the medication prescribed at home may not be approved in Sweden. It is best to ensure that you pack sufficient medication for the duration of your trip.

Pharmacy staff are well trained and can give good advice. Unfortunately, pharmacies can be hard to find in the

Pharmacy sign

countryside and they are not open on Sundays. A limited number of natural remedies are also sold in health food stores.

Out and About

Sweden has a varied landscape and climate and it is important to respect the forces of nature. In the mountains, the weather can change very quickly from still

and sunny one moment to fog or a storm the next. If you have the right equipment and follow the rules, a trip in the mountains need not be dangerous. The STF mountain stations offer good advice about safe trails.

Along the coast drowning accidents claim many lives every year. Avoid going out in flimsy craft and boats which are beyond your capabilities. Take advice from local people about the weather.

There is no need to worry about the forest predators – bears, wolves, lynxes and wolverines. They are shy creatures and prefer to avoid people. The same applies to Sweden's only poisonous snake, the adder. However, anyone bitten by a snake should seek medical advice.

Mosquitoes can be a nuisance from June to autumn, especially at dusk, along waterways and in the mountains. Pharmacies stock mosquito repellent. In the archipelagos, there is also a risk of being bitten by ticks, which carry a number of diseases. Ticks should be removed from the skin with tweezers as quickly as possible. If the redness around the bite area persists, consult a doctor.

Ambulance

Banking and Local Currency

Sweden has retained its own currency, the Swedish krona, rather than adopting the euro. A number of shops in major tourist areas will accept euros, but goods are almost exclusively priced in kronor. As many banks are now cash-free or do not offer currency exchange, visitors are recommended to change currency at bureaux de change in the main towns, which have longer opening hours. Automatic cash machines can be found outside most banks and in shopping centres across the country. Credit and debit cards are accepted virtually everywhere, and the larger stores will take traveller's cheques.

Bankomat ATM

Banks and Bureaux de Change

There are plenty of banks in the towns, all providing a good service. Their opening times vary, but the normal hours are 9.30am–3pm. Some banks stay open until 6pm at least once a week. All banks are closed at weekends and on public holidays, as well as the day before a public holiday.

Svenska Kassaservice, which handles the Swedish post office Posten's cash transactions, has almost 1,000 offices around the country. They are agents for certain banks and accept withdrawals on a debit card.

Various bureaux de change chains are represented in Sweden, including **Forex** and **X-Change**. In city centres there is always a bureau de change office close by. Changing money in your hotel is the most expensive option. It is worth checking exchange rates and commission charges, because the differences can be significant. Currency can be changed at international airports from 5.30am, and from 7am at city train stations seven days a week.

ATMs

There are nearly 3,000 automatic cash machines throughout the country. Foreign visitors can use all cash machines provided that they have a bank card with a PIN code that is linked to, for example, Visa or MasterCard. Machines usually have instructions in several languages. The charge for withdrawing cash varies according to the type of card.

Banks and Bureaux de Change

Forex
Service Center
Tel 0771-22 22 21.
W forex.se

Handelsbanken
Kungsträdgårdsgatan 2.
Map 4 C1.
Tel 0771-77 88 99.
W handelsbanken.se

Nordea
Hamngatan 12.
Map 3 D4.
Tel 0771-22 44 88.
From abroad: +46 771 22 44 88.
W nordea.se

SEB
Sergels Torg 2.
Map 2 C4.
Tel 0771-365 365.
From abroad: +46 771 365 365.
W seb.se

Swedbank
Brunkebergstorg 8.
Map 3 D4.
Tel 0771-22 11 22.
W swedbank.se

X-change
Tel 020-39 40 00.
W x-change.se

Credit and Debit Cards

American Express
Tel 0771-295 600 (lost cards).
Tel 020-79 51 55 (trav. cheques).
W americanexpress.com/sweden

Diners Club
(lost cards and other assistance)
Tel 08-14 68 78.
W dinersclub.se

Eurocard
(lost cards and other assistance)
Tel 08-14 67 67.
W eurocard.se

MasterCard Global Service
(lost cards and other assistance)
Tel 020-79 13 24.
W mastercard.com/se

Visa
(lost cards and other assistance)
Tel 020-79 56 75.
W visa.se

The head office of Handelsbanken on Kungsträdgårdsgatan, Stockholm

Forex bureau de change, situated in large towns and at airports

Credit and Debit Cards

All the well-known credit cards, such as **Visa, Diners Club, Eurocard** and **MasterCard,** are accepted across Sweden, but not all places accept **American Express** because of opposition to the relatively high charges that the retailer has to pay.

Cards can be used not just at larger hotels and restaurants, but at nearly all shops and services. If you pay by credit card, you will need a PIN code, because all transactions are electronically processed, or most shops will ask you to produce proof of identity. Some shops also offer a cash withdrawal service for small amounts in conjunction with purchases.

Cash machines can be used to make withdrawals using an internationally accepted credit card with a PIN code.

If your credit or debit card is lost or stolen, contact the company that isued the card immediately. In order to ensure your card works overseas, it is worth contacting your bank or credit card provider in advance of travelling.

Traveller's cheques are not accepted in all shops, but it is possible to exchange them for cash at banks.

Currency

Sweden's currency is the krona (plural kronor). The krona (abbreviated as SEK or Kr) is divided into 100 öre. The smallest coin is 1 Kr and the largest note is 1,000 kronor, which is not used much. If possible, it is advisable not to carry notes of more than 500 Kr.

Although Sweden has not adopted the euro, many shops in tourist areas and border towns will accept payment in euros, but will usually give change in kronor.

Notes

20 Kr (Selma Lagerlöf)

Swedish currency notes are issued in denominations of 20, 50, 100, 500 and 1,000 kronor. They depict famous Swedes, including monarchs, scientists and authors.

50 Kr (Jenny Lind)

500 Kr (King Karl XI)

100 Kr (Carl von Linné)

1000 Kr (King Gustav Vasa)

Coins

Coins are issued in values of 1, 5 and 10 kronor. The 1 Kr and 10 Kr coins depict Sweden's monarch on the obverse side while the 5 Kr has his monogram on the reverse side.

1 krona

5 kronor

10 kronor

Communications and Media

Sweden has a first-class public telephone system. A top-ranking telecommunications industry and high living standards have placed the Swedes among the world's biggest users of telephones. Although the fixed telephone system is well developed, there are now nearly as many mobile phone users as there are people in the country. With the advent of the 3G and 4G systems allowing video telephony and advanced data services, only a very small percentage of the population does not have coverage. Internet use is widespread, with impressive investment in broadband.

A modern Swedish phone kiosk

Local and International Phone Calls

Sweden is divided into 250 dialling code areas. The prefix for international calls from Sweden is 00. Then dial the country code and the phone number without the initial zero of the area code. To dial Sweden from abroad, the country code is 46. For enquiries such as whether your phone will operate in the mountains, call **Telia customer services**.

Local numbers can be obtained by calling directory enquiries on 118 118, or online at Eniro (www.eniro.se) or Hitta (www.hitta.se). The number for directory enquiries also provides listings of mobile numbers. Computer-to-computer phone calls allow visitors to call free of charge using the Internet. Popular service providers include Skype and Google Talk.

Public Telephones

The number of public telephone kiosks has shown a marked decline, as most Swedes have a mobile phone. The remaining public phones are mainly card-operated and are usually found in public places such as hospitals, airports and public-transport locations. They are owned by Telia and are cheapest to use with a Swedish phone-card. These can be bought at newspaper kiosks (for example, Pressbyrån) and in supermarkets and shops, and are available for 50 or 120 units. Instructions on how to use public telephones are also shown in English. The emergency number is 112. Some 020 and 0200 numbers can be called free of charge. Coin-operated phones are very rare.

Mobile Phones

Sweden's mobile network is based on GSM, and most foreign visitors will be able to use their GSM, 3G or 4G phones here. However, visitors from North America should check with their service providers to ensure their phones are GSM-compatible. The major network providers in Sweden include **Telia**, **Telenor**, Tele2/Comviq and 3 Sweden. Inexpensive GSM mobile phones can be purchased at a number of stores, including The Phone House (in Stockholm), Telia and Telenor, together with a prepaid SIM card for local phone calls.

Within the Stockholm area, mobile users must dial the area code 08 before a local number; the country code is not required.

The GSM network offers good service coverage outside the cities. Having a mobile phone is a good idea even out in the wilderness, although there is no guarantee that you will be able to call for help if you need it.

Internet

Although Internet access is offered in most hotels, you may be charged a daily fee. Hotels that focus on business travellers may have computers available for use in your room. Public computers are generally found at local libraries; users may be asked to present some form of identification.

Sidewalk Express offers pay-per-minute Internet access from computer terminals across Sweden, including at Arlanda Airport, Stockholm's Central Station and a number of Pressbyrån and 7-Eleven stores. The cost is usually around 25–35 Kr per hour.

Computer terminals at Sidewalk Express in Stockholm's Central Station

Wireless Internet (Wi-Fi) is widely available, with many public places, hotels and cafés offering Wi-Fi hot spots. Some are free of charge; others are inexpensive.

Postal Services

The Swedish postal service has an almost 400-year history, but many Swedes think the service has deteriorated in recent years. Post offices have been closed and replaced by a few large postal centres, mainly for companies. For the general public, there are small service points, primarily in supermarkets and at petrol stations. They have the advantage of longer opening hours in the evenings and at weekends. The disadvantage is a frequent lack of space and services. Perhaps the best service is provided in the really remote areas by mobile postal workers. Stamps can be bought at post offices, shops, Pressbyrån kiosks and tourist information offices. The basic postage for a postcard or letter under 20 g within Sweden is 5.50 Kr (non-denominated stamp) or 6 Kr (denominated stamp); for abroad the postage is 12 Kr. Postboxes are painted blue for local letters and yellow for other domestic and international mail. Collection times are shown on the postbox and sometimes take place in the early afternoon. In large towns there are last-minute postboxes, which are emptied in the evenings.

One of the country's many Pressbyrån kiosks

Post office logo

Yellow postbox for national and international, blue for local mail

Most international courier services – such as **DHL**, **FedEx** and **TNT** – are represented in the cities, and special services are also operated by the Swedish post office, **Posten**.

TV and Radio

Most hotels provide a television in the room with both national and foreign channels. The most frequently used are the Swedish SVT1, SVT2, TV3, TV4 and Channel 5, as well as the international CNN, Sky News, BBC and Eurosport channels. SVT1 and 2 are state-run public-service channels. SVT2 and TV4 broadcast local programmes in the morning and evening, including weather forecasts.

There are also a number of local radio stations, broadcasting mainly international and Swedish music. P6, SR International broadcasts programmes in eight languages (including English) on 89.6 MHz.

Newspapers and Magazines

Major foreign newspapers and magazines can be bought in the cities, at airports and at other transport hubs. Pressbyrån kiosks, tobacconists, department stores and some tourist information offices stock a limited selection of foreign publications.

TRAVEL INFORMATION

Stockholm Arlanda is the busiest of Sweden's international airports, although a number of other airports have international flights, notably Gothenburg's Landvetter and Sturup, near Malmö, in the south. Since summer 2000, Sweden has been linked with Continental Europe by a bridge over the Öresund Strait to Denmark for road and rail traffic. It is now possible to fly to Copenhagen and take a short train journey across the bridge to Malmö. There are still a number of car ferry services operating between Denmark and Sweden, as well as across the Baltic Sea from Finland and the Baltic States, and across the North Sea from Norway. In summer, an increasing number of cruise liners call into Swedish ports. Express buses operate services from cities across Europe.

Arrival by Air

Most major European cities have direct flights to one of Stockholm's three airports: Arlanda, Skavsta and Bromma. Landvetter near Gothenburg and Sturup outside Malmö also have international traffic. Arlanda is served by around 52 international airlines. It is also possible to fly via Copenhagen in Denmark. The leading Scandinavian airline **SAS** dominates. Other operators include **Lufthansa**, **British Airways** and **Finnair**. **Delta Air Lines** operates from the US to Europe with onward flights to Sweden via major airlines such as Air France or KLM; **American Airlines** flies to the UK with onward connections via British Airways.

Arlanda is 40 km (25 miles) north of central Stockholm and is also a hub for Swedish domestic flights and charter services. Bromma, situated 7 km (4 miles) from the city centre, may only be used by less environmentally damaging

Arlanda Express linking Arlanda Airport with central Stockholm

aircraft. Skavsta lies 100 km (60 miles) south of Stockholm, near Nyköping. Low-cost airline **Ryanair** flies routes to Skavsta, Gothenburg and Malmö from several UK airports and to other destinations in Sweden from other parts of Europe.

Getting from and to the Airport

All the international airports are served by airport buses to the city centre in conjunction with arrivals and departure times. Stockholm's Arlanda Airport has a **Flygbussarna** bus service, which operates every 10 minutes at peak times. Journey time is 45 minutes to the City Terminal at Central Station. An onward journey by taxi can be booked on the bus. The taxi ride into town from the airport is quicker, but more expensive. Most taxi firms have a fixed charge to the city centre. Avoid unauthorized taxis and check the fare before departure. The shortest journey time is by the pricier **Arlanda Express** train, a 20-minute trip to Central Station. Trains depart every 10 minutes at peak times from the two stations, Arlanda South (serving terminals 2, 3 and 4) and Arlanda North (for terminal 5).

Air Fares

Fare options are many and varied, particularly if you are flexible about departure and arrival dates, or can book well in advance.

Increased competition between the airlines has made it considerably cheaper to fly to Sweden from many European destinations, and now SAS offers low-cost tickets with a no-frills service to meet the competition. It is possible to find return flights from London, Paris or Frankfurt for less than £80. Tour operators often have packages with attractive air fares and accommodation included. Newspaper advertisements and travel companies' websites have details of last-minute deals.

Terminal 5 (International) at Stockholm's Arlanda Airport

Ferry from Finland on the way to its terminal in Stockholm

Arrival by Ferry

There are a number of ferry companies operating direct services across the North Sea and the Baltic to Sweden. The large car ferries used on most routes offer plenty of passenger comforts, including good food, entertainment options and shopping facilities.

Although the Öresund Bridge has reduced ferry traffic from Denmark, the short Helsingør–Helsingborg hop still has several ferries an hour operated by **Scandlines**. **Stena Line** covers the routes Grenå–Varberg and Fredrikshavn–Gothenburg.

The busiest route in terms of passenger numbers is from Finland with regular crossings from Helsinki, Turku and Mariehamn to Stockholm and Kapellskär. Both **Viking Line** and **Tallink Silja Line** have terminals in Stockholm – at Stadsgården and Värtahamnen respectively. The crossing takes about 15.5 hours from Helsinki and 11 hours from Turku. **Vasabåtarna** operates ferries between Vaasa in Finland and Umeå in northern Sweden. From Estonia, Tallink Silja Line operates the routes between Tallinn and Stockholm and between Riga in Latvia and Stockholm.

Polferries has the routes Świnoujście–Ystad and Gdansk–Nynäshamn. **Stena Line** operates the Gdynia–Karlskrona route.

Trelleborg is the major port for traffic from Germany. **TT-Line** goes from Rostock and Travemünde, while **Scandlines** goes from Rostock and Sassnitz, as does **Stena Line**, which also sails the Kiel–Gothenburg route.

Arrival by Train or Express Bus

There are excellent train links from continental Europe and Norway and a large network of express bus routes. To find out the best connections by coach or train to Sweden from Copenhagen, Oslo and Sassnitz (Germany), visit **ResRobot** website.

Arrival by Car

Motorists arriving from Denmark can use the spectacular Öresund Bridge between Copenhagen and Malmö *(see p185)*. On the Swedish side, the toll bridge connects with the E6 motorway to the north. Alternatively, there are car ferries.

Car ferries are also the most practical option from Finland and the Baltic States, since driving around the Baltic Sea can take two days.

The borders with Finland and Norway have customs posts which are often unmanned. However, the entry regulations still apply *(see p318)*.

Arrival hall at the Central Station in Stockholm

Getting Around Sweden

Flying within Sweden has its advantages considering the enormous distances between places, and in many cases the fares are reasonably priced. The high standard of overnight sleeper trains makes long journeys by train a comfortable option. The X2000 Express train running between the major cities often competes well in terms of time and comfort with domestic flights. Elsewhere in the country, buses provide much of the public transport. Travelling by boat offers exciting opportunities to discover Sweden's magnificent archipelagos and waterways.

SAS, one of the companies offering domestic flights in Sweden

Domestic Flights

The vast length of Sweden makes domestic flights a convenient option, and deregulation and increased competition in recent years have made prices more reasonable. Of the 45 airports offering scheduled flights, 12 belong to and are operated by state-owned **Swedavia**. Visit the **Luftfartsverket** website for links to information on all of Sweden's airports, including flights and current arrivals and departures.

Stockholm/Arlanda dominates the domestic flight scene, but several companies have chosen to fly from the capital's more centrally located Bromma Airport. Landvetter, outside Gothenburg, and Sturup, outside Malmö, are other major airports.

Flight times are generally short: Stockholm–Gothenburg takes 55 minutes. The longest direct flight, Stockholm–Kiruna, takes 1 hr 50 mins.

SAS is still the leading airline in terms of passenger numbers. Other operators include **Malmö Aviation** and **Norwegian**. Tickets can be bought at travel agents or directly from the airlines. Tickets booked online

can generally be paid for with a credit card, then printed out or collected at the airport. It is worth searching for the lowest prices, particularly if you book a long way in advance. Young people under 26 can buy cheap standby tickets.

Travellers to Malmö could consider flying to Kastrup in Copenhagen, as there is a fast train transfer to central Malmö across the Öresund Bridge.

Larger airports are served by airport buses, which operate in conjunction with arrivals and departures.

Travelling by Train

There is a well-developed train network covering parts of Sweden from the Öresund Bridge in the south to Riksgränsen in the north. Stations and services are good by international standards. The trains are run by a number of competing companies. The state-run **SJ** operates most long-distance routes. Other major players include **Veolia Transport** and **Tågkompaniet**, which have parts of the lines in Norrland. At county level, train services are run by local train companies in partnership with bus services and in some cases ferry services.

Travel involving different companies and forms of transport is administered by **Samtrafiken**, which is part-owned by each of the transport companies. Resplus is a unique cooperative service offering travellers one ticket for all journeys and all transport operators in the country.

Since the 1990s, airlines have experienced tough competition from the SJ high-speed train (formerly known as the X2000 Express), which links the cities of Copenhagen/ Malmö, Gothenburg, Östersund and Falun to Stockholm. The journey time is around 5 hours from Malmö and 3 hours from Gothenburg. The trains offer a business class service similar to that of airlines.

InterCity is the main long-distance alternative to the SJ, offering first- and second-class seats. The overnight sleeper trains are recommended for longer journeys such as Gothenburg–Östersund and routes in northern Norrland. The standard is high, and you can often have your own compartment with shower, if you wish. Compartments contain between one and six beds.

SJ logo

Train passing through the village of Storlien in Southern Norrland

Ticket prices vary considerably depending on the type of train. Discounts are worth searching for.

Tickets can be bought online and at larger stations. Buying tickets on the train attracts a fee of around 100 kr. Note that seat/berth reservations are necessary for the SJ and night trains.

The **Inlandsbanan** line operates in summer, offering the opportunity to travel through the Swedish wilderness, forests and mountains. It runs 1,300 km (800 miles) from Kristinehamn on Lake Vänern north to Gällivare in northern Lapland.

Travelling by Bus

In many places buses are the only public transport available and although services are patchy in rural areas, it is possible to get about. Local timetables are on **Samtrafiken**'s website.

Express buses compete with trains and airlines on longer routes. Journey times are longer, but ticket prices are lower and the buses are modern. See Samtrafiken's website for routes and times. Some bus companies, such as **Swebus Express**, do not require pre-booking. If one bus is full, another one is laid on.

Many express bus companies arrange special excursions in the tourist season. Contact the tourist information offices for information. Trips are also arranged to the southern Fjällen where there is no train line. **Fjällexpressen** is one of the operators running ski buses from Stockholm and Gothenburg.

Abisko's modest station building on the Malmbanan line

Travelling by Boat

Sweden's long coastline, vast lakes and extensive archipelagos make for busy boat services. In addition to the scheduled services, sightseeing trips and tours are offered in summer, occasionally on classic old steamers.

The Dalsland, Strömsholm and Kinda canals attract some charming boats, but the best tourist trail is the Göta Canal *(see pp150–51)*. Sweden's blue ribbon takes you 611 km (380 miles) in a relaxed three days, negotiating 65 locks, the country's three largest lakes and some of Sweden's most attractive scenery. Contact **Rederi AB Göta Kanal** for more information.

Boat services to the Baltic Sea's largest island, Gotland, are run by **Destination Gotland**; its high-speed ferries take less than 3 hours on either of the Nynäshamn–Visby or Oskarshamn–Visby routes. In peak summer season, there are up to eight departures a day. Although the ferries can take 500 cars per trip, it can be difficult to get a place for a car during holiday periods if you have not booked in advance.

DIRECTORY

Domestic Flights

Luftfartsverket
Airports, timetables, information
w lfv.se/en/About-us/Swedish-Airports

Malmö Aviation
Tel 0771-55 00 10.
w malmoaviation.se

Norwegian
Tel 0770-45 77 00.
w norwegian.com

SAS
Tel 0770-727 727.
w scandinavian.net

Swedavia
w swedavia.se

Train, Bus, Boat

Samtrafiken
Tel 08-762 44 00
(general enquiries).
w reseplanerare.resrobot.se

Train Travel

Inlandsbanan
Tel 0771-53 53 53.
w inlandsbanan.se

SJ
Tel 0771-75 75 75.
w sj.se

Tågkompaniet
Tel 0771-444 111.
w tagkompaniet.se

Veolia Transport
Tel 0771-26 00 00.
w connex.se

Bus Travel

Fjällexpressen
Tel 08-12 00 45 60.
w fjallexpressen.com

Swebus Express
Tel 0771-218 218.
w swebus.se

Boat Travel

Destination Gotland
Tel 0771-22 33 00.
w destinationgotland.se

Rederi AB Göta Kanal
Tel 031-80 63 15.
w stromma.se/sv/Gota-Kanal

Gotland's high-speed catamaran service approaching Visby

Road Travel in Sweden

Distances within Sweden are huge, and in the rural areas travelling in your own or a rented car is often the only way of getting about. The well-developed road network varies in quality, but the major roads are generally of a good standard. State-run ferries operate a free service in the archipelagos. Although traffic can be heavy in the cities in rush hour, it is never on the same scale as in the UK and on the Continent, and Swedish motorists are generally good-natured. For advice on driving in Stockholm, *see p332*.

Elk on the road, a hazard for motorists in the forests

Road Standards

Sweden has an extensive road network, with more than 210,000 km (130,000 miles) open for public use. Almost the same again is not accessible, primarily forestry roads which are closed with a boom. The majority of the public roads are sealed and of a good standard. The exceptions can be found in the forested counties of the northwest, where ice and heavy traffic can make the roads difficult to negotiate.

The national road network comprises *europavägar* ("European motorways"), *riksvägar* (national roads) and *länsvägar* (county roads). Motorways such as the E4 and stretches of the E20 and E6 make up less than 1,200 km (700 miles). With the exception of the Öresund and Svinesund bridges, roads are toll-free.

The three-lane highways require some attention for the uninitiated. The traffic runs in opposite directions along one or two lanes with a wire barrier to separate the flow.

Traffic Rules

Generally, Swedish traffic is comparatively well organized and most motorists follow the rules of the road. Road safety is good, despite occasionally dense traffic and severe weather conditions. The number of road fatalities is around 500 a year, the same level as in the 1940s.

The most common breach of the rules relates to speed limits, despite the presence of speed cameras and radar patrols. The fines are high and there is a risk of losing your licence for serious speeding offences.

The maximum speed on motorways is 120 km/h (74 mph), but the limit is more often 110 km/h (68 mph), 90 km/h (55 mph) or 80 km/h (50 mph), depending on the road. On country roads the limit is usually 70–80 km/h (43–50 mph) and in built-up areas the limit is 40 or 50 km/h (25 or 31 mph). The limit is reduced to 30 km/h (19 mph) around all schools and nurseries. Residential areas often have traffic calming measures such as road narrowing and speed bumps. By law, the driver and all passengers must wear seatbelts. Children under a height of 135 cm (53 in) must use child seats.

Beware of the strict rules regarding alcohol and driving. A driver is guilty of drink-driving with a blood alcohol level of only 0.2 per mil and gross drink-driving (from 1.0 per mil) is punishable by imprisonment.

Motorists must give way to pedestrians at crossings not controlled by lights. Vehicles must stop at junctions onto major roads, even if there is no Stop sign. At roundabouts, vehicles already on the roundabout always have right of way. Traffic lights with a continuous amber light mean "stop" and there are hefty fines for driving through a red light. Side-lights or dipped headlights must be used even during daylight hours.

Winter tyres must be used from 1 Dec–31 Mar. Studded tyres may be used, but not during the period 1 May–30 Sep, unless the road conditions require them.

Car Ferries

State-run car ferries operate free of charge in the archipelagos and across some of the larger rivers. Some places also have private ferries, which do levy a charge. You rarely need to book, but check the timetable carefully as the ferries may not run late at night unless in emergencies. **Färjerederiet Trafikverket** can provide information.

Uddevallabron on the E6, one of Sweden's many road bridges

Road Signs

Swedish road signs mostly follow the European standard, but the country also has some signs of its own. Signs carrying the symbol for elk, reindeer or deer warn drivers that there is a major risk of colliding with wildlife. Thousands of accidents involving animals occur every year and a collision between a car and a full-grown elk is often fatal. The risk is particularly high in the summer around 5am–8am and 10pm–2am, when visibility is poor. Fences along the roadside are no guarantee that animals won't suddenly appear on the road.

As in the rest of Europe, brown signs with white symbols indicate recommended tourist routes, heritage sites, tourist areas and attractions along the road such as a national park or a historic building.

Individual attractions may be indicated by a sign with a white "pretzel" on a blue background.

Warning sign for elk

Parking

There is usually a charge for parking in towns and built-up areas, especially in the centre of towns and cities. City car parks and on-street parking are often expensive. Sometimes charges apply 24-hours a day and at weekends, too. Many ticket machines accept credit cards and petrol cards, but they may not always work, so it is best to keep a good number of 10 Kr coins to hand.

Diligent traffic wardens hunt out illegally parked cars and the fines can be high, particularly if you have parked illegally in a space reserved for disabled drivers.

Where parking is free during the night, there is sometimes a parking ban on certain days for cleaning, so it is always important to check the signs – otherwise your car may be towed away. Supermarkets and other large stores often have free parking for a few hours, but be aware that sometimes they require a special parking ticket for your windscreen showing your arrival time.

Fuel And Services

There are plenty of service stations along the major roads and in built-up areas, but they may be few and far between in rural areas. Although some stations are manned 24-hours a day, drivers are often directed to automatic pumps which take cards and notes.

It is sensible to fill up before a night drive. In the event of technical problems, there are few places which can help outside working hours – garages are usually closed in the evenings and at weekends.

Assistancekåren and **Falck** offer emergency roadside assistance. They often have an agreement with motoring organizations and insurance companies abroad.

Renting a Car

In addition to the familiar international car hire chains, there are a number of local options, including the petrol companies' extensive rental service. Most places will have some form of car rental.

It is possible to pre-book cars at airports and major train stations, often for one-way rental where you leave the car at your destination. Bookings can be made from abroad via the Internet or by phone. You generally only need a valid driving licence to rent a car, but there may be an age limit of 20, or even 25 for exclusive vehicles. Prices vary considerably, so it is worth shopping around. Special weekend deals are common and considering Sweden's long distances, it is best to opt for offers which include unlimited mileage.

Traffic warden

Winter Driving

Road conditions in the winter vary depending on the severity of the weather and the location. Studded tyres are permitted in Sweden and their use is recommended, at least from central Sweden northwards.

Anyone not used to winter driving should not venture out if there is a risk of snow and ice. The major roads are treated with salt, and ploughing is generally good, but even in Skåne in the far south, snow storms can cause traffic chaos and in some years military tracked vehicles have had to be called out.

Getting Around Stockholm

Stockholm is a perfect city for pedestrians. Distances between sights are short, and there is always something interesting to discover among the eye-catching vistas and waterfront scenes. Cycling is popular and there are many cycle lanes throughout the city, although for the visitor a green area such as Djurgården might be more relaxing for a cycle trip. Public transport on buses, trams, underground trains, local trains and ferries is efficient. Apart from Gamla Stan, and during the rush hours, driving a car in Stockholm is relatively easy, although parking can be difficult.

Stockholm on Foot

In central Stockholm, walking is the best way to see the sights and get a feel for the place. Road users are more disciplined here than in many other cities. Pedestrians are not allowed to cross a road against a red light, but motorists must stop and give way to pedestrians at zebra crossings with traffic lights.

The clear street signs make it easy to find one's way around, and Stockholmers are always glad to help visitors. There are walking and cycling routes everywhere in the city. Take care not to step out in the cycle lane, which is often marked just with a white line to separate it from the walking lane.

Gamla Stan is a popular area for exploring on foot, and there is always something to see around Kungsträdgården as well. In good weather, nothing beats Djurgården, with its host of attractions set in beautiful parkland only a short distance from the centre.

There are pleasant waterfront walks along the quays, for example from Stadshuset along Norr Mälarstrand and the Riddarfjärden bay.

Walks with multilingual guides are organized regularly, often with a special theme – history, architecture or parks, for example.

Cycling

The capital's network of cycle paths is increasing all the time, but you need to be an

Taking a waterfront stroll along Djurgårdsbrunnsviken

experienced city cyclist if you want to explore the central area from the saddle. Otherwise Stockholm and its surrounding area are tailor-made for cycling. Djurgården is a lovely place to explore by bike. It is possible to hire bicycles from **Djurgårdscykeln**; they are free with an SL Access Card (*see Public Transport, opposite*).

Driving in Stockholm

Anyone familiar with driving in large cities will have no problems in Stockholm. It is relatively easy to get about by car, except during the rush hours (7.30am–9.30am, 11.30am–1pm, and 3.30–6pm). Cars are not really necessary in the city centre because of the short distances between sights and excellent public transport. However, a car is an advantage if you want to explore further afield.

Congestion charges were introduced in 2007 to tackle busy traffic and to improve the environment.

The speed limit is usually 50 km/h (31 mph), but near schools it is 30 km/h (19 mph). Speeds up to 70 km/h (43 mph) are permitted only on the main roads in and out of the city.

It is often hard to find a parking space. In some areas parking charges apply 24-hours a day, but usually parking is free in the evenings, at night and at weekends. Check for street cleaning times when parking is prohibited.

Stockholm's Tunnelbana

— T10 Kungsträdgården – Hjulsta
— T11 Kungsträdgården – Akalla
— T13 Norsborg – Ropsten
— T14 Fruängen – Mörby centrum
— T17 Åkeshov – Skarpnäck
— T18 Alvik – Farsta strand
— T19 Hässelby strand – Hagsätra

The city's traffic wardens are diligent. Being wrongly parked could cost you a fine of 550 kr or more. Do not leave valuables in your car, particularly in a car park.

Taxis

Distances between places in the city centre are short and brief journeys by taxi start from around 200 kr. There are usually plenty of taxis available, particularly at taxi ranks and major sights, with the exception of the rush hours. You can also hail an empty taxi, indicated by the illuminated sign on the car roof. The best method is to order a taxi by phone or book one in advance. It is always worth enquiring what the fare is likely to be, as many companies charge a fixed rate. Be careful about using unauthorized taxis without a taxi sign on the outside, or a taxi identity card on display inside, especially at night.

Public Transport

All public transport in the county of Stockholm is under the control of **Stockholms Lokaltrafik**, but the actual services are run by several companies. An extensive network of local trains, underground trains, buses and ferries carries hundreds of thousands of commuters in from the suburbs every day. In the city centre, the Tunnelbana (T-bana) underground system's green, red and blue lines are the mainstay, supplemented by city buses, a few tramlines and ferry routes.

On regular lines in the Stockholm area there is a choice of tickets: single-trip or 1-, 3-,

Ferry linking Gamla Stan and Djurgården

7- and 30-day travel cards. It is worth buying an SL Access Card, which can be topped up with credit and held to a card reader as you enter your chosen method of transport. The tickets are valid for one hour from the start of the journey. Single tickets can be bought on departure, while return tickets, SL Access Cards and travel cards are sold at Pressbyrån outlets and SL and T-bana stations.

The network of red city buses is built around a number of blue "feeder" routes. These run more frequently. Many streets in the city centre have special bus lanes which speed up the traffic. The best routes for sightseeing are 3, 4, 47, 62 and 69.

Run by **Waxholmsbolaget**, public transport in the archipelago is good all year round, with more frequent services from June to August. An excellent way to explore the archipelago is to take the ferries from Strömkajen, which stop off at countless picturesque jetties along the way.

Other recommended trips include Birka, Drottningholm and Mariefred/Gripsholm *(see pp116–17)* A popular way of getting to Djurgården is on the ferry from Slussen to Allmänna Gränd. SL's one-day and three-day cards are valid on the Djurgården ferry.

Sightseeing

A pleasant way of enjoying Stockholm from the water is to take an excursion run by Stockholm Sightseeing (**Strömma Kanalbolaget**).

A "Round Kungsholmen" tour departs hourly from the quayside near the City Hall. The "Under Stockholm's Bridges" and "Round Djurgården" tours depart from Strömkajen near the Grand Hotel, and passengers are also picked up from Nybroplan. Tickets can be bought at both these points. A commentary is provided on headsets in several languages. The tours generally run once an hour. Most tours are only available in the summer, but some run until December.

Sightseeing tours by bus include the **Open Top Tours** double-deckers, which run between strategic stops close to attractions in central Stockholm. Passengers can hop on and off along the way.

Red city bus and blue "feeder" bus

General Index

Acknowledgments

Streiffert Förlag would like to thank the following staff at Dorling Kindersley:

Publisher
Douglas Amrine

Publishing Managers
Jane Ewart, Anna Streiffert

Senior Editor
Christine Stroyan

Map Co-ordinator
Casper Morris

DTP Manager
Jason Little

Production Controller
Linda Dare

Additional Picture Research
Rachel Barber

Additional Photography
Ian O'Leary

Dorling Kindersley would like to thank all those whose contributions and assistance have made the preparation of this book possible.

Main Contributors
ULF JOHANSSON has produced Swedish guidebooks such as *Sverigeboken* and *Sverigevägvisaren*. He has also been a publisher and year-book editor at the Swedish tourist association Svenska Turistföreningen.

MONA NEPPENSTROM is an editor and travel journalist and has written a large number of Swedish guidebooks, including *Sverigeboken*, *Sverigevägvisaren*, *Turisttoppen* and rail company SJ's travel guide series *Längs spåret*.

KAJ SANDELL wrote the *Eyewitness Stockholm* travel guide. He is a journalist and formerly wrote for Swedish publishers Åhlén & Åkerlunds Förlag and Swedish daily broadsheet *Dagens Nyheter*.

Factchecking
Lena Ahlgren

Proofreader
Stewart J Wild

Index
Helen Peters

Artwork Reference
Svenska Aerobilder AB

Revisions Team
Namrata Adhwaryu, Kate Berens, Subhashree Bharti, Hilary Bird, Alannah Eames, Anna-Maria Espsater, Anna Freiberger, Amy Harrison, Yvette Holman, Shobhna Iyer, Alison McGill, Sonal Modha, Vikki Nousiainen, Susie Peachey, Rada Radojicic, Lucy Richards, Ellen Root, Marta Bescos Sanchez, Sands Publishing Solutions, Kathleen Blankenship Sauret, Azeem Siddiqui, Deepika Verma, Nikhil Verma, Alex Whittleton.

Photography Permissions
The publishers would like to thank all those who gave permission to photograph at museums, palaces, churches, restaurants, hotels, stores and other sights too numerous to list individually. Particular thanks go to the Guild of Museum Directors in Stockholm for permitting access to picture archives as well as making additional photographing of objects and exhibitions possible.

Picture Credits
a = above; b = below/bottom; c = centre; f = far; l = left; r = right; t = top. .

Works of art have been reproduced with the permission of the following copyright holders:

© ADAGP, Paris and DACS, London 2008: Paradise 1963 Jean Tinguely and Niki de sainte Phalle 53bl, 80clb; © DACS, London: Nils Ferlin KG Bejemark 239c; Concrete Jonas Bohlin 31tr; Noble Glass carafe Gunnar Cyren 304clb; The Dying Dandy Nils Dardel 86bl; The Child's Brain Giorgio De Chirico 85bl; The Dance Carl Eldh 107bl; Selma Lagerlof Carl Eldh 237bl; Einar Forseth 106tr; Simon Gate 157tr; statue of Evert Taube Gordon Willy Gordon 66clb; Hans Hedberg 30tr; Visby Wall Hanna Hirsch-Pauli 168tr; Altarpiece in Jukkasjärvi Church Bror Hjort 276c; Märta Måås-Fjetterström 30br; Orpheus Carl Milles 75tl; Poseidon Carl Milles 197cr, 204t; Sigurd Persson 31tl; Crux rug Pia Wallen 304bl; © DACS. London/VAGA, New York 2008: Monogram Robert Rauschenberg 86crb; © Sucession Picasso/DACS, London 2008; Breakfast Outdoors Pablo Picasso 84tr.

Every effort has been made to trace the copyright holders. Dorling Kindersley apologizes for any unintentional omission and would be pleased, in such cases, to add an acknowledgement in future editions.

Commissioned by the publisher, the book's main photographers, Peter Hanneberg, Erik Svensson and Jeppe Wikström, produced the majority of the photographs reproduced in this book. They have also contributed archive pictures which have been listed among the other picture credits. The publisher would like to thank the photographers and all the other individuals, organizations and picture libraries for permission to reproduce their photographs and illustrations:

Alamy images: Rolf Adlercreutz 324br; Annems 20; Arterra Picture Library 2-3; Marie-Louise Avery 292cl; blickwinkel 144; Matija Brumen 270tl; Frank Chmura 17b, 78; Peter Forsberg 293c; Niels Poulsen Kirke 188-9; Lphoto 211b; Nicholas Pitt 293tl; Prisma / Chmura Frank 210; Rohan Van Twest 198bl. **Amarok** AB: Magnus Elander 24tr, 24clb. **Armémuseum:** 270bl. **Áttje Fjäll- och Samemuseum:** Jan Gustavsson 28tr.

Bastard Mat & Vin: Per-Anders Jörgensen 298tl.
Brygghuset Restaurant: 297t.

Corbis: Bettmann 6-7; Bob Krist 162; Hans Strand 274-5.

Dreamstime.com: Alexander Bondarchiuk 14b; Byggam79 26-7; Kim Carlson 13b; Davthy 172br; Michael Elliott 25clb; Rose-marie Henriksson 11c; Inger Anne Hulbækdal 328b; Jensottoson 316-7;

Antony Mcaulay 13tl, 16bl; Sophie Mcaulay 10cl.
Drottningholms Slottsteater: Bengt Wanselius 115tr, 115bc.
Fagersta Turism: 143cl. **Hotel Fjällgården**: 288b. **Fjärils & Fågelhuset**: 103cl. **Fotolia**: Mikhail Markovskly 14 cr; Philipp Weiss 219br.

Getty Images: AFP 249cla; Christian Aslund 14tr; David Clapp 266; Dan Wiklund 174. **Gondolen Restaurant**: 295t. **Gunnebo Slott**:229cla. **Göteborgs Konstmuseum**: *Karin and Kersti*, Carl Larsson 241br. **Den Gyldene Freden Restaurant**: 294b.

HSB Malmö 2006: Ole Jais 185lbr. **Peter Hanneberg**: 4-5tc, 24cla, 24cra, 25tc, 25tr, 25cl, 25br, 27cr, 28bl, 29cb, 129b, 165bl, 165br, 173tr; 251b, 252c, 262bl, 263tr, 267b, 272c, 273br, 278cla, 279crb, 279br, 310bc, 312b, 313tl, 313b.

Christer Hägg: *East Indiaman Wasa*, Jacob Hägg 202bl.
ICEHOTEL Sweden: 282b, 301bl, 382b. **IMS Bildbyrå**: 49tl.

Jay Fu Restaurant: 296tl. **Jönköpings Läns Museum**: *Bianca Maria in Among Elves and Trolls*, John Bauer 29bl; **Jumbo Stay Hotel**: 284b.

Kosta Boda:Ann Wåhlström 31bl; Ulrika Hydman Vallien 156bc; Kjell Engman 157bc. **Kosta Boda Art Hotel**: 286t; **Kungliga Biblioteket**: 42br, 76bl. **Kungliga Husgerådskammaren**: Alexis Daflos 4br, 60tr, 60clb, 61tr, 113tc; 112cl, 112bl, 113bl, 114tr, 114clb; *The Triumph of Karl XI*, Jacques Foucquet 43tl; 52b; Håkan Lind 58cl, 58cb, 58bc; 59ca, 59cr, 60cla, 113cr; 139cl. **Kungliga Myntkabinettet**: 57crb; Jan Eve Olsson 62cl, 75tr. **Kungliga Operan**: Mats Bäcker 70tr, 73tl, 73c. **Källemo AB**: 31c.

Livrustkammaren: 43bl, 47br; Göran Schmidt 47cla, 57tl; Nina Heins 62bl.

Malmö Turism: Mårten Swemark 183tl; **Medelhavsmuseet**: Ove Kaneberg 70cla. **Moderna Museet**: 84br, 84bl; Per Anders Allsten 84bc. **Museum tre Kronor**: 61br. **Musikmuseet**: Nina Heins 76cr

Nationalmuseum: 30clb; *Flowers on the Windowsill*, Carl Larsson 30–31c; *Gustav Vasa*, Cornelius Arendtz 36; *Ansgar Preaches Christianity*, Georg Pauli 38bl; *Stockholm Bloodbath*, Dionysius Padt-Brügge 39t; *The Entry of King Gustav Vasa of Sweden into Stockholm, 1523*, Carl Larsson 40t; *Portrait of Erik XIV*, Steven van der Meulen 40c; *The Fire at the Royal Palace 7th May 1697*, Johan Fredrik Höckert 41tr; *Portrait of Queen Kristina*, David Beck 41clb; *The Death of Gustav II Adolf of Sweden at the Battle of Lutzen*, Carl Wahlbom 42bl; *The Crossing of the Belt*, Johan Philip Lemke 42–43c; *Karl X Gustav*, Sébastien Bourdon 43cr; *Bringing Home the Body of King Karl XII of Sweden*, Gustaf Cederström 43br; *King Gustav III of Sweden*, Lorens Pasch d.y. 44tl; *Portrait of the Bernadotte Family*, Fredrik Westin 44crb; *The Coronation of Gustav III*, Carl Gustav Pilo 46cla; *The Battle at Svensksund*, J T Schoultz 46clb; *A Noisy Dinner*, Johan Tobias Sergel 46bc; *Conversation at Drottningholm*, Pehr Hilleström 46–47c; *The Murder of Gustav III*, A W Küssner 47tr; *Bacchanal on Andros*, Peter Paul Rubens 53tl; 59br; *The Conspiracy of the Batavians under Claudius Civilis*, Rembrant 86cla; *Amor and Psyche*

(1787) Johan Tobias Sergel 86clb; 86bc; *Lamino Chair* (1955) Yngve Ekstrom photo Hans Thorwid 87clb;*The Love Lesson*, Antoine Watteau 86tr; *The Lady with the Veil*, Alexander Roslin 87tl; *Karl XIV Johan's Visit to Berga*, A C Wetterling 150tr; *Valdemar Atterdag Plunders Visby 1361*, Carl Gustaf Hellqvist 171br. **Naturhistoriska Riksmuseet**: Staffan Waerndt 102c. **Nordiska Museet**: Birgit Brånvall 94tr; Mats Landin 53tr; 94cl; Sören Hallgren 94bc; *Snowstorm at Sea*, August Strindberg 95cr; 95ca; *The Proposal*, Knut Ekwall 95tl.

Östasiatiska museet: 80tl, Erik Cornelius 82bl; Karl Zetterstrom 80cla.
Parken Zoo I Eskilstuna AB: 139bc. **Pontus Restaurants**: 291t. **Postmuseum**: 65crb. **Pressens Bild**: 5tr, 21b, 22tl, 29tr, 33br; Hans T. Dahlskog 49br; 59tl, 93tl; Jan Delden 74br; Gunnar Seijbold 77tl; Axel Malmström 105tr; 111br, 126tr, 302cr, 303tl, 308cr, 314tl. **Pumphuset**: 297bl.

Red Boat Hotel: 283b. **Rederi AB Göta Kanal**:151cra. **Laila Reppen**: 26–27c.

Salt & Brygga: 291b, 298b. **Scandic Hotels**: 285t, 287bl, 289t. **Sheraton Stockholm**: 283t. **Villa Sjötorp**: 290b, 299t. **Sjöhistoriska Museet**: 100c. **Skogskyrkogården**:111c. **Ingalill Snitt**: 26tr. **Statens Historiska Museum**: 90cla, 90clb, 90bl, 90br, 91tc, 91ca, 91cb, 91br, 91bl, 136br. **Steninge Slott**: 136t. **Stockholms Auktionsverk**: 47bl. **Stockholms Stadshus**: Jan Asplund 107br, 107tl. **Stockholms Stadsmuseum**: *Tre Kronor Palace*, Govert Camphuysen 42cl; *Newspaper Readers*, J A Cronstedt 45tl; *The Regicide Anckarström Punished in Front of the House of Nobility*, 47cr; 48clb, 49clb. **Strindbergsmuseet**: Per Bergström 75bc. **Superstock**: Age Fotostock 124-5; Anders Ekholm 35cr; Macduff Everton 50-1; Robert Harding Picture Library 128; Hemis.fr 35tc; Imagebroker. net 222-3, 264br; Image Source 68; Johner 250; Jonathan Larsen t; Naturbild 246-7; Nordic Photos 192, 263bl; Prisma 145b; Stock Connection 116cla, 152-3, 232. **Svenska Akademien**: Leif Jansson 46tr. **Rolf Sørensen**: 24bl, 25bl.

Thielska Galleriet: *Hornsgatan*, Eugène Jansson 99tl.
Vasaloppsmuseet: 249cra, 249br. **Vasamuseet**: Hans Hammarskiöld 53br, 96tc, 96cla, 96bl, 96br, 97tc, 97cra; 97br, 97bl. **Spritmuseum**: 93c. **Visit Karskrona**: Therese Hagstrom 193cr.

Claes Westlin: 30cla. **Jeppe Wikström**: 32br, 33t, 35bl, 62tr, 70bl, 71crb, 71bl, 74tl, 82br, 83ca, 92t, 103br, 105cla, 105br, 106br, 108t, 109t, 109bl, 116cr, 117tl, 117br, 308bl, 327t.

Front Endpapers: Alamy Images: blickwinkel Rbc, Prisma / Chmura Frank Lc. **Corbis:** Bob Krist Rc. **Getty Images:** David Clapp Lbl. **Superstock:** Johner Rcr, Nordic Photos Lcl, Robert Harding Picture Library Rbr, Stock Connection Ltr.

Jacket: Front - Getty Images: Jeppe Wikstrom main. Spine - **Getty Images:** Jeppe Wikstrom t.

All other images © Dorling Kindersley.
For further information see: www.dkimages.com

Special Editions of DK Travel Guides

DK Travel Guides can be purchased in bulk quantities at discounted prices for use in promotions or as premiums. We are also able to offer special editions and personalized jackets, corporate imprints, and excerpts from all of our books, tailored specifically to meet your own needs.

To find out more, please contact:

in the United States **SpecialSales@dk.com**

in the UK **travelspecialsales@uk.dk.com**

in Canada DK Special Sales at **general@ tourmaline.ca**

in Australia **business.development@pearson. com.au**

Phrase Book

When reading the imitated pronunciation, stress the part which is underlined. Pronounce each syllable as if it formed part of an English word, and you will be understood sufficiently well. Remember the points below, and your pronunciation will be even closer to the correct Swedish.

ai:	as in 'fair' or 'stair'
ea:	as in 'ear' or 'hear'
ew:	like the sound in 'dew'
EW:	try to say 'ee' with your lips rounded
oo:	as in 'book' or 'soot'
OO:	as in 'spoon' or 'groom'
r:	should be strongly pronounced

Swedish Alphabetical Order
In the list below we have followed Swedish alphabetical order. The following letters are listed after z: **å, ä, ö**.

You
There are two words for 'you': 'du' and 'ni'. 'Ni' is the polite form; 'du' is the familiar form. It is not impolite to address a complete stranger with the familiar form.

In an Emergency

Help!	**Hjälp!**	yelp
Stop!	**Stanna!**	stanna!
Call a doctor!	**Ring efter en doktor!**	ring efter ehn doktor
Call an ambulance!	**Ring efter en ambulans!**	ring efter ehn ambewlanss
Call the police!	**Ring polisen!**	ring poleesen
Call the fire brigade!	**Ring efter brandkåren!**	ring efter brandkawren
Where is the nearest telephone?	**Var finns närmaste telefon?**	vahr finnss nairmasteh-telefawn
Where is the nearest hospital?	**Var finns närmaste sjukhus?**	vahr finnss-nairmasteh shewkhews

Communication Essentials

Yes	**Ja**	yah
No	**Nej**	nay
Please (offering)	**Varsågod**	vahrshawgOOd
Thank you	**Tack**	tack
Excuse me	**Ursäkta**	ewrshekta
Hello	**Hej**	hay
Goodbye	**Hej då/adjö**	haydaw/ahyur
Good night	**God natt**	goongtt
Morning	**Morgon**	morron
Afternoon	**Eftermiddag**	eftermiddahg
Evening	**Kväll**	kvell
Yesterday	**Igår**	ee gawr
Today	**Idag**	ee dahg
Tomorrow	**I morgon**	ee morron
Here	**Här**	hair
There	**Där**	dair
What?	**Vad?**	vah
When?	**När?**	nair
Why?	**Varför?**	vahrfurr
Where?	**Var?**	vahr

Useful Phrases

How are you?	**Hur mår du?**	hewr mawr dew
Very well, thank you.	**Mycket bra, tack.**	mewkeh brah, tack
Pleased to meet you.	**Trevligt att träffas.**	treavlit att traiffas
See you soon.	**Vi ses snart.**	vee seas snahrt
That's fine.	**Det går bra.**	dea gawr brah
Where is/are …?	**Var finns …?**	vahr finnss…
How far is it to …?	**Hur långt är det till**	hewr lawngt ea dea till
Which way to …?	**Hur kommer jag till …?**	hewr kommer yah till …
Do you speak English?	**Talar du/ni engelska?**	tahlar dew/nee engelska
I don't understand	**Jag förstår inte.**	yah furshtawr inteh
Could you speak more slowly, please?	**Kan du/ni tala långsammare, tack.**	kan dew/nee tahla lawng-ssamareh tack
I'm sorry.	**Förlåt.**	furrlawt

Useful Words

big	**stor**	stOOr
small	**liten**	leeten
hot	**varm**	varrm
cold	**kall**	kall
good	**bra**	brah
bad	**dålig**	dawleeg
enough	**tillräcklig**	tillraikleeg
open	**öppen**	urpen
closed	**stängd**	staingd
left	**vänster**	vainster
right	**höger**	hurger
straight on	**rakt fram**	rahkt fram
near	**nära**	naira
far	**långt**	lawngt
up/over	**upp/över**	ewp/urver
down/under	**ner/under**	near/ewnder
early	**tidig**	teedee
late	**sen**	sehn
entrance	**ingång**	ingawng
exit	**utgång**	ewtgawng
toilet	**toalett**	too-alett
more	**mer**	mehr
less	**mindre**	meendre

Shopping

How much is this?	**Hur mycket kostar den här?**	hewr mewkeh kostar dehn hair
I would like …	**Jag skulle vilja …**	yah skewleh vilya
Do you have?	**Har du/ni …?**	hahr dew/nee…
I'm just looking	**Jag ser mig bara omkring**	yah sear may bahra omkring
Do you take? credit cards	**Tar du/ni kreditkort?**	tahr dew/nee kredeetkoort
What time? do you open	**När öppnar ni?**	nair urpnar nee
What time do you close?	**När stänger ni?**	nair stainger nee
This one.	**den här**	dehn hair
That one.	**den där**	dehn dair
expensive	**dyr**	dewr
cheap	**billig**	billig
size (clothes)	**storlek**	stOOrlek
white	**vit**	veet
black	**svart**	svart
red	**röd**	rurd
yellow	**gul**	gewl
green	**grön**	grurn
blue	**blå**	blaw
antique shop	**antikaffär**	anteek-affair
bakery	**bageri**	bahgeree
bank	**bank**	bank
book shop	**bokhandel**	bOOkhandel
butcher	**slaktare**	slaktareh
cake shop	**konditori**	konditoree
chemist	**apotek**	apoteak
fishmonger	**fiskaffär**	fisk-affair
grocer	**speceriaffär**	spesseree-affair
hairdresser	**frisör**	frissurr
market	**marknad**	marrknad
newsagent	**tidningskiosk**	teednings-cheeosk
post office	**postkontor**	posstkontOOr
shoe shop	**skoaffär**	skOO-affair
supermarket	**snabbköp**	snabbchurp
tobacconist's	**tobakshandel**	tOObaks-handel
travel agency	**resebyrå**	reasseh-bewraw

Sightseeing

art gallery	**konstgalleri**	konnst-galleree
church	**kyrka**	chewrka
garden	**trädgård**	traidgawrd
house	**hus**	hews
library	**bibliotek**	beebleeotek
museum	**museum**	mewseum
square	**torg**	tohrj
street	**gata**	gahta
tourist information office	**turistinformationskontor**	tureest-informashOOns-kontOOr
town hall	**stadshus**	statshews
closed for holiday	**stängt för semester**	staingt furr semester
bus station	**busstation**	bewss-stashOOn
railway station	**järnvägsstation**	yairnvaigs-stashOOn

Staying in a Hotel

Do you have any vacancies?	**Har ni några lediga rum?**	hahr nee negra leadiga rewm
double room with double bed	**dubbelrum med dubbelsäng**	doobelrewm med doobel-seng

alternatives for a female speaker are shown in brackets

twin room	dubbelrum	doobelrewm
	med två	med tvaw
	sängar	sengar
single room	enkelrum	enkelrewm
room with	rum med	rewm med
a bath	bad	bahd
shower	dusch	dewsh
key	nyckel	newckel
I have a	Jag har	yah hahr
reservation	beställt rum	bestellt rewm

Eating Out

Have you got a	Har ni ett	hahr nee ett
table for…	bord för…?	bOOrd furr…
I would like	Jag skulle vilja	yah skewleh vilya
to reserve	boka ett	bOOka ett
a table.	bord.	bOOrd
The bill, please.	Notan, tack.	nOOtan, tack
I am a	Jag är	yah air
vegetarian	vegetarian	vegetariighn
waitress	servitris	sairvitress
waiter	servitör	sairviturr
menu	meny/	menew/
	matsedel	mahtseadel
fixed-price	meny med	menew med
menu	fast pris	fast prees
wine list	vinlista	veenlista
glass of water	ett glas	ett glahss
	vatten	vatten
glass of wine	ett glas vin	ett glahss veen
bottle	flaska	flaska
knife	kniv	k-neev
fork	gaffel	gaffel
spoon	sked	shead
breakfast	frukost	frewkost
lunch	lunch	lewnch
dinner	middag	middahg
main course	huvudrätt	hewvewdrett
starter	förrätt	furrett
dish of the day	dagens rätt	dahgens rett
coffee	kaffe	kaffeh
rare	blodig	blOOdee
medium	medium	medium
well done	välstekt	vailstehkt

Menu Decoder

abborre	abborreh	perch
ansjovis	anshOOvees	anchovies
apelsin	appelseen	orange
bakelse	bahkelse	cake, pastry, tart
banan	banahn	banana
biff	biff	beef
bröd	brurd	bread
bullar	bewllar	buns
choklad	shooklahd	chocolate
citron	sitrOOn	lemon
dessert	dessair	dessert
fisk	fisk	fish
fläsk	flaisk	pork
forell	fooraill	trout
frukt	fruckt	fruit
glass	glass	ice cream
gurka	gewrka	cucumber
grönsaksgryta	grurnsahks-grewta	vegetable stew
hummer	humm1er	lobster
kallskuret	kall-skuret	cold meat
korv	koorv	sausages
kyckling	chewkling	chicken
kött	churtt	meat
lamm	lamm	lamb
lök	lurk	onion
mineralvatten	minerahl-vatten	mineral water
med/utan	mehd/ewtan	still/sparkling
kolsyra	kawlsewra	
mjölk	m-yurlk	milk
nötkött	nurtchurtt	beef
nötter	nurtter	nuts
ost	oost	cheese
olja	olya	oil
oliver	oleever	olives
paj/kaka	pa-y/kahka	pie/cake
potatis	potahtis	potatoes
peppar	peppar	pepper
ris	rees	rice
rostat bröd	rostat brurd	toast
räkor	raikoor	prawns
rökt skinka	rurkt sheenka	cured ham
rött vin	rurtt veen	red wine
saft	safft	lemonade
salt	sallt	salt
sill	seell	herring

skaldjur	skahl-yewr	seafood
smör	smurr	butter
stekt	stehkt	fried
strömming	strurmming	baltic herring
socker	socker	sugar
soppa	soppa	soup
sås	saws	sauce
te	tea	tea
torr	torr	dry
ungsstekt	ewngs-stehkt	baked, roast
vinäger	vinaiger	vinegar
vispgrädde	veesp-graiddeh	whipped cream
vitlök	veet-lurk	garlic
vitt vin	veett veen	white wine
ägg	aigg	egg
älg	ail-y	elk
äpple	aippleh	apple
öl	url	beer

Numbers

0	noll	noll
1	ett	ett
2	två	tvaw
3	tre	trea
4	fyra	fewra
5	fem	fem
6	sex	sex
7	sju	shew
8	åtta	otta
9	nio	nee-oo
10	tio	tee-oo
11	elva	elva
12	tolv	tolv
13	tretton	tretton
14	fjorton	f-yoorton
15	femton	femton
16	sexton	sexton
17	sjutton	shewton
18	arton	ahrton
19	nitton	nitton
20	tjugo	chewgoo
21	tjugoett	chewgoo-ett
22	tjugotvå	chewgoo-tvaw
30	trettio	tretti
31	trettioett	tretti-ett
40	fyrtio	furrti
50	femtio	femti
60	sextio	sexti
70	sjuttio	shewti
80	åttio	otti
90	nittio	nitti
100	(ett) hundra	(ett) hewndra
101	etthundraett	ett-hewndra-ett
102	etthundratvå	ett-hewndra-tvaw
200	tvåhundra	tvawhewndra
300	trehundra	treahewndra
400	fyrahundra	fewrahewndra
500	femhundra	femhewndra
600	sexhundra	sexhewndra
700	sjuhundra	shewhewndra
800	åttahundra	ottahewndra
900	niohundra	nee-oohewndra
1,000	(ett) tusen	(ett) tewssen
1,001	etttusenett	ett-tewssen-ett
100,000	(ett) hundra-	(ett) hewndra-
	tusen	tewssen
1,000,000	en miljon	ehn milyOOn

Time

one minute	en minut	ehn meenewt
one hour	en timme	ehn timmeh
half an hour	en halvtimme	ehn halvtimmeh
ten past one	tio över ett	teeoo urver ett
quarter past one	kvart över ett	kvahrt urver ett
half past one	halv två	halv tvaw
twenty to two	tjugo i två	chewgoo ee tvaw
quarter to two	kvart i två	kvahrt ee tvaw
two o'clock	klockan två	klockan tvaw
13.00	klockan tretton	klockan tretton
16.30	sexton och trettio	sexton ock tretti
noon	klockan tolv	klockan tolv
midnight	midnatt	meednatt
Monday	måndag	mawndahg
Tuesday	tisdag	teesdahg
Wednesday	onsdag	oonssdahg
Thursday	torsdag	toorsdahg
Friday	fredag	fredahg
Saturday	lördag	lurrdahg
Sunday	söndag	surndahg

alternatives for a female speaker are shown in brackets